MUSICAL TRENDS IN THE 20TH CENTURY

ARNOLD SCHOENBERG
(1874–1951)

Musical Trends in the 20th Century

By

Norman Demuth *1898-1968.*

GREENWOOD PRESS, PUBLISHERS
WESTPORT, CONNECTICUT

Library of Congress Cataloging in Publication Data

Demuth, Norman, 1898-1968.
   Musical trends in the 20th century.

   Reprint of the ed. published by Rockliff, London.
   Includes indexes.
   1. Music--History and criticism--20th century.
2. Composers. I. Title.
ML197.D37 1974   780'.904   73-6258
ISBN 0-8371-6896-1

To my friend, René Dumesnil

FOREWORD

THIS book is not a "History of Fifty Years' Music". It does not set out to include every name and every work which has come to light since the beginning of the century in every country. It is a study of certain composers who may justly be said to have played a part in the history of world music; consequently they have arrived at a state of maturity and have already influenced the future trend of music. They have formulated the several facets of twentieth-century music and have become representative of the first half of the century. In many cases the earlier works gave little indication of the future trend. Some of them are universally acknowledged as giants; others have played a great part within the limits of their own cultures without, perhaps, making a direct world impact. It has been considered necessary to include the latter because the tendency of insularity is to regard articles and persons unknown and unexperienced within the confines of that insularity as being somehow deficient in value and importance. The tendency also is to exaggerate the importance of the insular article, and although it may not be essential that a composer has a world or at least a European recognition, it is necessary that he be kept in due perspective.

Looking round at the scene to-day, it is obvious that in all countries there is an enormous creative activity, but economics and other factors work against universal recognition of many who deserve it. On the other hand, there are a great number of composers who write admirable music of no great importance. To include these side by side with giants like Sibelius, Vaughan Williams and Schoenberg would be unfair to the composers themselves and would make them look ridiculous.

Further, these composers are not yet mature. Their works may terminate in a technique altogether different from that of to-day—at least, one hopes so, for no creative artist has ever stood still in this respect. Quantity is not as important as quality, else were composers like Camille Saint-Saëns and Samuel Coleridge-Taylor among the greatest. It is only when viewed in retrospect that the position can be determined and although there are some among the younger composers who make their contemporaries look mere pygmies side by side with them, it is still not safe to prophesy as to the ultimate result of their labours.

One may prophesy, however, that the second half of the century will not witness as great a cleavage as that which divided the late nineteenth and middle twentieth. The composers studied in detail will be found to have led the progress which in turn will be continued by their successors. On the other hand, it would be altogether wrong to ignore many names which may be said to have been "in" but not "of" the twentieth century in that their technical and musical expression bears too close an affinity with late nineteenth-century ideals and aims. These composers are exceedingly important and cannot be ignored or derided. Without them the present-day music would be very different. The preliminary chapters, therefore, will concern themselves with setting the scene, which will in turn be followed by a closing consideration of the situation up to date.

I would point out one fact which does not always strike the older reader as forcibly as it should. The older generation was brought up during an immense upheaval when cultures underwent a complete change, and taste gradually took the place of judgement. Standards altered rapidly—they are still altering, but not so rapidly. To that generation a work like Debussy's *Pelléas et Mélisande* is more than a matter of a name. It is a reality. The same may be said of Stravinsky's *Petrouchka* and *Le Sacre*. To-day the young generation has to take much of this period for granted. The first work, to the majority, is only a name. There is no opportunity for hearing it in the theatre and radio performances are few and far between. Even in my day (and I write as one aged fifty-two) it was one of the most debatable works ever written. We absorbed it avidly, as we absorbed *L'Après-Midi*. We raved about the other two works—and, incidentally, how long ago were they performed as ballets? Such is the passage of fashion that few of the works which created furore after furore in the 1920's are played to-day, and when one or two do make an appearance, one wonders what the fuss had been about. Many of these composers are standard names now, but their life was not considered as certain of longevity in concert programmes, in their time.

What is lacking in music to-day is the element of adventure. Perhaps we have grown blasé, for there is not the spirit of enthusiasm and active partisanship now which marked the immediate post-Great War years. It is true, however, that there is much more thinking done now than then, and listening is more intelligent and enlightened; but critical faculties have been doped by the plethora of hackneyed classics which fill our concert programmes and young people are not given what they are entitled to in a world of their own, and are not allowed a balanced view of the progress of music within the past fifty years. It is not feasible, therefore, to take very much for granted.

This book not being a piece of propaganda, the reader must not expect to find that every composer has been mentioned, but I have made the choice after some consultation with colleagues. The reader may be surprised to find that Elgar is not given a chapter to himself; but Elgar no longer influences the twentieth-century trend, if, indeed, he ever did really make any impact at all on his young contemporaries. The name of Vincent d'Indy is comparatively unfamiliar here, but he was head of a school in Paris and numbered several great French composers among his pupils. Great men though both these composers were, they were not "of" the twentieth century. The name of Willem Pijper may similarly be completely unknown; but what applies to d'Indy applies to him, with the difference that he was definitely "of" the century. The period which saw German music in decline in the person of Richard Strauss also saw the ascendancy of the new school of Schoenberg which, after many years of active hostility on the part of the conservatives, has become recognised as a genuine expressive force. One may not like it—one may not like a good many tendencies—and one may not think that it has any future; but there is a trend in its direction, and personal feelings, in either direction, must not blind or dazzle one.

As regards the musical examples, I have not quoted from many works which are easy of access and for the greater part have confined myself to those not in immediate call, and to those whose quotation has seemed necessary to make points clear. As far as possible the examples have been made accessible for the piano, but in certain instances this has been impossible. In these cases I have written the actual sounds of the transposing instruments, although personally deploring this recent concession to laziness; but I am aware that not all readers are sufficiently practised in score reading.

Dates of composers and works have been given once only, usually at the first mention of them; but in a few cases I have deemed it wiser to repeat them when making comparison between different periods of different composers. It has not been possible in every case to ascertain the actual date of composition. The French composers usually place this after their names on the title-page of the scores, but where it has not been discoverable, I have quoted the year of publication. It is not expected that in the majority of cases there will be any considerable time-lag between the two.

Norman Demuth.

Paris,

Sept. 1950.

(The deaths of Charles Koechlin, Arnold Schoenberg, and Jerzy Fitelberg took place when it was too late to amend the text from present to past tenses).

CONTENTS

(Names contained within brackets are mentioned but not discussed in detail)

CONTENTS

(Names contained within brackets are mentioned but not discussed in detail)

ILLUSTRATIONS

ACKNOWLEDGEMENTS

I WOULD like to express my best thanks to my wife who, once again, has read through typescript and proofs with the greatest care and patience, and whose advice I have taken in the majority of instances. I must also thank those of my colleagues whom I have consulted on certain points over which I had some doubts, and who do not want their names to be disclosed—for obvious reasons.

I must also thank all those who kindly sent me photographs at my request, particularly Mr. Nathan Broder of Messrs. Schirmer Inc., New York, who went to infinite pains to obtain those of the American composers, and to Stichting Donemus of Amsterdam for those of the Dutch.

Without the friendly co-operation of the many publishers controlling the works discussed in these pages the value of the book would be considerably lessened, and I would like to express my deep appreciation of the kindness shown me in this respect by the following publishers. Every effort has been made to give the correct attribution in each case, but readers will appreciate that in so wide a field changes in copyright may occur.

MESSRS. ASCHERBERG, HOPWOOD AND CREW LTD.

Bax	*Romance*

MESSRS. BOOSEY AND HAWKES AND CO. LTD.

Bartok	*Second Piano Concerto*
	Third Piano Concerto
	Music for String Instruments, Percussion, and Celesta
	Sixth String Quartet
	Sonata for Two Pianos and Percussion
Delius	*Brigg Fair*
	Hassan

BRITISH AND CONTINENTAL AGENCIES
(BREITKOPF AND HARTEL)

Sibelius	*Second Symphony*
	Third Symphony
	Finlandia
	En Saga

xiv

MESSRS. CHAPPELL AND CO. LTD.

Bax   *Mater, ora filium*
To the Name above every name

The above as agents for MESSRS.
G. SCHIRMER, INC., NEW YORK

Schoenberg   *Second Chamber Symphony*

MESSRS. J. AND W. CHESTER AND CO. LTD.

Goossens   *Second Violin Sonata*
Jack o' Lantern
Phantasy Quartet
Silence
Pijper   *Second 'Cello Sonata*
Poulenc   *Mouvement perpétuel*
Sonata for Piano Duet

MESSRS. J. CURWEN AND SONS LTD.

Vaughan Williams *A Pastoral Symphony*

MM. DURAND ET CIE (PARIS)

Debussy   *Pelléas et Mélisande*
Reflêts dans l'Eau
Hommage à Rameau   [*qui fut*
Et la lune descend sur le temple
Sarabande (*Pour le Piano*)
Dukas   *La Péri*
d'Indy   *Jour d'Eté à la Montagne*
Symphony in B flat
Milhaud   *Sonata for Two Violins and Piano*
Second Violin Sonata
Protée
Ravel   *Sonatine*
Roussel   *Bacchus et Ariane*
Aubade (*Petite Suite*)
Sérénade
String Quartet

MM. MAX ESCHIG ET CIE (PARIS)

Satie   *Socrate*   [*un chien*)
Véritables Préludes Flasques (*pour*

MM. HAMELLE ET CIE (PARIS)

Fauré   *La Parfum impérissable*
Clair de Lune

MM. HEUGEL ET CIE (PARIS)

Milhaud   *Esther das Carpentras*
       Les Euménides
       Les Choéphores
       Les Malheurs d'Orphée
       Le Pauvre Matelot
       Salade
       First Violin Sonata
Martinet   *Orphée*
       Variations for String Quartet
Mihalovici *Toccata for Piano and Orchestra*
       Third String Quartet
       Ricercari

MESSRS. NOVELLO AND CO. LTD.

Holst   *Ode to Death*

The above as agents for MESSRS.

HANSEN, MUSIK-FORLAG, COPENHAGEN

Sibelius   *Fifth Symphony*
       Sixth Symphony

OXFORD UNIVERSITY PRESS

Pijper   *Piano Concerto*
       Third Piano Sonatina
       Second Violin Sonata
       Second Trio
       Flute Sonata
Sibelius   *Violin Concerto*
       (Rights for this country only)
Vaughan Williams *Fifth Symphony*
       The Shepherds of the Delectable
       Mountains
Walton   *Portsmouth Point*

PETERS EDITION

Schoenberg *No. 5 (Five Orchestral Pieces)*

REVUE MUSICALE, LA (PARIS)

Milhaud   *Polytonal Fragment*

MM. ROUART, LEROLLE ET CIE (PARIS)

Auric   *Les Fâcheux*
Satie   *Deuxième Sarabande*
       Les Fils des Etoiles

MM. SALABERT ET CIE (PARIS)

Honegger   *Concerto da Camera*
                         Jeanne d'Arc au bucher
                         Judith
                         Mouvement Symphonique No. 3
                         Prélude (Trois Pièces)
                         Phédre
                         Symphonie Liturgique
Milhaud   *Fantaisie Pastorale*

MESSRS. SCHOTT AND CO. LTD.

Stravinsky   *Concerto for Two Pianos*

MESSRS. STAINER AND BELL AND CO. LTD.

Vaughan Williams *A London Symphony*

STICHTING DONEMUS (AMSTERDAM)

Pijper   *Third Symphony*

UNIVERSAL EDITION (VIENNA)

Berg   *Wozzeck*
                         Violin Concerto
Krenek   *String Quartet (Op. 78)*
Satie   *Mercure*
Schoenberg   *Pelleas und Melisande*
                         First Chamber Symphony
                         Traümleben
                         Friede auf der Erde
                         Second String Quartet
                         Third String Quartet
                         No. 3 (Three Piano Pieces, Op. 11)
                         No. 14 (Das Buch der Hängenden
                            Garten)
                         Der Mondfleck (Pierrot Lunaire)
                         Valse (Five Piano Pieces, Op. 23)
                         Prelude (Suite for Piano, Op. 25)
Webern   *Sechs Bagatellen*
                         Das Augenlicht
                         Symphony (Op. 21)

" Il n'y a pas de musique nouvelle. Il n'y a que des musiciens nouveaux."

PAUL DUKAS—"Le nouveau Lyrisme"
Minerva—February, 1903.

CHAPTER ONE

THE FRENCH GENIUS

Saint-Saëns (1835-1921)—Vincent d'Indy (1851-1931)—Paul Dukas (1865-1935)—Guy Ropartz (1864)—Florent Schmitt (1870)—Charles Marie Widor (1865-1937)—Louis Vierne (1870-1937) — Albéric Magnard (1865-1914) — Gabriel Fauré (1845-1924)—Charles Koechlin (1865-1950)—Roger-Ducasse (1873)—Déodat de Séverac (1877-1921)—Louis Aubert (1877)—Gustave Charpentier (1860)

ALTHOUGH the history of music has shown a constant but gradual change from period to period, the cleavage between old and established traditional customs has never been so suddenly marked as in the twentieth century. In the 1920's there appeared a complete break and negation of everything which had come to be regarded as permanent ideals undergoing, nevertheless, smooth expansion. This period, and this sudden break, are unparalleled in earlier years; in the same way that it was a French composer, Hector Berlioz (1803-1869), who carried music on from the pleasantries of Haydn and Mozart to the *Symphonie fantastique,* written only twenty years after Haydn's death, so the new *avant-garde* of music in the present century may be said to have been declared in France. The difference between the composers who were actually making themselves felt in the early years of the century and their immediate predecessors of the late nineteenth is one of the phenomena of musical history; so much the greater the split in the 1920's. French music led European thought in some respects for a greater part of the nineteenth century, and when it was not actually in front of the German ideal, it ran parallel with it. By the end of the nineteenth century France had produced a line of symphonic composers in Franck, Lalo, Saint-Saëns, Chausson and Dukas, whose approach differed from the contemporary German and Austrian schools only in their attraction to a less thoroughly technical aesthetic. The technically

I

logical Teutonic mind was concerned with the eternal problems of "working out". Everything was "worked out" and developed, and provided that the technical mastery was complete, the emotional side was of secondary importance. It will be seen that even many years later this passion for technique still remained. The French symphonic composers were primarily not so concerned. They did not regard the symphony as the vehicle for profundity of thought, expressible only through this aforementioned technical mastery. They looked for more, and a single poignant phrase was more valuable to them than two pages of canonic invention. The neo-classicism of Franck had a highly-charged emotional appeal. That of Saint-Saëns paid homage to technical device and process but kept its Gallic clarity and lightness. Emotionally it lacked the essential quality of sincerity. Saint-Saëns' technique stood still, and his last works sound hardly any different from his early ones; in those few places where for a moment he departed from traditional custom, as in the Fifth Piano Concerto (1896), he seems to have been actuated by cussedness. He had talent, but no genius.

Franck and Lalo also showed that their neo-classicism was fully competent as regards the ordinary symphonic devices and processes; but there was a great difference between their approach to the problems. Lalo's continuity is spontaneous and not discursive; Franck depends upon the good taste of the performer to maintain his continuity and not to drag out his argumentative phrases. Failure to do this results in a sectional performance which completely destroys the original intention. Chausson followed Franck's example, but scored more picturesquely; his *Symphony in B flat* (1891) is written with all the skill of the born romantic colourist. Dukas' *Symphony in C* (1895-1896) said all the things which Saint-Saëns failed to say because with Saint-Saëns there was no necessity for concentrated thought. Even his most profound moment, the *Symphonie avec orgue* (1886), is superficial. The technique is too easy and he ranks as a second Mendelssohn—like others (including Gounod), he had been called the "second Mozart". Saint-Saëns regarded himself as the "Grand Maître" not of French music but of music in general. He suffered from frustrated ambitions, one of which was a desire to be known as the successor to Wagner; his several very charming organ pieces show that he was really a miniaturist. Dukas' technique at that time was traditional and neo-classic; but his was a plastic mind which absorbed a good many of the contemporary ideas without entirely relying upon them. He wrote but a handful of works and throughout his life exercised a Flaubertian self-criticism.

The symphonic stream was continued by Vincent d'Indy (1851-1931), the pupil and disciple of Franck. An aristocrat by birth and a true and faithful friend of Art—which he always spelt with a capital "A"—he viewed music from the symphonic angle and from no other. In his time he was a pioneer, but this love of adventure drew him to Wagner, in whose technique and aesthetic d'Indy saw the salvation of all symphonic music. d'Indy's own style and idiom, however, were very different from those of the Master of Bayreuth. Architecturally, he went to Beethoven and thus his whole creative efforts were directed towards the Beethovenian symphony and the Wagnerian music drama; he never got as near to the latter in his own operas as his detractors (and their name at that time was legion) maintained. His most Wagnerian operas were *Fervaal* (1881-1895) and *L'Étranger* (1898-1901). The former became known as the "French *Parsifal*", but only because of its mystical nature. Its technique nowhere resembles that masterpiece of German opera. *L'Étranger*, whose philosophy is the Wagnerian salvation by love, is more graphic and pictorial. It just enters the twentieth century. The only Wagnerian tinge is its continuity, which relies upon the metamorphosis of themes rather than the use of the *leitmotiv*. It and *Fervaal* penetrated recesses of greatness for which the history of French opera could show no earlier parallel. It was not so much the case of Opéra *versus* Opéra-Comique as that of Vincent d'Indy *versus* Camille Saint-Saëns and Jules Massenet. There were too many unable to see two points of view, and in their eyes either the d'Indy or the Saint-Saëns-*cum*-Massenet concept was the right one. In spite of the symphonic continuity of his two works, d'Indy maintained his Gallic temperament in the religiosity of *Fervaal*, which was mystical, and in that of *L'Étranger*, which was idealistic. Unfortunately, he tended to preach sermons, and although he wrote of the struggle between Good and Evil in much of his symphonic music, this struggle is implied and the listener is not fully aware of it. In the two operas, and also in the later *La Légende de Saint Christophe* (1908-1915), there was no doubt about it. The *abonnés* of the Opéra and the Opéra-Comique did not want uplift; they wanted a good evening's entertainment, and it should be remembered that at the period of the first two operas the battle of Wagner in Paris had not been completely won. Those therefore who blamed d'Indy for this alleged Wagnerian approach to a lyrical genre did not realise his inherent sincerity and goodness and that for him, opera, as well as symphonic and chamber music, represented something hitherto not experienced in the French concept.

As regards Beethoven, d'Indy viewed all symphonic music from the conception of the *Op.* 110 and 111, and the great Beethoven *Variation* in its most amplified style. This enthusiasm he inherited from Franck, who had studied the works of Beethoven's third period and had mastered all the implications contained in them. After Beethoven, symphony deteriorated. It lost the power to discuss great matters. The *Symphonies* of Schubert (those which were known), Schumann and Mendelssohn did not come up to that level of spiritual thought and exultation to be found in Beethoven's *Seventh* and *Ninth*. Franck had brought the genre back to a position of dignity and significance and d'Indy subconsciously attempted to supply the deficiency. It is true that his first surviving symphony, *sur un Chant Montagnard Français* (1886), was a work redolent of the French countryside and of peasant habits and, therefore, does not supply the full evidence for this claim; but previously he had composed *Le Chant de la Cloche* (1879-1883) for soloists, double choir and orchestra (to his own text), a work unprecedented since the days of Beethoven's *Ninth*.[1] His approach to symphonic music was easily definable at that period. The *Symphonie sur un Chant Montagnard Français* was written for orchestra and piano—note the precedence. Many regard it more as a symphonic "concertante" than as a symphony, but it proved that technical mastery in a classical framework was not the prerogative of German composers and that a Frenchman could be as symphonic as could one of any other culture and remain French. Yet while this serious-minded man was propagating the symphonic principle, a revolutionary movement had started quite unobtrusively in an obscure Paris café, the leader being an almost unknown (at that time), and, later, the most misunderstood composer of the century. The actual impact made itself felt upon only one composer for the time being and this was disclosed in 1894 when the *Prélude à l'Après-Midi d'un Faune* by Claude Debussy was performed at the Société Nationale, and was encored.[2]

[1] I omit Berlioz' "œuvres de circonstance".

[2] *Le Musique contemporaine en France*, René Dumesnil (Collection Armand Colin), but in the diary in *Debussy*, Lockspeiser (Dent, *Master Musicians*), Eric Blom comments that it passed "almost unnoticed". Mr. Blom obviously refers to the Press, but it is inconceivable that it was not talked about pretty generally the next day.

The new wave of what was known as musical "Impressionism" began to make itself felt, and its insistence upon the abolition of such terms as "tonality" and "discord" appeared as a serious rival to the classical symphony because it seemed that composers would need to use only their imagination and would be able to write "just what they liked" without any reference to technique or tradition. In 1900 d'Indy opened the Schola Cantorum as a general school of music—previously it had been restricted to the study of plainchant, a knowledge of which it had disseminated all over France, to the ultimate good of her church music. The training of the new general school was based upon the methods of César Franck and was a direct challenge to the Conservatoire. The old-established Conservatoire alternated between the Prix de Rome, the blue riband of French music, and Opera, the latter deemed the highest flight of French musical composition. One of the purposes of the Schola Cantorum was to raise the knowledge and standard of music among young people. The former appears to have been incredibly limited. In his inaugural address, d'Indy quoted an instance of a Conservatoire student who, hearing the "Allegretto" from Beethoven's *Seventh Symphony* and not knowing its composer, exclaimed, "Ah, that's pretty. It might have been written by Saint-Saëns." [1]

Debussy's *Nocturnes* had been performed in the previous year, scoring an instant success. The vague haze of "Nuages" and "Sirènes" was emphasised by the clear-cut brilliance and verve of "Fêtes", and composers learnt how to be picturesque without necessarily subscribing to all the tenets of the new musical Impressionism as exemplified in *L'Après-Midi*, or adhering to the neo-classicism of Saint-Saëns as seen in his facile symphonic poems. Earlier, Paul Dukas had fallen under the spell of *L'Après-Midi* and in 1897 had completed the scherzo *L'Apprenti Sorcier*, the work upon which his fame as a composer has rested. The harmonic approach of this work shows a distinct advance upon that of the *Symphony in C*; but although the use of the augmented triad and a suggestion of the whole-tone scale showed the influence of the Debussy work, it was, generally speaking, too clear-cut to be Impressionistic, the only vague and nebulous writing occurring advisedly in those passages which delineate the incantation. The other representative composer, Camille Saint-Saëns, remained unaffected by the new ideas and ere long fulminated against them. d'Indy, if unable to fall

<hr>

[1] *La Schola Cantorum*, Vincent d'Indy et Autres (Blaud et Gay), and see also: *Vincent d'Indy*—Demuth (Rockliff).

into line with them, at least viewed them as genuine attempts to take music a step further.

'd'Indy may have regretted the absence of that symphonic thought which, together with the strongest sense of tonality and key relationship, he regarded as the basis and the essential of all music, but while completing his opera *L'Étranger*[1] in 1901 and his *Symphony in B flat* in 1902-1903, he was able to write a most sympathetic and penetrating advance notice of Debussy's *Pelléas et Mélisande*[2] which was produced at the Opéra-Comique in 1902, and aroused the most violent opposition. In answer to those who expressed surprise at this article, he said that his only desire was that everyone, including his own pupils, should write "beautiful things". He had a certain breadth of vision.[2] The opening of the twentieth century, therefore, witnessed the completion of a French symphonic opera (*L'Étranger*), one composed upon a hitherto undreamed of technique (*Pelléas et Mélisande*) and the climax to the by then established tradition of French symphony (d'Indy's *Symphony in B flat*). It will be noticed that two of these achievements were by the same composer.

What manner of men were the two distinguished French composers, d'Indy and Dukas, whose climactic works were written in the twentieth century but which cannot be said to have been of it? They had a great deal in common; both were cultured and well read outside the confines of music. They may be regarded as the last of the *Grands Maîtres*. Both had an equally developed reverence for music and as teachers, reigned supreme. d'Indy left behind him the record of his lectures at the Schola in the form of his *Cours de Composition musicale*, a monumental work. Dukas, although a great writer, left no didactic tome by which he can be remembered in the classroom.[3]

The attitude of Vincent d'Indy may be summed up in a paragraph from Book I of the *Cours*:

An artist must be inspired by a splendid sense of Charity— "the greatest of these". To love should be his aim in life; for the moving principle of all creation is divine and charitable Love.

[1] For a detailed study of d'Indy's operas, see my *Vincent d'Indy* (Rockliff).

[2] He wrote objectively, for at the first performance he expressed the opinion to Jean Huré (1877-1930) that "this music will not live because it has no form" (*Histoire de la Musique*, Emile Vuillermoz. Librairie Arthéme Fayard); but he was prepared to accept it for the moment.

[3] Some of his dicta can be read in *Paul Dukas*, Georges Fauré (Collection Euterpe, No. 1, La Colombe Editions du Vieux Colombier).

These words were addressed to beginners, as it were, in composition. They immediately place the highest import upon creative art; d'Indy himself, for the greater part of his life, practised this tenet—it was only towards the end of his life, when music turned suddenly away from most of the things which he held most dear, that he showed any bitterness of feeling. His capacity for work was enormous. Pierre de Bréville (1861-1949) told the writer that d'Indy gave him an appointment for a lesson at—*five a.m.* d'Indy lacked a sense of humour, perhaps, yet he was intensely human. This lack of a sense of humour may be seen in his strong insistence that everything should be taken seriously. An American, Mrs. Elisa Hall, commissioned a number of works for saxophone. She had gone deaf and her doctor had advised her to study a wind instrument. The saxophone was a popular serious instrument at that time, and she determined to build up a repertoire for it. d'Indy and Debussy were among the first composers to be commissioned. Debussy had no heart for the matter and saw a ridiculous side to it. However, he managed to write a *Rapsodie* (1903-1905) with piano accompaniment which later was scored by Roger-Ducasse (1873). d'Indy approached the work with all reverence and composed a *Choral Varié* (1903) which from the musical and technical point of view can rank with any serious set of variations. This thoroughness, this sincerity for everything is illustrated further in the story told by M. Léon Vallas.[1] d'Indy took charge of a demonstration of the Dalcroze method, work which one would think was not very serious. d'Indy conducted it as if he were in front of the *B minor Mass* or the *Ninth Symphony*, and took the most minute care over little detail, learning the whole thing by heart. One result of this was that those who previously had respected, admired and even loved him now simply adored him. This was the type of man who maintained the serious side of French musical culture at the beginning of the twentieth century.

Nevertheless, he was not really megalomaniacal or pontifical in musical utterance, although strenuously maintaining that in every respect his word was the right one. Although he was at the height of his powers at the opening of the century, he did not gravitate very far in the direction of the new thought, but Debussy's *Nocturnes* awakened in him a latent romanticism which culminated in *Jour d'Été à la Montagne* (1905). Here Impressionism is only suggested because d'Indy could not get away from his strong sense of form, tonality and clarity.

[1] *Vincent d'Indy*, Vol. II (Editions Albin Michel).

His harmonic progress actually went hardly further than the use of the augmented triad which, to-day, seems no distance at all, and in *Jour d'Été* his deliberate orchestral colouring does not seem altogether happily contrived. Up to this time he was very much *of* the century, but the advent of Les Six, inspired by Satie and Stravinsky, roused his ire. His pioneering days had ended and he stormed against all the ideals which both these and Arnold Schoenberg represented. Apart from that of Honegger, he held all contemporary music in horror and steadily proclaimed his artistic faith in the symphonic forms. The picture of this very grand old man producing the mystical and spiritual opera *La Légende de Saint Christophe* in 1918, a work devised with orchestral interludes to denote the passing of time, composed at the moment when what became known as the "silly season" of music was about to burst forth, calls for whole-hearted admiration. The work was not popular, but the writer has a very vivid recollection of a concert performance given by the students of the Schola Cantorum in the Salle Pleyel, Paris, which appeared to contain everything of the highest inspiration and purpose. The reverence with which these young people greeted d'Indy was truly moving. d'Indy himself conducted it.[1] His later works are well worth playing to-day, particularly the *Poème des Rivages* (1919–1921), the *'Cello Sonata in D* (1924–1925), the *Diptyque Méditerranéen* (1925-1926) and the *String Sextet* (1928). In 1922-1923 he surprisingly wrote a *comédie musicale* in three acts, *Le Rêve de Cinyras*,[2] and was astonished to find that nobody took it seriously. The trouble, of course, was that it was not quite light enough, although sufficiently so to cause some comment. Much of the music is delightful, and it is an incredibly virile work for one approaching his eightieth year.

He was a great man, and the twentieth century may be proud and glad to have witnessed him. His influence was very strong in its own direction and although many of the unthinking scoffed, the majority admired. Among his many pupils were Albert Roussel, Arthur Honegger, and Marcel Mihalovici.

d'Indy succeeded in enforcing the cyclic style upon the symphony and sonata. This style is constantly adopted to-day and many of those

[1] When Sir Henry Wood played one of the Interludes—"La Queste de Dieu"—at a Promenade Concert, one critic, apparently oblivious of the fact that d'Indy was nearly seventy years old, objected to so much music "by young French composers" being performed at these concerts . . . !

[2] His life completed a full circle as in 1876–1882 he had composed an opéra-comique, *Attendez-moi sous l'Orme*.

who use it are not aware of the hostility and fury which d'Indy's insistence upon it aroused, if, indeed, they are aware of its development through d'Indy. Being an enthusiast, he saw signs of it where it did not really exist and some of his authorities for its earlier use rather strain the imagination. However, the fact remains that a study of the symphony from its earliest days to the present[1] revealed that the vast majority of symphonies are purely cyclical; at the time we are discussing the "d'Indyistes" were the only composers using it. It may be thought that a man like Debussy would have had little time for d'Indy. On the contrary; although disagreeing with the whole Franck-d'Indy concept, Debussy paid tribute to both composers as men and as musicians.

Vincent d'Indy is truly the father of all the later French symphonists, and not only the French, because his pupils numbered many from other lands; the number of South American students, for example, who came to the Schola Cantorum is altogether surprising. He may be said to have been the Nadia Boulanger of his time. His parallel as a teacher in this country is probably Tovey and as a composer one would say Elgar, surprisingly enough, perhaps. (This theory is not suggested because, like Elgar, d'Indy wrote his "popular" music, one particular work being *Marche du 76e Régiment d'Infanterie* (1903).) Mention should be made of his scholarly editions of the old masters, of Monteverde, Destouches and Rameau. In this respect he can be said to have accomplished for these composers what our Professor E. J. Dent accomplished in literature for Scarlatti, and for Mozart's operas.

Paul Dukas (1865-1935) was a different type of man. He may be credited with the fact of being the first French composer to write a *Piano Sonata*.[2] This he produced in 1901; it is a work of monumental proportions and sufficiently difficult to scare pianists away from itself. It combines the best traditions of the past as regards texture and form with the best contemporary outlook upon technique. It is classical in lay-out but romantic in import. Dukas followed it up the next year with his equally monumental *Variations, Interlude, et Final sur une Thème de J. Ph. Rameau* in which any latent romanticism is completely expelled and the work is neo-classic throughout. In 1907 he produced his opera *Ariane et Barbe-Bleu*, on the subject by Maeterlinck,[3] in

[1] The Symphony: Its History and Development. Demuth. (In preparation).

[2] d'Indy wrote the second—1903-1904.

[3] Bartok used the same subject in 1911. Dukas' opera is studied in detail in my *Paris and the Opera: The History of a Culture.* (In preparation.)

which he proclaimed his sympathy with the warm romanticism of the time. The work is symphonic in that each act is written in one of the classical forms. It displays the Gallic approach to the orchestra in its most coloured state, a state which lacks all the violence of Richard Strauss. It was written over a space of ten years, during which period Debussy composed *La Mer*; it was not published until 1909.

In 1912 the dance-poem *La Péri* made its appearance, and here Dukas applied the symphonic approach to a form entirely unsymphonic in resource. He may be said to have spoken the last word in this type of romanticism which for colour outvies Rimsky-Korsakov and for sheer beauty of lovely sensuous tone finds few equals.

The different outlook upon romanticism of d'Indy and Dukas can be shown in two examples on page 11.

Notice that in *La Péri* Dukas maintains tonality by means of the pedal point; but this does not relate the six-four chords to each other. The shimmering descending semitonal thirds give an impressionistic feeling to an already mysterious atmosphere. Notice that d'Indy avoids this "effective" writing. There is nothing grandiloquent about either of them.

As a teacher Dukas pursued the same idealistic course as d'Indy, but with infinitely more humanity. It is difficult to imagine d'Indy delivering himself of the following expression, no matter how much he might have felt it:

"Looking for imitations is the lowest form of musical cretinism."

d'Indy certainly would not have addressed his pupils in this way on the subject of Brahms or any other composer:

"Brahms! Clumsy, Germanic. There is a great deal of beer in his music."

This should not suggest that there was no depth of feeling in Dukas' teaching or that he did not view his work in this connection very seriously; but compare the utterance of d'Indy. [1]

Dukas was certain that the future of music lay in counterpoint, and in this he was not wrong, for the music of the 1920's and onwards has been drawing rapidly away from harmonic turgidity to contrapuntal clarity.

Dukas considered himself an "amateur" composer. When he sent in the score of *La Péri* he modestly added the note: "If you do not think it is good, I will tear it up." Debussy admired *L'Apprenti Sorcier*. He met Dukas at a concert in which the work had been played.

[1] See page 6.

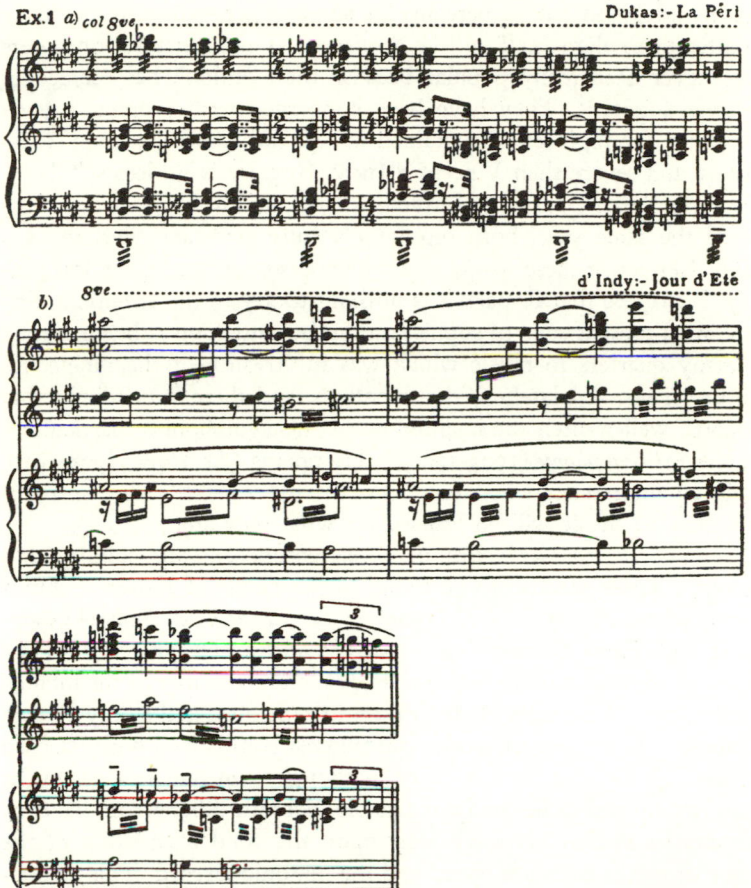

Ex.1 a) col 8ve............   Dukas:- La Péri

b) 8ve............   d' Indy:- Jour d' Eté

"How goes it?" said Dukas to Debussy. "Everything always goes well when I hear that work," replied Debussy. A great tribute from one who was not always kindly disposed towards his fellow-composers.

Of the same generation is Guy Ropartz (1864), now the only surviving pupil of César Franck. Ropartz' music has never made the impact that its quality demands because he has chosen to live in Brittany, isolated from the stream of current musical events. It seems that in France as well as in this country the personal absence of a composer places him outside the recollection of concert- and recital-givers. However, Ropartz is unconcerned over this. His style has steadily advanced but, as beseems his age and generation, it has made no attempt to align itself with *le dernier cri*. The Franckist composers have never been really popular because their outlook has seemed to be over-dogmatic. They have been concerned with keeping French music on the high level it attained at the turn of the century. Less austere and severe than Vincent d'Indy, Ropartz is no less scholarly. His *Fifth String Quartet*, published in 1948, and his *Sinfonietta*, completed the same year, both represent a fully alive and alert musical mind. Neither of these works could have been written in the last century. It may be that Ropartz has nothing to say to the twentieth century in its present state of sophistication; but attention is being turned in many quarters to music which was in advance of the nineteenth century if not absolutely *of* the twentieth, and there is no doubt that Ropartz' well-written and inspired music, his symphonies (particularly the *Choral Symphony* (1905-1906)), his operas (*Le Pays*, 1908-1910, made an impression when broadcast on the French radio in 1949) and chamber music will be realised for what they are.

Among the characteristics of these composers are solidity and strength. These are also to be found in the music of Florent Schmitt (1870) whose *Psalm XLVII* (1904),[1] *La Tragédie de Salomé* (1907-1910) and *Piano Quintet* (1901-1908)[2] add a substance to French music which makes it fall between its own stool and that of the inflated Teutonicism of the early twentieth century. Schmitt is the only French composer of his generation who can suggest comparison with Richard Strauss. Those who want solidity of thought can find it here, but it is unfriendly and rather unapproachable. Schmitt differs from his contemporaries in that his work rests upon the solid foundation of the major or minor common chord and the diatonic discord. This characteristic is responsible for much of the lack of tenderness which is noticeable even in his quieter moments; but when he becomes romantic, he does not hesitate to betray his indebtedness in a small way to Satie in accordance with his natural culture. He may be considered the most Teutonic of all French composers simply because of this hardness. Nevertheless, his work is important and adds to the evidence that France always has been in the *avant-garde* of music. *La Tragédie de Salomé* preceded Stravinsky's *L'Oiseau de Feu* by three years and

[1] In the Vulgate it is Psalm XLVI.

[2] Schmitt's works overlap each other and his opus numbers do not follow chronologically.

contains much that made the "Danse Infernale" so exciting. The rhythmic complexities of Schmitt's work bear comparison with the "Danse Sacrale" from *Le Sacre de Printemps,* composed in 1913. Here Schmitt accomplished, easily and simply, exactly what Stravinsky accomplished with so much labour and complication.

His setting of *Psalm XLVII* is masterly in its simplicity of technique. Magnificent brass fanfares proclaim glory to the Almighty, and the music generally is the direct antithesis to what a British composer would write. The reason becomes apparent when the language of the text is considered. In English it runs as follows:

> O clap your hands together, all ye people:
> O sing unto God with a voice of melody.
> For the Lord is high, and very greatly to be feared: He is the
> great King upon all the earth.

In Latin:

> Omnes Gentes, plaudite manibus: jubilate Deo in voce
> exultationis.
> Quoniam Dominus excelsus terribilis: Rex magnus super
> omnem terram.

In French, however, it becomes:

> Gloire au Seigneur!
> Nations, frappez des mains toutes ensemble.
> Gloire au Seigneur!
> Parce que le Seigneur est très élevé et très redoutable.

This comparison explains the difficulty of an English audience in following the rhetorical music which accompanies the salute to the Almighty. It also shows the inherent theatricality of Gallic worship; but theatricality is by no means a vice. Schmitt in this work regards the text as the utterance of a people released from captivity. He shows his direct descent from Berlioz; this is apparent in the general panoply of his ideas, which are on the large scale, but avoid being grandiloquent. Schmitt, therefore, must be considered in the panorama of Gallic culture as one who is traditional in technique and outlook. In this respect he is very much alone and it is this influence which has tended to his longevity of expansion; for Schmitt has never considered his listeners and makes no compromise with them. Consequently, many find it impossible to be with him throughout a work like the *Piano Quintet*, which is absolutely unassailable for its logic, but is repelling in its length.

Florent Schmitt views music from a Teutonic angle in the scope of his scores and the classical working out of his ideas. After Berlioz he seems to have been influenced by Liszt and, side by side with a man like Camille Saint-Saëns, he makes the latter look a pygmy; but he does not do so with d'Indy or Dukas. His music lacks a general sense of humour and is over-serious. Its composer would appear never to smile—but this is altogether a wrong impression and shows that the man and the music are not necessarily compatible in temperament. A photograph taken in 1920[1] shows Schmitt and Arnold Schoenberg standing together on a boat crossing the Zuyder Zee. It is significant that while the Gallic Schmitt looks extremely serious, the Teutonic Schoenberg, that most austere of composers, wears a broad grin—but perhaps this may be explained by quality of seamanship.[2]

Florent Schmitt is one of the glories of French music. He is a *Grand Seigneur* rather than a *Grand Maître*. He will probably be viewed by posterity much as Berlioz is viewed to-day. He is unpopular with those who prefer to think of French music in terms of ineffable grace and charm, for he gives this comfortable theory the lie direct. His music is basically Gallic, but it is a Gallicism influenced by foreign ideals. His technique is exceedingly clear. Even in his broadest development passages he never combines themes for the sake of so doing, in order to show the scholasticism of his mind. His guiding principle is one thing at a time, a principle he learned at the hands of Massenet and Fauré. Most of his important works were written in the twentieth century, but they do not contribute very much to the technique of the period. They go only a little further forward than d'Indy and Dukas, and it is unfortunate that Impressionism came at the moment when Schmitt's style and idiom had been formed. In the days of the battles at the Société Nationale, Florent Schmitt was loud in vociferation. His voice always rang out above that of the opposition with some terse and pointed suggestion. His influence will be felt as soon as music has settled down once more.

This somewhat cursory glance at the French situation at the begin-

[1] Reproduced in *Florent Schmitt*, P. O. Ferroud (Durand).

[2] The absolute indifference of the other passengers to the great men in whose presence they are sitting, is striking.

CHARLES KOECHLIN (1865–1950)

PAUL DUKAS (1865–1935)

(*Above*) GUY ROPARTZ (1864)

(*Left*) VINCENT D'INDY (1851–1931)

ERIK SATIE (1866–1925)   CLAUDE DEBUSSY (1863–1918)

ning of the century must content itself with mere reference to the names of Charles Marie Widor (1865-1937), whose set of excellent organ *Symphonies* are definitely in the century but not in the least of it, Louis Vierne (1870-1937),[1] whose similar works hold exactly the opposite position, and Albéric Magnard (1865-1914), whose isolated life culminated in an heroic death during the 1914-1918 War when he defended his house outside Paris single-handed against a troop of Uhlans. Attention must be directed to two figures, one of whom has been described as being the very "essence of French music", and the other a name rarely seen in concert programmes but always held in the highest regard among musicians.

An element which has been lacking in some of the composers already mentioned is that of spontaneous lyricism. Grace and charm have not been the prevailing features, and had Gabriel Fauré (1845-1924) not had this ineffable gift, French music might well have become something much more classical in nature. Fauré may be said to have formulated a concept of French music and his style has become recognised outside France as representing everything French music stands for. He was never an Impressionist, but he had the gift of delineation which enabled him to conjure up all kinds of romantic situations in music. These were objective. (Strangely enough, French music is rarely subjective. *La grande passion* may be a characteristic of the French temperament, but it seldom appears in her music.) The melody of Fauré and other composers is distinctly feline in quality, but it is never erotic. For that one turns to the brutal animalism of Richard Strauss and the adolescent sensuality of Alexander Scriabin.

Fauré held the appointment of Director of the Paris Conservatoire: his opposite number at the Schola Cantorum worked with him in perfect harmony. Previous to this, he had been Professor of Composition[2] and his pupils included Maurice Ravel. He was one of the prime movers in the formation of the Société Musicale Indépendante in opposition to the Société Nationale. His attitude to the position at the time may be summed up in his words at the inaugural meeting of the former: "It seems that we are going to conspire." He was a different kind of pioneer to Vincent d'Indy, who, although impatient with all

[1] This year was a fateful one for French music, as it saw the deaths of Roussel, Ravel and Pierné as well.

[2] Ambroise Thomas threatened to resign his directorship if the appointment were made, for Fauré had not won the Prix de Rome.

forms of academicism and pedantry, wished all reforms to be carried out in his own way, and usually succeeded in getting that way. Fauré, strange as it may seem to-day, was the nineteenth-century prototype of Professor E. J. Dent, who founded the International Society for Contemporary Music, and one must realise that the works put forward in Fauré's time sounded every bit as iconoclastic as did those in the early days of Professor Dent's Society.

Fauré was a musical poet, with ineffably charming ideas. There is hardly anything which does not bear the imprint of consummate craftsmanship and musicality. His songs and piano pieces hold positions of their own in music. Unfortunately, they have directed attention to but one side of his genius and it is too widely considered that he was a miniaturist. His larger-scale orchestral works have not the breadth and power usually expected in symphonic music. The *Ballade* (1881) and the *Fantasie* (1919) for piano and orchestra, for example, have all the elements of poetic grace but no epic strength. In all probability a stronger musical personality would have made *Promethée* (1900) and *Pénélope* (1913) broader and most certainly more violent; both these works, however, have a sense of drama and the tragedies are well unfolded. They are not familiar works either in part or whole and those misguided enthusiasts who lapse into tremors of ecstasy at the mere mention of Fauré's name have no idea as to the venomous cynicism of their idol when driven to it by a text. Fauré was extremely happy in the theatre, and his incidental music was written in many cases for production in this country, at the time when the over-swollen "Grand Manner" and the overbearing tide of Germanophilism had swept over all creative music here. Fauré, therefore, offered the obvious counter-blast to this tide and to our conception of French music which appeared to be centred in the neo-classicism of Camille Saint-Saëns.[1]

Again, this theatre music (which is small stuff) has attracted too much attention because, unlike the vast majority of such scores, the music had a certain concert value—like that of our own Sir Edward German (1862-1936). Incidental music in those days was not restricted solely to the stage action. It was less bound up with the play, and the composers were given plenty of opportunities in the entr'actes as theatres boasted "live" orchestras and did not depend on radiograms,

[1] There are still those alive who remember the tedium of his oratorio *The Promised Land,* which he wrote for a Three Choirs Festival in 1912. It appears that Saint-Saëns thought that English audiences expected and wanted twentieth-century Handel.

records and the kind permission or otherwise of the Musicians' Union to use them. Fauré's counterparts in this respect are found in the music to *Hassan* (Delius, 1862-1934) and *Mary Rose* (Norman O'Neill, 1875-1934). Sir Edward German was more symphonic in his approach and consequently incongruous; his music always betokened lavish production.

The graceful strain pervades such works as the Suite, *Dolly* (1893–1896)[1] and the *Pavane for Chorus (ad lib) and Orchestra* (1887). The quality of the melody is feline and sinuous. It pays no attention to key relationships or key sequences, but keeps a steady hold on tonality. Fauré holds the balance between the symphonic classicism of d'Indy with his emphasis on key relationship and the Impressionism of Debussy with its negation of key and discord. Fauré is strictly formal where Debussy ignored formalism, and is freely tonal where d'Indy would have kept within a key system.

He is one of the few composers to whom the word "exquisite" can be inoffensively and truly applied. His piano *Nocturnes* continue the tradition of Field and Chopin, and he inherited Chopin's gift of sustained cantabile melody. His pianism is never virtuosic and the Liszt tradition never appealed to him. Fauré's songs completely stylised the French manner. To all this music he brought a mind thoroughly equipped technically and founded upon a strictly classical tradition— no one otherwise trained could have written the piano *Variations in C sharp minor* (1897). His harmony is sometimes described as being careless; he was not concerned with niceties of preparation or resolution, but it is seldom that he uses parallel blocks of chords of the same quality and quantity. In a song like *La Parfum impérissable* (1897) the piano moves freely and chromatically. At the other end of the scale there is the reflective and lyrical diatonicism of *Clair de Lune* (1887).

Ex.2   *a)*   Fauré:- Le parfum impérissable

Mon coeur est em-bau - mé___ d'une o - deur im-mor - tel -

Notice the date and the harmonies of this song.

[1] Thousands of children "under five" know and sing part of this work, thanks to the B.B.C.

Fauré:- Clair de Lune

Tout   en   chan - tant   sur   le   mo-de mi - neur.

This music finished its work in 1918. From that moment it was supplanted by the slick Les Six and the uncompromising Stravinsky; but its day may not be completely over, for a post-war world torn between uncertainties and austerities is finding solace (and this is not the same thing as escapism) in the suavities of this exceedingly polished and not completely realised composer.

Our panorama leads into the realm of present-day actuality with a figure whose output has been large and for the most part has not been published, but whose influence as a teacher, again at the Paris Conservatoire[1] has been considerable. The author of many didactic books, he himself is a man of rare humanity and consequently he brings a breath of human feeling to harmony and counterpoint in their strictest forms. Although a certain amount of dogma is inescapable in technical teaching, Charles Koechlin (1867)[2] does not allow himself to be bound by the conventions of the schools. As a composer he holds the curious position of having anticipated all the "isms" and "alities" before they became fashionable; thus, like Satie, he has seen the "new music" catch up with him, but never pass him. He has never thrown over any style but uses whichever the situation demands. All the "isms" have been bent to his own necessity and in this way he has shown himself to be one of the most eclectic composers of his generation. This does not mean that his music is a mixture of styles, but it does imply that one has to look deeply into the technique before one recognises his individuality. It stands to reason, therefore, that he is not restricted to any single type of subject and he is at home in whatever presents itself. Impressionism suited his purpose in works like *L'Astre Rouge* and *Le Sommeil de Canope*, but in his *Etudes Antiques* he adopts a modal style with consummate ease. Similarly, in his Chamber Music, the thought turns to neo-classicism of a kind almost sparse in its economy and there is no feeling of uncertainty or unfitness anywhere. He is

[1] As a student, he left there without gaining a single award.

[2] News of Koechlin's death in 1950 came through after this section had gone to press.

one of the hardest composers to classify in detail because his characteristics are so eclectic, but one realises while listening that it is *his* music and no one else's. It must be said of him, therefore, that his individuality is indefinable in words.

His attitude may be explained by the fact that he regards classical harmony as the basis of all composition, unlike the Schola which placed the greater emphasis on counterpoint. He is insistent that the basic technique be mastered before the student attempts to write "free" harmony or counterpoint. In this way he guards his students against those extremist tendencies which often become evident too early in their careers and have no technical foundation. However, he is not a slave-driver and none of his students have ever complained of the relentless strictness of his training as did Georges Auric inveigh against that of the Schola Cantorum. One would say that Koechlin even now is more concerned with harmony in his own works than with anything else. It is easier to convince with the "new" harmony than with the "new" counterpoint, but his rhythm is rhapsodic and moves freely.

The exact reason for his neglect here is difficult to ascertain, unless it be that performances would show up the lack of originality in the thought of too many of the household names. It is difficult to proclaim a new prophet when that claim is liable to be found unjustified, and all the prophecies may be only echoes. It may well be thought that Koechlin should be regarded as a *Maître* rather than as a creative artist; but his personality precludes this. His capacity for work is as great as was that of Vincent d'Indy. It was Koechlin who orchestrated many of Fauré's works, a task of remarkable self-abnegation, for his name never appears on the scores.

Of all the composers born in the middle nineteenth century, he is the one who may be considered, with Erik Satie, as being most of the twentieth. One finds so much of both Satie and Koechlin in other people's music.

Our knowledge of French music is actually very limited. Of the older generation we know next to nothing about Roger-Ducasse (1873), Déodat de Séverac (1877-1921) and Louis Aubert (1877). Organists, however, play an elaborate and well-wrought *Pastorale* (1909) by the first-named, the second is vaguely remembered by his charming piece, *Où l'on entend une vielle boîte à musique* (1912), and the third received the honour of a solitary performance at a Promenade

Concert (at the time when those concerts really were the "Henry Wood Promenade Concerts") of his *Habanera* (1919), a work of prodigious warmth and passion.

One last figure must be mentioned since he may rightly be called the last of the Bohemians. Gustave Charpentier (1860) during his ninety years has written little and his reputation rests entirely upon one opera, *Louise* (1900), which from being reasonably well known over here seems to have passed into respectful oblivion.[1] *Louise* is a documentary. Charpentier realised that few operas were immediately concerned with the ordinary people who populate the big cities. It was written during the days of parental tyranny, when children could hardly whisper without first obtaining permission to do so. Charpentier was interested in the working girls of Montmartre, whose lives seemed to him to be drab and hard. He saw the contrast between the free life of the artist, insecure though it may have been, and the walled-up existence of the working girl. He was a picturesque individual in his younger days and had an eye for local colour, seeing the romance of Montmartre all round him and realising that here lay the material for a human opera which might support his venture, the "Conservatoire populaire de Marie Pinson", designed to give the working girl free musical education. (The workers, however, were not very responsive.) *Louise*, therefore, is an opera of the highest social significance.[2]

Charpentier wrote the libretto himself, sometimes adding it to the music, at others working at the two elements simultaneously. He told Gustav Mahler (1860-1911)[3] that at times he worked so enthusiastically at the music that it outpaced the libretto by several pages. *Louise* made an immediate appeal to Mahler. The scene of Paris by night, that in the sewing-room and the gala in honour of Louise herself ("The Crowning of the Muse") are among the most vital moments in opera. The scenes between Louise and her parents and her love passages with Julien are not great music and, indeed, sometimes touch bathos; but the whole technique of the opera is upon the conversational principle and there is only one aria which can be removed and performed separately—"Depuis le jour", within its context tolerable and understandable; outside it, sentimentally deplorable. The Nocturne and

[1] Its 500th Paris performance took place on January 18th, 1921.

[2] This seems to have escaped the notice of those who advocate the application of the principle to music.

[3] *Gustav Mahler: Memoirs and Letters*, Alma Mahler (John Murray).

sewing-room scenes, however, are effective by themselves and Charpentier shows his genius in dealing with big crowds in the latter and his sense of drama in the former.

This sermon on free love dates Charpentier's Bohemianism; the whole legend died rapidly during the first two decades of the present century. His Verism, however, manifested itself in Vienna. When Mahler produced *Louise* there, Charpentier insisted that Julien should be fitted with an electric lighting set beneath his costume, so that when he talked about his heart, the light illuminated a large-size model.[1] Charpentier, therefore, can claim to be both of and in the twentieth century, since *Louise* is written on twentieth-century principles (although its technique does not intrude very far over the borderline) and he himself embraced the fashionable philosophies of Social Realism and Verism.[2] The former, however, did not imply any Marxist tendencies. The sequel to *Louise*—*Julien* (1913)—failed as it was bound to do since the nature of the subject was not strong enough to carry further than the original impulse. Julien has succeeded in winning the Prix de Rome, and, according to the situations in the opera, lives in an atmosphere of almost unbridled licence. These situations may be romantic and poetic and they may show the dangers of free love (Louise is relegated very much to the background, preferring to be Julien's source of inspiration, etc., etc., etc.) but on the whole the entire work is too unreal. *Louise,* however, remains a masterpiece and a landmark in opera, its production in 1900 preceding that of Debussy's *Pelléas et Mélisande* by two years.

The infinite variety of French music makes it unpredictable, and he who would write about it without previous knowledge is rash indeed. The overlap of the centuries showed more signs of progress in France than anywhere else. The so-called *avant-garde* in music emanated from Paris, and she is still the home of present-day culture. The progress was slow, but most other cultures either stood still or tried to penetrate the heavy mists of tradition which had established an atmosphere of self-complacent smugness. Over the passage of the two centuries hovered the barbaric influence of the Teutonic eagle.

[1] *Gustav Mahler, op. cit.*

[2] Alma Mahler refers to Surrealism, but this represents an association of unassociated ideas.

CHAPTER TWO

ERIK SATIE
(1866-1925)

IN order to appreciate fully the distinction between French music at the end of the nineteenth and the beginning of the twentieth centuries, it is necessary to go back a matter of thirteen years or so and consider the revolution (already mentioned) which occurred in an obscure café, engineered by an equally obscure composer. The history of music shows, for the most part, a smooth evolutionary process, but now and again one finds a seed, which has been sown without any flourish of trumpets, growing to large proportions, making itself apparent quite suddenly and surprisingly.

In 1887 Erik Satie wrote three *Sarabandes,* the second of which contained the following passage:

This is by no means an isolated example and many others are to be found in the three pieces. Although this is often indicated as being one of the most influential moments in music, it must not be forgotten that a little earlier Emmanuel Chabrier (1841-1894) had written this:

which is not unlike the Satie extract, and, again, is by no means an isolated example. Chabrier's opera was produced in 1887 at the Paris Opéra-Comique, so that there is no question of its having being written after Satie's *Sarabandes*.

In 1888 César Franck (1822-1890) wrote the following progression:

The significance of this simple little harmonic process written by three independent figures indicates that at the time "a stir was in the air" which was to upset the balance of music in France. It sounded the emancipation of one particular chord, not in itself a particularly violent action, but one carrying with it the destruction of the principles of concord, discord and resolution. In 1896 Debussy wrote the next example:

which was equalled between 1892 and 1902 by:

Debussy, therefore, extended parallel discord to the dominant seventh, and elsewhere in this particular "Sarabande" evinced a still wider freedom. It is argued by some that the influence of Satie played no part in the formation of Debussy's technique; but, if that were so, Debussy must be reckoned the most original composer of the century. However, it is impossible to agree with this in view of the difference between Debussy's music written before and after his meeting with Satie.

Satie went further. In 1891 he wrote the following parallel progression in his *Le Fils des Etoiles*, described as "Wagnérie Kaldéene du Sur Péladin":

This harmonic superimposition of fourths was to be used by the vast majority of composers all over Europe in the first twenty years of the present century. It resulted in the fourth taking the place of the sixth, thus presenting a clear-cut underlining of a melody, which in sixths or thirds would not be sharp enough to bring it into relief. It will be seen that the notes form an inversion of the chord of the eleventh. Up to that time it was not customary to include the root in any inversion of any chord after the ninth. The custom became reversed and the inclusion of the forbidden root was one of the characteristics of the later composer, Albert Roussel.[1]

The point to observe is that from these moments the trend of French music completely altered. The peculiar charm and warmth allied, albeit, to Satie's almost classic grace, opened a vista to Debussy, which was to be considerably enlarged. It is worth commenting upon the personality and merit of Satie before proceeding to his twentieth-century situation.

It is customary among the learnèd professions no less than among the artistic circles to denounce any revolutionary spirit which does not depart from convention with dignity and a certain air of apology. Anyone showing a distinctly novel individuality of expression is regarded as a charlatan or a *farceur*. There is little search made for any possible hidden truth and the individual is the object of considerable indignation and laughter. This has been the case with Satie, and in spite of the writings of his champions, in spite of the professions of faith

[1] *Q.v.*

expressed by such authorities as P. D. Templier in France[1] and Constant Lambert[2] and Rollo Myers[3] in England, and also in spite of the confidence shown by Albert Roussel and other musicians of repute who knew him well, the highbrow still refuses to take Satie seriously. This type of serious-minded musician views Satie's music first of all from the point of view of title; he then opens the copy and, seeing unbarred music of no great length and, reading certain seemingly irrelevant sentences written above the notes, (in some cases, printed in red ink) decides that the man was mad, and pursues his investigations no further. It does not occur to this enquirer first to put on one side the somewhat unusual appearance of the music and then to examine its technique. If this were done, and an intelligent consideration given to what Satie wrote after 1903, it would completely alter the assessment of the music. True, Satie did not write symphonies or concertos. He did not write flamboyant rhapsodies; but he did write a *Sonatine Bureaucratique* (1917) which suggests that he was cocking a snook at this very type of superior person. Had Satie called the *Véritables Préludes Flasques (pour un Chien)* (1912), for example, *Trois Etudes*, there is little doubt but that they would have made an instant impression. However, there was method in what he did.

We are, of course, concerned here with the music of the twentieth century, and those composers whose output overlaps the turn cannot all be started at the year 1900. They must be discussed in relation to their twentieth-century work and the reasons for any change of technique examined with care.

In 1891 Satie outlined his concept of the technique of opera to Debussy, particularly in regard to the Wagnerian approach. Satie remarked that it was no more necessary for the orchestra to pull a face whenever a character appeared on the stage than it was for the trees of the décor to do so. Debussy was impressed and asked Satie what work was in his mind at that moment. Satie told him that he was meditating an opera, *La Princesse Maleine*, but was uncertain whether Maeterlinck would give the necessary permission. Later, Satie learnt that Debussy had obtained the Belgian dramatist's permission for the use of *Pelléas et Mélisande* and had started on the score. In spite of his apparent good humour, Satie was a sensitive soul, but he concealed

---

[1] *Satie* (Editions Rieder).
[2] *Music Ho!* (Faber and Faber).
[3] *Erik Satie* (Dobson).

his vexation and tore up his own score. He then told Jean Cocteau that he would have to change his own style or be lost to music for ever. In 1903 he took the plunge and entered the Schola Cantorum for the purpose of studying counterpoint with Albert Roussel. His friends were dismayed. Debussy tried hard to dissuade him, saying that it might alter his natural style and possibly ruin it for ever. Satie replied that if the latter happened, "tant pis pour moi".

The fact was that Satie had already tired of the overheated Impressionism which unwittingly he had let loose and which had sprung from his chaste *Sarabandes* (1887) and *Gymnopédies* (1888). Debussy's action over the opera had nettled him. On the austerities of counterpoint he fancied that he could formulate a technique which would be individual to himself alone.

Roussel, too, tried to dissuade him from taking this step, as he did not consider it necessary; but Satie was adamant. Roussel described him as *"prodigieusement musicien"* and related that he was a most exemplary student and that his counterpoint was impeccable. Satie acquired a whole-hearted admiration for Bach's *Chorales* and his enthusiasm for them infected the members of the organ class at the Schola Cantorum. Eventually Satie left the Schola with a certificate of proficiency.

From that moment his music became sharp and incisive, and never again did he indulge in what is now called (somewhat loosely) "romantic harmony". The titles of his pieces became even more outrageous—this has never been completely understood. Jean Cocteau supplies the reason:[1]

> One often wonders why Satie saddles his finest works with grotesque titles which mislead the least hostile sections of the public. Apart from the fact that these titles protect his works from persons obsessed by the sublime and provide an excuse for the laughter of those who do not realise their value, they can be explained by the Debussy-ist abuse of "precious" titles. No doubt they are meant as a good-humoured piece of ill-humour, and maliciously directed against "Lunes descendant sur le temple qui fut", "Terrasses des audiences du Clair de lune" and "Cathédrales englouties".

Cocteau goes on to say that:

> The public is shocked at the charming absurdity of Satie's titles

[1] *Cock and Harlequin*, trans. by Rollo H. Myers (The Egoist Press).

and system of notation, but respects the ponderous absurdity of the libretto of "Parsifal".

Still more to the point is his next statement:

> The same public accepts the most ridiculous titles of François Couperin: "Le tic-toc choc ou les Maillotins", "Les Culbotes Ixcbxnxs", "Les coucous bénévoles", "Les Calotins et Calotines ou la pièce à tretous", "Les vieux galants et les Trésorieres surannes".

Satie, therefore, moved further and further away from Debussy and Impressionism, but he had the mortifying if somewhat entertaining experience in the light of his new technique of hearing his early works praised to the skies by those who previously had condemned them.[1] The cynicism of Satie's bitterness is apparent. It would seem that in titles like *Véritables Préludes Flasques (pour un Chien)*, *Embryons desséchés*, *Descriptions Automatiques*, *Aperçus Désagréables*, he was deliberately forming an opposition party: it should be noted that these titles did not enter his list of works until the twentieth century; up till then *Gnossiennes* appears to be the most unusual one. Truth to tell, Satie was obviously hurt to the innermost depths of his soul, but his sense of personal loyalty would not allow him to come out into verbal abuse of what his erstwhile friend Debussy had come to represent. His titles, therefore, went in direct contradiction to the romantically beautiful ones used by Debussy.

The extraordinary craving for sensation (leading him into all kinds of absurdities, not the least being his arrival on the stage at the end of *Relâche* [1924], described as a "Ballet Instantanéiste", in a 5-h.p. car), with which his detractors charged him was nothing more or less than a deliberate revolt against everything which Impressionism was doing to art in general. Each new movement, Dadaism, Surrealism, Classicism, was taken up by Satie entirely with this end in view. He surrounded himself with the young composers of Paris. What originated in "Les Nouveaux Jeunes" finally resolved into "Les Six". Satie found himself proclaimed by Jean Cocteau as "the great Master who is the inspiration of the new school" and finally as "*Le Maître d'Arcueil*", the suburb of Paris in which he lived; there he gathered round himself the young men

---

[1] "The public only takes up Yesterday as a weapon with which to castigate To-day" (Jean Cocteau, *op. cit.*)

of the time, Roger Désormière (1898), Henri Cliquet-Pleyel (1894), Maxime Jacob (1906), and Henri Sauguet (1901). All these enthusiasts were pledged, so to speak, to purify French music from the enervating atmosphere of Impressionism, which they considered clogged up musical expression with thick mists of vague tone. Their cry was "simplicity" and with Satie as their leader the battle raged as fiercely as in the days of the Gluckists and Piccinists. Satie served his young followers well, since he was sufficiently notorious to give them a certain standing, even if only for abuse, and they did not make things at all easy for themselves. When the ballet *Relâche* was produced the audience found the theatre locked up. (It must be explained to those unaware of the fact that in France any theatre without a production in progress is locked up and the word *Relâche* is posted on its notice boards.) This was perfectly logical if one comes to think of it, but hardly practical or politic; it was all part of the plan of operation.

This work, incidentally, provided the first film score, for in it there was an "Entr'acte Cinématagraphique". Here, again, Satie was a pioneer; in this case it is irrefutable, and he had the technique of the trade at his fingertips. The music is sufficiently positive to underline the action and negative enough to draw no attention to itself. The principle was largely the same as in his *Musique d'Ameublement* (1920), which he designed as a background to conversation during the entr'actes of a play; the latter, however, had nothing to underline or bring into relief to a viewer or hearer. To Satie's chagrin, everyone stopped talking to listen to it.

It may be useful to see at this point how far Satie had progressed from the technique of the *Sarabandes*. Compare Ex. 1 with Ex. 7, on page 29, from the first of the *Véritables Préludes Flasques*.

The cold classicism of this little extract has no bearing whatsoever on its title or anything else; it is simply "pure" music for piano. This style found its fullest expression in the drama *Socrate* (1919) and the ballet *Mercure* (1924), and in the former case an interesting parallel can be found. Both these works require some study since they contain the elements of the mature neo-classicism of the present day, of which Igor Stravinsky is the High Priest.

Socrate was written just at the realisation of Milhaud and the rest of Les Six, and Milhaud's stage music will be found to bear some affinity of approach with it. It is described as a "Drame Symphonique en trois parties avec voix sur les dialogues de Platon" and was com-

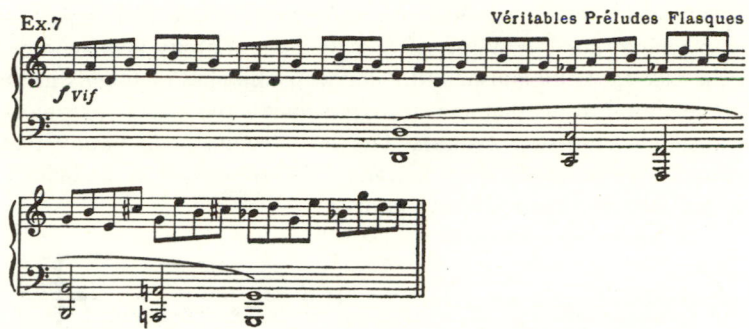

Ex.7   Véritables Préludes Flasques

posed for the Princesse Edmond de Polignac, to whom many composers owed a lasting debt of gratitude. The three parts are

1. Portrait de Socrate   (Alcibiade)   Le Banquet
2. Les Bords d'Illissus   (Socrate et Phèdre)   Phèdre
3. Mort de Socrate   (Phédon)   Phédon

The music is directed to be played in a perfectly level manner. There are no expression marks other than a "P" at the beginning of each movement, an occasional "PP", one "F" and crescendo and decrescendo. In this completely unexpressive approach the reader may remember Stravinsky's *Symphonies d'Instruments à vent en memoire de Debussy* which he wished to be played without any change of dynamic, albeit the expression lay (in spite of the composer's protests to the contrary) in the rise and fall of the notes.[1] It may be argued, therefore, that the music is negative, but in *Socrate* the negation is justified since the accompaniment underlines the text in such a way as to leave little impression. There is not the slightest hint at any dramatic expression until the end when, at the death of Socrate, the music adopts a square staticism on a pedal point.

The work requires four sopranos, flute, oboe, cor anglais, clarinet, bassoon, horn, trumpet, harp, kettledrums and strings.[2] Satie directs the solo voice to sing *en lisant*. Is it far-fetched to see here a parallel to the *sprechstimme* of Schoenberg? A feature of the technique and its particular "-ism" is that it makes performance with orchestra absolutely essential; with piano alone it soon becomes almost unbearably monotonous. This is a parallel at the other end of the scale with orchestral

[1] See page 281.
[2] See Holst's *Savitri*.

Impressionism which requires colouring to convince and impart its true meaning; but in the case of *Socrate* the monotony is engendered by the placing of the music which for wide stretches of time is in the same tessitura. In the first and third movements the music flows along in an almost non-stop manner. The accompaniment is simply that, and nothing else. There is no figuration. As an example of the melodic rise and fall, take the following phrase:

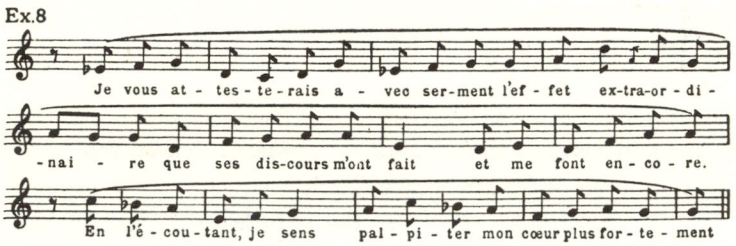

Ex.8

The line corresponds with the rise and fall of the spoken voice. At the end Socrate addresses Alcibiade in this way:

Ex.9

In the second movement the music moves along in 6/8 time and there is much more of an accompanimental figure which gives the feeling of a pleasant pastoral picture.

It is in the third movement that Satie shows how unnecessary it is to be graphic in the face of tragedy, and how full of poignancy polyphonically simple music can be. The music moves in blocks of triads and in open fifths, the latter giving the feeling of intense grief. In his book on the composer,[1] Rollo Myers quotes the music at the moment

[1] *Op. cit.*

(*Above*) MAURICE RAVEL (1875–1937)
(*Right*) ALBERT ROUSSEL (1869–1937)

Arthur Honegger (1892) 　　　　Darius Milhaud (1892)

when the Narrator tells how Socrate raised the cup of hemlock to his lips. This is one of those passages which must be quoted by every writer on Satie with music type at his disposal:

Ex.10

So-cra - te por-ta la coupe à ses lè - vres   et la but a-veɑ u-ne tran-quil-li-té

There is nothing "thematic". There is no definite theme which is extended or treated in any way. Now and again fragments are repeated in the orchestra while the voice proceeds along in its own course seemingly quite inconsequentially. If we think of the many operatic deaths by murder and suicide, with accompaniment of full orchestra and surging vocal lines, Satie seems to have put them all in the shade by means of perfectly clean four-part writing whose very negativism makes it own effect. That this work is "great" will not be claimed by its most fervent admirers; but, nevertheless, it does show certain signs of this in its unique character and idiom which are perfectly suited to the subject and in every way emotionally convince the listener. It is one of those works for which the radio is so admirably suited, given the right listening situation. Those who wish to study verbal accentuation for the purpose of setting a French text can do no better than to study it through this work.

Socrate is, of course, the most seriously intentioned work in the whole of Satie's large output. The ballets *Relâche*, *Parade* ("Ballet Réaliste") (1917) and *Jack-in-the-Box* (1899), posthumously scored by Darius Milhaud and intended originally for a pantomime, are among the high-jinks of music. They show just how far behind Milhaud and the contemporary music of the period Satie actually was. *Mercure* (1924), however, is different. This series of "Poses Plastiques" was a collaboration of all the best in the theatre world at the time—Picasso, Massine and Satie. The music is chaste and formal and can be seen to be in many respects the father of Stravinsky's *Appollon Musagéte*. In his painting of Night in *Le Sacre*, Stravinsky strains every instrument to its utmost. Satie gives an equally menacing picture in four parts, of which one is a pedal point and another only duplication at the octave of another part.

The music is divided into separate "numbers" of astonishing brevity. Again, it is impossible to obtain an adequate idea on the piano, but one would point to the Dance of the Graces

for delicacy; the Bath of the Graces

for chaste classic dignity, and to the Rage of Cerberus and the earlier Entry of Mercury

for strength of rhythm and, in the former case, no little natural humour. In the third tableau the music suddenly changes into polka style which, away from the *mise en scène*, strikes the ear as incongruous. It may be well to quote the final cadence:

Satie will always remain a legendary figure to whom lip-service and a certain amount of credit are given. He will always have his detractors who, for the reasons put forward, will never cease to regard him as the "phoniest"[1] figure in musical history. An understanding of his circumstances does not seem to ease the situation with the latter who are unable to see the defiance of his twentieth-century music.

[1] *Sic.*

CHAPTER THREE

CLAUDE DEBUSSY
(1862-1918)

THE year 1900 saw Debussy at the apex of his second "stage", which he had reached from the pre-Raphaelitism of *La Demoiselle Elue* (1887-1889), a stage which he never completely threw off, for it appears constantly in small places in his later work. From here he came under the influence of Symbolism, reacting to it from the poems of Verlaine and Baudelaire. A momentary return to the classical ideal appeared in the *String Quartet* (1893), but while composing this work he was thinking out the *Prélude à l'Après-Midi d'un Faune,* suggested by the poem of Mallarmé. It is from this work that he obtained his description as "Impressionist", a term which has been loosely handed about ever since and, in many instances, completely misapplied. Further experiments with the poems of Mallarmé and also with those of Pierre Loüys (*Chansons de Bilitis*, 1898) led to the three *Nocturnes,* which were produced in 1900 and made an immediate success.

The first and third of these, "Nuages" and "Sirênes", completely fulfil the impressionistic viewpoint. Both are vague in outline, particularly the latter. The second, "Fêtes", is far too clearly defined to be anything but an objective musical painting. It is not difficult to understand the reason for the success of this work. It lay very largely in its shape. This is perfect. "Fêtes", with its ebullience, forms a fitting centre to the triptych; its brilliance dispels the mists of "Nuages", and the veiled mysteries of "Sirênes" are a relief after the terrific drive of "Fêtes". This musical impetuosity with its swirling gaiety and suggestion of a gradually materialising brass band, is sufficient to give the lie to the too often repeated theory that Debussy was incapable of strength and could blossom only in the enervating atmosphere of the hot-house. The balance between these three movements is admirable,

It put a halt upon the generally accepted framework of "loud, soft, loud", and the quiet ending of "Sirênes" had an electrifying effect upon the audience at that time. I use the word "electrifying" advisedly, not in its sensational aspect, but as one which took the audience by surprise. Debussy here settled the question of the reflective coda. Its influence can be heard in the ending of "Neptune, the Mystic", in Holst's *The Planets*, which is pure Impressionism in its nebulosity.

The actual peak of Debussy's symbolism was realised in *Pelléas et Mélisande*, produced at the Paris Opéra-Comique on April 30th, 1902; he had commenced its composition in 1892. The reception, after a preparatory period of considerable travail, proved that no matter how subdued or "unoperatic" the work might be, it had vitality enough to sting the public into fury. Its impressionistic tendencies are by no means consistent, since the term can hardly be applied to a work governed by a text whose chief element is conversational declamation. In the purely orchestral passages the music can most assuredly be termed Impressionism; these places evoke a mood or a situation.

It is difficult to-day to imagine exactly how the audience must have felt as this monodic work progressed in a manner deliberately for-swearing all operatic conventions, unless one fully realises its pre-cursors and can place oneself in the theatre, so to speak, on that memor-able occasion. Here was a work with no overture, no choruses, no arias or ensemble numbers, no parts detachable from the whole and no actual tunes which could remain in the mind. Audiences were attuned to Massenet. They had become accustomed to the Wagnerian "*leit-motif*" or "guiding theme" which heralded the arrival of each character and symbolised certain actions. Debussy called these "visiting cards"; Satie referred to them as "grimaces". After some time the Wagnerian *leitmotiv* sinks into the consciousness of the listener. He recognises it easily and can take it away with him in his mind. The remarkable thing is that there actually are *leitmotivs* in *Pelléas et Méli-sande*, but Debussy does not always expose them and in many cases they have no particular bearing on what they accompany. Their use here, therefore, is in no way arbitrary and is dictated more by musical feeling and instinct than by any literary or symphonic reason. In *Pelléas* there was literally nothing that could be mentally referred to as approaching a theme or even a tune. Instead of singing, the voices recited and there was a veil of extremely lovely sound which appeared to have no cohesion, and no continuity. The subject itself was generally miserable and the sophisticated Paris audience, accustomed to the melodic loves of Manon and Thaïs, failed to see the point in such lines as "I am happy, but I am sad . . . I am not happy here".

Many opera-goers listen to the singing more than to the music. They are more concerned with a beautifully produced voice than with a beautiful work. In *Pelléas* there is no vocal display of any kind—and it was not the first time that a by now established opera failed on its production owing to an unusual attitude to singers. Gounod's *Faust* is a striking example of this. At the première the audience had come to hear Mme. Carvalho, a favourite singer, as Marguerite. They waited a long time for her appearance. Eventually in the second act she entered, declined Faust's attentions by saying that she was "not a lady",[1] and then went out, to remain out until the next act. Discontent in the theatre is usually caused through anticipation, and in the case of both operas this played a deciding factor, with the difference that after a few minutes, the audience for *Pelléas* realised what type of music they were to listen to, whereas in *Faust* they hoped, and hoped, and were annoyed at the postponement of their hopes.

All this seems a little elementary to-day, but it does not become one to be wise after an event. Opera and concert audiences do not consist necessarily of knowledgeable musicians. They are for the most part people who love music. They go for the purpose of an evening's enjoyment, and this does not merely mean "entertainment". The greater number have never been adventurous; they have never craved for novelty, although they accept it when it is not too far outside their immediate comprehension. They expect to be met at least halfway. *Pelléas et Mélisande* made no attempt to move one step in their direction. The concert-goer is far more prepared to listen than he who goes to the opera. The former expects to listen to long, slow movements. The latter is willing to do the same, but not when the movements are long. When this is the case, he subconsciously expects orchestral variety behind the voices.

The circumstances of the production are not without significance. Maeterlinck expressed final disapproval of the whole thing because he did not like Debussy's choice of singer for Mélisande, and he spared no pains to let the world know of his disapproval. An idea of the unique nature of the work had been spread round and the audience was inveigled into buying a spurious programme outside the theatre,

[1] This gave rise to loud guffaws.

which gave a parodied version of the opera. The "advance publicity", therefore, was not calculated to allay suspicion or repress latent hostility. Rehearsal had been complicated because Debussy had entrusted the copying of the parts to an impecunious friend and had neglected to check them. Consequently, absolute chaos reigned at times; but both Albert Carré, the director of the Opéra-Comique, and André Messager, the conductor, knew the value of the work and took infinite pains with it. What were the feelings of the audience when the opening bars stole in, quietly and unobtrusively, like this,

and the music proceeded to unroll itself in a continuous stream of quasi-recitative in which the orchestra played but a supporting rôle of a subdued nature, the singers declaiming rather than singing? The moments of drama are not pointed by music of enormous violence. In the fight between Golaud and Pelléas there is simply a short passage of arms culminating in Ex. 2 which is shown placed alongside bar three of Ex. 1 above. The deaths of both Pelléas and Mélisande are unattended by any symphonic urge like the "Liebestod" in *Tristan und Isolde*.

Pelléas et Mélisande remains a unique work. Its effects are gained by the simplest of means and Debussy is most effective when there is little movement. The principles underlying its beauty are, first and foremost, the conversational effect of the music which places the emphasis on the natural inflexions of the voice, and, second, the underlining of situations and statements by the orchestra. It is going rather far to consider the following passages as one of "the loveliest things in the whole score"[1] because there are plenty of others more beautiful and equally simple. From this point of view there is nothing which can be taken from the context as being superior to anything else. It may be noted that these two phrases, together with the two opening bars, reflect the Pre-Raphaelitism of Debussy's first stage. If Maeter-

[1] "Debussy", Lockspeiser (Dent, *Master Musicians*).

linck had but realised it, few poets have been so well treated by a composer, because Debussy regarded the text as everything but a vehicle for musical display. His attention to the rise and fall of the syllables is a model for all time. M. Léon Oleggini recounts an illuminating experience in this connection:[1]

> I was in the middle of a crowd of turbulent children. By accident I happened to tread on the foot of one of them. I then heard some words which astonished me: "Oh! Monsieur, vous m'avez fait mal!"[2] This cry of anguish was not unknown to me. Was it from a song or was it simply a natural exclamation? It was exactly the same melodic inflexion as the gentle "Petit père, vous m'avez fait mal" which escaped from the lips of little Yniold when his father trod upon his foot. This was a natural and spontaneous cry of reproach expressed emotionally in ordinary human language.

Here is the phrase:

If the reader will recite any sentence of the poem aloud, he will find a close analogy between his vocal inflexions and the rise and fall of Debussy's music.

However, this must not be taken to imply that there is no dramatic

---

[1] *Au cœur de Claude Debussy* (Julliard).

[2] French is necessary here.

force or strength in the music. Take that moment when Golaud grasps
Mélisande by the hair and swings it to and fro:

This is typical of the direct pin-pointing of the music, in direct
opposition to the technique of Wagner, of whom Debussy said that
"he sang too often".

The orchestra underlines throughout. Read the well-known phrase
when Mélisande lets down her hair from the tower window; as her
tresses glide down the wall, the orchestra glitters in a parallel manner:

The scene in the vaults is ominously graphic,

the whole effect being obtained by harmonic simplicity. On the other hand, Debussy could be quietly lyrical, as the following phrase (which might have come from a string quartet) shows:

The simplicity of Ex. 7 and, indeed, the first two bars of Ex. 1 and the following is only a question of degree:

Think of the swirling passion of Tristan and Isolde when they declare their love, and compare it with Debussy's extremely direct yet no less passionate utterance, "Je t'aime. . . . Je t'aime aussi", statements made with no orchestral background to suggest the physiological aspect of the situation.

Pelléas et Mélisande is a work which requires the full sympathy of the audience. Its primary obstacle to immediate acceptance was that it came too suddenly; it was too "novel". It is easy to make extravagant claims for it. It did not alter the course of things, although composers have learned lessons of pure lyricism from it. Debussy did not repeat himself in this way in any later stage work. *Pelléas et Mélisande*, however, marks the final disappearance of traditional and classical harmony. It also marks the centre of a curious trilogy. Wagner solved his problems symphonically in *Tristan und Isolde* and after that the way remained perfectly clear to him. Debussy solved his, declamatorily. Satie in *Socrate*[1] defined emotional expression in a purely classical manner which left the voice almost speaking its lines over a (for the most part) inconsequential accompaniment. From the association of Debussy and Satie there arose the *sprechstimme* of Schoenberg, a completely satisfactory cross between speech and song. Wagner opened the door of the hot-house; Debussy passed through it and Satie let in the air at the other end. Each work is a landmark, but only *Tristan und Isolde* has exercised a world influence because it alone has a primarily *musical* basis.

Whether it stands isolated or not, *Pelléas et Mélisande* remains a great work. It combines Symbolism with Impressionism; it has not extended the latter in any way because it is unextendable. Without it, Dukas could not have written *Ariane et Barbe Bleu,* which is more conversationally lyrical and more intensely musical. As Jean Lepine points out,[2] *Pelléas et Mélisande* is not, musically speaking, Debussy's masterpiece, because there is not enough actual music in it; but it is a masterpiece of the operatic and lyrical stage. Its influence on composers has not been as direct nor as strong as has that of Dukas' *Ariane et Barbe Bleu.*

It is an open question as to whether *L'Après-Midi* or *La Mer* is Debussy's "masterpiece". The former certainly exercised a world influence, but its limited scope prevented Debussy from exercising his latent powers of expansion to the full. In *La Mer* he was under no restrictions. With this work he entered upon his third stage, which may be described as Naturism (of all composers, Debussy appears to be inseparable from "-isms"). *La Mer* is fully symphonic and in this respect we may be permitted to wonder as to the genuineness of Debussy's fulminations against symphonies and symphonic music.

All readers of Debussy's musical criticism know that he never wrote of Franck, d'Indy or Chausson in terms other than those of the greatest respect and admiration. All three composers, particularly the second, represented everything that he fought against. His action in withdrawing the early *Fantaisie* for piano and orchestra (1889), after its rehearsal, on the score of its being too much in the *cyclique* style, is reasonable, as he was a young man at the time and wished to be original. The fact that the *String Quartet* is cyclical throughout suggests an inherent attraction to the style, and indicates that his powers of deriva-

[1] See pages 30 and 31.
[2] *La Vie de Claude Debussy* (Les Vies Authentiques, Albin Michel).

tion and variation were of an advanced nature. No composer with his face set firmly and irrevocably against what is known as symphonic development could have contrived *La Mer*, a work notable for its sustained development and continuity. It is impossible to find out anything from his letters in this respect, except that the whole thing was anathema to him and that he was determined to rid French music of anything applicable to the Teutonic classical ideal. One can read between the lines, however, and imagine a certain amount of frustration at the deliberate avoidance of everything which was basically latent within him and which was self-consciously thrust aside in the endeavours to be original, individual and prophetic at all costs. Drawn in two directions, one by instinct, the other by a sense of cultural patriotism, finding out as time went on that his self-formed idiom was gradually exhausting itself and finally having to return to a style of neo-classicism, his sense of disillusionment and his general attitude as displayed in his critical writings and in his personal relations with his contemporaries, are perfectly understandable. There are few composers who have been completely satisfied with themselves, but still fewer who have given evidence of such consummate disappointment. There are few who have accomplished so much and made such an impact on the progress of music while appearing to disapprove of the whole thing.

La Mer was Debussy's last large-scale purely orchestral work. It has been said that he wrote himself out with it and that subsequent music written in this style was a means of finding a way of expression which should crystallise all the three stages of his creative output. As we know, this crystallisation terminated in the neo-classical Sonatas. In the meantime, however, he enriched the world with some beautiful music. *La Mer* completely repudiates the theory of Debussy's nebulosity. In this work he does not give himself up to dreaming. The music is strong and vital. Some have complained that it in no way suggests its subject and that nowhere is the salt tang of the sea evoked; but Debussy was not writing three sea pictures of a conventional kind. There appears to be a standard for the musical portrayal of waves of all sizes, and none of the well-known works fail in this delineation. Debussy thought of the sea and expressed those thoughts in his own way. He made it musically tangible, he who never experienced it directly to any great extent—Roussel, the quondam naval officer, never once found it a source of musical inspiration. *La Mer* shows the difference between Debussy's Impressionism and Naturism, and many expected him to remain nebulous and filmy. There is nothing "pretty" about *La Mer*, nothing vague. The sea is not presented with sunshine glittering upon gentle blue wavelets. The music surges within the confines of its context. Many commentators see signs in it of the later neo-classicism, especially in the remarkable triadic phrase in the third movement. This is not altogether accurate. If anything, it suggests a backward glance at the early triadic music of *La Demoiselle Elue*, although, of course, considerably reinforced. Debussy might well have become the master of the common chord had he so chosen; but it would have entailed either a self-conscious archaicism or too much strength, and this was the measure (in his eyes) of that insidious Teutonic influence which he felt to be making an impression on French music. Yet the twentieth-century master of the common chord[1] has shown it capable of the fullest individual expression. After *La Mer*, Debussy's Naturism, which he expressed by means of "Impressionistic" harmony, was compressed within the small forms.

There are not many composers whose piano music is divisible into two such completely different categories as is that of Debussy. It is extremely difficult to place many of the earlier *Suites* within the compass of the twentieth century because their composition, or at least their assembling, was spread over a wide space of years. The *Suite Berga-masque*, for example, was commenced in 1890 and finished in 1905, while *Pour le Piano* ranged from 1896 to 1901. The former went through several stages of indecision before coming to fruition. Debussy intended that it should consist of

> Prélude
> Menuet
> Promenade sentimentale
> Pavane

and somewhere or other *Masque* and *L'Isle joyeuse* were to be included. It finally appeared as

> Prélude
> Menuet
> Clair de Lune
> Passepied

The two rejected pieces were published separately in 1904. It is possible to associate the third movements under one idea, but

[1] Page 142.

one is tempted to regard both *Suites* as collections of isolated pieces written at odd moments and assembled for the purpose of publication.

These works are written in the spirit of the old clavecin composers, with the exception of "Clair de Lune", which is pure pianism throughout. The superior person despises them as he does *not* despise the *Children's Corner*, a suite composed between 1906 and 1908, because it is a succession of characteristic little pictures, each with a sentimental appeal. This sentimentalism appears also in the dedication. Actually the quality of the *Children's Corner* is not as high as either of the other two *Suites* and it is very much *une œuvre de circonstance*. The clarity of the texture is striking in both *Suites*. In the "Prélude" to the *Suite Bergamasque* Debussy shows diatonic strength and bravura. In the "Menuet" he uses the inner thumb melody of the right hand which characterises the later "Minstrels" and "General Lavine eccentric" while the interlocking hands traces back to Rameau's "Le Lardon" upon which Dukas raised such monumental *Variations*.[1] The "Passepied" (in duple time) is similar in character to that in Delibes' *Le Roi s'amuse*, its mediant pedal point being quite Franckian. "Clair de Lune" is an oasis in what otherwise is a *Dance Suite*. Its prettiness has made for undue popularity, this finding its outlet in countless disarrangements for salon orchestras. It has a certain kinship with some of Gabriel Fauré's slender thoughts, but its pianism is by no means subtle.

Pour le Piano opens with a detached and Toccata-like "Prélude" and is diatonic until the reiterated chords in the middle; it is then rather spoilt by the augmented triad which gives a suggestion of the wholetone scale. This "Prélude" is actually much more Toccata-like than the so-described finale, which is not nearly so brittle. The "Sarabande" has already been mentioned.[2] It is in the "Toccata" of *Pour le Piano* that one of the few contacts with Ravel can be found, the general texture of the piece corresponding with that of the third movement in Ravel's *Sonatine for Piano*. It was in 1901 that the impact of Ravel was felt by Debussy. This was the year of *Jeux d'eau* which immediately opened a new vista to Debussy and other members of the band known to themselves as the Apaches. The first results of Debussy's study of this work are to be found in *L'Isle joyeuse* (suggested

[1] See page 9.
[2] See page 23.

by Watteau's picture, "Embarquement pour Cythère") and shortly afterwards in "Reflets dans l'eau" (1905) which was the first piece in the first set of *Images*. The influence is not clearly noticeable in the set of *Etampes* (1903) of which "Pagodes" and "Soirée dans la Grenade" are picturesque and evocative, while "Jardins sous la Pluie" reflects the diatonicism of the early *Danse* (1890). In the two sets of *Images* Debussy established Impressionism as a pianistic style. The titles became fanciful, particularly in the second book whose pieces are called "Cloches à travers les feuilles", "Et la lune descend sur le temple qui fut" (a title added after composition at the suggestion of Louis Laloy) and "Poissons d'Or", suggested by a piece of Oriental lacquer, not by goldfish swimming round a bowl. Impressionism thus became combined with Naturism. Of these two books of *Images*, "Reflets dans l'eau" owes everything to Ravel's *Jeux d'Eau* without in any way resembling it. It is beautifully evocative of a summer scene. A phrase such as this descends directly from Satie:

while this shows point of contact with Ravel's pianism:

"Hommage à Rameau", the second of the first book of *Images,* moves with chordal dignity, evoking the majesty of Versailles. The piece is described as "dans le style d'une Sarabande mais sans rigueur". The chordal progress of the right-hand part in the following extract needs extreme care:

Here this block pianism is successful; it is not so in "Et la lune descend sur le temple qui fut" because the quality and quantity of the chords are too similar.

The only impressionistic movement in the *Children's Corner* is "The Snow is Dancing", which gives a remarkable evocation in sound of a soundless element. The regrettable *La plus que lente* (1910) may have been a "pot-boiler"; Debussy himself scored it for orchestra and it has suffered a fate similar to "Clair de lune" at the hands of Salon combinations. The years 1910-1913, however, saw the two books of *Préludes* for piano which rank among the most notable achievements of the twentieth century.

In order to emphasise the pictorial intention of the pieces, Debussy placed the titles at the end of each piece. In this way we stroll round a picture gallery, and study each picture in turn, referring to the catalogue, not in ignorance or unawareness, but to see the exact wording of the titles. This idea is not dissimilar to Moussorgsky's *Pictures at an Exhibition* (Debussy was one of the first in France to recognise Moussorgsky's greatness) save that in Moussorgsky's case the scene is actually laid, so to speak, in a picture gallery and there are short "Promenades" which take us from exhibit to exhibit.

In only two cases are there fanciful titles—"Les sons et les parfums tournent dans l'air du soir" and "La Terrasse des audiences au clair de lune". In one case, "Les Tierces alternées", the description becomes technical and this particular Prélude might well have suggested the later *Douze Etudes*. From the analogy of the picture gallery it seems as if an abstract design has slipped in by mistake. In certain cases the descriptions are not convincing. Without looking at the title one would not guess at "Hommage à S. Pickwick Esqre P.P.M.P.C." which, in spite of M. Cortot's eulogy,[1] is both silly and dull. On the other hand, "General Lavine eccentric", "Ministrels", and "Ondine" are distinctly personal studies, the first two quaint and the third nebulous. Debussy simply gives a picture of Ondine rising from the waves; Ravel, in his large-scale movement of the same title, presents her in person in all her sinister beauty and cruelty. In "La Cathédrale engloutie" Debussy paints a musical scene which has made an appeal everywhere, especially among those moderate pianists who can manage the not very difficult pianism, and whose imagination is stirred by the solid organ-like quasi-ecclesiastical chords. The same may be said of "La fille aux cheveux de lin" whose chaste virginity is as simple-minded as "Le petit berger" in the *Children's Corner*. Préludes such as "Les collines d'Anacapri", "Le danse de Puck" and in a small way, "Bruyères", are perfect. "Feux d'artifice" does not come off, in spite of the Marseillaise.

It is often very loosely said that in these *Préludes* Debussy used the whole-tone scale and produced nothing more than musical "atmospherics". Neither of these statements is true. Only in one—"Voiles"—did he concentrate upon the former, and then not consistently, since he found its limitations very quickly. As for "atmospherics", he evoked atmosphere, and objection to this is taken only by those who worship at the shrine of Teutonic classicism.

The pianism in these *Préludes* is Debussy's own. He established this little form as a picturesque piece, and no longer "always founded upon some particular figure". It is the idiom of the *Préludes* which has drawn attention away from the earlier *Suites* which, by comparison, sound rather faded and *démodé*; but in due course it will very probably be these *Suites* which will survive. Impressionism already sounds dated; this is very true, also, of *L'Isle joyeuse*, and a dated style does not take many generations to become a mere period piece.

From this point Debussy discarded Impressionism and Naturism and turned Neo-Classicism. The first large-scale indication of this was revealed in his music for Gabriele d'Annunzio's play *Le Martyre de Saint-Sebastien* (1911), commissioned by Ida Rubinstein. This work

[1] *La Musique Française de Piano* (Vol. I) (Presses Universitaires de France).

came under the veto of the Roman Catholic Church, the Archbishop of Paris forbidding the faithful to have anything to do with it, firstly because the principal dancer was a Jewess, and secondly because he did not consider Debussy a fit and proper person to enter the realm of ecclesiastical music.

Still further refinement of texture came in the *Six Epigraphes antiques* which followed the *Préludes*. These are transcriptions of early pieces and are purely classical. The *Douze Etudes* (1913) for piano, in two books, are simply performers' pieces, the aesthetic appeal not being very strong. They say very little, but serve to show the direction his mind was taking. *En blanc et noir*, three pieces for two pianos (1915), are impelled more by orchestral than by pianistic thought.

By the twentieth century the songs had shown his complete departure from symbolism, although the *Trois Poémes de Stephane Mallarmé* (1913) indicate a glance back in that direction. Two of the *Poémes* ("Soupir" and "Placet futile") were set by Ravel and the settings should be compared. [1] In the *Trois Ballades de François Villon* (1910) the shadow of the future "Claude de France" made its appearance, to become established in the *Trois Chansons de France* (1914) for mixed voices in the polyphonic style, and in 1915 in the *Sonatas* for 'cello and piano, and for flute, viola, and harp, to be followed in 1916–1917 by one for violin and piano. These were described as being composed by "Claude Debussy, Musicien français" and in them Debussy tried to align himself with the spirit of Rameau. These chamber works sound laboured and suggest that he had reached the limit of his capacity. Only in the early *String Quartet* does he satisfy as an abstract composer, and even in that genre he was unable to avoid delicate romanticism as in the slow movement.

There are certain works which are rarely heard. Among them is *Jeux* (1912), a ballet which he wrote for Nijinsky. This most unballetic music, written to an equally unballetic scenario, is despised by the Debussy specialists, but it has many lovely moments. It is too serious for its subject, which amounts only to the loss of a tennis ball by two players, subsequent love-making, and a second tennis ball thrown on to the court by an unseen hand. This has been interpreted as a psychological conflict between the two sexes. This is as may be, but Nijinsky was notoriously insensitive to music. Debussy's score is not divided into ballet movements. There are no set dances and the work is con-

[1] See *Ravel*, Demuth (*Master Musicians*, Dent).

tinuous although not in any way symphonic. The slow sections suggest Dukas' *L'Apprenti Sorcier* with the difference that Debussy makes the music even lazier and hazier; but the work as a whole is completely individual and shows no "influence" whatsoever. One feels that one is done out of something by being prevented from hearing it.

Debussy's position in the history of music is assured. He accomplished more indirectly than directly. He placed the laws of tonality and key relationship completely in the background and, without any preliminary manifesto or pamphleteering, gave composers a fresh orientation of values through his own technique. Yet this quiet rebel admired César Franck, Vincent d'Indy and others whose outlook was very different from his own; it is noticeable that in this regard he was more respectful to his seniors than to his contemporaries, in spite of his impatience with Franck who, while listening to Debussy extemporise, called out in desperation, "Modulate, modulate; for goodness' sake modulate," to be met with the rejoinder, "Why should I? I am perfectly happy in this key." M. Daniel Chennevière describes Debussy[1] as "the most profound reflection of Modernity; indeed, he is Modernity itself". It is perfectly true to say that he was the most highly organised individual composer of the end and beginning of the centuries. The influences which have been mentioned were more those of the spirit than of technique, although that of Satie cannot be gainsaid—the fact that many do gainsay it is the result of their attitude to Satie. He stands alone, for he exhausted his own researches. Nothing further can be said in that language. His claim to greatness will always be maintained by the fact that he took the leading step to abolish classical and traditional concepts, and upon these negations he formulated his own completely individual expression, which is recognisable amid all others.

[1] *Claude Debussy* (Durand).

CHAPTER FOUR

MAURICE RAVEL

(1875-1937)

DEBUSSY and Ravel have always been placed in juxtaposition by the unthinking as the representatives of a single ideal. Nothing could be more inaccurate in this respect, but, as it happens, the pairing is not so loose in other directions. Ravel was the last French composer to write picturesque stylised music and he took his approach from that of Debussy; both composers were concerned with an objective romanticism impelled along lines essentially Gallic. After the death of Ravel French music proceeded no further in this direction; actually Ravel himself had forsaken his earlier paths for the more venturesome neoclassicism of his last two *Sonatas*. After the upheaval of the 1920's both Debussy and Ravel were regarded as *démodé*. The former was not alive to witness this, but the latter found himself no longer regarded as a young composer's rallying point. In such ways do the mighty fall.

The revelation of *Jeux d'eau* (1901) was no smaller than that of the *Prélude à l'Après-Midi d'un Faune* in 1894, but its impact was more immediately felt because it was an accessible work and also because a certain amount of the ground had already been prepared. The difference in the music preceding *Jeux d'eau* was less marked than that preceding *l'Après-Midi*. Debussy, therefore, had done most of the spade-work and it remained for Ravel to run concurrently with him but along his own track, Ravel not placing so much importance upon researches in sonorities as did Debussy.

Ravel was essentially a composer for the piano. Although at home with other instruments, his achievement in all fields taken together was greatest in this addition to piano literature. Debussy had nothing to place alongside Ravel's *Gaspard de la Nuit*. *La Mer* may possibly be classed with *Daphnis et Chloé* and even *La Valse* for its orchestral colouring; but in spite of the delightful skill and technique of *L'Heure espagnole*, it still remains of less importance than *Pelléas et Mélisande*.

Importance or lack of importance does not in any way affect the musical value of a work. This is something altogether outside the scope of position, and every work must be judged in relation to what immediately preceded and went with it. *La Vestale* (Spontini) and *Les Huguenots* (Meyerbeer) are important, historically. Both are of high value in their own sphere and period. The quality of the music in relation to their period is of the highest. Posterity, however, has placed them in the background, not because anyone later has written anything of better quality, but because a good many composers have written things which are very different. This touches upon the question of high values, quality and standard. In this consideration many composers have written opera "as good" in their own way as *Figaro* or *Don Giovanni* in theirs; those who have attempted to write in the same way have not succeeded in being different in any respect save in that of quality. If we look at the progress of opera there is very little between Mozart and Wagner which has survived. Intermediate composers have been relegated to the museum for the attention of studious musicologists[1] —although it would seem that this period has not appealed to a vast number—but many of these works are excellent examples of their times. One hundred years on may view *Pelléas et Mélisande* and *L'Heure espagnole* much as we view *Robert le Diable* and *William Tell*. One does not know and one cannot tell. However, as things are now, *Pelléas et Mélisande* and *L'Heure espagnole* are two landmarks, the former for the reasons discussed in the previous chapter, the latter because it solves the question of twentieth-century conversational lyrical opera; but it could not have existed without Charpentier's *Louise* which does the same thing according to the lights of 1900. Doubtless there will be many who will raise their hands in horror and curl their lips in scorn; but if the two scores are studied from this point of view, the principles will be seen to be similar. *Louise* and *L'Heure espagnole* are both *sung* music. The melodies with which both works abound are lyrical. The aesthetic is the same; the technique (of course) is different. Neither work stands in any relation whatsoever to *Pelléas et Mélisande*.

[1] "Rats du Bibliothéque", *Le Théâtre d'Opéra*, Bronislow Horowicz (Editions de Flore).

Debussy and Ravel are aesthetically poles apart, but the one is neither greater nor smaller, neither better nor worse than the other. Ravel had the benefit of study with Gabriel Fauré; Debussy had a sympathetic but nervous teacher in Ernest Guiraud (1837-1892) who viewed the theories of his pupil with interest tinged with apprehension. Fauré was the more receptive and the more amenable of the two professors. He could align his own aesthetic more closely to Ravel than could Guiraud his to Debussy. Debussy was iconoclastic; Ravel was progressive in that he adapted certain existing processes and methods to his own thought.

Nevertheless, Ravel was not found easily acceptable even by 1911, the year of the *Valses nobles et sentimentales,* by which time audiences had become accustomed to the *Nocturnes* and *La Mer* of Debussy and might have become so to anything; but those were the days of verbal protest when feelings ran high and the conventional concert-goer could still give expression to his opinions. The new music was played in front of audiences; to-day whenever it *is* played, it is done so in radio studios either with no audience or in front of one "specially invited" and in this country sufficiently cowed into expressing nothing more than respectful approval.[1]

Ravel's style is much easier than Debussy's, simply because it is not experimental. His was an altogether different personality. Elegance personified, with the best tailored suits, the neatest folded pocket-handkerchiefs, he cut a figure where the unkempt, unhappy Debussy made a mild sensation. Yet none shall say that the one was a better or more of an "artist" than the other. Ravel's refinement of appearance and mode of living found their reflection from the very first in his music. Ravel's works are the acme of neatness and precision. Everything is calculated in terms of effective presentation. His pianism lies under the hands so exactly that the fingers work automatically. The interlock of the two hands, so complicated at first sight yet so natural in execution, betrays the touch of the consummate artist. Not for Ravel the principle of "what I have written, I have written, and that is what my thoughts dictated". He refuted the theory of the artist's carelessness.

This neatness of technique is exemplified in all his piano music, and although the music looks as if it could be simplified in execution, in

[1] In Belgium, for example, the whole situation (with the exception of the announcement) is exactly as in a concert hall, and the applause is immediate, spontaneous, and unrestrained.

point of fact the results are not similar. The opening bars of the *Sonatine* for Piano (1905) could be played thus:

Ex. 1.

Sonatina

but in so doing there is no equality of tone in the two melodic lines, the bass becoming too prominent. In *Jeux d'Eau* the interlocking is equally effective for the same reason. Ravel edited every note and every phrase. Nothing is left to the imagination of the player. When rubato is required, he says so; when the pace needs slowing or quickening, he says so also. Unless these directions are given, it is highly impertinent for pianists to indulge in them. The *Sonatine,* for example, is pellucid in its texture and simple in its aesthetic. The tempo-rubato player, however, cannot possibly be expected to grant the composer the knowledge of how his music should be played to obtain its greatest effect and, consequently he rubatos it from the first bar to the last, making the first movement into a flaccid and sentimental drawing-room ballad. A similar massacre is made of the middle section of the "Rigaudon" from *Le Tombeau de Couperin* which, perky music in itself, is made to sound ludicrous by too slow a pace, excessive rubato destroying the lines and complicating something perfectly straightforward. The trouble is that so accustomed have we become to pianists' "interpretations" that when a French player announced the performance as being authoritative from the composer himself, one critic queried the entire performance.

Herein lies one difference between Debussy and Ravel, for the former requires rubato treatment in innumerable places. Another can be seen in their approach to melody. Ravel is very much more direct. Debussy's melody was to stand on its harmonic basis; Ravel's stands upon its own feet. It is always singable and has considerable length and shape. Beneath their translucent pianism, the themes of *Jeux d'Eau,* the *Sonatine* and *Ondine* are clearly defined. This is obvious in whatever one looks at until the two later *Sonatas* where Ravel attempts a different aesthetic. Only once did he approach Impressionism and that was in the *Rapsodie espagnole* (1907), which is evocative music.

One will not find much "development"—his most popular chamber work, the *Introduction and Allegro* for harp, string quartet, flute and clarinet (1905-1906) consists entirely of the repetition of two themes; this may account in no small measure for its popularity. Yet he could draw a fine line of some range and continuity as in the much-loved "Dawn of Day" in *Daphnis et Chloé*, while the *Trio* for piano, violin, and 'cello (1914) is planned upon a scale far outreaching anything that Debussy aimed at.

Ravel wrote only one actual orchestral work for the concert hall. The other orchestral works are either transcriptions, concertos or works for the theatre. With the exception of the much-abused and completely misunderstood *Bolero* (1928), his ballets are as suitable for the concert hall as for the theatre—indeed, the matter goes in the other direction where *Daphnis et Chloé* (1909-1912) is concerned since it was found to be too linear, too symphonic for choreographic purposes. *La Valse* (1919-1920) is entirely satisfactory in the concert hall even if its programmatic background is not fully understood. Neither of these works is written in Ballet Form, but in both cases Ravel had something better to go on than the slight script given to Debussy for *Jeux*. The *Rapsodie espagnole*, therefore, remains Ravel's solitary contribution to the orchestral concert hall and in that work the third movement, the "Habanera", dates from 1895-1899 where it formed part of the two-piano work, *Les Sites auriculaires*. Even *Ma Mère l'Oye* was born as a suite for piano duet. We may be glad that all this is the case since otherwise he would not have made the direct impact which has influenced so many composers; those who deal with young students find that when these begin to branch away from their traditional basic technique, it is Ravel who appears to give the direction (from there they dally with the whole-tone scale under the impression that it is Debussy, and thence proceed to their own individuality—in due course).

Ravel's two operas are well contrasted. The first, *L'Heure espagnole* (1907), is a perfect example of the Spanish *goût* and of the adoption of a formalised framework. The precision with which Ravel sets the clocks ticking, each with its metronomic mark, and the extreme daintiness with which the Spanish dance styles are fitted into the conversational situations carry the Debussy concept of declamation further than that envisaged by the technique of *Pelléas et Mélisande*. A less distant parallel with Debussy's work is the opera *L'Enfant et les Sortilèges* (1920-1925), a work whose pointillage is very near *Pelléas et Mélisande*. Here Ravel pared down his ideas to the barest essentials. The music underlines every situation and every statement. There is less actual music in it than in *Pelléas et Mélisande*. It is written in accordance with what later became the principles of the film score, entailing the complete inseparability of music and screen. In this way *L'Enfant et les Sortilèges* approaches the incidental music to a play, the dialogue of which is "musicalised" rather than spoken or declaimed. Ravel touches upon realism here, not hesitating at literal representation of cats on clarinets. This caused some discussion at the time, the critics deploring what they felt to be a descent into the music-hall. Honegger pointed out, however, that since the situation required cats, it was up to Ravel to delineate the animals in the most suitable manner. Many find this work the quintessence of delicacy and musical pointillage. Others find it extremely infantile, placing it alongside *Hansel und Gretel* for child-appeal and rating that work higher—it is not unenlightening to imagine how Ravel would have dealt with this subject and also to consider the Teutonic approach to a light-weight fairy story.

When Ravel became neo-classical, he was more successful than Debussy. This phase opened with *Le Tombeau de Couperin* (1917) whose graceful and charming technique is even more convincing for its purpose than Debussy's *Hommage à Rameau*. This was only "ad hoc", and it was not until 1920-1922 (the *Sonata for violin and 'cello*) and 1923-1927 (the *Sonata for violin and piano*) that he found himself coming "up-to-date" with his contemporaries; the two *Concertos* (1931, simultaneously) *for Piano (both hands)* and *Piano (Left Hand) and Orchestra*, had an extra-abstract impulse.

These two works are altogether remarkable, because although they were actually composed at the same time, they are completely dissimilar. The *Concerto in G (both hands)* is more a "Divertissement" than a Concerto-proper, although written in the established forms. Ravel himself admired Saint-Saëns for his clarity—nothing else—and in this work he took the concertos by this composer as his model, writing it *for* rather than *against* the piano, in the true Saint-Saëns manner.[1] The result is a succession of altogether delightful and unassuming movements, of which the second has a rare beauty of melody. This was castigated in some circles as being too straightforward and

[1] I have heard Americans claim that Gershwin provided the "motive and means" for Ravel's *Piano Concerto in G*.

easy of execution for a Concerto. He himself felt that he had got near to the spirit of Mozart. The *Concerto in D (Left Hand)*, written to commission from Paul Wittgenstein, is quite different. Here Ravel composed what is really a big work. The grandeur, breadth and opulence of the first section are magnificent, the Scherzo (the work is in one continuous movement) sufficiently impertinent to be a real scherzo, while the closing Cadenza reveals a knowledge of the resources of the left hand to its ultimate degree. Ravel, therefore, began and closed his life (for after this work there was nothing of any moment) with piano music, the repertoire of which he so nobly enriched.

His big work, *Gaspard de la Nuit* (1908), in three movements, "Ondine", "Le Gibet" and "Scarbo", reveals virtuosity of writing and requires similar playing. He received the impulse for this from a casual remark of Debussy who, at a meeting of the Apaches, said that he wanted to write something on the largest scale for piano which would combine musicianship with technical virtuosity. Ravel seized upon this idea—Debussy had himself seized upon somebody else's earlier on[1]—and this work was the result. Pianists who play *Gaspard de la Nuit* admit the difficulties, but also admit that the pianism, which looks so frightening, is all perfectly pianistic, lies under the hands, and is never clumsy. In none of them does Ravel make any experiments in sonority. The only "atmospheric" state is in "Le Gibet" which conveys its motive through a repeated pedal point and gives the acme of effect through musical means. "Ondine" and "Scarbo" are pen-painting. "Ondine" has a theme whose line was to be equalled later in *Daphnis et Chloé*, while "Scarbo" is the very epitome of impish scintillation. Let it be admitted that pianists seem to prefer "Ondine" to either of the others.

If Ravel avoided sonorities for their own sake in his piano music, he took full advantage of them when he wrote for the orchestra. A Ravel score is a marvel of ornate ingenuity, suggesting in many places a deliberate avoidance of the obvious. Again, the editing is superbly done and every note has its directive. It may be that his scores glitter and that he was too much addicted to glockenspiel and celesta, too much, that is to say, for the ears of those who cannot rid themselves of Teutonic classicism; but this is Ravel himself, and betokens his infinite patience over small details. Ravel does not emphasise his climaxes with a bang on the cymbals. He achieves them thematically

[1] See page 25.

and by accumulation of orchestration. The Wind Machine in *Daphnis et Chloé* is justified by the stage requirement. In the concert hall it is unnecessary. *La Valse* pays particular attention to the "confectionery" department once it has got wound up; but, again, Ravel had the justification of the glitter of the ballroom—one suggests, however, that he would probably have used this department in this way without such justification. The process simply indicates the difference between the Gallic and Teutonic outlook on the orchestra. The former, regarding it from all its pictorial aspect, uses its full resources in a pictorial and romantic way; the latter, always impelled by the tradition of classicism and thematic expansion, eschews such things as flippancies and extra-musical effects, thus emphasising the thematic pre-eminence of the thought. Neither the one nor the other is wrong. It is purely a matter of personal taste. If one finds oneself listening to a work which might be either Gallic or Teutonic, a situation not quite so far-fetched as might be imagined, the horns will always indicate the origin. The Gallic use of them will be sparing and thematic, the Teutonic generous and thick. The Teutonic angle is to pad up with good velvety horn tone; the Gallic requires no such padding. There is in all genuine Gallic scoring a lightness and deftness of touch which the Teutonic composers can neither find nor imitate. This is paramount even in a composer like d'Indy who, although under the sway of Teutonic classicism, could not lose his innate Gallicism, and this blessing he imparted to Albert Roussel and others who came under his influence. It is obvious, too, in the dignified Dukas, the erudite Albéric Magnard (1865–1914), and Florent Schmitt with all his weight of symphonic continuity and development.

Ravel and Debussy represent two facets of French music. The 1920's, with their sudden cleavage with the past, found no place for Ravel and from being a figure-head and director of young French thought he retired into the background as a strongly cultured composer, very much of a period. His neo-classical technique did not fit happily upon his shoulders; it was either so advanced as to seem artificial, as in the *Sonatas*, or not advanced enough to proclaim any position among the "newer" aspects of music. It was impossible to forget the romanticism of *Daphnis et Chloé* and the *Sonatine*. Young France looked elsewhere for its lead and inspiration. It found that the *grands maîtres* like d'Indy seemed to be as antagonistic to the new neo-classicism as they had been to the older Impressionism. They continued to respect these *maîtres,* but ceased to follow them. Youth was as intolerant of age as it has ever been, seeing that age did not advance further than that extreme to which it had already attained. The upshot was the unintentional formation of the group known as "Les Six". In the meantime, attention became focused upon one who was quietly carrying on the work formulated by the older composers, and whose technique, while in no way iconoclastic, was distinctly in the *avant-garde.* This figure subconsciously was showing the young idea how to combine the best of the old with the best of the new.

CHAPTER FIVE

ALBERT ROUSSEL

(1869-1937)

It was Albert Roussel who formed the eventual rallying point and through whom the mature works of the two most important members of Les Six can be traced. Roussel maintaine̓d a steady progress along lines which were considered *démodé* and proved that once Impressionistic and Wagnerian influences were swept away from French music, there would remain an individual Gallic symphonicism.

Older than Ravel, Roussel came to music later in life than most other composers. Until 1894 he served as an officer in the French Navy and he was twenty-five years old before he threw up his naval career to devote himself to music. I have told elsewhere[1] of the subterfuge which decided Roussel's future. He studied first of all with Eugène Gigout (1844-1925) at the Ecole Niedermeyer, but when the Schola Cantorum was founded in 1896, Roussel was attracted by the sincerity and personality of Vincent d'Indy. In 1898 he became a student at the Schola, remaining there until 1907.[2]

The French symphonic school inaugurated by Lalo, Franck, Saint-Saëns, Chausson and Dukas was approaching its first climax which, in effect, was signalled when d'Indy produced his *Symphony in B flat* (1902). *Pelléas et Mélisande,* it will be remembered, had been produced the same year. 1902 also saw the first large-scale work of Roussel, a *Trio for Violin, 'Cello and Piano* which, although unacceptable to-day, bears certain signs that the future of French neo-classical music was to rest in the hands of its composer. Roussel's first representative work, a setting of *Quatre Poèmes* by Henri de Regnier appeared in 1903 and were indicative of his later first manner. During this period he produced

[1] *Albert Roussel* (United Music Publishers).
[2] *La Schola Cantorum,* Vincent d'Indy et autres (Bloud et Gay, Paris).

a *Symphonic Prelude* after Tolstoy's *Resurrection*, a work thoroughly Franckian in construction and in its approach to tonality. More significant, however, was the symphony *La Poème de la Forêt* which immediately showed a direct avoidance of the pitfalls of Impressionism while adopting certain of its principles.

Impressionism was regarded askance at the Schola, the training being on the rigorous classical lines of the teaching of César Franck. Roussel, therefore, found himself in the happy position of combining pictorial thought with classical upbringing as regards questions of both tonality and form. In this work one sees what the older Vincent d'Indy attempted in his *Jour d'Été à la Montagne*, but which he attempted too late in life to be really convincing. Roussel spent the years 1904-1906 in the composition of *La Poème de la Forêt*, in the meanwhile producing the piano pieces *Rustiques* and the astonishing *Divertissement* for flute, oboe, clarinet, bassoon, horn and piano. This work remained isolated until the masterly *Evocations* appeared in 1911.

La Poème de la Forêt is not without interest and of its type has everything to commend it. Had Roussel stayed at this point, he might very well have been just another French pictorial composer with a sense of advanced harmony. Having reached maturity in years and sensibility, he was able to recognise the dangers attendant upon delineative music, and it was here that his innate sense of symphonic thought stood him in good stead. Formally he was perfectly at home. *La Poème de la Forêt* is orthodox in design and construction, conforming fully to the cyclical principal; but, being an objective work, the Schola could not regard it as a real symphony, for although classical in framework it was not so in impulse and at that time the Schola demanded a completely abstract approach. Whatever Impressionistic tendencies Roussel might have felt within himself were kept under control by the Schola. *La Poème de la Forêt* is too clear-cut to come under the category of Impressionism. There is nothing vague about it, for Roussel's strict contrapuntal writing was definitive and although much of the music is harmonic in thought, there is behind it a strong feeling for and ease of polyphonic line.

It is in the first movement—"Forêt d'Hiver"—that Roussel indicated his mature harmonic outlook and in the fourth—"Faunes et Dryades"—one finds the initial suggestion of the bounding vitality of his mature rhythms. There are many cases of early works being revised by their composers in later life. Such a process with *La Poème de la Forêt* would have been utterly impossible because it would have entailed completely re-writing it; consequently the result would have been an altogether new work. Roussel, however, even at that time was not sure of his musical future. Hence the *Divertissement* served as an experiment and such a successful one that it presaged all the rhythmic brittleness of Les Six and their uncompromising attitude to harmony. This was a sudden flash in the pan, however, and until 1919 Roussel's output shows a curious alternation of romanticism and classicism. The *Suite for Piano* (composed in 1909-1910) showed that he was not at home in the medium, and this became increasingly obvious as time went on. The *Suite* in question consists of a "Prèlude", "Bourrée", "Sicilienne", and "Ronde" in which the old dance styles are present in name only. The pianism is clumsy and awkward and the difficulties not commensurate with the results obtained. This work hovers between the two "-isms". Roussel appears to have had some fanciful ideas in his head which his technique forced him to keep in the background.

He was appointed Professor of Counterpoint at the Schola Cantorum in 1902—since it is on record[1] that he was still a student at that time, he may have started as a pupil-teacher, becoming fully fledged in 1907; he resigned in 1914. It was in 1910-1911 that a revelation came to him which was to influence the whole of his mature music. During a tour in India he listened to the Hindu music which suggested that herein lay a certain way of avoiding Impressionism yet at the same time adding something new to European technique. The result of this tour was the tryptich *Evocations* for soli, mixed voices and orchestra which at once placed Roussel on a level with the greatest and most significant names in French music. It had a still further significance in that it led to the vast opera-ballet *Padmâvati* in which he used Hindu scales as fully as is possible in European music. From these two experiences sprang his mature technique which was to ripen in 1919-1921 with the severely classical *Symphony in B flat minor*, one of the most profound works in French music. Together with Debussy's *La Mer* and Dukas' *La Péri*, Roussel's *Evocations* place French music on a level with that of any other culture. While Germany was blowing herself out with the distended exaggerations of Richard Strauss; while the Grand Manner was synonymous with "great music"; while complexities were rapidly becoming complications, this French music pursued its own way, maintaining a steady hold on clarity and economy of means. Roussel

[1] *La Schola Cantorum, op. cit.*

learnt clarity from Vincent d'Indy through counterpoint. This it was which drew to him such varied pupils as Satie, Varèse and Martinů.

Impressionism had now reached an *impasse*. Debussy himself had realised its limitations. The way out was not to come until a little later; in the meanwhile the time had become ripe for a resumption of classicism in France which, to be really significant, had to be essentially French. Between the *Evocations* and *Padmâvati* Roussel had composed a *Sonatine* for piano in 1912, a work curiously abstract and pianistically awkward in which he appears to have cleared his mind of any extraneous thoughts and to have written "pure" music. There is none of the brittleness of the *Divertissement* or the showy technique of the *Suite*. The music is condensed to essentials. Of what is known as "pianism" there is none, and the rhythms are taut and unsupple. With this work Roussel bade farewell to a negative thought almost inapt in its blockish squareness for any medium. He had also been brought into ballet, a genre which at the time did not in the least interest him, but which in later years was to prove most suitable for his mature suppleness of rhythm.

Le Festin de l'Araignée (1912) is an attractive and altogether charming little work, written, as it were, with the point of a needle, scored for a minute orchestra, and absolutely perfect for the medium. The earlier experience of *La Poème de la Forêt* helped Roussel in painting musically the pictorial warmth of a landscape, and the subject itself allowed him to work a considerable amount of still dormant romanticism out of his system. It is not Impressionism, for Roussel was not an Impressionist. Not even in the magnificent *Evocations* did he align himself with this school. Roussel was to write other ballets, but they were not romantic or expressionist. *Bacchus et Ariane* (1930), one of the strongest ballets in the repertoire, did not paint any scene or picture, and *Aeneas* (1935) for chorus and orchestra was hardly graphic because it had nothing to delineate.

By this time, however, he had become recognised outside his own country. The composition of *Padmâvati* was interrupted by the 1914-1918 War in which Roussel, like Ravel and others, served in the French Army. Having assimilated the Hindu scales before the interruption to his work, Roussel had begun to think instinctively in them. When he resumed work upon *Padmâvati* after his discharge from the Army owing to ill-health contracted while on active service, he was able to take it up without any hesitation, and the seam which might well have been apparent with other composers, cannot be distinguished. He himself had no doubt whatsoever that everything "after the war", including music, would be different, yet so far in advance of pre-war musical thought was this work that through it Roussel was able to take his place in the *avant-garde* without any strain or difficulty. *Padmâvati* is distinctly more genuinely Oriental than *Evocations,* although the latter could not be mistaken for anything but what it is. *Padmâvati* had to wait until 1923 for production, although it was finished in 1918. Its production coincided with works like Stravinsky's *Les Noces,* Honegger's *Antigone* and Milhaud's *Christophe Colombe*; it was a splendid period for the new music. All these composers were younger than Roussel, but the older man took a place beside them and was not incongruous in that circle. Paris audiences were being initiated into the latest works of Schoenberg, Webern, and Bartok, and they found that their native Roussel fitted perfectly into the general trend of things.

Roussel returned to music with all the enthusiasm which younger men experience. He wrote the "Scherzo" for a *Symphony* at enormous speed—and then hesitated. This movement was inclining to Impressionism, and, in this case, real and true Impressionism. This was not the direction to which he looked, but rather than destroy the movement, he issued it under the title of *Pour une Fête de Printemps.*[1] This was his last romantic work, although he turned towards it in the "Aubade" in the *Petite Suite* (1929), but henceforth he tried to banish permanently anything from his mind except pure musical thought. The result of this self-criticism was the *Symphony in B flat minor* (1919-1921) with which work French symphony took up its interrupted progress. Be it noted that this austere and severe work was composed at the very moment when French music began to seethe with the efflorescence of Les Six; when both Impressionism and Symphony (in its fullest meaning) were regarded as completely outmoded and outside the canon of the Gallic *goût.* Roussel continued in this manner, but not as severely because the working of the *Symphony in B flat minor* had formed his abstract instinct. He himself regarded it as a work of human aspirations. It indicated the goal towards which he had set his feet. Later he was to regard the (third) *Symphony in G minor* as signifying human achievement. He arrived at his maturity,

---

[1] Spring has always attracted French composers—Debussy's *Printemps,* Roger-Ducasse's *Nocturne de Printemps,* and Milhaud's *Concertino de Printemps* come to immediate recollection.

therefore, in his fifty-second year—he was to live but sixteen more.

His music is not divisible into the usual three periods, but remains in two. Had he come to music earlier, had he undergone his course of serious study at the usual age, it is impossible to hazard a guess as to where he would have finished. His was a genuine musical instinct. His late start and the interruption of the 1914-1918 War delayed but did not stultify his progress, and from this point he provides the answer to those who still maintain that French music is something ineffably slight and charming but entirely lacking in profundity—which means that it has a culture of its own and owes nothing to the Teutonic caucus which for so long has maintained a firm hold on European music elsewhere.

Roussel shows his innate classicism in chamber music, the *Sérénade* for flute, violin, viola, 'cello and harp (1925), the *Trio* for flute, viola and 'cello (1929), the *String Quartet* (1931-1932) and the *String Trio* (1937), even more than in his symphonies. The chamber works are not attractive music to listen to from the aesthetic point of view, as are the chamber works of Debussy and Ravel. They make no concessions at all and the ear is aware of scholarly texture, always pure, and always in exquisite taste in which any suggestion of effect is completely absent. These works are *musicians'* music and they exemplify a severity of outlook which might have quelled even the serious Vincent d'Indy. On the other hand, the *Second Sonata* for violin and piano (1924) is lyrical to a degree, and combines strength of material with grace of line.

The *Symphony in B flat minor*, representative as it is, does not present us with the characteristics by which we recognise Roussel after a few bars. The themes are terse and move fairly evenly. The first work to give us full knowledge of the distinctive characteristics of Roussel is the orchestral *Suite en fa* (1926) which is full of the most astonishing vitality and leaping themes. Such is its vigour that a well-known conductor told me in all seriousness that it frightened him! This ebullience reappears in the *Symphony in G minor* and, to a lesser degree, in the *Symphony in A* (1934). Contrary to the usual procedure, increasing years did not quieten his music in any way and both the choral-ballet *Aeneas* and the *Rapsodie Flamande* (1936) show no lessening of the Roussel vigour.

Roussel's most recognisable qualities are the astringency of harmony and the wide range of theme. When he spreads his melodic thought over a wide compass, the guiding spirit would still appear to be the voice and not the instrument. It is, of course, utterly impossible to sing the wide compound leaps at their true pitch, but they do not require supporting harmony to bolster them up. The majority of them have more than harmonic implications; they are definitely chordal in themselves. It was this approach to melody together with his contrapuntal ease of movement which makes his massive setting of *Psalm LXXX* so eminently singable.

Terse themes will always be found in the quick movements. When writing a slow movement he let his lyrical inspiration have full freedom. Consequently at times the continuity is almost too unbroken. One thing leads perfectly smoothly to another. His lyricism sometimes fails to convince at first hearing, particularly in the ballets and most especially in *Bacchus et Ariane*. In *Evocations* and *Padmâvati* the sinuosity of the lines is dictated entirely by the particular scale in use at the moment. The essential angularity compared with European ideas seems to jolt the ear, but this is entirely due to the exigencies of the scale in question. It was this unfamiliar melodic technique which baffled such experienced musicians as Florent Schmitt and Emile Vuillermoz, who commented upon the banality of the melodies in *Padmâvati*, a curious comment when one comes to think of it. What they meant was that from the traditional point of view the melodies were far too angular. *Padmâvati* does not contain the melodic warmth of *Evocations* because it is a truer Orientalism, although it would not be right to regard the latter as India through French eyes, in the way that Saint-Saëns' *Caprice Arabe* may be regarded.

Another feature of Roussel's themes is their vital rhythm. This may also be accredited in a number of cases to Les Six. There is no felinity as in Gabriel Fauré, for example, because Roussel was more direct. He was essentially dramatic in those places where drama would not seem to play a part. Hence a little work like *La Naissance de la Lyre* (1922-1924) (which still awaits a performance in this country in spite of certain radio qualities) bears the stamp of the theatre even when a character is declaiming alone. Here Roussel proved himself as much at home with the Greek scales as with the Hindu, and the purity of the diatonicism rendered imperative by the scales present this work as a cooling draught. A particularly suitable illustration of the way in which a suggestively banal melody is covered up with harmonies, thus detracting attention from it to the whole, may be seen in Ex. 1 on the following page.

As regards his melodic rhythm, the following passage will show exactly how each line has its own freedom and its own pattern, and it appears as if no one line were of any more importance than another:

This melodic rhythm gives his music its magnificent drive and impulse. The music exults, whether it is in the ever-pressing forward virility of the *Symphony in G minor* whose first movement sets the pulses throbbing, or in the sharply patterned ballet necessity of *Bacchus et Ariane*. The opening of *Aeneas*, which might be any polyphonic passage from a chamber work, saves itself by its taut rhythm.

Harmonically he is as clear as water. His astringency he obtains by the simple process of including the root in all inversions of discords and by arranging the position of the chords in such a way that the third clashes with the eleventh while the sharpened seventh pierces its way through the mass of sound. He uses harmony in a manner individual to himself, not hesitating to indulge in tonic and dominant but killing it, as it were, by means of bi-tonality.

This he acquired from *Padmâvati* where the scalic material forbade unessential and chromatic notes. Broadly speaking, he took away some of the Hindu semitones and made them diatonic in the European manner; thus the latter state is even stronger than the original. He knew the value of the augmented triad which makes a shattering climax at the top of an enormous drive. Superficially it would appear that he was incapable of any tenderness, but this proves a fallacy when one comes to examine the elements which make up the technique, for Roussel is never overtly sentimental. It can be seen in innumerable quiet places such as the following which needs string "thinking" to convince:

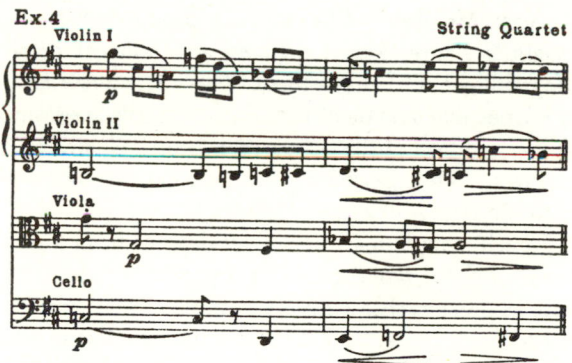

In the case of the slow movement from the *Symphony in G minor*, it lies in the graceful curve of the music. He may be credited with writing an original type of "Pastorale" in the *Petite Suite* which completely disposes of the conventional compound time and shepherd's pipes. This short relapse into objective romanticism formed a good answer to those critics who accused him of lack of feeling.

His use of the orchestra is carefully detailed. Never a colourist in the sense that Ravel was, he contrived the most beautiful results from the normal application of classicism. This was easy in *Evocations* and *Padmâvati* through the nature of the subjects. Elsewhere, especially in the "Sarabande" from the *Suite en fa* he attained a massive dignity which impresses as well as stirs. He was detailed with the percussion and in his violent moments he enjoyed himself immensely with it. This was a lesson learnt from Vincent d'Indy, who himself played the timpani and other instruments in the group in Paris orchestras, thus gaining an insight into the subject which few other composers have really troubled about. A hearty thump on the bass drum too often suffices some composers, when more careful consideration of the percussion "department" would give better results.

The importance of Roussel will be seen to lie in the fact that he maintained the French symphonic school and kept French music vitalised in line with certain aspects of tradition, always looking forward and never backward. The strength of Roussel was an example to all. The young composers saw in it the means of associating themselves with tradition and at the same time holding their position in the *avant-garde*. They saw that continuity and symphonic development were not relics of the past. Mr. Edward Lockspeiser comments[1] on the curious fact that Gabriel Fauré, Maurice Ravel and Vincent d'Indy left no "outstanding followers" behind them. This, of course, is a matter of opinion. It is a peculiar statement to make, to say the least, since Vincent d'Indy left the tradition of the Schola Cantorum, illustrated in Roussel himself, and from him it passed on to Honegger throughout his whole career and to the later Milhaud.

All the French symphonists trace their descent from d'Indy through Roussel via the Schola, whether as direct pupils or as indirect disciples. An influence as great as this is not discernible at once and it is possible that when Mr. Lockspeiser added his footnote he was not fully aware of the trends of French music further than Debussy and Ravel. The inclusion of d'Indy, therefore, is an unfortunate shot in the dark,

[1] *Debussy, op. cit.*

especially if the name of Marcel Mihalovici (1898) is remembered.[1]

Roussel stands at the top of the stairs, beckoning his musical successors to follow him in the clarity of his neo-classical Gallicism and the absolutely individual style which he formulated for himself.

[1] Page 331. Mr. Lockspeiser may be excused in this instance since Mihalovici's music has only just begun to make itself known; but his remark is typical of the generality of thinking which does not recognise as outstanding or important anyone not firmly established in the repertoire of this country.

CHAPTER SIX

LES SIX AND THEIR AIMS

THE formation of this coterie was accidental and arose through a casual meeting in 1916 between Darius Milhaud (1892) and Arthur Honegger (1892). The former invited the latter to a studio concert at which a young French composer named Georges Auric (1899), a pupil of Vincent d'Indy at the Schola Cantorum, would be present. Milhaud and Honegger had been fellow-students at the Paris Conservatoire in André Gédalge's (1856-1926) counterpoint class. The meeting took place at the studio of the poet Blaise Cendrars and also present were Erik Satie, a young woman, Germaine Tailleferre (1892), (a pupil of Charles Marie Widor at the Conservatoire) and Louis Durey (1888). It was suggested by Cendrars that a number of concerts devoted to the works of young composers would be a good thing, and Erik Satie remarked that instead of following the example of other societies and playing other people's works, they would concentrate on their own. This proved a popular suggestion in every way and as time went on the party was joined by Jean Cocteau (1891), the poet and dramatist, and another composer, Francis Poulenc (1899), a pupil of Charles Koechlin.

The composite group took on the name of the "Nouveaux Jeunes". Milhaud was waiting to travel to Brazil, where he had a diplomatic appointment; consequently the earlier activities were carried on in his absence. For some while the group worked together, but on January 16th and 23rd, 1920, the critic Henri Collet (1885) wrote an article in *Comœdia* entitled "Les cinq Russes, les six Français et Erik Satie". In this article Collet suggested that, in Les Six, France had a coterie which might be as influential upon French music as The Five had been upon Russian.

The members had only one thing in common, the rejuvenation of French music and its purging of the baneful influence of Teutonism which had been proclaimed by Camille Saint-Saëns. This purge, however, tended away from the hot-house atmosphere of Debussy and the Impressionists. It was to be effected by a return to simplicity, to a neo-classicism of the twentieth century having no contact with that of the nineteenth, but, if anything, reflecting the seventeenth and eighteenth. The whole approach to music was to be reorientated. Symphony, for example, was to return to its original meaning, "sound" for orchestra; the established conditions of symphonic music were no longer to be regarded as *sine qua non,* everything being pared down to a minimum commensurate with directness of statement. Middle sections would no longer be the hall-mark of the truly symphonic composer and the exigencies of "form" would be entirely at the disposal of the individual—actually this has never been otherwise and the idea of composers contentedly pouring their ideas into a ready-made mould is one confined strictly to those who have never written symphonies or sonatas but have taken certain evidence for granted. Above all, Wagner was to be completely obliterated from Gallic thought. Here there was a certain divergence of opinion. Honegger regarded Wagner as the saviour of classicism; Milhaud cried, "Down with Wagner." After an entertaining ballet to a scenario by Jean Cocteau, *Les Mariés de la Tour Eiffel,* in which each member of the group wrote a section, the whole thing split up, and apart from the general principles governing the association, the members worked in complete independence, each solving the problems in his own manner. The "Nouveaux Jeunes" broke into two parties, Satie forming his own coterie. Les Six, however, had become a name established in music-lovers' minds and the name remained. The association, therefore, became such only in terms of personality and principle.

It was mere chance that there happened to be six at that first meeting. There might have been any number; indeed, in an article in the *Chesterian,* Albert Roussel added three names who at the time might very well have been regarded as belonging to the group. Of these three, only Roland Manuel (1891) is familiar to-day; but his technique is altogether too refined and slender to find a place beside the regular members.

Those were the days of Diaghileff and the Russian Ballet, when *le dernier cri* was the rage. The principles of Les Six, therefore, seemed in every way suitable for this purpose. Diaghileff asked Cocteau to "astonish" him. This Cocteau did with Auric's *Les Fâcheux* (1924), following it with *Les Matelots* (1925). Poulenc contributed *Les Biches* (1924), Milhaud *Le Train bleu* (1924), Durey, Honegger and Taille-ferre remained aloof. This music was admittedly slick, but it was obvious that if the aims and ideals of the group were to carry any influence and attract attention, it would be necessary to show an immediate break with the prevailing fashions. Stravinsky (1882) provided the authority and example. His *Symphonies d'instruments à vent* (1920), composed in memory of Debussy, together with *Les Noces* (1923) formed the starting point of what may be called the "back to" movement. "Back to Bach" was the cry, but this, like so many other such cries, was entirely misunderstood. It implied that the future of music lay in abstract counterpoint rather than in romantic harmony and vague impressionism. However, none of Les Six went as far as Stravinsky, at that time in his complete negation of emotion and shading.

Only two of the group have been drawn to the large forms. Durey soon retired to the country in order, in his own words, to compose "a page a day". Tailleferre, after creating a mild sensation with her *Ballade for Piano and Orchestra* (1923), *String Quartet* (1919), and her *Concerto* for two pianos, chorus and orchestra (1934)—in which the pianos play an entirely doubling rôle in the concerto grosso style—vanished into musical oblivion. Poulenc has proved himself the essence of ele-gance and polish in a number of works which are rather higher than salon music, but approach it very nearly—and in this regard they have their value—and he may be said to illustrate one aspect of the French *goût* in its purest form. Auric has made a name principally in films, an exceedingly remunerative field, but one which is ephemeral, to say the least. His music lacks what that of the other members can never be accused of lacking, namely, variety. One film score sounds very much like another and all sound like everything else he has written. For some unknown reasons, film producers in this country have fallen beneath his sway and no film dealing with the East End of London seems to be complete without music by the Parisian, Auric. To such an extent has his sense of timing developed that it appears that he can now write a complete score without ever once seeing the film, a feat in which he is assisted by the ever-constant lack of variety I have mentioned. This leaves Milhaud and Honegger, two figures of prodigious strength—

the one French, the other Swiss by birth and blood, but French by training and culture.

The amount of power wielded by this small coterie was remarkable. Rarely has such an unrepresentative body of young people contributed so much in general to the music of a continent. They cleared the air, so to speak, of all subjective vapourings and picturesque delineations through the haze of Impressionism. They were largely responsible for the wave of *snobisme* which characterised the 1920's; but further than this, they can be said to have reorientated a complete culture. That this was accomplished at all is nothing to wonder at, as it had been done before; but that it should have been accomplished by a group of completely unknown composers is a striking testimony to their personalities and also to the "power of the Press", which directed attention to their work not only in praise, but in abuse—and the latter invariably makes rather than mars a cause when it is violent, spiteful or reactionary.

The musical means with which these reforms were carried out are not without interest. It was first of all an age of reaction against old values and customs. There was, for example, a distinct revolt against the third and the sixth, these consonant intervals having become exhausted through over-constant use. The natural tendency, therefore, was to use any intervals but these. In France the interval of the fourth and seventh took the places of the third and sixth. In this country it was the fifth in its complete triadic form which provided the fullest means of breaking away from tradition. The fourth has from time almost immemorial been regarded as a discord. It is but the fifth inverted, and since that interval is perfect, it is difficult to understand how or why its inversion, while still so described, can be regarded as a discord. Such imperfection in perfection is unreasonable. In any case, concord and discord in their fullest sense had been abolished and every chord had become its own entity. The doubling of a part at the third or sixth had become monotonously emotional, and to adopt this process was merely to fall in line with a preconceived habit. Further, aural custom had removed all edge from the main line itself because the doubling effected too much consonance, too much melting of one line into another. It may look as if the result of these early steps to destroy tradition were pure cussèdness, as if the composer deliberately set his face against the two culpable intervals and used any rather than them; but this was no more cussèd than the earlier habit of avoiding the second, fourth and seventh. It was simply a change of values. It was found that underlining a theme at the fourth below not only preserved the clarity of the theme itself by giving it edge, but drew attention to the two-part basis of the line. Consequently, the process of super-imposed fourths was devised; but even then the mass of sound became divisible into two interlocking sevenths. It could be softened by forming the mass into two interlocking sixths, and by widening the extreme intervals to fifths, but still keeping interlocking sevenths.

This removed the superimposition of fourths, but the outside ninth, whether major or minor, still gave the required edge and prevented the music from settling anywhere to a finality of phrase. The chord of the added sixth in open formation accordingly took the place of the triad and it became fashionable to end a piece with it.[1] Like most fashions, it became a cliché since everybody did it, and instead of making for contrast of cadence it only added a tinge of variety from the ordinary traditional cadences. It added to cadential resources without finding a substitute for the old ones.

Much of this doubling at the fourth sounded crude at first, but with custom the ear became acclimatised to it as in the normal course of events and it soon ceased to astonish. Other separations of the ordinary diatonic discords were utilised, but so intriguing became the new freedoms that all processes were worked to death and it was not for some time that composers acquired the habit of mixing the spacings so as to obtain contrast. The greatest stumbling-block to variety was that everything moved in the same direction; this made for too much parallelism. Examples of the use of following fourths and ninths can be seen here:

Ex. 2 a)   Milhaud - Sonata for Two Violins & Piano (1914)

[1] A textbook attempt at explanation described it as "a discord resolving upon evaporation", which is as good as any, should any be necessary.

Of these the second appears to be expressive of the braying of a donkey; this is pure fancy and must not be taken for fact. Play the right hand as B flat, G, B flat—E flat, G, E flat, and the dividing line between the old and new technique becomes apparent. The fourth, however, was not restricted to the Gallic composers of the time and frequent use of it can be found in the works of Sir Arnold Bax (1883), whose aesthetic is far removed from that of Les Six.

The uncompromising approach to the so-called discord can be found everywhere, and it will suffice to quote but two examples:

Atonality made little real impact upon Les Six. They were drawn more to polytonality, the horizontal parallel of the vertical pantonality, a term which Arnold Schoenberg (1874) prefers since it implies an extension of tonality. Milhaud in an article in *La Revue Musicale* dated 1923, pleads the cause of polytonality, claiming as his authority a little canon by J. S. Bach which forms an answer, but hardly a far-reaching or convincing one. The right hand is in the tonic and the left in the dominant, and up to that point the authority is provided; but it does not go far enough, since Bach deliberately avoids the danger-points. The twentieth century, however, cultivates those snags which

Bach by-passed and turns what in Bach would have been a vice into a virtue. This little canon is none too happy in itself, but Bach exercised considerable care in its devising. Milhaud forswore this care and went head first into the issue. He himself composed an example of poly-tonality for the article mentioned above and it will not be out of place to quote it here:

Ex. 4 — Milhaud - Polytonal fragment

Polytonality will be seen to consist of a combination of different tonalities viewed horizontally. The basic thought, therefore, is con-trapuntal rather than harmonic. When, however, it becomes harmonic, it can lead to a situation such as Ex. 5, on next page, from the Overture to Act III of *Les Euménides*.

It is but fair to add that a similar build-up of thirds appears in *Le Roman de la Momie* (1886), by Ernest Fanelli (1860-1917). The reproach that the composer has no need to hear what he is writing applies equally well to traditional technique and it is equally possible to concoct a work along traditional text-book lines by obeying the "rules" as laid down for preparation and resolution of discords, etc. This has been done over and over again and can be found in all the dull and uninspired music which was poured out in this country during the late Victorian era, the implication being that the basic training and technique had not been placed in the subconscious but

Ex.5   Milhaud - Les Euménides

had been allowed to become the determining factor in what was genuinely believed to be creative art. Les Six, however, were all sufficiently sensitive to realise that no music can be written from a negation. Atonality denies all tonality. Polytonality insists upon it. Consequently, the composer in the former case has always to remember what he must *not* do, whereas he in the latter has always to bear in mind what he *must* do. One difference between the old and the new can be seen in the method of passing from one point to another. As long as the start and finish of a passage are satisfactory, what happens in between times is a matter for the conscience of the compose   Thus Milhaud writes uncompromisingly as follows:

Ex.6   Milhaud - Esther de Carpentras

Mon nom, des   cris   et   des   san - glots   et   vous, Pè - re?

This is an extension of the passing note principle to that of the passing chord.

With this freedom of harmonic and contrapuntal movement came an equally free use of rhythm which, from being contained inside the context or marked as a characteristic regularity, found itself in many cases to be the chief ingredient of the music. In his incidental music to Paul Claudel's *Protée* (1922)[1] Milhaud writes a completely rhythmic movement for percussion instruments—cymbals, side-drum, bass drum and gong—which form the accompaniment for male voices singing in unison. In other places the combination of rhythms is complex but never complicated. Each of Les Six had the Gallic characteristics of clarity and clear-thinking. A free use of quintuple time and subdivision of the ordinary quadruple measures came to be part and parcel of the stock-in-trade with composers in all countries.

One irritating thing to be found in these composers' works is their fondness for a constantly recurring bass. (The reader should bear in mind that we are discussing the first appearances of this revolutionary musical process and that many things have altered since then.) This obviously cleared up the earlier tendencies to constant change, but for the moment appeared to be a line of little resistance. The ostinato is the easiest form of bass to manage simply because it requires

[1] And in many other works.

no managing. It just goes on and on and ultimately stops when the work is ended. So far as it itself is concerned there is no reason for its ever stopping, and as long as the first and last points are left and met the intervening moments all fall logically into place in the succession of ideas, the ostinato continuing regardless of any harmonic, contrapuntal or melodic sense of fitness.

Les Six, however, were not all drawn to the "-alities" and only Milhaud and Honegger may be regarded as being really serious-minded, in that they were attracted to the large forms. Poulenc provided an altogether novel approach to music herself by definitely stating that his *Sonata* for piano duet was a "Sonata for pleasure", thus signifying that the higher reactions to musical composition and reception were no concern of his. Scores became cynical and witty instead of prosy and dogmatic, terse and simple in statement instead of long-winded. Orchestral instruments were no longer used mainly for that much-abused purpose, "colour", and the entire facet of orchestral writing returned to the classical ideal. Looking back at the music which upheaved the trend of creative art, one is astonished now at its tameness. Things which made one sit up in astonishment now appear altogether easy and obvious. The music of the 1920's is rarely heard at the present time because its purpose has been fulfilled; but there are isolated works which appear now and again as if to remind us of what the past was like. There are also some works which have fallen into undeserved oblivion, for Poulenc, Milhaud and Honegger have been prolific, especially the two last-named.

The fact is that nothing can shock us now. The battle of *Le Sacre* has been won, the campaign on behalf of the twelve-note-row system mastered, the one-time new trends of Les Six have now become almost commonplaces. Composers have been set the task of consolidating the new positions and if it sometimes appears that they are turning to the past, it will be found that this is no actual *volte-face* but simply the discarding of certain processes or assimilating them into the technique of the past. For the first time in many years the word "contemporary" seems to be justified; there are no signs of the future.

Nevertheless, the 1920's actually saw very little which was "new". All the "-alities" had been practised in the past by such people as Antonin Reicha (1770-1836), who in point of fact left behind him concrete examples in his works of polyrhythm, polytonality, polymodality and other processes practised in the 1920's. Reicha was never given the opportunity of reaching fulfilment as a composer, and his ideas made little impression outside the circle of his own pupils; his textbooks are infinitely more progressive than most of those in use to-day and he may be regarded as one of the most advanced pedagogic revolutionaries in the history of music. If authority be required for the technique of the 1920's, it will be found in Reicha, but, unfortunately, he was never an authoritative composer.

As a group Les Six means nothing now—incidentally, they very soon became Les Cinq when Louis Durey seceded from the movement; but the description "Les Six" has remained in order to differentiate it from "The Five". Collectively the group has accomplished everything it set out to do. It established the new French *goût* which had its basis in Couperin and Rameau rather than in Bach and Beethoven. It completely abolished all Wagnerian tendencies which had invaded the lyric stage and turned French dramatic thought into its own personal channels. After purging French technique of the "-isms", it gradually produced an essentially French school of symphonists which bears the stamp of its culture and in due course will take its place with that of all countries. It definitely removed the taint of superficial prettiness from the general regard of French music and showed that the established forms need not be the framework for pompous and sententious ideas although holding those of a serious and scholarly impulse. Of the protagonists of the period, those who made contemporary music what it is (for the ideas of Schoenberg have not yet become universally accepted and are practised only by a select few), two demand detailed consideration.

CHAPTER SEVEN

DARIUS MILHAUD
(1892)

MILHAUD is neither slick nor thoughtless, although composition comes quickly to him; he devotes sufficient consideration to everything he writes for him to be completely satisfied that what he writes is the sum total of his thoughts at that particular moment. Milhaud is not highly stylised, and it is difficult to explain exactly what his idiom entails. In the earlier days when he was thinking in terms of polytonality his path was perfectly clear; but this path reached its dead-end in 1922 with the completion of the polytonal work *Les Euménides* which seemed to him to represent the final achievement of polytonal thought.

Milhaud's progress is interesting. A pupil of Gédalge, his early works were strongly redolent of Franck; indeed, the *First Violin Sonata* (1911) contains all the elements of the Franckian harmonic approach plus bar after bar of the most banal arpeggio writing. Milhaud had a chequered career as a student. He was incapable of falling into line with traditional technique and his own style evolved itself from the freedom of thought which youth has always claimed but has seldom been able to carry out. It would be wrong to say that he was entirely self-taught, for his leading mentors, Gédalge, d'Indy and Widor, guided his ideas into something like order. His harmonic researches caused some qualms among his teachers, but they saw what was beneath the surface and realised that time alone could bring them into fruition.

Music owes a great deal to Milhaud who, in the face of much active opposition based largely upon misconception, has steadfastly turned his face against the easy way to success. Everything which was hissed and derided in the 1920's now seems perfectly normal, but at the time appeared to flaunt every cherished tradition. The most harmless musical entertainments were viewed as professions of aesthetic faith. In many cases they were indeed so, but in these instances there was more than entertainment behind them. His amusing ballet *Le Bœuf sur le Toit* (1919), founded upon South American themes and rhythms in Old Rondo Form, called forth a storm of abuse in spite of the fact that Milhaud had previously established the foundation of his career as a serious composer with such dramatic works as the music for Claudel's *Agamemnon* (1913) and *Les Choéphores* (1915). He was regarded as a buffoon simply because he and his collaborators, particularly Jean Cocteau, provided Paris with gay shows of no pretensions whatsoever.[1] His use of the term "symphony" in the *Six Petites Symphonies* (1917, 1918, 1921, and 1922) which referred back to its primitive implication of "sound" for orchestra was laughed to scorn, Milhaud being accused of clowning by the one side and lacking symphonic instinct by the other. Neither was right, of course, but the public and the critics expected lengthy developments in the symphonies; instead they received miracles of condensation expressed in sheer delicacy of texture, little mood pictures which were, literally, sounds for small orchestra. The battle of *Le Sacre* was no worse than the reception given the first performances of some of Milhaud's earlier works. Such was the riot at the production of the opera *La Brebis égarée* in 1913 that Albert Wolf turned to the audience and called out, "You had better come to-morrow; they are performing *Mignon*."[2] This kind of thing lasted for quite a number of years, the highest pitch of opposition being reached at the first performance of the Symphonic Suite from the music to Claudel's *Protée* (1919—performed 1920)[3] during which the organist of the church of the Temple de la Victoire was slapped on the face by Louis Durey and the critic of *Le Ménestrel* was led out by the police, much to Milhaud's joy.[4] Gabriel Pierné rebuked the audience in the middle of the Fugue by saying that the work was in the programme because he thought it deserved to be and that they would play it again the following Sunday. He also stated that while agreeing with the principle of free expression of thought, he believed it to be customary to withhold it until the end of the performance. At this the audience called out, "à Charenton! à Vincennes!"

[1] He was accused of similar flippancy when his *Machines agricoles* (1919) and *Catalogue de Fleurs* (1920) were first performed, although they, like the ballet, were composed in all seriousness.

[2] Ambroise Thomas.

[3] 1921, *Darius Milhaud*, Collaer (Massé, Paris).

[4] *Notes sans Musique*, Milhaud (Julliard, Paris).

All this is past history and it but repeats other similar occurrences, for Milhaud was one of the world's pioneers and prophets. Everything he foretold in his early works has come true and has been assimilated into present-day technique. French music was purged from Teutonic influences, but the way was hard. Milhaud, therefore, is a landmark, more so than his friend Honegger, who has not shown such a marked cleavage between his early and mature music.

Milhaud has touched every genre and has proved his eclecticism and universality. He may be said to have established the idea of making the resources fit into the framework of the music. Not for Milhaud to have his MS. paper printed in advance with the instrumental force which tradition has laid down. He has never confined himself to any single constitution and the present-day search for new orchestral sonorities is but an echo of his pioneer work. His discipleship of Vincent d'Indy taught him the value and resource of the *batterie* and the possibilities of placing it in the centre or forefront of the score rather than letting it fill a subsidiary rôle. Thus, in the ballet *L'Homme et son Désir* (1918) he uses a vocal quartet, twelve solo instruments and fifteen percussion. In 1929-1930 he wrote a *Concerto for Percussion* accompanied by a little orchestra consisting of two flutes, two clarinets, trumpet, trombone and string quintet. In his impressive *Les Malheurs d'Orphée* (1924) he uses flute, oboe, two clarinets, trumpet, harp, glockenspiel, percussion and string quintet, a modest score. The three "Opéras-Minutes" require even smaller forces. This places the works within the economic range of all, but Milhaud does not hesitate to issue more than one version. The ballet *La Création du Monde* (1923) is available for two flutes, oboe, two clarinets, bassoon, horn, two trumpets, trombone, piano, two kettledrums, percussion, two violins, saxophone, 'cello and bass, and also for piano and string quartet. *Le Pauvre Matelot* (1926) exists in two versions, one for normal orchestra and one for thirteen instruments, while the later ballet *Jeux de Printemps* (1944) can be found in three styles; chamber orchestra of flute, clarinet, bassoon, trumpet and string quintet; piano (four hands); full orchestra of three flutes, three oboes, three clarinets, two bassoons, four horns, three trumpets, three trombones, tuba, percussion, harp and strings. In the *Six Petites Symphonies* he varies the constitution to suit the moods.

On the other hand, he does not hesitate to write boldly for "extras", none of which can be dispensed with. In what many believe to be his greatest work—certainly it is one of the most important in the present century—*Les Euménides,* he adds four saxophones, four saxhorns and fifteen percussion instruments to an already outsize orchestra of three flutes, three oboes, three clarinets, four bassoons, four horns, four trumpets, three trombones, tuba, harp, percussion and strings. Thus he almost outvies our Josef Holbrooke[1] in the vastness of some of his requirements but, like Holbrooke, he never uses his forces extravagantly; he is equally at home in both large and small styles.

In consequence of his polytonal researches and instincts, Milhaud is essentially contrapuntal. He is the scholar of Les Six, but this does not preclude poetic imagination. This can be seen in his poetic explanation of polytonality. He himself has said, "When I find myself in the countryside on a dark night, plunged in silence, if I look at the sky it seems to me that in an instant I am assailed from all directions by shafts of rapidly moving lights; all these shafts of light carry some kind of music, each one different, and the musical infinity criss-crosses from all directions, each sound ray scintillating in its own distinctive manner." This explanation of silence as an association of chaotic ideas is suggested also in Eugene Goossens' *Silence* (1922)[2] and in Holst's *Ode to Death* (1919) at the words "The night in silence".[3] Fancifully, therefore, Milhaud justifies a technical process which in itself is perfectly clear in expression, for Milhaud has all the clarity of Couperin, Rameau and the great French heritage.

As in Ex. 1, on paper much of the polytonally contrived music

Ex.1 Orestes — Les Euménides (1917-1922)

Qu'el-le vienne à mon se-cours.   A el-le de ga-gner sans

[1] Page 111.   [2] Page 294.   [3] Page 139.

seems a mere jangle of sound. To read it in silence requires extreme concentration. To play it on the piano is painful, to say the least. However, on its proper medium it comes off perfectly well. When Milhaud is polytonal on the piano, the music is delightfully suggestive. His *Second Violin Sonata* (1917) amply illustrates this. The poetic impulse directs him to a pastoral style which appears in many works, although it is not in the least standardised. Milhaud here combines the extreme simplicity of semitonal common chords with a diatonic tune. In this way he obtains an effect of nocturnal Impressionism, one would say. Thus, in the ineffably beautiful third movement of this particular *Sonata,* parallel shafts of light descend in motion contrary to the plain and unadorned violin theme.

Ex. 2   Second Violin Sonata (1917)

During the war a brother officer played this work with me to a volunteer audience of soldiers. After the performance one of them, a man of no musical culture or even with great musical interest, told me that this particular movement explained exactly what he had experienced so often when on guard during a summer night and which had hitherto eluded all attempts at verbal explanation. I believe a thorough understanding and appreciation of Milhaud's fanciful polytonal experience to be essential for the complete comprehension of the music. It is more actual romanticism than that of Schumann as expressed in terms of slightly deviating traditional harmony. I believe Milhaud to be in this connection one of the greatest romantic poets of the twentieth century, a romanticism which he expresses in twentieth-century musical language, in "sound" for instruments of music. He is equally poetic and evocative when he writes in terms of pure lyrical melody (of which more anon) as in the piece for violin and piano known as *Le Printemps,* which started life as the "Bacchanale nocturne" in *Protée.*

Milhaud's pastoral moments, unlike those of Vaughan Williams, are evocative through the material, through the themes rather than through any modality. It is easy to explain Vaughan Williams by this term. With Milhaud the explanation lies in the music itself—I do not refer here to the ebullience of the Provençal country fair which he paints so well and which has some slight parallelism with the Hampstead Heath of Vaughan Williams' *A London Symphony*. It must be ascribed to the particular type of Impressionism which Milhaud himself has explained and which avoids all the vague warmth of the Debussy variety.

Milhaud's polytonality is admirably shown in his *String Quartets* which have none of the latent romanticism seen in the *Second Violin Sonata* and which are abstract from start to finish. The *Fourteenth* and *Fifteenth* (1948-1949) which, together, make an *Octuor* and, separately, two single Quartets, are a reminder that Antonin Reicha (1770-1836) did much the same thing; but in his case one of the bodies was a wind combination, the two bodies being in different modes. When Hans Richter first heard Strauss' *Ein Heldenleben* he remarked that one could combine a hundred different themes provided one did not mind the resultant sound. Those who do not agree with Milhaud's technique are of the opinion that this applies equally well to him and to polytonality generally. The proof lies in the results. If the works sound satisfactory both together and separately, there can be no objection. Milhaud has succeeded beyond doubt. The *Fourteenth* is balanced in its violence by the *Fifteenth* in its quiet charm. It is strange that he waited until 1947 before composing a *String Trio*.

His scholarship can be found in the *Cinq Etudes pour Piano et Orchestre* (1920). Milhaud himself explains his intentions:[1]

> I had studied a process of writing which was basically traditional; each Study deals with a different problem of sonority and construction (Bach in the *Art of Fugue* and *The Musical Offering* set himself the most complicated problems). I used polytonal writing and thus obtained the utmost subtlety in the quiet movements and the utmost intensity in the noisy. The Third Study—Fugues—is a study of four simultaneous fugues; that played on the wind instruments is in A, that for the brass in D flat minor, those for the strings in F; the piano unites in one of the two parts the

[1] *Notes sans Musique, op. cit.*

notes common to the three keys and expresses the subject and answer of the fugue while orchestral fugues form variations. The Fourth Study, dramatic and violent, is constructed . . . so that the piece is divisible into two; the second half is exactly the same as the first but is inverted. From the middle onwards it continues as it began. The violence of this work astonished the public, who were not slow to show it.

Again, no romanticism and, again, hostility. In the concerto manner Milhaud has been both successful and otherwise, and it is in one of these works that he shows his rhythmic strength in its most complicated form. The *First Violin Concerto* (1927) has been described as one of the worst in the repertoire because, musically, it has hardly anything to commend it and its entire being depends on complicated cross-rhythms. Its second movement has been misunderstood. Milhaud served in the French Legation in Brazil during the First World War and while there absorbed South American tunes and patterns. The second movement of the *Concerto*, if viewed entirely as a movement in a serious-minded work, is lamentably banal; but as soon as it is realised that it is a typical South American tune, the situation alters. The content of the Finale is lamentable and consists simply of rather cheap abstract sounds. The rhythmic puzzles which Milhaud delights in presenting can best be seen in the following extracts:

This is the only complication of its kind that I can find in Milhaud's output, and from this it is refreshing to turn to the *Concertino de Printemps* (1934) also for violin and orchestra in which Milhaud's texture is particularly happy and in which, as in the *First Concerto for 'Cello*

and Orchestra (1934) and the *Fantaisie Pastorale for Piano and Orchestra* (1938), he uses a small orchestra. In all these three works the rhythm is contained in the musical melodic texture, Milhaud achieving a rare tenderness and grace in the *Concertino de Printemps* and the *Fantaisie Pastorale*. Milhaud's use of rhythm *per se* is striking and has developed alongside his ever-growing interest in percussion. It can be seen in both small and big ways.

He is perfectly at home with an alteration of accents which displaces the normal flow of the measure. Such displacements as the following are achieved perfectly naturally and fall easily upon the pulsation of the music:

The use of rhythm by itself is one of the strongest points of the music dramas and other stage works. Here the objector may be justified in maintaining that this is an extra-musical effect since the text is merely spoken upon a rhythm. The effect of this, however, is impressive.

The ballet *Salade* (1924—later known as *Le Carnival d'Aix* (1926),
a "Fantasie d'après Salade") may be studied in this respect and can
be multiplied in other works.

For Ex. 5 *b*) see page *90*.

Few who have heard the "Présages" and "Exhortation" from *Les
Choéphores* can ever forget the dramatic intensity of the syllabic
rhythms of the recited solo and chorus through a rhythmic side-drum
ostinato. The extremely early works owe most of their hostility to
what at the time appeared to be an over-emphasis on this element.
Rhythm with Milhaud is not the same as that with Stravinsky in *Le
Sacre* and *Les Noces*; Milhaud is content in a great many cases to leave it
unadorned with actual musical sound and he does not use the orchestra,
either large or small, as one big percussion instrument. Nevertheless,
in a work like *L'Homme et son Désir* (and in others) the initial impulse
springs almost entirely from Stravinsky; but they part company over
melody.

It is doubtful if he has as yet composed what commentators would
call "a great melody"; few composers have done so, but he has proved
himself capable of a lyrical charm and beauty which is essentially
Provençal. As may be expected, this is to be found mostly in his pastoral moments where it assists by implication the formation of the
picture and impression. This pastorality is both serene and proletarian.

Ex. 5 b)

Les Choéphores (1915)

In the latter case the music is hard and uncompromisingly easy. Some would call it commonplace and even vulgar, but this is what it is intended to be, and in those movements which represent the clod-hopping junketings of the crowd at a Provençal fair, Milhaud is akin to Emmanuel Chabrier (1841-1894), who in some of his *Piéces Pittoresques* and other ebullient works reveals a thorough sympathy with country folk. Milhaud's most popular orchestral work, in this country at any rate, the *Suite Provençale* (1936), is a complete musical picture of a Provençal country fête. Milhaud's pastoral romanticism in its lyrical beauty and poise can be seen in Ex. 6 on page 91. The dividing line between the actual use of polytonality in all its con-sequences and that of no fixed tonality appears as early as 1926 in the opera, described as a "Complainte", *Le Pauvre Matelot*, where Mil-haud uses second inversions of triads and diatonic discords where-

Ex.6 a) Second Violin Sonata

b) Fantaisie Pastorale (1938)

c) Protée

soever and howsoever he wills. In this particular case, where the more sophisticated polytonality would be out of place, the music foreshadows the later harmonic principles of the works of the period of his American exile, for Milhaud's output divides itself into two main sections. The opening of *Le Pauvre Matelot* is simple and direct, and the whole work is remarkably free from chromaticism. The few bars in Ex. 7 on page 92 at once suggest his later rather unfortunate habit of slamming the orchestra about, but there can be no doubt as to its directness and bluffness. This work, incidentally, was written in thirteen days.

It would be both profitable and fascinating to consider Milhaud in complete detail, but such study is outside the scope of a book whose purpose is to outline some of the trends of twentieth-century music. It will not be out of place, however, to explain the enumeration of his many works, which fall into two categories, the first reaching to 1940 and for the most part written in the complete French milieu and

Ex.7   Le Pauvre Matelot (1926)

uninfluenced by anything outside that orbit save the Brazilian "Saudade", the second stretching to the present day, culminating in *La Fin du Monde* (1949), an orchestral work for radio use, the greater number being composed under an American influence which, although not in any way affecting his technique, led him to expansion of resource. The works in the first category go up to Op. 217, those of his American exile, sixty-three in number, take the sum to 280, while the remainder up to the time of writing achieve the magnificent total of 299 (doubtless he has reached 300 by now). The American period includes the enormous opera *Bolivar* (1943) in three acts and ten tableaux, which takes four hours to perform.[1]

Milhaud waited until 1939 before composing his *First Symphony* for full orchestra, designed on the established and traditional lines. This was an impulse from America, from Chicago. Milhaud was in the depths of despair at the time and could find no impulse for composition. When the Chicago commission reached him, he was not interested for the immediate moment, until he suddenly realised that his work would be the only French one to be so commissioned. He found that his frustrated patriotism had an immediate outlet, and the work was completed in November of that warlike year. From that moment his outlook changed and there were no more *Petites Symphonies*; indeed, he joined the ranks of the traditionalists in this respect and in the peace-haven of Mills he produced in all tranquillity four works of classical proportions but not of classical design; the *Fourth Symphony* bears the legend, "Océan Pacifique, Océan Atlantique, Aôut-

[1] Milhaud's complete dramatic output is studied in detail in my *Paris and the Opera: the History of a Culture*. (In preparation.)

Sept. 1947. Orch. Genval Oct. Aix Dec. 1947". The exile returned home greater in stature than when he left, for he had overcome all the frustrations and disillusionments of the war years and had emerged recharged with vigour and a sense of direction.

In these last symphonies Milhaud makes his contact with Berlioz. It is true that in *Les Euménides* he has produced a second *Les Troyens*, but elsewhere the relationship is not in any way apparent. One may, perhaps, connect a work like the *Suite Provençale* with *Le Carnival Romain*, but the topography is different and Milhaud's *Suite* does not glitter. Although adhering to the multi-movement symphonic style, Milhaud does not restrict himself to the traditional type of succession. The first movements of the *First* and *Second* are described "Pastoral" and "Paisible" respectively. This places the danger of a certain lack of contrast between the second and third movements and it is only a composer with technique sufficiently advanced to vary itself that can avoid this pitfall. Remembering the circumstances of the *First Symphony*, it is interesting to see how Milhaud at once reacts in his true pastoral Provençal manner with music exceedingly happy and gay. The following forms a neat comparison with the pastoral theme of the *Second Violin Sonata*[1] which may be described as general in application rather than locally rural.

The *Second Symphony* (1944), composed in memory of Nathalie Koussevitsky, is more sober, but while duly serious-minded does not wallow in grief and can in no way be regarded as a symphonic "Requiem". One notes that the movements headed "Paisible", "Mysterieux", "Douloureux", and "Avec serenité" are moods rather than pace-marks, the music in each case being quietly mobile with some fine climaxes. The Finale, described "Alleluia", is a magnificent fugue of considerable power and verve.

[1] Page 91.

When the French Government in 1946 commissioned a *Te Deum* from Milhaud to celebrate the Liberation it is significant that he was not contented with simply a setting of the hymn but immediately let loose a flood of music which found its climax in the *Te Deum*. There are few more impressive moments than the opening of the second movement when, after a strong sustained orchestral chord, the chorus enters quietly with a vocalised one. This may be an effect, but it is strangely moving and Milhaud showed his old skill in dealing with mixed voices, skill so splendidly shown in the big Claudel works. Again there is a "Pastorale", but let it be noted that the noun is used in this case and it is a reversion to the earlier *Second Violin Sonata* rather than the expression of a pastoral mood. The significance of this large work lies in the fact that Milhaud returned to his original state of fecundity and proved that increasing years does not necessarily imply the adoption of simplicity and small forms.

The *Fourth Symphony* (1947) is the one in which he most nearly approaches Berlioz. This work, composed for the Centenary Celebrations of the 1848 Revolution, is the least musically satisfactory of the four, probably because the events it celebrates belong to past history and the idea of liberation had been hymned by Milhaud in the *Third Symphony*. In any case, a work which labels its movements "L'Insurrection", "Aux Morts de la République", "Les Joies Paisibles de la Liberté Retrouvée" and "Commemoration 1948" is asking for a good deal of faith, especially when it simply celebrates an event and nothing more. Two "Liberation Symphonies" in such close succession defeat their own object. The music itself is not particularly inspired— this is a common deficiency in political music.

Milhaud is one of the greatest figures in contemporary European music. It remains to be seen to what extent his influence has permeated musical composition in America. That it has already begun to do so cannot be doubted, and musical America in time will not fail to show the benefit of his sojourn. He is not immediately acceptable as is Roussel, for example, and he relies too often on sheer violence to get his intention across. He has been accused of a complete lack of human feeling. This is difficult to understand since feeling is patent in all his quiet moments.

His lyricism lately has lost much of its free-heartedness, but it has been replaced by a steady symphonic growth which, although showing no signs of cyclicism or germination, is a binding factor in his big thoughts. He stands in the direct line now from d'Indy and Roussel He is at the head of French musical thought, a *maître*, although by no means one of the d'Indy type. In the same way that Guy Ropartz represents Brittany, so does Milhaud represent Provence and both stand for everything which is finest in eternal France.

CHAPTER EIGHT

ARTHUR HONEGGER

(1892)

THE dictionaries describe Arthur Honegger as a Swiss composer. Although of Swiss parentage, and although he did his military service in the Swiss Army, he was born at Le Havre and, with the exception of two years at the Zurich Conservatoire, his pupilage was spent entirely in Paris, first at the Conservatoire from 1911-1913 and then privately, under Vincent d'Indy and Charles Marie Widor. His entire cultural background, therefore, is French and it was in Paris that he spent the greater part of his mature musical career and made his reputation. On the outbreak of the Second World War he moved to Switzerland. This may be misunderstood, but France has every right to claim him as one of her composers. His style and idiom are essentially French and his fondness for the big forms emanates entirely from d'Indy, who impressed upon him the necessity and importance of a strict consideration to form. He was long considered the only serious member of Les Six because he did not take part in any of the high jinks broadly associated with the other members, and when Milhaud and others repudiated Wagner, Honegger proclaimed his constant faith and admiration for him. Further, even in his earliest pieces—he commenced to compose seriously in 1914—there is an almost classical sense of design. It is true that he was drawn to Verism, an attraction which was evidenced by *Pacific 231* (1923) and *Rugby* (1928)—the latter as unsuccessful as the former was successful—but elsewhere, and earlier, in the *Pastorale d'Été* (1920) and *Le Roi David* (1921) he displayed a strong feeling for romantic beauty and dramatic force.

If Milhaud was the scholar of Les Six, Honegger was the logician. His pupilage with Vincent d'Indy and the study of this composer's works gave him a strong grasp of the exigencies of form; but Honegger was not content to take things as they were. His logical mind detected one flaw in the classical design, a flaw in his eyes which viewed the design as a continuous entity rather than as a succession of three sections. Honegger practised what certain earlier composers had tentatively experimented in. It seemed more logical as regards balance for the second subject to reappear before the first in the recapitulation section, since in this way the music unfolded itself more continuously. Instead of A, B, C, A, B, Honegger adopted what he called the "Façade design", A, B, C, B, A. The two designs may be planned in this manner:

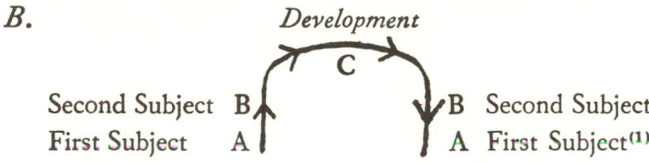

This was nothing new, but Honegger adopted it consistently in his sonatas and symphonies. Vincent d'Indy's opinion of this is untraceable, but one may be sure that if he disagreed with it, and this disagreement would have arisen over the different outlook which he himself held, he must have viewed the experiment on the grounds that his pupil had, at least, a strong faith in the necessity for form. It is a shape which, like the cyclical and germinal principles, has commended itself to other composers; but it destroys the discursive and argumentative nature of the earlier design.

Another equally logical principle also made itself manifest in his earlier works and has appeared with unfailing regularity all through his output; this is his love of contrary motion. Rather than double an important fragment in similar motion, Honegger persists in contradicting it in the bottom line. Here are some examples of it:

[1] Instead of moving perpetually downwards, the music moves up and then down.

In time this becomes almost tiresome and it can be regarded as a Honeggerian cliché; but it is all part of his manner and is one of the signs by which one recognises him.

The contrast between Honegger and the other members of Les Six shows that the coterie was bound together only in one single aim, and that stylistically and idiomatically they had nothing in common. Honegger has never propagated any "-ism". That his music is polytonal at times can never be denied, but he does not self-consciously, as it were, write in that "-ality" or, indeed, in any other. If one may be applied to his music, it is that of tonality, another legacy from d'Indy, and also from Widor. Honegger, even in his most frantic moments, never loses sight of tonality. He regards each central note not as a tonic, but as a dominant from which the music proceeds naturally from one key to another, and to another and so on. His polyphony is hardly traditional, but it is less iconoclastic than that of Milhaud. Being intensely chromatic, the counterpoint has a constantly changing harmonic implication which gives a feeling of restlessness. It is this use of what has been called the "sinew of music" which gives his music its immense power and drive, its forward impulse becoming increasingly noticeable once the quasi-ostinato habit, previously referred to,[1] had been discarded. While Milhaud in his polyphonic moments is concerned with linear tonality alone and seemingly pays little attention to the harmonic implications, Honegger is concerned with the lines in themselves, the combinations having to form a perfectly solid harmonic block at every moment when viewed vertically. It is at those moments when the texture is thin that Honegger is least interesting, and he depends very largely on rhythm to maintain the nervous interest. It is when the polyphony appears inside the context of the technique that he proves his strength and ability to enthral us. He is probably aware of this, for he rarely writes a deliberate "Fugue"; indeed, one calls to mind only the short *Fugue* for organ and the *Prélude, Arioso et Fughette (for Strings) on the name BACH.* Fugal he often is, but this occurs incidentally. This manner differs from that of Milhaud, who compels attention through rough edges which the traditionalist regards merely as crudities.

Honegger's admiration for Wagner is stamped on almost every orchestral page he writes. He does not use the Wagnerian formulae or processes and his themes have much more line; but he depends upon solid effects and warmth of harmonic colour. His use of the brass is Wagnerian, but with the small orchestra he is not so successful. It is a salient feature of his orchestral writing that in no instance can any Berlioz ancestry be detected, and this is equally absent from the elaborate oratorios, from *Le Roi David* (1923) to *Jeanne d'Arc au bucher* (1935) and *La Danse des Morts* (1940). His choralism and, indeed, his polyphony generally traces back to the Quintet in *Die Meistersinger* in the first place and to J. S. Bach in the second. His massive orchestral thoughts are the direct descendants of *Der Ring des Nibelungen.* Brahms, Bruckner and Mahler escaped him as they escape most Latin composers, but whether Honegger is Latin in anything save training is an open question. This Wagnerian admiration which led Honegger at once to the great forms without in any way touching the grandiloquent was another trait which commended him to Vincent d'Indy; but the panoply of orchestral tone with Honegger lacks Wagnerian dignity and majesty, and one is never overwhelmed by the two in quite the

[1] See pages 78 and 79.

same way. When Honegger exults and carries the listeners with him, it is the romanticism of the thought which makes the appeal. He is never miserable and his music proclaims the joy he feels in the act of living. This may well have been the initial impulse in some of the earlier *Symphonic Movements,* as I have suggested. His expressionism did not last long, but out of it grew the symphonic intensity of the later *Symphonies.*

Honegger has never lost his initial vein of pure lyricism. He is the most directly lyrical of Les Six and, indeed, of the greater number of composers of his period, because his themes are so often symphonic in content and suggestion. Even in the shorter works it is difficult to find one which does not offer immediate possibilities for expansion. In the *Second Violin Sonata* (1919) this is very obvious, and the lyricism stands out in bold relief from the pianism because the former is unaffected and diatonic. Honegger likes to take his themes high up and let them poise and soar over a moving accompaniment. Here he shows the influence of Roussel, but, in the *Violin Sonata* mentioned above, there is one, and practically the only, direct reference to a habit contracted by d'Indy which is to be found in the use of the rhythmic figure, ♪♪ ♩♩. This plays an important part in d'Indy's *Symphony in B flat,* a work which would make an instant appeal to a latent symphonic mind like that of Honegger. If Milhaud was mainly lyrical when pastoral, Honegger is lyrical throughout. It is only in the *Pastorale d'Été* that he shows any tendency to melodic immobility and he does not get his impulse from rural scenes or customs. It is curious, therefore, that the isolated example of pastoral music should prove the exception in his lyricism. A few typical Honegger melodies may be quoted here:

Ex. 2 a)   2nd Violin Sonata (1924)

Prélude - Phaedre (1930)

b)

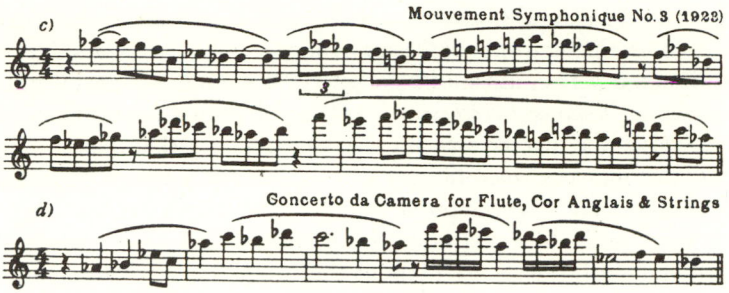

This melodic mobility is matched by the extreme vigour of most of his works, a vigour which becomes somewhat exhausting after a short while, although it is not in any way nerve-tearing; but Honegger has always been a man of intense physical energy and, consequently, fifteen minutes of his company is as good as a tonic. His personality is of the strongest. When conducting an orchestra he stands firmly, with feet slightly apart, and his beat is notable for its precision. He and Milhaud, incidentally, are among the few composer-conductors who convince their performers that they actually and really know their own music inside-out and backwards. Honegger's extraordinary energy manifests itself in his *Symphonic Movements*—"Pacific 231", "Rugby" and "No. 3" (1933), the last-named an abstract outburst of physical exuberance. It is found also in the Mimed Symphony *Horace victorieux* (1921), *Chant de Joie* (1923) and *Overture for The Tempest* (1923). The first of these has never been performed in its original state, and Honegger concocted the present work from the material of the original. The second appears to be largely a sudden outbreak of enthusiasm. The third is one of the most graphic pieces of musical dirty weather in the repertoire, and all the effects are gained by legitimate thematic means. It may be argued with some justification that it overbalances the play which follows; but Honegger did not compose any other music for it and it is likely that it was a reaction to the play itself. In all these works the form is logical and clear. A similar symphonic energy and logical working-out is found in the later *Symphonies*, of which there are four dated 1930, 1941, 1945-1946, and 1946 respectively; his first actual *Symphony*, therefore, preceded the *First* of Milhaud by nine years—it was not in Honegger's nature to wait for his fiftieth anniversary before embarking on what at that time was regarded as being still the natural climax to maturity and experience. In his works for solo instrument and orchestra Honegger shows remarkable restraint and a perfect sense of balance. He is entirely successful in his *Concerto for 'Cello and Orchestra* (1931) and it would appear from this work that at the time he was approaching (rather earlier than in other cases) that moment when his thought was naturally simplifying itself; but the succeeding works proved that he was merely taking things a little more easily. The texture of this particular *Concerto* is remarkably slight and clear. There are none of the complexities which appeared in earlier works—and with Honegger complexity often implied complication. This, however, lies more in the resources required than in the actual material. It reached its highest point in the monumental *Jeanne d'Arc au bucher,* his enormous "mystère" to text by Paul Claudel.

It is at this point that we consider his dramatic music, and the position of dramatic composers in France in the period 1920-1939 in this respect. It goes without saying that the invention of radio opened vast possibilities for dramatised music, not only in the sense of heightening an invisible situation but in removing certain incongruities which live performance accentuates and in which respect certain film scores reach the ridiculous. It may well be that people commit suicide to the accompaniment of a full symphony orchestra; I do not know for certain, but over and over again in the cinema we are invited to watch the death-throes of some villain or other, and to listen at the same time to the writhings of an orchestra, all the members seemingly about to commit similar suicide. This, apparently, is called "stylisation", but we would not be rid of it for the world because it undoubtedly heightens the' tragedy and poignancy of the situation. In radio, music is an essential part of drama, and by drama I do not refer to the conventional type of play. A Greek tragedy without music can be a deadly affair and the listener requires a subconscious lift. The trouble comes before the ear has accustomed itself to absorbing music and recitation simultaneously, and it is noteworthy that, although vigorous protests at the inclusion of music are invariably received by the B.B.C. after some notable production, in the majority of cases it is passed by unnoticed or at least without comment. Consequently, it may be a sign that ears in general have by now become acclimatised to the required conditions; but it should be remarked that listeners' reactions are stirred more by the casual phrase than by the lengthy "band". Honegger has composed several dramatic scores which have been necessitated by the authors themselves. He has been lucky in working with such dramatists and poets as René Morax, André Gide, Romain Rolland, Paul Claudel and Gabriele d'Annunzio. This galaxy of stars has inspired him to write some of his finest music. Now, one of the most lamentable features of much film and theatre music is that it is utterly useless away from its original purpose. This, which the French call *musique de scène*, is a source of revenue, but is hardly conducive to making a composer feel happy, since once the play has finished its run or received its allotted number of broadcasts, the music counts for nought. Honegger, although writing his share of "incidental music", has always managed to get involved with something needing more than this. His dramatic music has always been expandible and, consequently, he has been able to keep it in the repertoire in the form of concert suites. This, it may be argued, signifies that the music and the text are not one indivisible entity which, from the idealistic point of view, they should have been; but it does not necessarily follow. One may single out the music to *Le Roi David* (Morax, 1921), *Antigone* (Cocteau, 1922), *Judith* (Morax, 1925) and *Phaedre* (d'Annunzio, 1926) as being remarkable dramatic achievements which were fully supplemented by Honegger's music and which were written with music as one of the express purposes of the production. It all depends, therefore, upon the attitude of the poet and dramatist towards music. Some dislike it, regarding their lines as being all-sufficient, and the addition of music an impertinence and almost an avowal of incompetence (Shakespeare was not one of these). Others, while not deliberately writing a drama for acting and music, acknowledge that their work should and must be performed with the latter. The composer in this situation is ón happy ground. In certain cases, such as those of *Antigone* and *Judith*, the original idea has been developed into operatic proportions, while *Le Roi David* became a symphonic oratorio. All these form perfectly satisfactory concert works if the intentions are made clear on the programmes. The music to *Phaedre* should be in the permanent repertoire.

The "mystère" design has appealed to him and his initial reputation was made by *Le Roi David* when performed in this style. *Jeanne d'Arc au bucher* (1935) is monumental. It includes every available resource for spectacular production. Great actors find every opportunity for declamation, great singers for interpreting thoughts of the highest musical inspiration, while the addition of wordless choruses to the orchestral accompaniment (if such a word may be used) forms one of the most intensely moving works of the century. That the emotion is not restricted to spectacular production has been proved by radio performance which, at the other end of the line, has on each occasion resulted in a most moving experience. The form of this work disturbed the critics who found it ill-balanced and considered the music as having been conceived as a huge film score. They did not realise that it was a revitalised approach to oratorio whose classical design of solos, ensembles, and fugal choruses died a natural death with Parry's *Judith* (1888) and Saint-Saëns' *The Promised Land* (1912). In *La Danse des Morts* Honegger was not so successful, partly because there was too much recited text, and partly because that text was taken in too liberal an amount from the Bible; it became, therefore, too much like a Biblical reading. There was not enough music in it.

One may note the manner in which Honegger parts company with Milhaud in his use of the spoken word. It has been seen that Milhaud contrived much impressive rhythmic declamation in works like *Les Choéphores* and *Les Euménides*. Honegger avoids this, and lets the spoken word become entirely a matter for the reciter. Massed recitation does not appeal to him in this respect, and he feels that it is too near a musical expression to be convincing. Milhaud's enterprise is thoroughly successful in its own milieu and one does not want every composer to imitate it. Honegger, therefore, would seem to be more definitely musical than Milhaud, since he does not approve of an extra-musical element trying to have contact with actual music; but this is entirely a personal affair and proves nothing. From the unforgettable closing "Alleluias" of *Le Roi David,* through the moving and thrilling moments in *Jeanne d'Arc au bucher* to the infinite variety of the music to Denis de Rougement's *Nicolas de Flue* (1939), in which Honegger has provided a score of limpid lucidity and simplicity, dramatic music has been adorned so as to become as important as opera and Honegger (together with Milhaud) has raised the genre to the highest level, lifting it up from the depths of obscurity and self-effacement.

This Franco-Swiss composer occupies one of the highest positions in the musical hierarchy to-day. Without being in any way experimental, without subscribing to any definite "-ism" or "-ality", he has placed himself in the forefront of contemporary musicians. He is more universal than Milhaud since he does not find himself attached to any province of the world. With Milhaud, he has fought a winning battle, but he never considered it necessary to be iconoclastic and from the first saw that music could be continued along the lines laid down by Vincent d'Indy and transmuted by him to Roussel, and to Honegger himself. He is among the most symphonic of French twentieth-century composers; certainly he is the most so of his own generation and he has never shown signs of being anything else. He and Roussel add virility to French music, Honegger maintaining an equal balance between romanticism and classicism, Roussel deliberately eschewing the former. Of the young music written in the 1920's, that of Honegger is the only kind which does not date, and one can play any of it without aligning it with any specific period except that of the last thirty years in general. This can be said of few composers. His present-day maturity is recognisable mainly by its use of increased resources and its growth of thematic detail. Honegger is the "great" figure of French twentieth-century music. He is not eclectic in style and is not immediately derivative—one does, in fact, look in vain for derivation among the composers of his period and age, although possibly finding some authority in the older Stravinsky. Honegger is not as approachable as Roussel because his music is more weighty. Roussel had the knack of making himself immediately acceptable and comprehensible, while one has often to look for hidden truths in Honegger. He forms an expansion of the Roussel ideal, an expansion which would not have bothered Roussel himself and which he would not have felt it his bounden duty to carry out or equalise. One would say that, of the twentieth century, Roussel, Honegger and Milhaud propagated most of the new ideals. Roussel owes nothing to Stravinsky. Milhaud certainly acquired some ideas from him, but Honegger was hardly touched by him. Prophets invariably emerge slowly. It is highly probable that in due time these three composers will be found to have laid the foundation of later twentieth-century music in Europe.

CHAPTER NINE

THE ENGLISH PANORAMA

Parry (1848-1918)—*Stanford* (1852-1924)—[*Cowen* (1852-1935)—*Mackenzie* (1874-1935)]—*Corder* (1852-1932)—*Bantock* (1868-1946)—*Holbrooke* (1878)—*Smyth* (1858-1944)—*Elgar* (1857-1934)—*Scott* (1879)—*Dale* (1885-1945)—*Bridge* (1879-1941)—*Bliss* (1891)—*Ireland* (1879)—[*Moeran* (1894-1950)—*Jacob* (1895)]—*Howells* (1892)—*Warlock* (1894-1930)

THE Victorian age in this country had a depressing effect on creative musical activity. Having thrown over the yoke of Handel which, after all, had some kinship with that of Purcell, the cult of Mendelssohn and everything German took its place. Students looked to Leipzig for enlightenment, and studentage there appeared to be the hall-mark of respectability. The Teutonic influence permeated every walk of life, thanks to the inclinations of the Prince Consort. When, in 1870, Hubert Parry (1848-1918) produced his setting of *Prometheus Unbound,* it was felt that English music had at last come to its renaissance. This turned out to be a slight exaggeration. It indicated that we had one composer at least capable of writing good, sound, solid stuff, which had no bearing upon the elegancies of Mendelssohn; but in place of these elegancies, the contemporary composers were donning the mantle of Johannes Brahms (1833-1897). This influence worked indirectly. It is noticeable, for example, in the manner of writing for violas and 'cellos common to Parry and Stanford, although to a lesser degree with the latter. The *Song of Destiny* appeared to the writers of cantatas to be the model of perfection and one which could be pondered upon and translated in terms scarcely differentiated. The representative composers at the turn of the century, therefore, had produced nothing which could be termed either definitely British or English.

From another direction came the ravings (to ears of those days) of Richard Strauss and the Grand Manner.

While the scholastic Parry and Stanford turned to Brahms for their direction, the wilder spirits such as Granville Bantock (1868-1946) and Josef Holbrooke (1878) found creative excitement in the Strauss model, scorning the academic approach and arousing complacent English audiences to frenzies of enthusiasm on the one side, among the younger generation, and of indignation and fury on the other. One figure stood aloof, Edward Elgar (1857-1934) who, being independent and attached to no school, college or academy, had a hard fight to wage against the conventionalities of the era, being quite unsupported by any influential element. Elgar, living in the country and outside the musical swim of London, knew few influential people—in this country it has always been necessary for the composer struggling for recognition to "know" somebody or other in a high place. The outsider, the "provincial composer", therefore, was regarded at that time as highly impertinent if he dared intrude upon the preserves of Dr. This or Sir Somebody That. Imagine the rage when this provincial composer told the Royal Philharmonic Society that he did not "submit works" for performance.

It was, indeed, a hard struggle for anybody not claiming some kind of official backing, and this, musically speaking, meant an adherence to the established rules and regulations for the setting forth of musical tunes in writing. The wonder is that anyone ever got anything played anywhere. The representative composers at the end of the nineteenth century were Parry, Stanford (1852-1924), Cowen (1852-1935) and Mackenzie (1847-1935). The rebels were Elgar, Bantock, Holbrooke and Cyril Scott (1879). The phenomenal position of the last-named will be explained later. Parry and Stanford were turning out orchestral works by the score, all of a pedestrian nature. Of the two, Stanford had style and a flair for orchestral colour which showed him to be a long distance ahead of his colleague, in this field at any rate. Both showed a distinct descent from and membership of what is known as the English Choral Tradition. In chamber music both were complete failures. They excelled in organ music, each leaving behind some perfect specimen of this medium which will surely live as long as there is one diapason left in English churches. Stanford gained a reputation on the Continent as an operatic composer, assisted (so it is surmised) by personal acquaintance with operatic magnates. Parry's one attempt made no impact upon the many directors to whom Stanford showed the score. Parry was concerned with turning out festival cantatas in quick succession, the supply hardly keeping level with the demand. Consequently, there is much which is dull and uninspired among the threads of gold[1] inevitable with a composer of his ability. His best works may be said to be the *Songs of Farewell* which he composed towards the end of his life. Into these he put his innermost soul and the result is a set of motets which can rank with any others throughout the history of music. However, they have nothing in common with those twentieth-century ideals which had come to the surface in France and elsewhere.

Mackenzie was an orchestral player. Parry and Stanford viewed everything from the vocal and pianistic point of view. To his dying day Stanford believed in the "black and white test", and an orchestral score which did not sound convincing on the piano was stigmatised as "atmospheric". Mackenzie thought orchestrally in the first place. He brought to his music an essentially instrumental impulse and although of the three composers his is the music which finished its earthly life first, it had more variable qualities about it. The same may be said of Cowen, whose symphonies are not negligible in their way and fashion. A composer who never got his true deserts was Frederick Corder (1852-1932) whose *Elegy for Twenty-four Violins and Organ* and *Motet in Fifty (real) Parts, with Orchestra,* have considerable value. Of the four composers, his was the most eclectic style. He was a colourist and might have made a European conquest had European music not been under the sway of the greater colourist and virtuoso composer, Richard Strauss. Of the four, knighthood eluded Corder— yet his would have been a deserving case, more so, in fact, than Sir Frederick Cowen (Parry and Mackenzie were Director and Principal of the Royal College and Royal Academy of Music respectively). Stanford claimed his honour purely as a representative composer, many-sided but not eclectic, paradoxical though this may seem.

In the words of Professor Adolf Weissmann (1873-1929),[2] in England "learning is sedulously cultivated". It accounted for the enormous pull that those connected with universities and teaching institutions had over the independents and recalcitrants. It accounted for the exaggerated importance placed still upon the holding of a university degree by examination instead of by achievement; but this

[1] Among these are *De profundis* (1891) and *Voces clamantium* (1903).
[2] *The Problems of Modern Music* (Dent).

had a certain good point about it as at the time it lifted the status of the musician from that of a mere fiddler to one of social recognition. The first to suggest that the composer was worthy to rank with the poet and painter was Sir Arthur Sullivan (1842-1900) who, incidentally, sprang from humble surroundings. Parry was one of the landed gentry of England and in spite of his (at the time) deplorable Liberal tendencies, he was at home in the highest circles and accepted for what he was by birth. This later led to recognition of his artistic merits and the world was surprised to find out that musicians knew how to behave themselves in public. Stanford was an Irishman whose family had certain social connections in Ireland.

The twentieth century augured well for the recognition of the composer as a more than tolerated individual and in some cases the old patron system came back into operation. This was all to the good. Actually the system has never since gone out of operation, although it comes more from societies formed for the purpose than from the individual. It is difficult to see the difference between the commissioned picture or bust and the commissioned orchestral score. No matter how high and mighty the great composers may have deemed themselves, history relates no instance of a refusal of a commission. However, this did not in any way deter the unfavoured composer from composing, because it was his very life's blood to do so; but at the beginning of the century he did not go out of his way to make things easy for himself.

The Grand Manner entailed virtuosic writing for the orchestra which strained the abilities of the players to their utmost—to-day these very same works simply make them take a little more trouble. From Richard Strauss and his symphonic poems, his operas, particularly *Elektra*, came the idea that the greater the noise, the greater would be the value of the music. Consequently, the larger the orchestra, the more significant the work and the harder it was to play, the greater was the position held by the particular composer. These tenets held fast until the Great War of 1914 which, in retrospect, can be seen to have been the inevitable result of over-swollen tendencies. The Teutonic composers blew themselves out in a blast of megalomaniacal self-importance. Nevertheless, it would be altogether wrong to regard the native music of the first fourteen years of the twentieth century as either negligible or inferior in quality. I refer, of course, to the representative music; there were quieter forces at work which were not allowed to materialise until the Great War had ended, and then many of them were *démodé*.

The virtuosic influence of Richard Strauss was reflected largely in Bantock and Holbrooke. The former left behind him a vast number of works of magnitude, many of which have never been performed as far as one can make out. His fine choral ballet, *The Great God Pan* (1915), for example, is a work worthy to rank with the very finest of Strauss. *Fifine at the Fair* (1912) and the *Hebridean Symphony* (1918) have remained in the repertoire, while *The Witch of Atlas* (1902), an infinitely more approachable work, has vanished. Bantock was a composer of enthusiasms. Whenever he found himself in contact with some kind of movement, he entered into it whole-heartedly. Hence the many choral works, ranging from the simple part song to *The Vanity of Vanities* (1913), an alla capella work of large proportions. His experience with choirs at competitive festivals showed him such organisations at both their best and their worst and he knew exactly how to provide music of the right standards for all occasions.

At the level of the large-scale choral and orchestral work, he requires no out-of-the-way instruments as does his friend Holbrooke; but he often made difficulties by duplication. In *Sea Wanderers* (1906), for example, a work of considerable beauty and power, he makes the situation economically and practically difficult by using a solo string quartet which plays an independent rôle throughout the work. Unfortunately, it does not confine itself to essentials and the work is placed out of the reach of the ordinary provincial and country resources, for let it be remembered that the composer relies more on these for performances than he does upon the town and city municipal choir.

Nothing small appealed to Bantock when thinking orchestrally—his first student work was called *Satan in Hell*—and he laid on his colours with a thick brush. English music might have become significant on the Continent had he not been wrongly considered as being derived from Strauss. His only connection with that composer lay in the virtuosic nature of his writing and his passion for broad subjects. By the 1920's his style and idiom had become standardised and he ceased to deliver any message of note to a brave new world that hardly knew what it wanted. Fortunately, Bantock was an opportunist. He saw just how the wind was blowing and he was able to adapt himself to the small-size part-song and—the brass band, for which he saw a future, and for which he adapted several of his orchestral works.

Sir Edward Elgar (1857-1934)   Sir Granville Bantock (1868–1946)

(*Above*) Sir Hubert Parry
(1848–1918)

(*Right*) Sir Charles Villiers
Stanford (1852–1924)

Josef Holbrooke (1878)

Richard Strauss (1864–1949)

Dame Ethel Smyth (1858–1944)

Florent Schmitt (1870)

Bantock wrote three music dramas—his *Seal Woman* (1924) was on a small scale—no concertos and no chamber music except two *Sonatas*. Holbrooke has written for almost every instrument in existence and has touched every genre. His is a more eclectic style than Bantock's and, like Bantock, he has been drawn mainly to the largest forms. His association with T. E. Ellis (otherwise Lord Howard de Walden) enabled him to compose a dramatic triology of enormous proportions. *The Cauldron of Anwyn* if written by a foreigner would command more than respect. As it is, it remains a curiosity and in its original state completely unproducible with any possibility of economic security. Being given a free hand, Holbroke included saxophones and sarrusophones together with a multiplicity of brass and wood-wind that makes fascinating reading and hearing but precludes performance save on special occasions when a wealthy guarantor may be handy. The difficulties of his string writing exceed those of Strauss, but with all the wealth of material placed in the scores, it is impossible to reduce them or simplify them in any way.

On the other hand, works like *Queen Mab* (1904) and *The Bells* (1903), which do not require ultra-ordinary forces although calling for a few "extras", are magnificent and do not deserve the comparative oblivion into which they have been allowed to drift. His so-called "Illuminated Symphony", *Apollo and the Seaman,* made a sensation at the time of production (1908) and would do so now; but it needs an outsize orchestra. This work anticipated television and the radio incidental music score. The text was shown on the screen by means of a magic lantern and the orchestra, concealed behind the large sheet, played music delineating the poem. The lantern operator had to be a musician capable of following the score and arranging the synchronisation. Film musical directors of to-day who think they are on new ground deceive themselves. This score also appears to be unreducible to reasonable requirements and therefore it looks as if it, too, will pass into limbo or remain a work for scholars, for Holbrooke can teach orchestration through his own works.

His symphonies and chamber music have all come in for their share of abuse. Holbrooke is belligerent and his music tells us so; but it is often magnificent. Few composers have written such vital sea music as appears in *Dylan* (1910), the second of the Trilogy. Incidentally, Holbrooke was responsible for yet another innovation; in this work, in order to get convincing flights of wild fowl, films were made in the

Outer Hebrides and projected on to the stage. This, of course, was in the days of the silent film, when there was no means of deadening the whirr or hum of the projector and the films themselves resolved into a series of flicks. The scoring, however, was vivid enough to cover the sounds, and this incipient film music was infinitely more successful than some of the over-vaunted high-level scores heard to-day. The theatre, however, was not ready for such an innovation, and the extra-musical effects were not taken seriously.

The position held by Holbrooke in his heyday was exceedingly high and he certainly had every claim to be regarded as the English Strauss or Berlioz. His idiom, like that of Bantock, did not advance up to the 1920's and he, again, has no message for the younger generation. Yet his is more than a period genius, for genius Holbrooke undoubtedly is. After the Great War people looked for terseness of expression and directness of speech. Holbrooke remains an honoured name in the twentieth century. Before 1914 he was undoubtedly of the century. It is still possible that the pendulum may swing in his direction again.

Such a possibility may well happen in the case of Dame Ethel Smyth (1858-1944), a composer as tempestuous in her music as in herself. She, like Holbrooke, was a fighter. Obsessed by the fact that as a woman the usual channels of performance would be closed to her, she determined to storm those channels and swim across them. She succeeded. She insisted on her opera *Der Wald* (1901) being performed in Germany, at the Kaiser's own Imperial Opera House, during the South African War, when it was dangerous for an English person to stop at a shop-window, such was the hatred for this country. She brushed aside all opposition and succeeded in everything she attempted to do. Her *Mass in D* was performed by the Royal Choral Society under Sir Joseph Barnby in 1893. From that time it remained dormant until 1924, when Sir Adrian Boult revived it. Opposition only made her the more determined. A chance remark by the publisher to the effect that he feared the *Mass* was dead served to give her the courage to prove how wrong he was; and she proved it. Her superhuman energies and sincerity placed her in the fore-front of the Suffragette Movement. She fearlessly demonstrated in the usual places and was proud of her sojourn in prison as a result. This energy is well shown in her greatest work, *The Wreckers* (1904),[1] an opera of which any country and any

[1] Mahler intended to produce it in Vienna (1907), but resigned before he could arrange it. The same thing happened in 1905 with Nikisch in Leipzig, and in 1914 with Bruno Walter in Munich.

period can be proud. It was once said that she proved her femininity by writing louder music than would ever occur to any mere male to do. This is true only in the fact that she scored generously and boldly. *The Wreckers* never flags. It has all the stagecraft of the experienced hand. The music swirls and surges and the singers find that strain is unnecessary because their voices are allowed to top the orchestra even in its wildest moments. The style is often accused of being Wagnerian. Actually Dame Ethel denied this and said that she was not particularly attracted to that composer. The accusation came about simply because she had Wagner's sense of the drama, and this has never been a strong point in the hundreds of failed British operas. Of the period, and its music pre-dates the twentieth century, this is the only British opera which could stand the test of time and be acceptable to-day.

Her lighter operas, *The Boatswain's Mate* (1915), *Entente Cordiale* (1925), and *Fête galante* (1922) are not so successful. The first-named is first-rate music—too first-rate for the subject. The tunes are perfectly delightful—one thinks of "When rocked on the billows" and "Perhaps at times you want to meet a friend"—but the humour is a trifle obvious, the cats on the tiles, Fate knocking on the door, as in Beethoven's *Fifth Symphony*, when the village policeman appears, for example; but, all the same, it makes splendid entertainment even though the lessons of Women's Suffrage and feminine superiority are allowed to influence the whole thing. The two other operas are lighter in texture, but still not light enough to escape charges of commonplace.

Dame Ethel was a wide reader and an earnest philosopher. The latter can be seen in her beautiful choral and orchestral "symphony", *The Prison* (1930), one of her last works and one of her best, written just before deafness closed her in. By dint of her own endeavours, therefore, Dame Ethel Smyth forced her music into the repertoire. She may be regarded as the last of the fighters, the last of those who refused to acknowledge the possibility of defeat.

Sir Edward Elgar may justly be said to have represented everything which the spacious Edwardian Era stood for. He became in course of time a kind of unofficial Music Laureate and he found it as easy to hymn the glories of pomp and circumstance as to utter deep philosophies. Of all British composers since Purcell, Elgar was probably the name most familiar to the man in the street. This figurative person, of course, was not aware of the large-scale works which were outside his orbit. He knew Elgar for *Salut d'amour* (1889), for *Pomp and Circumstance,* for *The Crown of India* (1912) and particularly for "Land of Hope and Glory" (1902), which itself comes in *Pomp and Circumstance*. Elgar did more than is generally recognised to bring the uninterested outsider into the concert hall. It is an affectation to decry these *œuvres de circonstance*. They were very real to him at the time and also to the man in the street.

The Edwardian Era was one of growing social consciousness. Reforms were in hand, but progress was slow. It took some while for the Brotherhood of Man to become a reality, although there were plenty willing to acknowledge it—on paper and in theory. The word "democracy" was admitted, but feared. The leading artists held themselves aloof from public gaze. The native conductors, Henry Wood, Landon Ronald, Thomas Beecham, Julian Clifford and Dan Godfrey, were, in the first three cases, legendary figures who appeared on the concert platform and vanished into thin air between times. They were not to be found in fashionable grill-rooms or in other places where they make life gay. In the last two instances the inhabitants of Hastings and Bournemouth realised their approximation to eminence and in these smaller milieux the two conductors were familiar figures—but even then they kept a certain amount of distance between themselves and their public. The fact was that they all had to work. The London men were virtuosi, the country ones propagandists. Clifford and Godfrey had the menace of the balance-sheet hanging over their tenure of office; but the remarkable achievements of Godfrey in Bournemouth far outvied London. Unfortunately, London was the Capital and the centre of the life of the whole country. This insularity, which even now has not been lived down, produced a snobbishness which rated a perfect performance at Bournemouth or Hastings of lower value than an indifferent one in London. Such cities as Birmingham, Manchester and Liverpool might as well have been in the African desert for all the weight they carried in London.

This snobbery had its unintentioned counterpart among composers. Parry and Elgar may have lived in the country, but they knew nothing about it apart from its amenities. Their knowledge of and interest in folk songs were practically nil, and it would never have occurred to either of them to take down a tune from the lips of an old man at death's door rather than that tune should be lost for ever. Such greetings as were passed to them by the locals were acknowledged in a patronising manner, which both would have deplored had they realised it. A casual word of appreciation in the street from a complete stranger would have seriously embarrassed Elgar. He would not have known what to do and would in all likelihood have given offence. Parry would have dealt with the situation a little better, but would not have felt absolutely comfortable. Elgar was completely unapproachable by strangers, Parry less so; but in both cases it was a matter of unintentional snobbery. Whether this aloofness of the artist was good or bad,[1] it had a tendency to place the musician on a pedestal and to turn him into a member of a race apart. Like all other such things, it went a trifle too far and in their anxiety to democratise themselves, musicians have now over-reached themselves. The theory that the composer is a superior person, however, is a recent discovery by certain cliques who seem to desire some social grievance at any cost. In actual fact, no composer of any note ever has so regarded himself.

A realisation of the situation in the Edwardian Era (which filled the first decade of the twentieth century) is of vital importance if the art of that era is to be understood. Art in terms of political and social realisation is no recent discovery. In the case of Elgar, it made for a dual personality. There was the Elgar prepared to hymn the glories of the British Empire who could appear as the perfect courtier. There was the Elgar who ruminated in the countryside, pondering over the spiritual influences on life and philosophising upon the mysteries of the Hereafter. Elgar looked the retired colonel no matter what he wore. His looseness of dress was rather stiff and formal, for "country clothes" at that time amounted to a Norfolk jacket and "'bockers", with a stiff collar and tie. It can be remarked from contemporary photographs that the most sensitive of French composers during this period invariably wore bowler hats. Placing them alongside Elgar, the country man, it would appear that clothes make no difference to the artistic sensitivity of the wearer. Whence, therefore, came the idea that the artist must necessarily be dirty, unkempt and loose-living? From a few isolated instances in Paris and from a number of nonentities who, noting a certain carelessness in some of the Great, exaggerated it in themselves, thus drawing attention to a kind of spurious Bohemianism which flourished like a bay tree. Elgar in his conventional clothes, Parry in his dark suit and white carnation maintained a constant bulwark against artistic sartorial formalism. The hand that wrote *Pomp and Circumstance*, the *Imperial March* (1897), and *The Crown of India* was the

[1] Personally, I think it was good in many ways, as it made for respect.

same that wrote the *Introduction and Allegro* (1905), *The Dream of Gerontius* (1900), and the second movement of the *E flat Symphony*—and who will say that the last three works lack sensitiveness?

Elgar's musical proximity to the man in the street was phenomenal. He gave that man something he could sing, something he could take home with him, something he could grasp at a single hearing. He was a composer of the greatest social significance in this direction and the technique he used was exactly the same as that of his more serious works. This explains why Elgar in his *Symphonies*, in the *Cockaigne Overture* (1901), *In the South* (1904), the *Serenade for Strings* (1893) and the *Introduction and Allegro for Strings*[1] has always found a more widely spread response from the public at large than any other composer.

Elgar demonstrated his musical individuality at a very early stage. His training was haphazard, to say the least, and his was an innate musical instinct. His style hardly altered from start to finish. The various little clichés by which he is recognisable appear in every single work. These are clichés simply because he made them himself and used them unsparingly. Various influences can be traced, but these do not detract from the essential Englishness of the idiom or make it any the less individual and distinguishable from all others. So strong is the personality that it is quite untranslatable in other hands. It is perfectly easy to copy—and this partly explains why Elgar made hardly any direct impact on his younger contemporaries. This, of course, applies to many other composers. The ingredients which make up the style and idiom originate mainly in César Franck; many see traces of Brahms, but of this I am not so sure. I do not know to what extent Elgar was familiar with Franck's works. Both were ardent Roman Catholics, but this by itself is not sufficient to have caused the adoption of certain harmonic processes and melodic twists by the younger composer (otherwise all music by Roman Catholics would sound the same, *quid est absurdum*). However, the chromaticism of Franck, his use of sequence and ornamented repetition, his square-cut melodic rhythmic patterns and the shape of his themes, to say nothing of the cyclical approach to symphony (which by 1900 had become in general use in France, at least) all find their opposite places in Elgar; yet in no case can Elgar ever be mistaken for Franck. In one respect only does Elgar outbid Franck, and that is in his use of suspensions.

[1] But not in *Falstaff* (1913) or the *'Cello Concerto* (1919).

Those who are out of sympathy with Elgar's style are repelled first and foremost by his excessive use of sequence. He had the uncanny knack of devising development sections which actually develop nothing at all and convince simply through the masterly and unashamed use of plain and sequential repetition. The first movement of the *Violin Concerto* (1910) is an extraordinary example of this. However, the development section does not necessarily imply what the text-books maintain, namely, "presentation of themes in different ways". This middle section is much more accurately defined as a "Free Fantasia". The processes of development or differing presentation come in the category of variation, and it may be remarked that only once did Elgar write in this manner. It is, of course, a commonplace to say that the *Enigma Variations* (1899) remains one of the most outstanding works of its kind; nevertheless, it must be remarked that each variation is a short piece in itself and as such requires no spacious length or continuity. When it came to the middle section of the symphonies and concertos, Elgar showed a certain short-windedness, but if one regards this section as a "Free Fantasia", no fault can be found constructionally, but only regrets expressed at the sometimes irritating repetition of phrase.

The *Symphony in A flat* (1908) was the first such work by a British composer capable of taking its place beside the other massively representative works of Brahms, Bruckner, Franck and d'Indy. Its enormous length, the power of the material, the extreme beauty of the slow movement make it notable. One may point to certain traits such as I have mentioned, but the quintessence of Elgar can be found on every page. This is what cannot be said of the symphonies by other British composers of the period. The quality of the long tune with which the work opens and closes is one of the earliest indications that such long-drawn-out melody was reaching its end and that future twentieth-century composers would think differently. The quality of a theme may not matter in the long run; it is what the composer does with it which is important and, truth to tell, Elgar does hardly anything with this one save repeat it; and the same applies to the material of the *Violin Concerto*. The student of form will find some interesting derivation of material in the *Symphony in A flat*. In the *Symphony in E flat* (1911) the work is held together more by quotation than derivation. It, therefore, is cyclical while the one in A flat is germinal.

The *Symphony in E flat* sang the Edwardian Era to an end. Intended as an act of homage to King Edward VII, it represents the act of fealty of subject to sovereign. It closed the earlier manner of dedicating works to royalty, an act hitherto carried out in terms of abject humility which both present-day sovereign and subject would find almost nauseating. This, of course, was no Victorian or Edwardian innovation. One has but to read the dedications of the Tudor and Stuart playwrights to realise the apparent urgency to flatter a patron. The Victorian and Edwardian royalty were patrons to nobody in a material sense, while the aristocracy played with music as cultured amateurs of any social stratum play with it. At the time this meant a great deal to the composer. It signified a kind of official approval, the common ground of the concert hall being one of the few upon which sovereign and subject could meet on terms of common interest and equality. To-day the whole outlook has become humanised, and present-day democracy, so natural and so spontaneous, makes the earlier attempts at it seem deliberate and self-conscious.

To the end of his life Elgar remained uninterested and uninfluenced by any prevailing fashion. The egocentric acrobatics of Strauss left him unmoved and untouched. It is reported[1] that the only work which really interested him was Berlioz' *Symphonie fantastique*. He never talked about music and when his own was mentioned, he adopted an off-hand manner which may have been the result of shyness, but bore unmistakable signs of affectation and often offended those who would have done him honour.[2]

He was the only prominent composer in this country at the beginning of the century with any real breadth of vision, the only one capable of writing "big" or "great" music.

With Elgar, tonality and key relationships were carried to a degree which Parry and Stanford would have thought almost iconoclastic. Symphonic music ceased to be an interplay of opposing related keys. Elgar's tonalities depended entirely upon where his thought led him, and this was propelled by modulating sequences, giving a spurious impression of forward movement. Nevertheless, the "home key" is always paramount, and it has a binding effect upon the whole. Elgar may be said to have been the last of the unapproachable and the last of the tonal composers, in the same way that Mahler (1880-1911) has been described as the last of the diatonic composers. He belongs to

[1] The late Filson Young in a radio talk.

[2] *Farewell, My Youth*, Sir Arnold Bax (Longmans, Green).

the twentieth century because he represented all that the first decade and a half stood for; his technique goes no further than 1914-1920. This in no way detracts one iota from the value of the music and in no way lessens its importance. He left no disciples, for the younger generation faced a world differently orientated and alien to the ideals he so strongly upheld. Until the advent of Vaughan Williams' *A London Symphony* Elgar was the only twentieth-century British composer in the repertoire with any distinctive style of his own, a style which, although mannered, was consistent. The words "in the repertoire" should be noted carefully, for there were some others equally distinctive who did not become an essential part of the repertoire until much later.

Of these, the most interesting is Cyril Scott (1879), over whose treatment artistic Britain should hang her head in shame. Scott received his training in Leipzig and remained independent of the native schools. He has always been quite aloof from musical centres of activity, but his works are for the main part published and available for those who run, to read. A prophet is often unhonoured in his own country, but the complete neglect of Scott is something inexplicable.

His output is large. He has written few large-scale works, but has enriched the literature of the piano. For some while he suffered under the misapplied description of "the English Debussy". Such a soubriquet invariably leads to misunderstanding and in any case is a back-handed compliment since it hints that the victim is entirely lacking in individuality and even originality. Cyril Scott's music was completely different from the standard native article at the time which was concerned with classical and traditional harmony. He was attracted to romanticism of an objective nature at a time when native composers hesitated at giving vent to such feelings. Further, a curious legend grew up round him which suggested that he was over-concerned with mysticism and occultism, two pursuits foreign to the average Britisher of the period. However, it so happened that he was drawn to these after he had established himself as a composer. Scott was one of the most sensitive composers of his period and had nothing in common with the then ordinary trend of things.

I have used the word "prophet". Further study of twentieth-century music will show that nearly everything which became the standard language of the 1920's had actually been postulated by Cyril Scott. It would be invidious to make comparisons or to single out individuals, but had Scott become established in the repertoire, certain later composers would have cut very different figures. However, Scott has never publicised himself or figured as one with a grievance. His advocates have not been vocal or vociferous and any apostleship has been passive rather than active.

Scott, therefore, forms a parallel with Satie in that both composers were far in advance of their contemporaries and were talking in tongues later to be adopted as ordinary twentieth-century technique. Scott showed an early disinterest in classical harmony, and although by no means an Impressionist, he formulated a certain chromaticism as sensitive as anything emanating from Paris, and as foreign to the English or British *goût* as can be imagined. He bears not the slightest resemblance to Debussy, for he is neither "atmospheric" nor pictoral. The early charge of being the "English Debussy" was due to an incomplete realisation of that composer. Such pieces as *Lotus Land* (1905), *Asphodel* (1906), *Sphinx* (1908), trifles in themselves, say more in their few pages than is said by others in their many, and contain all the elements of clarity and imagination. At the other end of the scale, there are the stirring *Handelian Rhapsody* (1909) and the massive *Prélude solennelle* (1913). The former originated as part of a discarded *Piano Sonata*—incidentally, there is a fine example of such a work, written in 1935. His *Piano Concerto* (1913-1914) and opera *The Alchemist* (1918) achieved some reputation abroad. The former is a brittle and scintillating work of no great pretension and is acceptable in a genre too notable for empty display and rhetoric.

Scott has been an opponent of the exigencies of form for many years. In his book, *The Philosophy of Modernism* (1917), he came into the open in the broadest possible manner, and shocked a good many susceptibilities by his outspoken denunciation of ideas hitherto taken for granted. Scott's deliberate avoidance of formalism has not resulted in any convincing substitute, and many of his pages are marred by strings of sequential repetitions which hold up the progress of the music and would suggest to the unknown a lack of invention. The well-known *Danse Négre* (1908) is an example of this. The texture, however, is extremely delicate, for Scott wrote in neither a British nor an English way; yet the style is certainly not Gallic. Even his most youthful works have no connection with the nineteenth century and there are no "early works" to avoid. There are certain divisions—he was under the Pre-Raphaelite influence for some time—but Scott's output as a whole is surprisingly equal and consistent, and it is usually impossible to date any particular work in relation to the others. He is one of the few composers to bridge the 1920's successfully and smoothly, and to leave nothing meriting concealment as being "unworthy". In spite of his neglect, Scott has never ceased to compose, and at the time of writing he appears concerned with large-scale works. His early Continental reputation does not seem to stand him in any stead to-day. Memories are short. In another direction he led composition in this country because at a time when the generality of composers either avoided the piano or were incapable of writing for it, Scott devised his own pianism, and his contribution to the literature of the instrument is even more significant than that of Scriabin (1872-1915), to whom pianists owe a lasting debt but, be it noted, no larger and no longer-lasting than that owed to Cyril Scott.

It was a remarkable act of faith that induced Benjamin J. Dale (1885-1945) to compose, at the age of seventeen, a *Piano Sonata* of monumental proportions. This work, lasting close on an hour, is full of masterly construction and requires a virtuoso to do it justice. If one can take it at its face-value without considering that its style became outmoded after a fourteen-year life, this work may truly be said to rank with that of the Liszt *Piano Sonata* for resource and design. Unfortunately, its difficulties are supreme and pianists have little opportunities in these days of rush to make study of it worth the enormous trouble. The style is impassioned, to say the least, and hints at the Grand Manner—and piano works in this manner are not found in profusion. The music has character; it also has stamina, but it is overwhelming. Dale did not rise to these heights a second time. Apart from the exquisite little choral work *Before the Paling of the Stars* (1912) and the vigorous *Suite for Viola* (1913) his output was not remarkable, and, more disarming than anything else, his style did not advance as he grew older. His last work, *The Flowing Tide* (1945),[1] however, showed that the invention was still there and it was written with all the old youthful enthusiasm.

Dale holds a curious position in twentieth-century music for there appears to be no earthly reason for the impasse in which he found himself. He was surrounded by young people and he read voraciously and objectively many works with which he could not see eye to eye. Many

[1] This work had a tragic history, as Dale died within a few moments of finishing the last rehearsal.

young composers who came under his care at the Royal Academy of Music have reason to bless him.

Somewhat older than Dale, Frank Bridge (1879-1941) suffered much the same neglect as Cyril Scott, and since his death his music has passed almost into oblivion. Being a conductor as well as a composer, Bridge was able to keep his name in the public eye and as an experienced string-player brought to his chamber music a rare practical knowledge. His output was not large, but shows consistent progress, the most modern height being that reached in the *Sonata* for 'cello and piano (1918) and the last *String Quartet* (1939). Romantic to the end, he only fringed the twentieth-century ideals, but the two works mentioned suggest some leaning for the misnamed atonality. His orchestral works, particularly *Summer* (1914) and *Enter Spring* (1927), show a picturesqueness which placed him apart from his fellows. His best-known work, *The Sea* (1920), bridges the gap between nineteenth- and twentieth-century points of view. Bridge himself regarded it as old-fashioned. His picturesqueness is not in any way Impressionistic and is admirably conveyed in the titles, which fall into line with the music, a combination not always convincing in such music. His neglect is undeserved, for although never quite achieving completely up-to-date technique he approached it more nearly than many who are still played. His later works are among the most cosmopolitan in the English repertoire of the period and should be acceptable abroad.

If Dale and Bridge never advanced to full twentieth-century significance, the same cannot be said of Sir Arthur Bliss (1891), whose output shows a remarkable *volte-face*. A pupil of Stanford at the Royal College of Music, he quickly discarded the style absorbed there. The Great War came at the right moment, since it drew him away from the then current trend of musical affairs and on his return to civil life, he found music in the hands of Stravinsky and Les Six. This was a revelation to him and he quickly fell into line with *le dernier cri,* producing works whose value surpassed those of many of the *avant-garde* because of his intrinsic basic training. Such cheerful things as *Rout* (1920), *Madame Noy* (1920), *Conversations* (1919) and the brilliant *Mêlée Fantasque* (1921) suggested that in this country there was a composer fully capable of equalising the ideals of Les Six; but the *Rhapsody* (1923) for flute, cor anglais, string quartet, bass, soprano and tenor showed that Bliss had a vein for lyrical beauty absent from the composers on the other side of the Channel. However, these works had their dangerous points for they were not entirely individual. In those days knowledge of Stravinsky was limited and anything which sounded at all *outré* was immediately stigmatised as being a reflection of this composer's latest thoughts. Consequently, a good deal of unenlightened and cynical criticism was levelled against Bliss on this charge. The *Colour Symphony* (1922), however, took attention away from these slender works and proved Bliss to have a symphonic instinct which denied the then convenient theory that such works were outmoded. Further compositions revealed quite an astonishing drift. The *Serenade* (1929) for voice and orchestra wavered between the two lines of thought, but the charming *Pastoral* (1929) for voices and strings and the colossal *Morning Heroes* (1930), a symphony for orator, chorus and orchestra, left no doubt that Bliss had turned away from the earlier style and was following a technique obviously more in line with his basic traditions as an Englishman. The *Piano Concerto* (1939), written for the Chicago World Fair, made a bid for virtuosic popularity and tried to combine the Grand Manner with mature twentieth-century thought. If such a thing be possible, then Bliss succeeded. His ballets *Checkmate* (1937) and *The Miracle of the Gorbals* (1946) confirmed that his rhythmic strength was admirable for this kind of work. The former was exceedingly impressive, while the latter proved that human feeling was not yet an abandoned musical cause. The opera *The Olympians* (1950) did not impress the experts, but pleased those who liked the humour and honesty of the work.

It is usual to regard early works as representative of an earlier period whose technique is less advanced than that of the present. Such works are not really acceptable because they are, to put it tersely, old-fashioned. Bliss' early works are old-fashioned, but not in the generally accepted sense of the term. They were slap up-to-date in an idiom which has not altogether vanished as yet. It is true to say that composers view things more seriously now, but, remembering that Bliss was born in 1891, it is interesting that this discarded music (for one rarely hears it now) should date from his early thirties and that there should be nothing earlier—in point of fact, there are a few chamber works, but these are in the possession of the composer's personal friends and are not, so to speak, for circulation. It takes a wise and a sane man with no little courage to turn his back so completely upon what he apparently believes in no longer, and to realise that it was driving towards an impasse. Of these works of the 1920's the aforementioned *Rhapsody* is truly the only one which does not date. The *Colour Symphony* contains all the ingredients of what could be achieved in the style—the description bears upon the composer's personal statement that when he composes he always has some colour in his mind's eye. It has certain traits which betray its Englishness, for English and British music are not one and the same things—this is what puzzles foreigners so much. The use of a lyrical theme over a succession of six-four chords, the whole resting upon a firm pedal point, is one of these indications.

At a time when music in this country lacked stamina, when in attempting to avoid sentimentality on the one hand and sheer cerebrality on the other it adopted a flaccid and uncertain technique, Bliss stood out by reason of his energy and vitality. It was once remarked of him that he could not write *pianissimo* if he wished to do so, and certainly most of his music bears this out; in those places where the dynamic is necessarily low, the thickness of the texture precludes any gentleness or tranquillity. Although it would not be true to say that he now writes in a *démodé* fashion, his style has ceased to be applicable to the present time. Bliss is one of the sanest of living English composers; this may account for his situation, as a little madness goes a very long way. The solidity of his thought, his essentially English choral technique—the unaccompanied writing in *Morning Heroes* and the *Pastoral* is a natural advance from Parry—and the directness of his orchestral scoring which seems to carry itself along by the sheer force of dynamics make one a little fearful for the future. He has long since ceased to influence the young idea, and older people not sympathetic to *le dernier cri* can listen to him with full understanding. He is one of the few composers of whom it can be said that he has progressed backwards because the quality of his present style *in* the century is superior to that of the earlier one, *of* the century.

A composer who has earned the respect and admiration if not the affection of everyone is John Ireland (1879), who also rose to fame upon the crest of the 1920's. Ireland's output is not very large, but it is of a uniform quality and substance. His *Second Sonata* (1917) for violin and piano had a phenomenal success on publication, for the second edition was sold out before the actual appearance of the first. Few other works have aroused more enthusiasm or interest. Ireland is not a composer spectacular in nature. His moods are quiet and restrained. He is not sensational and his place in the history of music is assured by the influence he has exercised over certain names whose music bears some distinct relationship to Ireland's own, yet does not in the main remind one of it.

Ireland's greatest chamber work is the *Sonata* for piano (1920), a work of profound thought and of original pianism. In it he showed that excessive decoration and ornamentation need not obscure lines. The pianism is crowded and he seems averse from letting a single finger be unoccupied. Consequently, the harmonies are full of added sixth effects which in many composers would seem an artificial affectation and a means of "going modern". This *Sonata* is approachable and accessible. It draws attention to the piano as an instrument of chordal percussiveness. Few composers have used the inner thumb melody as successfully as Ireland. The technique is consistent. It appears not only in the *Sonata*, particularly in the second movement which betrays his fondness for the punctuation of the inner theme, but in such delightful pieces as *Ragamuffin* (1917) and *Chelsea Reach* (1917). He is full of poetry—play *Amberley Wild Brooks* (1921), but do not imagine that there are any cascades or waterfalls there. The arpeggio cadenza in the middle is actually suggestive of the peculiar type of breeze which those familiar with the locality know to spring up suddenly, sweep across the fields, and die away immediately. *Merry Andrew* (1919) is another cheerful piece which does not fear a possible vulgarity in keeping with its subject. Ireland's titles are convincing. He is a twentieth-century composer who has never been afraid of using his imagination.

Nevertheless, in spite of the poetry contained in these exquisite piano pieces, he has energy and strength. His music is not all climax, although it does not eschew such achievement. It is well balanced. Ireland is also one of the few who can write in a light vein. He has contributed one of the most cheerful and happy piano *Concertos* (1930) to the repertoire, a work which requires no concentrated listening and yet completely fulfils the concerto essentials. When serious he is inclined to be gloomy, as in the *'Cello Sonata* (1923); but this gloom is philosophical, not morbid or pessimistic. He can rise to great heights. *These Things shall be* (1937) for chorus and orchestra could only have emanated from someone trained at the Royal College of Music and experienced in choral music. There are few works with such unselfconscious uplift as this. Certain moments suggest Elgar, but it does not rant nor rave, neither does it achieve itself in any chromatic manner.

Ireland's songs are all excellent. *I have Twelve Oxen* (1919), *Sea Fever* (1915) and *Blow out, You Bugles* (1918)—this last a much-neglected song—reveal a sensitiveness to poetry which forms a striking parallel with that of the piano pieces, and these include the later *Sarnia* (1941) which is full of delicate French harmony. Yet Ireland is essentially English; his *London Overture* (1936) is a cheerful Cockney work, far removed from the West End pageantry of Elgar's *Cockaigne* and from the human picturesqueness of Vaughan Williams' *A London Symphony*.

There are signs in the *Trio in E* (1938) that Ireland may be flirting with ghosts of the past, but he stands further from the Stanford tradition than does Bliss at the present moment. Ireland's influence can be seen in certain harmonic twists in the music of E. J. Moeran (1894-1950), whose own particular Englishness extends the range of Ireland. The Englishness of Herbert Howells (1892) and Gordon Jacob (1895) traces its way from Stanford and Vaughan Williams. The former made a brilliant start with a *Piano Quartet* (1916) and a *Rhapsodic Quintet* for clarinet and strings (1919), together with orchestral works, and then faded out from the panorama of English music. This was a pity, for Howells is a genuine creative artist. His organ music is magnificent and shows a deeply-stirred imagination, while his *Concerto for Strings* (1939) is a model of twentieth-century polyphonic texture. His *Hymnus Paradisi* (1950) is one of the loveliest works of the century. It is time that some of the facilities which seem to cluster round other composers were directed to Howells. Jacob, although more prolific and more advisedly scholarly, has less significance and individuality. His Englishness does not go further than the bounds of a healthy out-of-doors atmosphere.

Not all this music is for export. It is too modest and self-effacing. This does not matter, since English music is for the English.

An exception to this can be found in Peter Warlock (1894-1930), whose real name was Philip Heseltine. In the person of Peter Warlock he had a peculiar and natural insight into an Englishry which, by its free rhythms, was directly connected with the early type of English melody while the sensitive harmonies, in keeping with the twentieth century, were sufficiently delicate to balance the melodies with no sense of incongruity. His love of English poesy was unrivalled, and he had a happy knack of spontaneous association between metre and melody. Such exquisite things as *Bulalalow* (1922)—one of *Three Carols*—and

GUSTAV HOLST (1874–1934)    FREDERICK DELIUS (1862–1934)

Sir Arnold Bax (1883).

Ralph Vaughan Williams (1872)

Sleep (1924) will not be equalled. As a song-composer posterity may well regard him as the twentieth-century Schubert. In this way, his Englishry is universally acceptable. Music lost a notable figure when he died. *British* music is exportable—the names which made it noticeable on the Continent were Bantock and Holbrooke; it is doubtful if Strauss' efforts on behalf of Elgar had many repercussions in Germany once the initial surprise had worn off.

The classical ideal in this country is Bach. This leaves Couperin and Rameau out of account. Even to-day England is a stronghold of German music, although there are signs that the Gallic tendency is becoming increasingly recognisable; but it is not always the right tendency which is propagated. The House of Hanover established the wave of Germanophilism, which had become deeply-rooted and taken for granted by the beginning of the century. It gave us Handel, but it also gave us Mendelssohn, directly, and Brahms, indirectly. A quotation from a letter received from a German friend by the writer in 1934 may not be without significance: "When we want to hear good German music, we listen to the B.B.C." Complaints are heard nowadays which change the word "German" to "French". If this be true, it is a refreshing sign, although not one bringing very much comfort to the native composer, be he British or English. However, he should be used to it by now.

CHAPTER TEN

FREDERICK DELIUS

(1862-1934)

THERE have been some composers considered in these pages whose early works have fitted into the general panorama of their output without very much incongruity. Others have shown too great a dividing line. Of these latter, Delius stands at the head. It is significant that with one exception all the works reasonably familiar to concert-goers by Delius date from the first year of the twentieth century. The exception is the *Piano Concerto*, composed in three-movement style in 1897, and revised in one movement in 1906—one would add the Nocturne *Paris* (1899) but this is not very familiar. The *Piano Concerto*, even in its revised form, is regrettable since it conforms to the Grand Manner of its original period and has no bearing whatsoever on Delius as he is known in his maturity. Pianists, however, like to play it because it is "big" music, shows off their virtuosity and gives them a reputation as players of "modern music". This is one of those early works over which it is best to draw a veil.

The whole situation of Delius' music in this country is as scandalous as that of Cyril Scott. Earlier, on the few occasions when a performance took place, the music was considered freakish and unmanageable. It was not until he was old, blind and paralysed that a complete week's Delius Festival took place, during which all the mature works were played. The occasion was one of high pitched emotion. The sight of the stricken composer, the homage paid him by Sir Thomas Beecham and the sentimental tinge of much of the music struck the consciences of everybody who might have done something while the composer was well enough to benefit from it. Delius died not long after the Festival, doubtless cyncial to the last, and his music returned to the shelves of the hiring libraries, making, it is true, less rare reappearances but not often enough to warrant the long-term policy of the Festival being regarded as successful. Contrary to expectations, Delius' music stood the test very well. A highly stylised composer does not usually come out of this ordeal as popular as when he started upon it, and to expect that Delius' particularly chromatic technique would not have been unendurably monotonous was quite reasonable.

This lack of variety is a charge which the unthinking appear unable to forget. In every work there appear the same little harmonic and melodic twists which go to make up the Delius individuality. The Festival having proved that these were not monotonous suggests that Delius is one of the most original and individual composers of the century. Certainly, few others have shown such an innate sense of beauty, for even in his violent moments Delius is always intrinsically beautiful. His music is sensuous, but never sensual. It is always serene and this comes strangely from one who hardly knew what it was to be tranquil in both body and mind. When Delius sings of the English countryside it is not in terms of English folk song (I exclude for the moment the variations on *Brigg Fair*). It is in terms of poised chromatic harmonies, infinitely gentle and redolent of sheer laziness. The music is indeed the countryside itself even if at times it appears rather well ordered, and this applies to *In a Summer Garden* (1908), which is full of neatly arranged clumps of flowers surrounded by well-trimmed hedges. This excessive tidiness is one of the chief characteristics of Delius' technique and is rivalled only by that of Ravel, with whom, of course, Delius has nothing otherwise in common. That he was so sympathetic to the English countryside is opposed to his early upbringing, which had had a commercial background in Bradford followed by a period of orange-growing in Florida (during which time he cultivated a love for Negro melody), a short stay at the Leipzig Conservatoire and ultimate residence outside Paris. His visits to this country were few and far between, the performances of his music even rarer. He became embittered, as one might expect, for no matter how well a composer is received abroad, neglect at home rankles. Perhaps at the back of his mind there was a nostalgia which bit into him. Certainly his pastoral music suggests this. *Brigg Fair* (1907), even if the initial impulse came from the tune itself and not from any local associations, is a clear indication. *On Hearing the First Cuckoo in Spring* (1912) might very well have been suggested by either a French or an English cuckoo, but it is possible to associate it with the English downs and hills, and

Summer Night on the River (1911) with the Cambridge Backs—it is well to remember in thinking about these things that Delius' garden at Grez-sur-Loing was fringed by a stream. *In a Summer Garden* is too efflorescent, too herbaceous, so to speak, to be anything but a richly coloured pleasaunce.

These pastoral works, therefore, are topographically indeterminate, unlike the similar works by Vaughan Williams and Milhaud, which are definitely English and Provençal.

In the early days of the century Delius was writing heavenly serenities while Strauss was exhausting his genius and his players in megalomaniacal monstrosities. Delius' technique appears to have changed suddenly and unaccountably. As proof of this, play the well-known "La Calinda" from the opera *Koanga* (1895-1897) and follow it by the equally popular "Walk to the Paradise Gardens" from *A Village Romeo and Juliet* (1900-1901). His mature style appears to have arrived at a definite moment. It was the antithesis of the outlook surrounding him everywhere but in France, and contact here lies only in the aesthetic qualities of the music which aimed at beauty of sound rather than at classical abstract processes. Delius went to live at Grez-sur-Loing in 1899. He experienced musical activities in Paris at one of their most exciting moments; but nowhere is there evidence that he mixed with the musicians or that he had any music of consequence played there. He appears to have lived quite aloof from his own kind and to have been more or less a recluse. Even the Nocturne *Paris; the Song of a Great City* was performed for the first time (in 1901) at Elberfeld. There are points of contact with Elgar, therefore, not only in their common segregariousness but in their rather haphazard training. Both were musicians by instinct.

The only common denominator between Delius and the French *goût* may be said to be the habit of dreaming in a manner that suggests formlessness, but yet proves on examination to be complete conciseness. Here there is a slight parallel with Debussy; but Delius was never a real Impressionist. It may be said that he used the same chords as Debussy, but in a completely different way. Delius' sensitiveness is often dispelled by his strident use of the brass, especially the trumpet; but this is actually a strong factor in the technique and prevents its sensuousness being overwhelming. The charge of formlessness which was a matter for disapproval among academic minds is quite unfounded. It is true there are no "symphonies" and that the early concerto-manner was but a single example of flirtation with the then contemporary ideal. It is also true that not one of Delius' works opens with a gigantic pre-oration (with the exception of the *Piano Concerto*); the opening theme of the extremely lyrical *Violin Concerto* (1916) is not an introductory flourish, short though it is. In no case is the listener's attention claimed by some statement in the Grand Manner. *A Mass of Life* (1904-1905) commences immediately with the full chorus, a departure from the custom in this country which demanded that such a work should open with an orchestral mood-picture of some kind. *Sea Drift* (1903) has an orchestral prelude, but this is not rhetorical, of course, and it is necessary for the setting of the musical mood of the poem.

There are, therefore, no "development sections", no processes of expansion of material betraying a scholastic mind. Delius was neither a doctor of music nor a professor of composition at any conservatoire. Such things as thematic working-out and processes of development did not concern him. Instead of the usual multi-movement design he used either the early English phantasy which combines the several movements in one whole, the middle section being either a slow movement or a scherzo according to the quality of the first and third, or that of variation. It is true that sometimes the shape becomes loose, but it is invariably tightened up by some linking figure like that of the opening of the *Violin Concerto*.

With variation Delius was quite at home; his usual style was decorative rather than ornamental, harmonic rather than melodic. In *Appalachia* for chorus and orchestra (1902—it had been originally written for orchestra alone in 1896), *Brigg Fair*, and *Dance Rhapsody No. 1* (1908) the actual theme is not cleverly disguised, if disguised at all. He prefers to decorate it with varying qualities of accompaniment, but he shows himself fully capable of fragmentary treatment and one thing leads to another in this way. When he does ornament the theme it is rare that he goes further than rhythmic altertion, as shown in Ex. 1 on the next page. This is not going very far, but it is all in keeping with his outlook, which withdrew from cleverness of classical device. The charge of formlessness, looseness if you will, is levelled at a work like *In a Summer Garden* which is described as a "fantasy" and consequently pursues its way as the composer's thoughts dictated. It is held together by the exactness of phrase lengths and this prevents it becoming a loose type of improvisation. If Delius improvised upon the orchestra, he did it wonderfully well, for the genius of improvisation

lies in the ability to make the music sound like a written-down work.

Delius had a wonderful sense of orchestral tone-colour and contrast. His use of the heckelphone called for stupid comment in the early days and the lusciousness of the scoring appeared thick to those ears accustomed to either the severely classical manner of Brahms or the virtuosic style of Strauss. This was mainly because the music had a very strong harmonic basis. Another reproach laid against him was that he was no contrapuntist. One has yet to learn that this is a fault. In the case of Delius, who wrote no fugues and canons, it is a complete misunderstanding, for although it often looks as if he wrote the harmony first and then "contrapuntalised" it, there is a strong polyphonic underlay in what the old writers on music used to call "the march of the parts". Where another composer would have written merely counterpoint, Delius backs it up with the implied harmonies, thus altering what otherwise would be an abstract idea into a romantic one. He may be said to overdo sequence sometimes and to make the music too semitonal. His use of parallel chords when he wishes to move from a high register to a low appears to be very easy, but Delius effects it in a perfectly convincing manner, even if he does it too consistently.

His harmony is curiously static at times, and certain little characteristics appear with unvarying frequency. He became obsessed with the rhythmic figure ♫ ♩ ♩ (it appeared as early as 1890-1892 in the opera *Irmelin*) and used it not only during the course of a movement, but at the final cadence which he delayed in a most ingratiating manner by turning the tonic chord into a dominant seventh and returning without resolution to the original state. This immobility of harmony is apparent in the progress from idea to idea in *In a Summer Garden*, where certain passages remind one of an organist moving from manual to manual—this, curiously enough, is a reproach which I have not seen him charged with, and it is one upon which the carping critic seizes in the case of other composers, notably César Franck (but, then, Delius was never an organist). He has a love of chordal wood-wind writing and a Delius score cannot be "edited" or "cued-in". It appears that once upon a time a University Doctor of Music expressed the opinion that the more notes removed from a Delius score, the better the music sounded, a fatuous remark suggesting that it would sound best of all if there were no notes left.[1] We have got past that kind of stupidity now—one hopes—but if we take any progression of Delius in its orchestral context, it becomes obvious that the removal of a note alters the particular chord at that moment; for Delius' habit of moving in parallel and complete chordal entities precludes all omission or transference.

The free use of discord, even when used in this parallel manner, gives the music an intensity of emotion which is overwhelming. When he uses diatonicism it is strong but not altogether convincing, and it appears to be an artificial strength. The opening chorus of *A Mass of Life* is an example of this. One has but to think of the poignancy of *Sea Drift* and the extreme emotion of the unaccompanied chorus part in *A Song of the High Hills* (1911-1912) to realise the masterly manner in which he could let his feelings move unrestrainedly. In a smaller way, the two unaccompanied choruses "to be sung of a summer night on the water" and the vocalised mixed chorus in the incidental music to Flecker's *Hassan* contain an equal amount of intensity—and here we are faced with an interesting point.

Delius' choral technique is sometimes "apt" for strings. The two unaccompanied choruses mentioned above sound equally beautiful and convincing on strings, while a glance at the *Hassan* extract on page 134 will show that the approach is as string-like as is it vocal. It is in the choral works, particularly the large ones, that Delius shows his contrapuntal mastery. He never regarded the orchestra as a poly-phonic medium. The choral works contain everything which should delight the heart of the musical scholar except, of course, formalised fugues and fugato. Sometimes the writing is awkward for intonation—it is recorded that at the first performance of *Sea Drift* in this country the soloist had to put a finger in each ear[2] to shut out the choral

[1] *Delius,* Philip Heseltine (The Bodley Head).

[2] *Delius, op. cit.*

Ex.2   Hassan

disturbance—but it is never impracticable, and although some leads suggest that he had little actual choral experience, the difficulties can always be overcome by listening to the instrumental cues. The unaccompanied part songs *On Craig Dhu* (1907) and *The Spendour Falls* (1924) offer some awkward moments where control of breath in the former and speed of musical thought in the latter are essential. Delius requires his singers to think quickly, sometimes quicker than is comfortable, and it is in this respect that he shows his practical inexperience.

It is also said that Delius is not a dramatic composer. *A Village Romeo and Juliet* has never had the success it deserves because it is altogether too remote from the usual run of operatic aesthetics. At its period, it stood up against Strauss' *Die Feursnot* (1900) and the later *Salome* (1906). If Delius' work is placed against these, and if the opera-goer requires bloody murder, rape, violence and colloratura singing, then *A Village Romeo and Juliet* is tame indeed; but these elements only constitute what appear by custom to be salient features of opera. The critic does not appreciate the poetry of the music and complains that the action flags, forgetting the liveliness of the Kermesse and the sardonicism of the Fiddler. The two leading characters are simple-minded and childlike, even neurotic and escapist (to use jargon popular to-day); but this does not detract from the beautiful music which, after all, is the main element in the genre named opera. Those who care to listen to this music are entranced by the way Delius' somewhat sophisticated technique aligns itself with the simplicity of the two central figures. In *Margot le Rouge* (1902) Delius wrote a blood and thunder work which amply fulfilled the requirements of the "corny" operatic stage, but his sensitive spirit recoiled from it once it had been worked out of his system. Of *Fennimore and Gerda*

(1908-1910) we know nothing, it having been produced at Frankfurt-am-Main in 1919 and never in this country.[1] *A Village Romeo and Juliet* stands isolated; it is a lovable work.

Delius could be dramatic when he wished—who can forget the tremendous shout of the chorus in *Eventyr* (1917) which, coming unexpectedly as it does, is almost staggering in its effect; and the Wagnerian drama of the fifth part—"Night reigneth"—and the opening of Part Two—"On the Mountain"—in *A Mass of Life,* the latter orchestral movement being interrupted by a tremendous double chorus, "Arise! Now, arise, thou glorious noontide".

His only failures are found in the chamber music, where the medium of the string quartet appears too cramping, and his sensuous beauty of tone requires a larger palette. His pianism, as disclosed in three short *Preludes* (1924) and the *Dance for Harpsichord* (1919), is deplorable, although the *Dance* is more satisfactory by reason of the instrument's crispness. The accompaniments to his songs, and *Violin Sonatas* (two), do not show this pianistic incompetence. The *'Cello Sonata* (1917), however, is one of the squarest works in the repertoire.

I have used the word "lovable". It can be applied to nearly everything Delius composed in his maturity. He was capable of great spiritual exaltation, as in the string variation in the first *Dance Rhapsody,* in portions of *Brigg Fair,* in the little *Song before Sunrise* (1918) and elsewhere. His music needs strict attention to pace. Few works sag so much when played too slowly; when taken too quickly they become a jumble of sound. He stands unique in his generation and so far music has not produced a counterpart. He may provide the justification for the isolation of the artist, for his music could have been written only in complete seclusion. Stylised it may be, and it is noteworthy that the generous Eric Fenby, who gave part of his life that Delius' later works should be written down for all time, was able to comprehend the trend of Delius thought because of this. Stylisation, however, is but a part of a composer's individuality and the test lies in whether the interest can be maintained along one particular style. He was the last composer to whom beauty of sound was the beginning and end of music. Others have been romantic, sometimes defiantly so, but few have reached the innermost soul of sensuous sound as did Delius.

[1] Delius left five operas.

CHAPTER ELEVEN

GUSTAV HOLST

(1874-1934)

THE rise and fall of Gustav Holst is something almost incredible. For the greater part of his earlier life he worked in obscurity as far as the general public was concerned and suddenly came into prominence in the middle of the 1914-1918 War. After a period when his name was absent from hardly a single concert, he relapsed into obscurity once more. Since his death he has passed well-nigh into complete oblivion, with the exception of *The Planets* (1915-1916) which still calls forth respectful admiration as a large-scale British orchestral work. It is quite usual for those in charge of musical youth to be asked if he wrote anything else. Such is the result of being once fashionable.

Whatever romanticism there may have been in other composers, there was none whatsoever in Holst; according to those who knew him well, any such suggestion made him shrink in horror. He was a fine example of the honest-to-God sincere musician who would cycle miles and miles to take a rehearsal of some country choir, for the sheer love of music, with small material reward. (What came to him did so through his trombone-playing in various professional orchestras.) The flesh-pots of life seemingly made no appeal to him, and it was not until Sir Hugh Allen (1869-1946) became Director of the Royal College of Music that an official position came his way. Gregarious among his fellows, but shy among others, he was at his best in those places where ancient customs were revived and although he enjoyed Queen's Hall triumphs, he was happiest in places like Thaxted, in Essex, where the old May Day revels were practised, and among his Whitsuntide Singers in their Downland rambles. The former impelled one of his best works, the choral ballet *The Morning of the Year* (1927), a work of the highest value and one which should not be allowed to fall into neglect. Although dealing with the spring festival, it is going a little far to describe it, as I once heard it described in all seriousness as "the English *Le Sacre*".

His was a simple character, but he had learning. This never obtruded itself in ordinary conversation, and one unknowing would have been hard put to find out exactly what his calling and hobbies might be. This excessive modesty placed him in a niche apart from the majority of composers, and he relied chiefly upon his friends to push him forward. He certainly had no enemies, and many young musicians at the Royal College of Music and elsewhere adored him.

His scholarship outside music lay in a knowledge of Sanskrit and English poesy. The former he studied in order to fit himself for the musical setting of various *Choral Hymns from the Rig-Veda,* the composition of which was spread over a fairly wide period. These were not great music and, indeed, in places touched the commonplace; but they were different from the usual settings of usual texts. Choral societies, however, were too bound up in the classics to venture with them very often. It was with some surprise that English concert-goers listened to the big suite *The Planets* by this unknown composer, who found outsize orchestral requirements no obstacle to performance, and they quickly took him to their hearts. Holst's *magnum opus* came just at the right moment, for it supplied a significant counterblast to the new ideas which were coming over from the Continent.

He was over forty years old before he made his impact on the world. Up till then his compositions were not particularly original or surprising, although one picks out from the list the chamber opera *Savitri* (1908—produced 1916), *Beni Mora* (1910), *St. Paul's Suite* (1913), together with such miscellaneous things as *The Cloud Messenger* (1910) and *The Hymn to Dionysius* (1913) as being works which are still heard. Earlier efforts like the choral ballad *King Estmere* (1903) and the two orchestral *Songs without Words* (1906) show no signs of any future development to anything original or striking. He owed his first performances to the enterprise of H. Balfour Gardiner (1877-1950), who, being blessed with means, was also blessed with generosity and love for music; his own works were few, but not negligible.

What has been the cause for this almost complete extinction from the repertoire? We have seen what caused the sudden rise and it was the very same qualities which caused the fall. Holst accomplished a very great deal in the freeing of rhythm and the liberation of harmony from early twentieth-century tradition. He may be looked upon as one of the most successful of the systematic composers. Although actually obeying no systematic technique which can be labelled with any definite description, it is always perfectly easy to see just how the music was made. This transparency is a good thing in many ways, but the musical joinery was too apparent and too consistent. The results he achieved were all successful, but they were so much pioneering and got no further. In due course his technique became mannered, and one could anticipate more or less accurately just what he was going to do the moment he started. His tunes were often manufactured upon a hardly concealed process. When he tried to write one in the older tradition, he became self-conscious, as in the big tune in "Jupiter, the Bringer of Jollity" in *The Planets* which seemingly has no immediate contact with what has gone before and may be described as avuncular and exceedingly "hearty". This tune alone made his name felt all over the commonwealth of nations. Not only was it adapted as a school song for St. Paul's, Hammersmith, but it was found to fit (more or less) the hymn "I vow to thee, my country", by Cecil Spring Rice, which aroused all the patriotic emotions when sung by large crowds. The incongruity of this extraction from an astrological context was apparent only to those who knew *The Planets*. Although this is the only actual tune in Holst's original output which offers these possibilities, much of his technique was adaptable to the exigencies of any moment.

The Planets has by now become almost past history; not so several other works of more level quality, and it is noticeable that these are not impelled entirely by music alone, but are dictated by poetry or prose. Such a wonderful and at first hearing breath-taking masterpiece as *The Hymn of Jesus* (1917), which opened the eyes of all to the possibilities of "effective" choralism, and the ineffably beautiful *Ode to Death* (1922) indicated that Holst was really in his element when dealing with the medium of voice and orchestra, more so than when treating the orchestra alone. Now and again there are lapses which appear incomprehensible in a man of his good sense. The *First Choral Symphony* (1926), to words by Keats, graphic though it is in its scintillating moments, is a striking example of manufactured music written entirely upon technique. The second movement, "Ode to a Grecian Urn", is beautiful, although the square harmony and commonplace tune at the words "Who are these, coming to the sacrifice?" detract from the lovely sounds evoked from a succession of superimposed perfect fifths in the orchestra, and an almost whispered choral part.

Holst knew the capacity of the human singing voice, but in the Scherzo of this work ("Ever let the fancy roam") he expected too much, and the movement is infinitely more successful as an orchestral work than in its original form—another instance of unbalanced adaptability. It may be argued that the words he chose for the last movement ("Spirit who reignest") are not suitable for music, but there was no reason why he should have chosen them other than that he thought he could clothe them successfully with his particular kind of quasi-recitative.

This mastery of choral technique, combined with his elasticity of rhythm, always bent to suit the text, placed him in the forefront of choral composers. A certain tendency can be found to sustain a pedal point over which a voice declaims in recitative fashion in free rhythm. He is one of the few composers who have been able to use quintuple and septuple rhythms without self-consciously subdividing them. That some are so subdivisible cannot be denied, but his natural elasticity and syllabic pliability made it all perfectly smooth.

Thoroughly imbued with the "English Choral Tradition," he did not fear to go outside that tradition in order to use the voices for the purpose of effect and background. This is seen in a marked manner in *Savitri*, an opera which is mainly declamatory so far as the solo singers are concerned, and, of course, at the end of "Neptune, the Mystic" in *The Planets*. Knowing exactly how far voices could go, he was able to write two of the most astonishing passages in the whole realm of English choral music. The wonderfully contrived music in the *Ode to Death*, at the words "The night in silence under many a star, the ocean shore", is frightening on paper but perfectly easy to sing, provided that each part minds its own business. It is worth quoting.

Ex. 1

This, of course, sounds hideous on the piano and represents one shaft proving the fallibility of Stanford's "black and white test". A well-trained choir finds no difficulty in this, and the pitch is not a hard factor to control.[1] The other is in *The Hymn of Jesus*, where the semitonal descent of one choir against the sustained harmonic pedal point in the other reveals a beauty of spiritual and musical sound unparalleled by any other composer. That few could write so well when truly inspired can be seen in his setting of *This have I done for My True Love* (1919), which sang his ashes to their grave in Chichester Cathedral in an unforgettable manner, and in one of which he himself would have thoroughly approved.

With Holst, earthly joy seemed something far away, but spiritual satisfaction was part of his character and impelled such music as this little alla capella setting. His simple, unaffected manner made his ending of a letter, "Looking forward to the joy of your fellowship", perfectly natural where, in another, it might have seemed artificial.

However, this joy could be eradicated objectively and this Holst did in *Egdon Heath* (1927), the last word in musical despair and despondency. According to Edwin Evans (1874-1945),[2] Holst was not altogether sure if it was music at all; but the work remains one of his strongest, a strength the greater for its intensity of gloom.

In this work there are few signs of the carpenter's bench; it abounds elsewhere. His constant use of 6/4 chords, his obsession with the harmonic and melodic potentialities of the fourth, an obsession seemingly strengthened by its starkness which at once appealed to his romantic-shy soul; his love of pedal points and ostinatos—this has been laid down to certain physical complaints which made the act of writing a painful process[3]—his passion for long stretches of quasi-recitative so amply illustrated in the opening of the *First Choral Symphony* where the voice fights a hard battle to maintain its note against fearfully contradicatory harmonic odds; these are among the features of his work which strike the ear and eye before the aesthetic message can be received.

His own mannerisms helped him in the concoction of the opera *The Perfect Fool* (1923), which parodies nearly every style of operatic

---

[1] I did it with an amateur choral society in West Sussex, and there was no difficulty whatsoever.

[2] Article in *The Dominant*, April, 1928.

[3] *Gustav Holst*, Imogen Holst.

writing and even Holst's own, although I am not sure that this was an intentional *parody*. Anyhow, the best thing in the whole work is the opening ballet movement, where he uses septuple rhythm to great effect. Generally speaking, one would regard this work as a waste of time in its composing and of money in its production. It was a good joke—once—but an expensive one.

Holst was most successful when at his simplest. *The Planets* holds its own partly for this reason. That one can see the elision of the woodwind chords in "Venus, the Bringer of Peace", the open-handedness of "Mars, the Bringer of War", the cross rhythms of "Mercury, the Winged Messenger", the construction of both harmonies and themes in "Jupiter, the Bringer of Jollity", the wonderful means whereby he portrays physical tiredness in "Saturn, the Bringer of Old Age", and the bi-tonality of "Neptune, the Mystic", does not detract from the work and, incidentally, this last movement together with certain pages of *The Morning of the Year* and other isolated works show Holst to have been one of the first of the modern bi-tonal composers.

Holst's importance outweighs his creative achievement. He counterbalanced the experimental stages of Les Six and the early neo-classicism of Stravinsky. He showed that this country was not behind others in these respects. Nevertheless, his music is not human, taken both wide and large. We are told[1] that it was not until the last period of his life that he heard Schubert's *Quintet in C*, and that this suddenly revealed to him what he had missed. He was more constructive than creative, but remains a notable figure in twentieth-century music.

[1] *Gustav Holst, op. cit.*

CHAPTER TWELVE

RALPH VAUGHAN WILLIAMS

(1872)

On page 425 of his *Histoire de la Musique*[1] M. Emile Vuillermoz (1878) writes: "The French influence—Debussy and Ravel—makes itself felt on Granville Bantock (1869) whose activity and fecundity are considerable, on Ralph Vaughan Williams (1872), Frank Bridge (1879) and Eugene Goossens (1893)." My copy is that of the 14th Edition. The evidence shows that it has been brought up-to-date in certain respects but that the early information has not been altered. In the two complete pages devoted to English music there lies a wealth of significant food for thought—not engendered by the information given in itself, but in the fact that our music appears to have made such little impact upon the musical consciousness of a leading French writer on music. It would seem that nothing has resulted from the activities of the propagandists and that our "splendid isolation" (to quote M. Vuillermoz again) has caused us to live in a little world of our own and to imagine a situation rosy enough, but entirely one of wishful thinking.

It may be strange that the very composer who has formulated a completely English style should be accused of Gallic influences; but this is not as paradoxical as it may appear, since the French have never got over the fact that Vaughan Williams studied for a short time with Ravel; although his studies were mostly confined to orchestration.[2] Previously he had been a pupil of Parry at the Royal College of Music, and of Max Bruch.[3] The only work which may in any way be aligned with his French teacher is *The Wasps* (1909) which incidental music,

[1] *Les Grandes Etudes Historiques*, Librairie Arthème Fayard (Paris).
[2] Page 174, *Ravel*, Demuth (Dent, *Master Musicians*).
[3] Page 181.

by reason of its faint flirtation with the augmented triad and whole-tone scale, can with some stretch of the imagination be said to show a Gallic influence, but certainly not one suggesting Ravel.

Nevertheless, before this Ravelian tutelage, Vaughan Williams had produced certain works which stand out for their Englishness because of their inherent folk-tune influence, their breeziness and, technically speaking, the use of the common chord and clearly defined tonal qualities. Among these works one would single out *Songs of Travel* (1905), *Toward the Unknown Region* (1907) and *A Sea Symphony* (1903-1910). The second of these was revised in 1918, but to what extent I do not know. Vaughan Williams joined the English Folk-song Society in 1904, spending some considerable periods in collecting from the very mouths of the old people in the countryside a great many valuable and genuine folk-songs which otherwise would have fallen into oblivion. He became inoculated, so to speak, with the modal feeling of these tunes and in due course absorbed this feeling into his musical sensitivity.

I have said that the Gallic influence is hard to find outside *The Wasps*, but now and again it reappears at moments when he touches a certain aspect of spirituality. In "On the beach at night alone" (the second movement of *A Sea Symphony*) he uses a poetic chromaticism which, if one did not know that Vaughan Williams has always been anti-pathetic to César Franck, would suggest distinct contact in the semi-tonalism of certain brief phrases. Otherwise, the whole work is as bluff and breezy as only an Englishman can be. The breadth of the first movement which always thrills by its very grandeur, the sweep of the scherzo ("Waves") with its diatonic swinging tunes, and the triadic basis of the fourth ("The Explorers") immediately denote a directness emanating from a composer like William Boyce (1710-1779), who sang so nobly of "Heart of Oak". There is a similar defiant bluffness, although probably unintentional, in the closing chorus of *Toward the Unknown Region,* at the words "Then we burst forth". This little work, which years later was to wedge itself into the hearts of all choralists in England, indicated a path which led away from the usual run of the "Cantata", avoiding a definite "story" and painting a metaphysical condition intelligible to the unenlightened, yet still fulfilling the inner meaning of the text. Here are the first signs of a refusal to grapple with philosophy in terms other than basic prose, as it were, and to bring forward that philosophy in terms of music easily assimilated by all, thus underlining the teaching in a manner approachable by the masses rather than in an esoteric study for the few.

In these early works Vaughan Williams struck out technically from the habits of his older contemporaries, and when Parry described *A Sea Symphony* as being "full of noble things together with some impertinences"[1] he meant that the thoughts were great but their expression in terms of occasional consecutive fifths betokened some disregard of the established musical proprieties, for at that time the letter of the music and obedience to "the rules of the game" meant more to musicians than was actually admitted.

Vaughan Williams' sane attitude to music was emphasised by the *Fantasia on a Theme by Thomas Tallis* for double string orchestra, and *String Quartet* (1909) in which he showed the common chord to be as capable of intensity as all the chromatic heavings of the contemporary romantic Continental composers. If *A Sea Symphony* was "impertinent", this *Fantasia* was a downright insult to everything the "schools" held dear at that time; but it presaged the future which, in the light of retrospection, seems perfectly obvious.

It was not until the 1918 performance of *A London Symphony* that the name of Vaughan Williams stamped itself ineffaceably upon the concert repertoire—the earlier production in 1914 had made an impression, but people's minds were set upon things other than music at that time. The work went through many revisions as, indeed, have all Vaughan Williams' works. It is no sign of the amateur to take the advice of others. Vaughan Williams has always striven after perfection. This has meant more than just personal satisfaction. Asking for, and acting upon, the reactions of others is often mistaken for uncertainty. This does not entail following the dictates of the ordinary critic whose duty it is to criticise and do nothing else.

A London Symphony revealed something new at the time. It pictured London not in terms of Elgar's *Cockaigne* with its military parades, lovers in churches and general West End Edwardian opulence, but in those of the real London, the London of the Thames, of the City workers, the whistling messenger-boys, the junketings on Hampstead Heath and the terrible plight of the unemployed. This was the London that everybody could understand, and when the chimes of Big Ben faded the work away, the listener realised that the music had been all about himself. The most significant feature was the way in which

[1] *Hubert Parry*, Charles L. Graves (Macmillan).

Vaughan Williams showed a form of English musical Impressionism in the second movement which, with its hazy massed effect of strings playing complete common chords in root position against a gentle tune on the cor anglais, painted an unforgettable and faithful picture of an autumn evening mist on the Thames Embankment and hinted at the tragedies which were an every-night occurrence.

One of the charges against Vaughan Williams' triadic technique has always been that it lacks contrast in its limitations. That this is nonsense was proved in the *Fifth Symphony* (1943—note the date) in which the technique of the slow movement is identically the same as that in the slow movement of *A London Symphony*; yet while the latter is distinctly objective, the former is a deeply felt spirituality.

Vaughan Williams was writing like nobody else. He was one of the outstandingly original composers in Europe; but the full realisation of the English style did not come until 1922, when *A Pastoral Symphony* was performed for the first time. Parry's *Promethus Unbound* may have heralded English emancipation,[1] but it was Vaughan Williams' *A Pastoral Symphony* which heralded her complete renaissance, for it at once demonstrated a culture applicable only to England. Its peaceful serenities placed it as a symphony apart from all others. even apart from Beethoven's *Pastoral* and Mahler's *Third*, for

[1] See page 106.

Vaughan Williams made no attempt at delineating impressions or feelings, but simply took the spiritual and emotional messages of the Surrey hills, Cotswolds, or Sussex downs (we who live in Sussex like to think that it was our Downs which inspired him) as they came and translated them into terms of music. There are no scenes by any brook, no thunderstorms or prayers of thanksgiving, no village bands. This is the music which one, standing in the complete silence experienced only on the English hills and downs, heard, and which revealed itself during the course of many such sojournings and journeyings. It is not the music of the pure imagination of the town-dweller. It is too intimate, too sincere, and too true to life.

The basis of this work showed the complete breakaway from all traditions. It used nothing but common chords, and its strings of consecutive fifths gave it the requisite vagueness and modality; there are no folk-tunes anywhere. It came at the time when music was at the peak of one of its most sensational periods, and the passion for bizarre effects was at its height. As composers drew away from romantic Impressionism, *A Pastoral Symphony* acclaimed both in its own way.

This quasi-Impressionism has its strength engendered by strong common chords which are used freely and at length, and grow with the power of big oak trees. Their similarity of motion does not cloy and Vaughan Williams can move in block chords with no fear of monotony as is the case with Delius. The following passage is entirely parallel in quantity. The variety lies in the qualities.

Outside its immediate serenities, therefore, there is a rugged strength about the quasi-folk-tune subject of the second movement which is borne out by its diatonic background. Vaughan Williams used much the same principle in *Job, a Masque for Dancing* (1930) and, indeed, it appears constantly throughout the mature period. Vaughan Williams became prolific once he had established his maturity.

The voice sung "off" at the beginning and close of the finale of this *Symphony* is unforgettable in its rhapsodic poise. The alternative version upon the trumpet is altogether less satisfactory, for the voice defines that eerie quality which the matter-of-fact trumpet tone can only convey. *A Pastoral Symphony* is one of those works whose greatness lies in its restraint—there are few such. Greatness no longer lies in its association with the Grand Manner. It is achieved by force of originality and individuality, and its expressive qualities may be either noisy or quiet. This particular work is great because not only did it say something which has never been said before, but because it formulated the pure English style of the folk-tune idiom. It took expressive feeling on to a completely novel plane. It formed the natural culmination of the *Tallis Fantasia* which, itself, does not altogether escape the village green in its middle section; the village green plays no part in *A Pastoral Symphony*.

The triadic approach was continued in *O vos omnes* (1922) and the *Mass in G minor* (1922), where the thought became primitive. It was said that in this *Mass* Vaughan Williams wrote what other composers wanted to write, but did not dare do so. Here all the "laws of musical progression" are thrown to the winds in a way unique to the work itself. It is a far cry from *Lord, Thou hast been our refuge* (1913), which enjoyed a vogue at one time. The *Mass* formed a stepping stone to *Sancta Civitas* (1926), where the 6/4 chord plays a basic rôle. In this work Vaughan Williams proclaimed himself the master of the common chord. This element proved itself capable of infinite variety, and the ineffable beauties of *The Lark Ascending* (1914) are in no way related to those of *The Shepherds of the Delectable Mountains* (1922), in which Vaughan Williams provides the ideal ecclesiastical opera which in any surroundings other than those of a cathedral, sounds distinctly uncomfortable.

Although the early enthusiasm for this little opera seems to have burnt itself out, it should be maintained in the repertoire of small yet capable operatic societies. After Walt Whitman, Vaughan Williams came under the sway of John Bunyan, upon whose *Pilgrim's Progress* there exists a complete opera. The pathos of feeling in *The Shepherds of the Delectable Mountains* is so simply expressed that it almost hurts by its intensity.

Ex. 3   The Shepherds of the Delectable Mountains

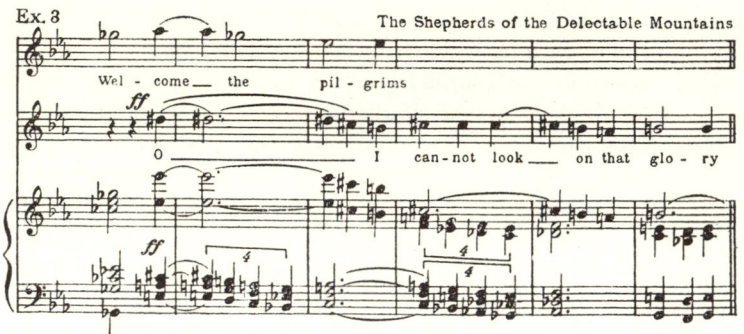

The closing "Alleluia's" which ring through the pages like a distant peal of village church bells, recurring over and over again, illustrate the thought of a believer and an idealist who has seen the vision and has understood it.

However, Vaughan Williams has not been content to wander permanently in the land of dreams and ideals. He put his foot down very hard upon the earth in the *Fourth Symphony* (1935) and the *Piano Concerto* (1934), whose technique is unrelenting and uncompromisingly firm. It would appear that he suddenly became defiant; this *Symphony* has a European appeal through its harmonic acidity. The *Concerto* is not such a convincing or satisfying work—it was re-written for two pianos; but not even this suggested that the piano was Vaughan Williams' instrument. He is not interested in pianism and the abstract thought of the work is foreign to his nature when expressed in this medium. The reposeful Vaughan Williams of *A Pastoral Symphony*, *The Lark Ascending*, *The Shepherds of the Delectable Mountains* is now considered as being slightly dated by those who, with few qualifications for so doing, draw up our concert programmes. We could do with a month's Vaughan Williams Festival, covering all the ground.

That his *Sixth Symphony* (1944-1947) reached its hundredth performance during 1950 is remarkable, but quite understandable. In an unsettled world where anything tranquil is regarded as being escapist, this symphony finds its natural surroundings. It should be noted, however, that Vaughan Williams' reaction to the 1939-1945 War was the *Fifth Symphony*, whose spiritual beauties preached the lesson of human dignity (a well-known Doctor of Music expressed the opinion immediately after the first performance that it "reeked of the organ loft", whatever that may have meant). It may be mentioned that Holst wrote "Mars, the Bringer of War" some time before anyone had the slightest idea of what a modern war would be like. Reaction, therefore, to immediate surroundings often appears contradictory; but Vaughan Williams has never been escapist and he faces facts while striving after ideals.

His English style did not make an immediate appeal to all and sundry, since it came too suddenly and formed too great a contrast to the European idea. Many found it enervating and too vague—the word "wandering" was often used. This meant that the usual divergence of material did not make an instantaneous impact upon the ear. There appeared to be an insufficiency of opposition between "subjects", although the truth lay in the situation which made one "subject" reasonably mobile and another less so. The sense of immobility came from the uncertain tonality and key relationships which, previous to the upheaval, had always been clearly defined. Symphonic modality was something quite fresh.

In *Hugh the Drover* (1911-1914) and *Sir John in Love* (1929) Vaughan Williams established a definitely English style of opera. The first is a folk-song work which succeeds in pleasing both those who consider folk-song to be the basis of all true music and those who find it irritating. The latter are convinced because the ear is not always made aware of the origin of the tunes and their elements. The harmony is not always modal either in content or feeling. The work goes with a swing. Some of the situations are a trifle fortuitous—for example, it is obvious the moment he enters that the Sergeant will recognise Hugh. The conversational effects are carried out in sheer music and there is a refreshing scarceness of recitative, that easy way of getting over certain difficulties. There is constant *music* all through the work. The ensemble movements are masterly. The Fair moves and is thoroughly alive. Hugh's introductory song is vigorous and sincere, and that which he sings in the stocks is beautiful. This is unaffected music which may be said to have closed the composer's first manner.

Sir John in Love will always suffer by unthinking references to Verdi and Nicolai. The Italian approach to the fat knight turns him into an international prototype which, no doubt, he is—or was, perhaps. The English attitude naturally keeps him within the confines of English historical legend, and within the Shakespearian concept. Comparison with the German Nicolai usually confines itself to a generality suggested by the Overture, since the whole opera, as far as I can ascertain, has not been performed in this country since 1920 (when the Carl Rosa Opera Company produced it at the Lyceum Theatre, London). It certainly approaches the English idea of Falstaff, but does not reach it entirely. It is interesting to compare the manner of *Sir John in Love* with those of Holst's *At the Boar's Head* (1925). Of the two, Vaughan Williams' treatment is more essentially operatic since there is more actual music in it, and although there are folk-songs, the majority of the pages are original. These two operas are not for export. Vaughan Williams has written English operas for the English.[1] He is not interested in international repercussion and does not consider it necessary that his work should penetrate the musical consciousness of foreign countries. He is also more sympathetically inclined towards English performers of his works than to foreigners; the latter cannot really get beneath the skin of the essentially national, insular if you like, idiom and style.

The Poisoned Kiss (1936), described as "An Extravaganza", does not, to my mind, seem altogether happy. It is music outside the generality of its composer and doubtless he enjoyed writing it; but the situation is rather similar to that of d'Indy and Roussel, who attempted "light operas" as a change from their usual seriousness, and did not quite succeed in them. That Vaughan Williams has humour can be seen in his *Five Tudor Portraits* (1936), but the humour in this opera lies in the text more than in the music. This is a personal point of view which two performances have not altered.

Riders to the Sea (1926), a different matter, is a tragic one-act work written somewhat on the lines of the musical quasi-recitative of *Pelléas et Mélisande,* but otherwise bearing no resemblance to that work. It is almost continuous recitative with small orchestra and wordless chorus. It is easy to say that it is unique—such a word can apply to many works. In this case one can find no parallel either in Vaughan Williams or in any other composer, for its idiom is completely isolated. One hears the inner consciousness of the characters in full expression and the whole work is not far removed from Impressionism; but Vaughan Williams cannot avoid being clear-cut for long. Of all his operas, this is the only one which might make a European appeal;

[1] Like the Arthurian and other operas by Rutland Boughton (1878), but these failed mainly because they are more "regional" than general.

it is extremely improbable that the others will ever appear in the great Continental opera houses of either this continent or that of America. This might not apply to *The Shepherds of the Delectable Mountains*, which, as I have said, requires the balance of a cathedral for its full realisation. Its ecstasy is personally rather than spiritually inclined. It is the longing of a human being for an ultimate goal and sings no glory save that of a just reward.

This insularity of style does not apply to all the orchestral works. The *Fourth Symphony* and, to a certain extent, the *Sixth* are universal since their Englishness is not quite so much on the surface; yet one doubts if the sporting second subject of the last movement in the *Fourth* would convince a Continental audience. *A London Symphony* is altogether different. Its topographical qualities, which an Italian could apply to Rome and the Tiber, scored a vociferous success there in 1935 when the audience in no uncertain manner bade Sir Henry Wood play it right through a second time (of what other symphony can this be said?). It could not apply to Paris and the Seine because that city is more sophisticated than either London or Rome.

The *Mass in G minor* finds its place naturally in any cathedral or church, whether Anglo-Catholic, Old Catholic, or Roman Catholic. The work itself is catholic—that is, general. The text is not the per-quisite of any one particular sect, whether in Latin or in English. It is music which carries the twofold aesthetic of primitive beauty and religious ecstasy. Even on the radio it seems out of place, because listening conditions are too bound up with its spiritual message. Simi-larly, the *Fifth Symphony*, with its lovely weaving and interweaving contrapuntal lines, its heavenly beautiful third (slow) movement and its dignified second and fourth, is out of place in a garish concert hall. Its real milieu would seem to be radio, and Vaughan Williams quite unconsciously has created an ideal radio symphony. This does not suggest that *A Pastoral Symphony*, therefore, should be played only out of doors on the top of a high hill or down. Its beauties are not as rarefied as those of the *Fifth Symphony* and it is tolerable in the concert hall, although, again, infinitely preferable in private. Neither of these works can stand communal listening; they require the withdrawal of oneself into bodily and spiritual solitude. They are not escapist, and they cannot be considered as "dope". They are too intrinsically beauti-ful for the usual listening situations and conditions. One who had the joy of hearing each work for the first time on the radio testifies to this.

During their progress, the slightest little distraction, be it a movement or a slight cough, completely upsets the balance of the mind. The attitude, therefore, to these unique symphonies is purely a selfish one, but in both cases selfishness is a requisite quality.

However, let it not be thought that Vaughan Williams is for the few, that he is for the aesthetic specialist or the enthusiastic amateur choralist. He makes an appeal to the "ordinary chap" through his *Folk-Song Suite* for military band and through the breadth of his setting to "For all the Saints". The latter made an almost unbelievable conquest of prejudice. The sentiment of the words had become wedded to the sentimental tune by Sir Joseph Barnby (1838-1896) and the two appeared to have become an indissoluble association. The whole was a complete misfit, the rhythm of the words frequently causing false accentuation owing to the strictness of the musical metre and the faulty rise and fall of the notes. For years and years the most conservative of all music-lovers, the hymn-singing public, had been content to sing the utmost rubbish in the hymn "For all the Saints" where the notes had gone up at the word "drear" instead of down, thus placing undue emphasis upon a mere adjective. It was a super-sentimental association which in any other milieu would have aroused scorn and derision. Vaughan Williams turned it into a paean of triumph. His fine, broad tune, in every way singable, was easily picked up, and the majestic pace was maintained by the steadily moving bass. When the notes descend upon that word "drear", the faithful find themselves singing sense at last, and in other verses they subconsciously adapt the tune to the accents. This setting fully brought out the vision of the poet. The fact that the tune completely broke down the prejudice of years without calling for any objection save a momentary initial disappointment was a major triumph in a small way. The "ordinary chap" loved the tune at once and was stimulated by its manliness.

Thus we have two great composers able to appeal to the "man in the street", Elgar doing so through his sense of imperial patriotism, Vaughan Williams through his latent spirituality and masculinity. Both composers achieved this through the breadth of diatonic melody. This may be a small matter in a study of a very great composer, but it is a very significant one.

Vaughan Williams, like Elgar, has also written his music for great occasions. The *Coronation Te Deum* (1937) surprised many by its directness; festival *Te Deums* usually finish up by being miniature cantatas—that written by Parry for the Coronation of King George V failed because it was too elaborately contrived. Vaughan Williams' was almost "congregational". *A Flourish for a Coronation* (1937) and *Thanksgiving for Victory* (1945), written to miscellaneous texts, are among those unfortunate works which can be applicable only to their proper occasions, and since coronations happen rarely and the need for thanksgiving after victory, it is to be hoped, even more so, one assumes that it will be some time before we hear the works again. The *Flourish* has all the Vaughan Williams melodic and harmonic qualities, not the least notable being the suave dignity at the words "O Prince, desire to be honourable; Cherish thy folk and hate extortion", and traces in spirit right back to Purcell.

I have used the word "dignity" several times and it is applicable to the humanism and easy sense of approach of so much of Vaughan Williams' music. Elgar's dignified moments are full of disdain. Vaughan Williams, both in himself and in his music, is dignified without being pompous or superior. Once more the "ordinary chap" finds himself met by a great man with hands outstretched to welcome and subconsciously uplift him. This type of person finds *Job* an acceptable work—rather surprisingly, perhaps. After some careful enquiry, I found that it was the majesty of such moments as the "Saraband", "Pavane" and "Galliard" which made the appeal. The swinging tune of the "Galliard", however, caused some hesitation, and it was described as being too "churchy". Its modality made the uninitiated listener feel slightly uncomfortable; but it was an unconscious tribute to its genuineness. The slow movements did not impress. The "Minuet" caused some irritation, the opinion being that the sons of Job would have to sin much more spectacularly if their offences were to cause Divine wrath. Satan was not quite understood until the explanation was given that *Job* was not intended as a macabre work. This enquiry, let it be said, was made with the aid of the gramophone, and while it would not be right to say that one and all determined to go and hear the work at the very next opportunity, it would be just to feel that the result of the enquiry showed that nervous hysteria on the orchestra is not the only way to convert the heathen and that honest sincerity can make itself apparent even through mechanical reproduction. At the other end of the scale, the *Serenade to Music* (1938) moved the most callous by its sheer loveliness.

All this goes back to the power of the common chord and the

diatonic melody. Certain elements play an integral part in Vaughan Williams' melodic equipment. One is the interval of the fourth, which is apparent from the opening bars of *A London Symphony* and continues straight through the *Fifth* and *Sixth Symphonies*. Its quality ranges from impressive Impressionism in the first case, passing through extreme violence in the *Fourth Symphony* to the serene spirituality of the *Fifth*. Another is its constant revolving round a focal point, and swinging upon a fulcrum. When rapid and forceful, it acquires a boldness of utterance typical of English bluffness and plain speaking. Comparison of these with earlier examples from *The Wasps*, *A Sea Symphony* and *Toward the Unknown Region* shows the difference between diatonicism and modality.

Harmonically, he has proved that invention can find means of contrast and variety in a technique which on the surface appears extremely limited. Vaughan Williams' modality is more genuinely English than the chromaticism of Delius. That it is capable of expansion, time alone, and Vaughan Williams himself, can show.

Vaughan Williams is absolutely unpredictable from one work to another. Few men of his age have produced such constant variety upon such a consistently high level of inspiration during the last fifteen years. In the same way that Gabriel Fauré is often regarded as being the personification of French music, so can Vaughan Williams be looked upon in the light of English music. He is a greater composer than Elgar because he is more original.

CHAPTER THIRTEEN

SIR ARNOLD BAX

(1883)

THE unsophisticated Englishness of Vaughan Williams finds its opposite parallel in the romantic Celticism of Sir Arnold Bax, whose music is the child of a vivid and sensitive imagination almost wholly free from subjectivity. While folk-song forms the direct musical basis of Vaughan Williams' inspiration, folk-lore plays the guiding rôle in that of Bax, and whatever folk-song influence there is lies in an occasional modality and a melodic focal centring which shows what is called the "folk-song influence". Bax is no musical idealist, and is not in the least aspersive or optative. He is a visionary, and his world is peopled with phantasms of which the non-Celt is unaware. Bax, however, is not unaware of living forces, and it would be wrong to imagine him as a being apart from the world or aloof from his fellow-men. Like every other creative artist, he retires within himself while in the act of creation, but he is no dreamer with his head in the clouds. At one time he stood almost alone in his pursuit of an aesthetic from which the majority recoiled. During the time when romanticism was regarded as a kind of period piece, and composers' one aim was to be slick and original, and different at all costs, Bax wrote some of his most powerfully contrived music which openly avowed his romantic aims. For this reason, and for the fact that he has lived outside the main stream of musical talk and activities, he has stood alone throughout the greater part of his life. In his younger days he was regarded as a composer of exceedingly difficult music, difficult both to play and to listen to. To-day, with technique so much advanced, the actual playing of the notes offers few nuts to crack; but the question of balance is a concern which has to be given full consideration if clarity is to be maintained, and it is this extremely necessary attention to detail which causes performers to hesitate. In the older and more leisurely days, performers could afford to spend many hours in sorting out knotty points. There were fewer concerts and, consequently, more time for concentrated study. Nowadays, when performers are liable to be called át a moment's notice to fill a gap or to prepare as many as five programmes simultaneously, the tendency is to take the line of least resistance, and when the old battle-horses are put aside, it is the modern composer of music easily assimilated who reaps the benefit. Deplorable though this may be, it is none the less true and, to a certain extent, understandable. The fault lies, however, with those who control programmes.

Bax has written enough piano and chamber music to fill many programmes; but one seeks in vain among the lists of recitals, both live and radio, for any full realisation of this. Orchestrally, his works do not actually invite performance because they often call for extra resources and thus strain finances. Nevertheless, a composer who has written seven symphonies should be less ignored by the rich man of music—namely, the B.B.C., whose financial responsibilities are not as acute as is often maintained. If a composer is an ornament to his native culture, it is altogether scandalous that he should not be performed as a matter of course; but here, again, one is up against the time factor. When conductors scurry here, there and everywhere, conducting concert after concert in ceaseless succession, they have neither time nor inclination to study complex scores which, performed rarely as they are, they have little opportunity of hearing elsewhere. This is one of the gaps in our musical life which the death of Sir Henry Wood accentuates daily.

Pianists sometimes complain that there are "too many notes" in Bax' music. The fact is, that if one is content to view music in terms of a tune with an accompaniment, this is, to a certain extent, true. One of the features of Bax' pianism is his habit of adding a secondary theme in conjunction with the main one. Often he places the principal material in the middle of the keyboard, while above it there is a musical commentary which, if omitted, leaves but the bare bones of the matter; at the same time firm control of dynamic is required in order that it should be a commentary and nothing else. This is apparent more in the pieces than in the *Sonatas*, the latter in themselves constituting an invaluable contribution to the repertoire. This point may be illustrated by the following extract from one of his least-known pieces, and one of his best:

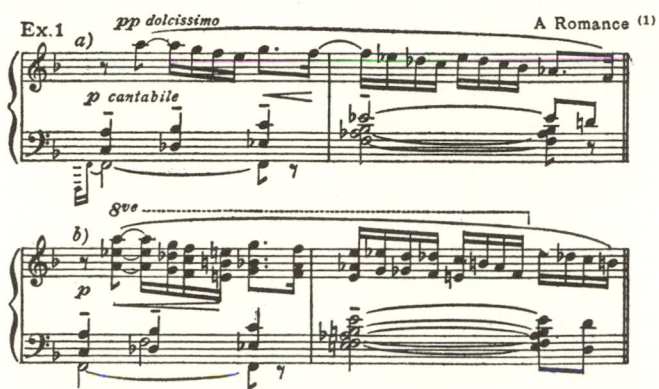

Ex.1 a) *pp dolcissimo*   A Romance [1]

This trait appears over and over again. It is as much part of the essential Bax as are clusters of notes the essential Ireland. In the case of the works for two pianos, the *Sonata* particularly in this instance, it is a danger, for Bax is not inclined to regard the medium as music for two individuals but as music for one large piano. The early *Moy Mell* (1917) largely escapes this, but Bax' technique and idiom increased in thickness as he grew to maturity. Those who play Bax have to be thoroughly in sympathy with his style. They have to be ultra-sensitive in their comprehension and response. His contact with his performer is closer than in almost any other composer outside the systematic note-row stylists, and even here the contact is more sympathetic than spiritual. The exercise of the imagination, always essential with romantic music, has to be used to the full with Bax, otherwise the music becomes a mere jumble of sound. The performer has to exercise a continuous *ricercare*, as it were, and seek out the innermost secrets of the music.

Although having nothing in common with the Impressionism or research in sonorities of Debussy, Bax is not dissimilar from that composer. His Impressionism lies in the mental picture which he is painting in the music. His titles are always fanciful—*Apple Blossom Time, A Hill Tune, The Maiden with a Daffodil*—a Rossetti picture less chaste than Debussy's *La Fille aux cheveux de lin,* but equally evocative. As with Debussy, however, one looks at the catalogue to see the description of the picture, but more frequently, since Bax does

[1] This is used in the slow movement of the *Fourth Symphony* (Chappell & Co., Ltd.)

not delineate at all. Occasionally, however, one does find suggested delineation, as in the case of *In a Vodka Shop*, which implies indeed some kind of clumsy Russian dance, but does not necessarily indicate the impulse of vodka. It is this piece, and this piece alone (and that mainly through its title), which has led the unthinking critics and commentators to say that Bax has gone through a Russian influence. Without being in any way flippant, one would suggest that if the piece had been called *In a Gin Palace* it would have been hailed as a picture of one facet of English life (gin has, I understand, an effect somewhat similar to vodka in its middle stages). If one finds a certain affinity to Moussorgsky's *Gopak* in this piece, it is only through the repetitiveness of the material, for Bax outvies the Russian composer in rhythmic violence. At any rate, this is but a small piece upon which to lay a general charge, and one suspects that these critics and commentators write from unawareness of Bax' style in general; perhaps they do not like music sufficiently well to find things out for themselves.

Whatever absence of delineation there may be in the piano pieces, there is plenty in the orchestral works, apart from the symphonies. The waves beat upon the shore of Cornwall in *Tintagel* (1917) and the sea undulates in the sunshine in *The Garden of Fand* (1912), while the wind soughs through the forest in *November Woods* (1917) in an unmistakable fashion. This music uses the orchestra virtuosically, but artistically. Bax' efflorescence, latent in the piano pieces, finds its full achievement here, as, indeed, may be expected. Bax' approach to the orchestra forms the complete contrast with that style emanating from the Royal College of Music which turned out Vaughan Williams, Holst and Bliss, for under the aegis of Frederick Corder the Royal Academy of Music (where Bax studied) was drawn to Wagner and Strauss. Bax, therefore, does not score in the neo-classical manner of Brahms-cum-South Kensington and such music coming from that side of Hyde Park is unthinkable. In his sense of colour Bax is able to compete with any European model, be it French or pre-revolutionary Russia. His is a more elaborate Delian attitude; the two composers use the wood-wind in an almost identical manner, and when the older writers of text-books on orchestration refer to this department as "the flower-garden of the orchestra", they might have foreseen both Delius and Bax.

From the wealth of detail which a Bax score contains, the main material stands out only if the conductor meticulously observes the dynamics. The listener must be prepared to concentrate. Once attention has flagged, even momentarily, it is impossible to pick up the thread. It is easy to sit back and bathe in the sound; but it is not the function of Bax' music to be content merely with "sound". The Impressionists may not have been concerned overmuch with themes; it is one of Bax' chief cares that there shall be some definite thematic material throughout the work which should at all times be obvious through the weaving of the texture. This closely-knit colour has drawn the reproach upon him that his music is "thick". This is not so; it may be dense, but it is not impenetrable. The wood is clearly distinct from the trees.

In this respect he forms a much closer parallel with Ravel, if with anybody, than with the Impressionists. Harmonically, of course, he is far in advance of both, yet he does not eschew the ordinary common chord. His orchestration is faithful to his intentions and these are always perfectly clear. The strings soar up into the highest registers and sweep and swoop in the correct virtuosic manner; but these sweeps and swoops are thematic and not mere effects. He does not elaborate a simple passage as does Ravel, but takes care to avoid the easy way. Orchestral players, therefore, have few opportunities for relaxation and must keep on the *qui vive*. Their alertness is rewarded because they know that they are contributing something essential to the work and not merely decorating it. Bax' tone-poems form the direct antithesis to those of Strauss in that they are not pretentious. Bax is not concerned with vital problems. His constant care is to paint a picture and take his time over it. In this respect he will probably be the last orchestral romantically objective composer for some little while; but when the present passion for cerebrality and systemisation of composition has run its course (and even now it is approaching its end), it will be to Bax that composers will turn for example and authority.

As regards his *Symphonies*, the situation is a little different. Only in the *Third* (1929), and *Fifth* (1930–1), does he show any purely romantic tendencies, at least, as far as the outside listener is concerned. The former reveals his Celticism in its most advanced degree. There are no mists or twilights, however; instead, the air is highly charged with portent which not even the ebullient finale really dispels. His fondness for quasi-folk-tune is seen in the second subject of the first movement, which he covers with a veneer of chromaticism. This does not in any way conceal the implied modality of the tune itself, but the general effect is a trifle top heavy. His subjects are invariably clearly divided and he seems to leave and approach them with difficulty; the second subject is often a long time coming and one waits with some suspense and a little impatience. In the latter *Symphony*, dedicated to Sibelius, he adapts his own style to that of the great Finnish composer. This is done not by a deliberate avoidance of his own individual harmonic idiom, but by using the Sibelian principle of germination. I do not know if this was deliberate or not, or if it was the result of a close study of Sibelius' scores, but the result sounds as if Sibelius dictated the manner while Bax wrote the matter. This does not end in pastiche and Sibelius could not have composed the work; but it shows how a composer can actually adapt himself to the manner of another and still keep his own personality. Of all Bax' *Symphonies*, this one is the easiest to follow for the reason that its construction is patent all the way through. I do not think it is the best, for it falls below the *Third* in the use of the imagination. Its colour is Sibelianly sombre for the most part and echoes in this respect the *First* (1922), in E flat minor which shows Bax ruminating over serious things and setting himself in a philosophical framework, albeit a slightly pessimistic one.

The *Third Symphony*, however, can rank with any other of the century, with that from any other culture. Students could use it as a guide to orchestration, for it contains nearly everything which need be exemplified. The *Fourth* (1930-1931) is most objectivist and the most immediately acceptable. It is certainly the best "introduction" to Bax' *Symphonies* because it is entirely himself. I find the *Sixth* (1933), the least satisfying, and repeated readings and hearings confirm the original impression that it slams the orchestra about too much. There seems to be little real impulse and it leaves few thematic or textual impressions behind it. Nevertheless, it is of importance because of its range and magnitude, which is not altogether free from an unconscious grandiloquence. The majesty which now and again penetrates the *Third* and certainly directs the *Second*, does not ring quite true in the *Sixth*.

Bax' *Symphonies*, with those of Vaughan Williams and the earlier ones of Holbrooke, take their place in a culture to which they add lustre, and the three composers illustrate the infinite variety of British/ English music. Bax' considerable works, neglected in those places where they might be expected to be welcomed, raise the tone of our music everywhere. They may not be exportable—they are too long for the Latin temperament and too efflorescently romantic for the

Nordic—but, as I have said, this is not a concern which need bother us. His chamber music, particularly the *String Quartets* and *Nonet*, however, by its very media exclude this excessive romantic flowering. That they have not made their full impact as yet is one of those questions which remain unanswerable save for the possibility that they make no appeal to the inexperienced minds which are responsible for our most authoritative programmes.

There is one field which I have deliberately left until the end because I believe Bax to excel in it over many others and because it is even more ignored. I refer to Bax' magnificent motets and large-scale choral and orchestral works. The neglect of these works is the result of regarding Bax as an essentially instrumental composer. In this country our composers are categorised too much, and if they write a majority of works in one particular medium, any in another are regarded rather in the light of freaks or momentary aberrations.

The home of *alla capella* choral music is in South Kensington. There they have always nurtured the English tradition as the primary factor in our music. In Marylebone they view things differently. The English choral tradition is nurtured there, to be sure, but they regard instrumental music as of equal importance. This situation dates from the appointment of Sir Hubert Parry to the Directorship of the Royal College of Music, for Parry was essentially a vocal and choral writer. Sir Alexander Mackenzie, Parry's opposite number at the Royal Academy of Music, was essentially an instrumentalist and an instrumental writer. It is curious that the heads of two great institutions should subconsciously have so directed the two policies through their own activities. One may say with some freedom that had Bax been trained at the Royal College he would have written more choral music, and even if his output had been its present size, it would have appeared more often.[1] As it is, our big choral societies ignore the motets and appear to be blissfully ignorant of the choral-and-orchestral works.

The primarily orchestral writer is not always at home with a choir—there is the evidence of Beethoven for this theory. One finds it difficult to realise that Bax shows an intimate choral knowledge; from what one can tell from his book,[2] he has had no practical experience with choirs, has not sung or trained and conducted one. In spite of the combined difficulties of his choral idiom, the individual lines are all per-

[1] The one exception to this is, of course, Eugene Goossens (page 290).
[2] *Farewell, My Youth* (Longmans Green).

fectly singable, and if not particularly easy of execution are all written "in the tradition". Certain aspects of this have been mentioned in the chapter on Gustav Holst.[1] In these works Bax shows complete polyphonic mastery and he thus places himself in the direct line from the Elizabethans, carrying the choral principles of Parry's *Songs of Farewell* several steps further. Traditionalists like Parry and Stanford would probably fight shy of these works and describe them as orchestral choralism. Bax knows the overwhelming force of contrapuntal choralism, as did Bantock before him, but not quite in the same way.

In *Of a Rose I Sing* (1921) for small choir, harp, 'cello and double-bass, *Now is the Time of Christymas* (1921) for male choir, flute and piano, and *The Boar's Head* (1923) for male voices and others, Bax shows a certain affinity with the mediaeval spirit. However, it is in the two great motets for unaccompanied choir *Mater Ora Filium* (1921) and *This Worlde's Joie* (1922) that he puts himself upon the highest level of inspiration. These works, particularly the former, appear to have been written in a state of white heat. They are as intense as the *Tallis Fantasia* of Vaughan Williams, which in its orchestral manner proclaims the tensity of passion achievable with common chords. Bax' harmony is not restricted to the triad, but it is patently non-semitonal.

Of these two works, *This Worlde's Joie* is the more approachable since the text does not call for elaborate counterpoint. It is just within the capabilities of the average choir provided that the singers have sufficient patience and reasonably good eyesight—I say this advisedly because both these works are printed in microscopic type and the price of a larger copy is outside the range of the normal choral financial position.

One cannot place these works, as far as their technique goes, in relation to any earlier period. It is very much of the present century. The spirit, however, is unmistakable. This is one of Christian devotion, and the manner in which Bax writes a kind of undercurrent recitation is suggestive of muttering prayers, of monks telling their beads. The atmosphere is of the monastery and cathedral.

[1] Page 136.

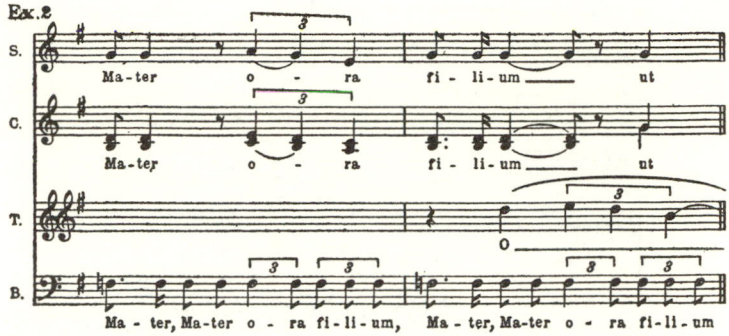

The general style is far in advance of the primitive simplicity of Vaughan Williams' *Mass in G minor* and while complex, it is never complicated. The four bars preceding Ex. 2 will give an idea not only of Bax' contrapuntal mastery, but of his unerring skill in achieving overwhelming climax through traditional means.

It will be observed that the work is only for first-rate choirs.[1]

I have commented upon Bax' fondness for a melodic commentary over the main material in his piano music. In Ex. 4 *a* and *b* he uses the same principle which succeeds without doubt in this genre:

[1] It was written for Charles Kennedy Scott's Oriana Choir.

I make no excuse for quoting the closing bars: because they form the climax to some of the most overwhelmingly powerful choral music in existence and show how the cadential effect can be emphasised by a sudden change from counterpoint to harmony (Ex. 5, page 166).

This work is stigmatised by many as being spiritual and mystical hysteria. This depends upon the psyche of the individual, but it has a burning sincerity running through it. One hesitates at making comparisons, but I doubt if J. S. Bach at his most inspired and greatest moments is any more impressive and moving than this. I would earnestly beg students who are facing the borderline of text-book harmony and free composition to buy this work and study it closely. I do not suggest that they immediately write a work of similar proportions and combined difficulties, but they will find choral possibilities at their maximum of expression.

Ex. 5

To the Name above Every Name (1923) is a setting in truncated form of Richard Crashaw's long mystical poem. It was composed for the Worcester Three Choirs Festival of 1923 and, as far as I can ascertain, has received precisely one performance. In it can be found most of the choral technique of the motets, but the writing is not so devotional. Bax uses a kind of spurious plainsong to give the right atmosphere.

Ex. 6   To the Name above Every Name

The effect is gained mainly by the repeated notes which imply recitation; the harmonies are of the same nature as those in Debussy's *La Cathédrale engloutie* and always succeed in suggesting a quasi-ecclesiastical atmosphere. Generally speaking, the choral writing is harder than in the motets, probably because Bax knew that the voices would be assisted by the orchestra. The work, therefore, is not particularly approachable. Its ecclesiastical atmosphere precludes concert-hall performance where its use of Gregorian tones would be quite incongruous, and since works commissioned for the Three Choirs Festivals are, for the most part, apparently doomed to one solitary performance, it seems doubtful if we shall ever hear it again. Through these choral works one sees how Walton came to write *Belshazzar's Feast*.[1]

Bax' later style appears to have thinned itself out and his ideas are less complex. The *Concerto for Piano* (*Left Hand*) (1949) revealed a simplicity of expression which sounded almost tame in comparison with the works associated with his name; but this simplification of style is not deliberate or self-conscious. Bax does not issue manifestos explaining why one work does not sound like the others or giving reasons for a change of style. Those who must talk about their idiom are usually uncertain about themselves. The true creative artist is unself-conscious. He creates his work as it comes to him and leaves it at that, knowing that there are always plenty of commentators and specialists who will not hesitate to tell him exactly what he has done and whither he is progressing, knowing much better than he himself.

Bax' position remains secure in that he will represent a rallying point when the days of cerebrality have worn themselves to a shadow. As there has been a swing away from romanticism to austere neo-classicism, so in turn will the pendulum swing back again. The future romanticism will be very different from that of the past and may well prove to be a happy combination of itself with neo-classicism. One envisages a compromise between Milhaud and Bax, a compromise on the surface seemingly absurd to contemplate, but not altogether so, when one considers the next figure in the panorama.

[1] Page 175.

CHAPTER FOURTEEN

SIR WILLIAM WALTON

(1902)

THE rôle played in the life of Milhaud by Paul Claudel may be paralleled by that played in the life of Walton by the Sitwell family. Milhaud's monumental dramatic music was set to texts by Claudel; Walton's monumental *Belshazzar's Feast* (1931), a work which still awaits its equal, was set to text by Sacheverell Sitwell. Milhaud scored one of his first "succès de scandale" with Claudel's entertaining *Protée;* Walton scored his first with *Façade* (1922), described as an "Entertainment", to words by Edith Sitwell. Both composers ere long rose above these initial uproarious works and have since progressed to serious things. The chief difference between them lies in the fact that Walton is almost completely self-taught, while Milhaud went through a stormy and chequered but otherwise reasonable period of regular study. Walton, like every other ex-cathedral chorister, started twenty years ahead of those not so happily situated, and at Christ Church Cathedral, Oxford, he subconsciously absorbed all the best traditions of English choral music during the impressionable times of his life. This indirect tuition is realisable, of course, only after maturity, and it is indeed interesting for a composer who has been through this fascinating mill to notice for himself how instinctive his polyphonic manner becomes and how he knows without any hesitation or query exactly what not to do in vocal writing. It is, of course, necessary to have an initial feeling for music. It is also necessary to be under a sympathetic choirmaster who rejoices in latent talent and fosters interest. It was Walton's good fortune to be under Dr. Henry George Ley (1887), himself an erstwhile chorister (at St. George's, Windsor) and an organ prodigy— one of the few prodigies who have fulfilled their early promise. With this early encouragement, together with some lessons from Sir Hugh

Allen and good advice from Professor E. J. Dent (1876) and Busoni (1866-1924), Walton at the age of sixteen commenced the composition of his first big work, a *Piano Quartet* of prodigious proportions. It should be recorded that a year earlier he passed his first B.Mus.; no small achievement. Later lessons from Nadia Boulanger (1887) and talks with the famous Ernest Ansermet (1883) brought clarity and directness of purpose to his style.

It is sometimes convenient to disparage the activities of the International Society for Contemporary Music by describing it as a "closed shop" and a "zoo". Whatever may be the strong and weak features of this estimable Society, it will have to its everlasting credit the fact that it spread the knowledge of Walton's music round Europe, and, consequently, established the fact that this country had once more produced a leading European figure sufficiently young to indicate the future direction of music here. Walton's *String Quartet*, an early work of great scope (to say the least), was performed at the first I.S.C.M. Festival in 1923, *Portsmouth Point* in 1926, the *Viola Concerto* (1928-1929) at the Festival in 1930, and the oratorio *Belshazzar's Feast* (1931) at that held in 1933. From that moment Walton arrived, so far as European music was concerned, and since it is the admirable custom of the London Centre of this Society to refrain from recommending works by composers who have become established, his name has not appeared again. Those who put it forward in the early days can claim credit for vision. It is interesting to note that one criticism levelled at *Belshazzar's Feast* by the foreign critics and musicians was that its style was too conventional and traditional to come within the scope of the I.S.C.M. This charge of reactionary tendencies levelled at this particular work was a striking testimony to the pioneering efforts of the Society and to the improved receptivity of new music by listeners in general. The activities of the Society through its Festivals and Concerts given by the various national "sections" have undoubtedly orientated composers in no uncertain measure, and although one sees the same names over and over again in the Festivals, the Society has long since ceased to concern itself with experiments, the period of consolidation having set in some time ago.

Walton's early career, however, was besought with a danger. His reputation was made with *Façade* (1922). It appeared at the time when the "silly season" was in full swing. It consisted of the recitation of some poems by Edith Sitwell, recited through a mask called a "Sengerphone" which was invented by the singer Senger for his performance of *Fafner*.[1] The recitation required well-marked rhythmic articulation. Walton's music formed the background, being composed for flute, clarinet, saxophone, trumpet, 'cello and percussion. There is a certain parallel here with Milhaud's declamatory recitation in the Claudel works.[2] The substance of Walton's music, always witty and polished, was such that when he compiled and re-scored two *Suites for Orchestra* out of the pieces, incongruity and lack of the spoken voice was hardly noticeable. These *Suites* beat the high jinks of Paris at their own game, for they combined a wholesome respect for scholarship which French composers like Auric either eschewed or lacked. The perkiness of Auric's ballets was defeated by English wit, the quality of which was always restrained, but never restricted. This was strange music for an introvert and a B.Mus. Walton has always been of a retiring nature and has never been prominent in those places where they talk. Doubtless he was drawn out of himself by his collaborators, the Sitwells and Constant Lambert (1905)[3] and they might have influenced his path along the easy way. Walton might have continued with this inconsequent music and have thus kept alongside *le dernier cri* which the style was supposed to represent; that is why I have suggested that the path was fraught with danger. In his next work, however, he showed exactly where he intended to go.

The overture *Portsmouth Point* (1925) was suggested by the painting by Thomas Rowlandson (1756–1827) which portrayed sailors and ships with peculiarly graphic skill. Walton had shown his rhythmic potentialities in *Façade*. In this overture we see the continuation of these in the field of symphonic music. It may be described as his last complicated work; henceforth he became merely superficially complex. These complications, later removed in a revised version, lie in the matter of accents which, in order to bring them out in no uncertain manner, entailed many changes of time signature. It was disconcerting to both players and conductors to find themselves faced with the following quick changes in succession—3/8, 2/4, 3/8, 5/8, 2/4, 4/4, 3/4, 4/4—and, in point of fact, the accents sorted themselves out naturally without these changes, the players being perfectly capable of stressing any beat at any moment. This spiky work showed the essence of Walton's thought,

[1] "William Walton", Edwin Evans (*Musical Times*, 1944).
[2] See page 81.
[3] Died 1951.

which was not to alter radically in the succeeding works, but which was to appear in the normal course of his polyphonic lines, for, from this moment, Walton indicated that he was basically in the tradition of classicism, of classical forms and technique.

Portsmouth Point is indeed a cheerful affair with a distinct tang of salt sea air. It avoids a deliberate hornpipe, but such a dance is there by implication. There are, however, no surging waves or stately ships sailing by, and to think of it in terms of the first movement of Vaughan Williams' *A Sea Symphony* would be misguiding. The listener must prepare himself for a scene of bustle and confusion as attendant upon Portsmouth Point on pay-off in those breezy and ribald days of Rowlandson. The nautical flavour, as it is called, lies in this approach, and not in any pictorial suggestion, although the work was impelled by painting. As this work is not seemingly played very often to-day, having been supplanted by the later *Scapino* Overture (1940), it will not be redundant to indicate a few of the salient rhythmic points which characterise the writing of Walton at that time, and which can still be found in the more respectable symphonic genres. Whatever the jazz-mongers have thought about the originality of their rhythmic spasms, they had nothing on Walton, who showed that syncopation was not the prerogative of Tin Pan Alley. The original jazz-mongers claimed syncopation as almost their own discovery, disdaining the serious musician's claim that the shifting of accents could be found all through the history of music. The jazz-mongers distorted and exaggerated it, of course, and the whole atmosphere was one of pure "jitters" from start to finish. This St. Vitus's Dance period played havoc with the nerves of its addicts.[1] Walton simply took the ordinary technique of syncopation and placed it in the forefront of *Portsmouth Point*. Four bars from this work will illustrate the meaning:

Ex. 1.

This fragment has for its bass the following pattern:

[1] A case was brought to my notice in 1944 of a jazz drummer who was taken to hospital, almost a gibbering idiot.

Ex.2

Portsmouth Point

Here can be seen the essence of that *dernier cri* which had pervaded the dance-hall and which composers attempted to "keep pure" by transferring it to the concert hall. It says more than Lambert's *The Rio Grande* (1929) because the technique was not used either as a parody or as a technique in itself. Lambert wrote a work in the jazz manner. Walton used that manner in a work for which it was eminently suited. The slickness of *The Rio Grande* with its self-conscious purple patches finds no place in *Portsmouth Point,* which is snappy without being slick. Walton immediately proved that he was going no further in this direction by his *Sinfonia Concertante* (1927) which immediately made him realisable as a serious-minded symphonic composer. Here are no pictures, even if the third movement does suggest that it originated in a fragment discarded from *Portsmouth Point,* for its nautical flavour is very pronounced. Walton took the concertante manner as his starting point, and the piano is placed in the centre of the orchestral *mêlée* rather in the same style as d'Indy's *Symphonie cévenole;* both works require virtuoso players. The smashing diatonic discords with which Walton's first movement opens compel attention in the same way as did the early introductions, with their emphasis on some rhythmic figure rather than on thematic content which made no later appearance. Walton's first section, however, contain germs which appear constantly in different ways. The work, therefore, grows from itself. In this respect he is one of the first English composers to use the cyclical style. His neo-classicism traces its descent through the Franckian concept, but in no instance is there any other connection. If one were looking for a Continental parallel in this respect, one would find it in d'Indy, but, to a greater extent, in Albéric Magnard, a composer with whom Walton is probably not familiar—there is no French composer of Walton's own generation with whom he can be stylistically paralleled.

It is in the dexterously wrought second movement that we find the contextual connection I have mentioned with *Portsmouth Point.* Here Walton's natural polyphony indulges in complete linear interdependence. His accents fall naturally at each moment in their own melodic consequence, and he contrives high emotional feeling. The extreme power of the climax, one huge sigh for piano and orchestra, lingers ever in the memory. I can think of only one similar moment in a work by any of the composers to the forefront at that time, and that is in Honegger's *Le Roi David* at the words "God be with us" from "The Dance before the Ark". Walton's work is a magnificent example of instrumental polyphony whose complexity of interwoven lines reveal the perfect neo-classicism of the twentieth century, and combine the traditional manner with the contemporary technique. The final pages of the work in which Walton ties up the whole thing with the opening music afford momentary relief from the onrush of the finale.

This work, which has since been revised—certain critics considered it overscored, but that was not very apparent—presaged Walton's future strength and mobility, which were to increase as time went on. From this violence, however, he reacted to a gentleness, which surprised many, in the *Viola Concerto*. Here he joined the ranks of the polymodalists; the alternating major and minor modes of the first movement sounded an ingratiating note where the central Europeans were acid and bitter with the same technique. Although the contrapuntal lines of the second movement in the *Sinfonia Concertante* had certain lyrical qualities in themselves, it was not until this *Concerto* that Walton showed himself in a clearly lyrical vein. Here, throughout, the viola sings unashamedly. The gentleness of the first movement achieved a fine and emotional middle climax in which a slight disturbance of accent may be detected, but otherwise there is nothing to connect it in this respect with *Portsmouth Point*. The second movement pays tribute to the then popular superimposition of fourths which is often found in Vaughan Williams and which Walton himself used in the Fugue subject of the last movement in the *Symphony* (1935). One other characteristic, which found an echo later in the *Symphony*, appears in this scherzoso *Concerto* movement, a rapid reiteration of one chord or note—in the *Symphony* the reiteration is not so rapid.[1] In the third movement Walton inverts the superimposition of fourths by turning them into fifths. The movement consequently obtains more range and shape. Its closing pages where, over an *ostinato* Walton refers to his previous material, are a romantic patch whose warmth contrasts the delicacy of the first.

This work had the honour of being played by Paul Hindemith at its first performance at a Prom. in 1929. This was indeed an honour, for Hindemith, although not by that time fully realised for what eventually

[1] It is also one of Bax' much-used characteristics (*q.v.*).

he turned out to be, was already respected as a leading contemporary composer, if a much-abused one. Formally, some critics found fault with two slow movements; but here there is actually no fault to be found save in the processes of listening. Doubtless if he had used the normal fast, slow, fast design they would have complained of the vigour and violence. The two movements in question are sufficiently dissimilar in style and content to provide the necessary contrast, but they do rather show up the middle one because the content is naturally neither so rich nor so varied. To many, therefore, this movement appears superficial. The variety, however, is not contained in the purely thematic content, for Walton applies the orchestral instruments to his polyphonic thought. Each one sings its own lines, and while it would be altogether wrong to regard Walton as an orchestral colourist, he adds an uncommon tint to the orchestral palette by his use of the bassoon which, as in the third movement of this *Viola Concerto,* for example, comes straight to the fore in a manner in which another composer might use the 'cello. This occurs constantly throughout Walton's music, and in this respect he forms an interesting parallel with Tchaikowsky and Bax (in the opening of the *Third Symphony*).

The lyrical serenities of the *Viola Concerto* were followed by the tempests of *Belshazzar's Feast,* in which the impulse comes from Berlioz. The general outline of the *Sinfonia Concertante* had suggested that he would be for long content to confine himself to a normal scale, but even those who had an inkling whither he was progressing were staggered by the proportions of *Belshazzar's Feast,* its dramatic force, and breadth of conception. It is no exaggeration to say that it was overwhelming, and it continues to have this effect after repeated hearings. It outvies Mahler's *Eighth Symphony* (1906) and Schoenberg's *Gurre-Lieder* (1900-1901), for the result in these works is obtained more by sheer weight of tone than by thematic content. One has to look back to Berlioz' *Requiem* (1837) for the real parallel. Nevertheless, Walton fulfils his object without having recourse to extremes. It is true that he writes for two brass bands and a few additional wood-wind instruments, but these can be dispensed with, if necessary. They are not exaggerations, but luxuries. Walton, accordingly, is perfectly reasonable in his demands and such is his mastery of orchestration that the reduced forces do not diminish the necessary weight behind the choral tone. The additions add volume, but not intensity.

Belshazzar's Feast, by its scope and resourcefulness, by its suggestion of barbaric splendour, by its total lack of pretentiousness and bombast, makes every other work of its kind sound small and pygmy-like by comparison. Others have tried to do the same, but have succeeded only in showing their own grandiloquence, or proving their inadequacy.

Walton's cathedral choir experience is here shown in the opening chorus, "By the Waters of Babylon", which could have been written only by one familiarised subconsciously by the music of the early polyphonic composers. Elsewhere, the choir has a difficult but not insurmountable task. The chief difficulty is that of fatigue, and there are few works which so require a vital conductor on the top of his form to sustain the performers in their efforts. A conductor lacking in imagination can make the whole thing flop. All the performers, players and singers together, have to imagine themselves *in the scene*. Questions of attack are not as difficult in execution as they appear on paper, and Walton does his choir the honour of realising that they would not tackle the work were they not an able body of singers.

The immensely dramatic passages are thrilling. To single out any one is invidious, but one may point to those at the words "Thou, O King, art King of Kings" and "O King, live for ever", for here is the maximum amount of effect obtained with the simplest of harmonic means. The choral writing for the songs of praise to the gods is actually more satisfactory and convincing than that for the rejoicing at the liberation. Perhaps the barbaric splendour of Belshazzar's Court made a greater appeal to Walton's imagination; but all through there is complete mastery of medium. The shout when Belshazzar is slain may, perhaps, have been suggested by that of "Barabbas" in the *St. Matthew Passion*, but, if so, it in no way affects its effectiveness. The Narrator's part, in a kind of ornamental recitative, is very cleverly done and one now regards the old-fashioned type of narration, with its punctuating chords, as being perfunctory to an extreme. This one single solo voice rather underbalances the rest of the work, since the single voice seems disproportionate to the rest. A sense of strain on the part of the singer is inevitable, but one can think of no other way of doing it. Sacheverell Sitwell's text, drawn from various parts of the Bible, was considered unsuitable for a Three Choirs' Festival. This is a narrowminded attitude. Whenever the story is read in the First Lesson, the moral remains, and some of the actual words appear with no noticeable act of vengeance taking place. Since the whole thing preaches the sermon of religious morality and principle, it is difficult to discern the objection, especially since the singers are not *really* praising the God of Brass, etc.

The splendours of *Belshazzar's Feast* were followed by the *Symphony* which was "bound to come".[1] Here Walton showed admirable restraint, and his action in first forbidding performance and later permitting it without the last movement, reserving completion of the work until he got the right thoughts, was a lesson to the many "Smart Alecs" of composers who write an opera before breakfast, a symphony during the meal, and a orchestral work before lunch, with a quartet or two thrown in in case anyone should think they have been lazy. Walton was reproached in some quarters for allowing incomplete performance, but his hand was forced by Sir Hamilton Harty (1879-1941), who knew that excitement over the work had already risen high and must not be allowed to die down. In this *Symphony* Walton provides the purely orchestral parallel to *Belshazzar's Feast*. I have suggested elsewhere[2] that the opening of the work refers unexpectedly to Bruckner's *Romantic Symphony*, where the music moves, horn-like, equally leisurely and suggestively. This is no disparagement, and does not imply that Walton deliberately followed this example or that he even thought of that work. It suggests, however, that Walton's capacity and scope reminds one of Bruckner, and also of Mahler. It is possible that he may finish up by forming a complete link with the older Viennese School of symphonic composers.

Walton's *Symphony* is wider in resource than either of Elgar's, the only British works with which it can be paralleled, but it is infinitely less approachable. Again, he shows his vitality and power, and listening to the work is an exhausting process. This does not apply to the *Violin Concerto* (1939), which was composed for Jascha Heifetz. This is purely virtuoso music. Once more the order of the movements is altered, the first being an andante, and once more Walton subjected the work to revision—this is always disconcerting to those who have bought the first edition or version and try to follow from that copy, although it is extraordinarily instructive. It may be said of this *Concerto* that the wealth of material is considerable and that never once is the solo violin overbalanced or driven to a losing contest with the orchestra.

The *Symphony* and *Violin Concerto* are notable contributions to world music, for Walton, although never in any instance following

[1] *César Franck*, Vincent d'Indy (The Bodley Head), apropos Franck's *Symphony*.
[2] *The Symphony: Its History and Development*. (In preparation).

the central European ideal, is immediately exportable. The two works contain a level consistency, the *Concerto* naturally being the more lyrical of the two. Walton does not abide by any formal customs in either work, although analysis shows thematic continuity and expansion. As in the case of the *Sinfonia Concertante*, the material grows out of cellules. The issues are joined with some considerable strife, but the results are never in doubt.

I have already referred to the supplanting of *Portsmouth Point* by *Scapino*, and the disappearance of the former is as surprising as the lack of impact made by Walton's other choral and orchestral work, *In Honour of the City of London* (1937), a cantata composed for the Leeds Festival. Perhaps it is but following in the steps of similar festival cantatas, but it is difficult to understand why. Formally, it is most interesting since it is devised as a set of variations upon the theme associated with the praise of London. Another work which has disappeared is the ballet *The Quest* (1943) written for Sadler's Wells. This is completely incredible, since Walton's peculiar rhythmic sense is admirable for ballet and such a sense is not a frequent feature in our music.

Within the last few years Walton has turned to chamber music, his contrapuntal facility being in every way suitable for the purpose of the *String Quartet*. He has also written a *Sonata* (1939) for Yehudi Menuhin. This apparent reaction from the big forms has caused some unrest, many critics being unable to dissociate themselves from his usual style. I quote from a criticism which is typical of much unthinking nonsense written about these works. It concerns the *Violin Sonata*:

> . . . shows still more markedly than the *String Quartet* the decline—or relaxation—of his powers that this composer has allowed to take place. The old vitality and originality is replaced by easy-going reliance on a certain type of harmonic cliché, rightly disdained by many composers far inferior to Walton, and with far less mastery even of such clichés.[1]

This is unreasonable, and suggests that Walton should spend the rest of his life composing an endless succession of Belshazzar's Feasts. The fact is that Walton, even if his chamber works may not be sensational, is but right to give his brain rest and refreshment, and since whatever he has written so far has added something to the richness of

[1] Colin Mason in *The Chesterian* (July, 1950).

music, these works are acceptable in every way. His opera will be awaited with the greatest interest.

It remains to mention Walton's film music. This is often a sore point, for there are many who have succumbed to the necessary but fatal fascination of the pound sterling and, in their anxiety to keep other people out, have turned themselves into film studios' hacks. A composer has to be extraordinarily eclectic to refrain from specialisation, if he is to convince on the screen. Few are so gifted to the extent that they can turn out music for contrasted types of films and remain genuine. Walton's *Crown Imperial* (1937) showed him gifted with an eye for pageantry and grandeur, even if Elgar gave his pen an inevitable prod in the middle section. Consequently, *Henry V* and *Hamlet* were almost made for him. It must be admitted that the excerpts from these scores are not as satisfactory as some try to make out because of the exigencies of the footages. The same applies to the "Spitfire Prelude and Fugue" from *The First of the Few,* which, lively and vital as it is, is over all too quickly. On the other hand, *Went the Day Well* contains some good "bands" which, as far as I can ascertain, have not been released for separate performance.

Walton has always brought the fullest sense of artistic integrity to whatever he has been doing. He has not had the advantages which have fallen in the paths of some others, for the first requisites for constant performance in this country are publication and money. Performance can be obtained to a limited extent without the former, but not universality. Financial resources which enable guarantees to be given against box-office loss and the costs of production, no matter from where they emanate, are becoming more and more essential and the composer so fortunate to have these behind him can make a comfortable income from performing rights alone which, in the aggregate, mount up to a considerable sum. Hence the composer with money can do more than he without, and while it would not be at all right to deprecate every composer who has such luck on his side, the principle works to the disadvantage of music in general and can give completely false valuations. Walton, therefore, does not deride the film score, and he saves his fame artistically by accepting only those which appeal to him.

His position is that he leads twentieth-century native music and is well ahead of his contemporaries by reason of his scope, his resource, and his genius. There are plenty of composers (there always have been) with talent and knack. Walton drives his genius hard and rarely lets it rest, for he ponders upon his thoughts and will not release them until he is sure that he can perfect them only in small details. Of all composers in the present-day repertoire, he is, as I have indicated, one of the few really exportable as a model of English music because he has never gone a-whoring after Continental systems, "-isms" and "-alities". His polyphonic strength gives his music its sinews, as, indeed, it would do to any composer; but there is more in it than mere contrapuntal facility. He is the only composer of his generation with sufficient stamina to claim descent from the earlier figures who have made music as powerful as his. He stands in his own time as did Berlioz in his, and Strauss and Holbrooke in theirs. It is difficult to see any signs at the moment that he is likely ever to become dated; but this is naturally not a point upon which one can dogmatise at this stage. He is a figurehead to which the rising generation should look, and from which they can learn. His characteristics lie in certain harmonic and rhythmic twists which have to be looked for rather than in anything directly tangible; but these are by no means clichés. While composers have been experimenting in the expansion of harmony or deploring the fact that harmony is no longer expandible, Walton has been quietly (paradoxical though it may seem) showing that the solution lies in counterpoint.

His is the music of one with but a single target in view, and he refuses to be deflected from it. It is the music of an honest and sincere man, like that of Bliss.[1] Walton's musical masculinity and his masterly workmanship—every composer worthy of the name can stand examination of his craft—place him in the forefront. In this respect he takes his place beside the older Roussel, Milhaud and Honegger, and from this quartet the future is likely to become manifest.

[1] See page 122.

CHAPTER FIFTEEN

THE GERMAN TRAGEDY

Bruch (1838-1920)—*Reger* (1873-1916)—*Pfitzner* (1869-1950)—*Strauss* (1864-1949)—[*Rheinberger* (1839-1901)]—*Karg-Elert* (1877-1933)

TOWERING over the musical scene at the change of the centuries, the figure of Richard Strauss (1864-1949) completely dominated musical thought in all the Nordic countries of Europe. The Latin races, with their Gallic lightness, their Roman passion for theatrical display, and their Hispanic craving for rhythm and colour, generally resisted the influence (an exception was the Italian composer, Ottorino Respighi (1879-1936) whose *Sinfonia Drammatica* (1914) is written in the technique of Strauss). By 1900 Strauss had composed most of the works by which his name will be remembered, and from then to the end of his life his output showed a decline and a revival in a few stage works which differ in style from his concert music. Strauss represented the militarism of Kaiserdom and the superiority of the German people as a "master race"—this aspect of the later Hitlerian theory was nothing new. The difference between the Straussian and Elgarian representation of their respective periods and cultures was the same as that between English and German Imperialism. Germany was rapidly approaching the moment when she was bound to explode. The inherent gross coarseness of her culture, and her insolent attitude to that of others tended to this one end. In England the new Sovereign attempted, with some skill and with no little sense of humour (which he kept within due diplomatic bounds), to stem the tide of German military and naval expansion, and while he lived the Kaiser remained in awe of this country. Consequently, there was almost universal peace among big nations. However, cultural expansion could not be prevented, nor was there any occasion for so doing. In Germany this expansion implied not a forward progress in artistic aesthetics, but a building-up of the *kolossal* in every direction—pictures on grandiose subjects, sculpture more than life-size, and orchestras swollen out to ever-increasing proportions. Nothing small made the slightest appeal.

Here, German musicians, particularly conductors, held key posts, but on the other side certain British composers (Stanford, Elgar and Smyth, for example) received performances in Germany—the last-named winning a battle against odds completely overwhelming to anyone less persistent. At the same time there was always the feeling over our music that it served to demonstrate the superiority of German-ism. That this was not absolutely universal was shown when Strauss promoted the performance of *The Dream of Gerontius* at Düsseldorf in 1901, and after the performance raised his glass in honour of "the *Maestro*, Edward Elgar".

The other composers in Germany were a good workaday lot with-out any special marks of genius. Max Bruch (1838-1920) remains alive through his first *Violin Concerto in G minor*, a work strongly redolent of Brahms; the beautiful second movement is typical of the best type of German romanticism. The two other *Concertos* made no impression for the reason that they sound too similar. Max Reger (1873-1916) was a figure apart, with a basically contrapuntal technique. Remarkably prolific in the polyphonic manner, composition appeared to come easily to him. He was the first post-Bach composer to think instinctively in terms of counterpoint, and his music is as complicated as Bach's is clear. Reger wrote quantities of organ music which require a second person to control the registration. Both hands and both feet are kept so fully occupied with playing the notes that there is no oppor-tunity for stop-changing. He brought this polyphonic style to the orchestra, with the result that a work like the *Sinfonietta* is a mere jumble of sound. On the other hand, his mind was particularly suited to *Variations upon a Theme*. Here the thought is usually pianistic, and, consequently, the texture is markedly clear. His many sets of *Variations* upon themes by Ferdinand Hiller, Beethoven, Mozart and himself provide students with the perfect text-books for amplified variation. The themes in some of these disappear almost as soon as they have been announced, reappearing triumphantly at the conclusion as if to say, "Here we are. Had you forgotten us?"[1] These works usually conclude with a well-wrought fugue, which is exhilarating, and in the case of the *Variations on a theme by Mozart* (the theme

[1] Paul Dukas.

being that of the *Piano Sonata in A* (K.·331)), there is an unexpected
air of delicacy which, in the ordinary way, was absent from Reger's
nature. His was the most scholarly mind of the period in Germany,
and he combined classicism with romanticism extremely successfully.
A man of overbearing egotism, a beer-drinker *par excellence*, he typi-
fied a certain Teutonic type which thought nobody any good except
itself, and no music outside Germany of the slightest interest or significance.

Reger excelled in chamber music, and his *Violin Sonatas* are remarkable works, worthy to be placed beside those of Brahms. The *String
Quartets* do not sound as crowded as one might expect, although the
texture is as thick as he could make it, and there is a general atmosphere
of busy-ness about them. The great strength of his music is artificially
contrived, and he often obtained the semblance of power through sheer
contrapuntal impulse. His setting of *Psalm CL* can be placed next
to Bruckner's (1824–1896) *Requiem* and *Te Deum*, but Reger's
work lacks the imaginative qualities which characterise the Austrian
composer, and he treats the Almighty as an equal.

The romanticism of Strauss had its counterpart in that of Hans
Pfitzner (1869-1950), a composer completely unknown in this country,
although vaguely familiar by name through his opera *Palestrina*,
a masterly and lengthy work, for the most part in the polyphonic
manner. He was a thinker and a metaphysician. *Palestrina* is funda-
mentally a revelation of the composer's aims and objects, and indicates
that final victory which will surely crown the endeavours of the
true artist. Pfitzner was an admirer of Schumann and Wagner. From
the latter he received the doctrine of redemption through sacrifice;
Der arme Heinrich and *Die Rose von Liebesgarten* both signify this.
From Schumann he took the warm-hearted romantic feeling expressed
in Schumann's Symphonies. *Palestrina* is written in the mould of
Die Meistersinger. If one can say that Pfitzner ever wrote a work
popular in his own country, then *Palestrina* is that work. Pfitzner
was a man of strong feelings and dogmatic expression. The battle
he fought for romanticism against the contemporary modernism
made him many enemies and, as usual, personal feelings stood in the
way of his music. His final joy came when he was presented with the
"Ehrenring" of the Vienna Philharmonic[1] a few weeks before his
death. This was certainly a very late joy, but it gladdened the old man's

[1] The equivalent of the Royal Philharmonic Society's Gold Medal.

heart and softened the material wants of his last days. He forms a striking parallel in this respect with England's treatment of Delius.[1] Pfitzner, who has been called the last of the romanticists emanating from Weber and Schumann, had the misfortune to be swamped by the more spectacular and virtuosic Richard Strauss.

Strauss did not score instantaneous successes with those works for which he is admired to-day, but by 1898 he had become established and had reached the apex of his career with *Ein Heldenleben,* which was to have its autobiographical parallel in 1903 in the *Symphonia Domestica.* In the former, Strauss played the rôle of the persecuted martyr, constantly harassed by enemies (the critics). The vainglory and bombast of this work epitomises the whole German individuality. Between this work and 1900 Strauss wrote nothing but songs. He then produced the opera *Feuersnot,* completed in 1901. This was but the prelude to the *Symphonia Domestica* and *Salome* (1906). *Feuersnot* was the last word in eroticism and human lust—or so it seemed at the time. Its powerful tragedy was just the thing to satisfy the prevalent animalism of the Germans which was to culminate in sheer brutality and barbarism. The virtuosic use of the orchestra reached its attainment here, and in no later work did Strauss combine so much musical sensuality with sheer technique.

Salome signifies the final word in what opera-mongers describe as "dramatic force".[2] The situations require not only magnificent staging, but vivid imagination. At the climax, Strauss shows the banality of thought to which he could descend at moments when it might be imagined that he would have risen to great heights. The "Dance of the Seven Veils", which should be the very perfection of climax, comes right down to earth, and the poor quality of the themes is barely covered by the purple-patched orchestration. What in that period was regarded as great music and great opera is now slightly entertaining. One admires the genius of the orchestration and the obvious ability to handle immensely powerful situations, but the whole thing has become tawdry and garish. Its sickly passion no longer appeals to generations nurtured on war and long since bored with pornography. The Grand Manner in the theatre, the out-Wagnered Wagnerism, very nearly sang itself to a standstill. There was to be one more drama

[1] Page 128.

[2] The Italian counterpart can be seen in the earlier *Cavalleria Rusticana* (1889), by Pietro Mascagni (1863-1945), that composer's only successful work.

in the inflated manner, *Elektra* (1909), which gained respect rather than admiration and was as beastly as the others, for Strauss had found the secret of over-emphasisation of subject in the music. In 1911 came the revelation of *Der Rosenkavalier*, a work equally erotic, but expressed in such a charming manner as to be utterly inoffensive.

Strauss was fortunate in his librettist. Hugo von Hofmannsthal (1874-1929) may not have been a great poet or a greater dramatist than the famous Eugene Scribe (1791-1861), that inveterate purveyor of libretti to Parisian composers, but both were magnificent writers of "opera books" and knew the essentials to their fullest extent. The collaboration between Strauss and von Hofmannsthal was perfect, although it may be that the Strauss apparatus was too heavy for the subject. Strauss in *Der Rosenkavalier* turned to Vienna, translating the colour of that city and her history into beautiful music. It was from this moment that he began to be approachable, forsaking nastiness for delightful coquetry. *Der Rosenkavalier* is his only opera really to have established itself in the repertoire, in spite of many attempts with the others. However, *Capriccio*[1] made such a deep impression at the Edinburgh Festival of 1950 that it may possibly find a niche for itself. The same Festival revived the two-way affair called *Ariadne auf Naxos* and *Le Bourgeois Gentilhomme*, composed in 1912 and revised in 1919. This charming little work, however, is not Gallic in quality where it ought to be. *Ariadne auf Naxos* is the opera contained within Molière's play *Le Bourgeois Gentilhomme*; it represents the work written by M. Jourdain's music-master and performed, together with a burlesque, in M. Jourdain's house. The suite named after the play consists of the incidental music and attendant ballets. In isolation this music is perfectly delightful and sparkles from start to finish. The "Entrance and Dance of the Fencing Master"—full of bluster and sword passes— the "Dance of the Tailor"— a charming minuet-quasi-waltz—the "Dinner", are all in every way ingratiating and delightful. Strauss makes one concession to Molière's period in the Lullyian Minuet, which he scores in the style of his own period while maintaining the older spirit. In the full stage setting the music simply does not fit and it has a tendency to switch from Versailles to Schönbrunn. Doubtless it were better that Strauss should have remained himself rather than have written pastiche. M. Romain Rolland[2] mentions Strauss' enthusiasm for Charpentier's *Louise*, an enthusiasm shared equally

[1] Described as a "Conversation Piece".   [2] *Musiciens d'Aujourdhui.*

by Gustav Mahler. *Ariadne auf Naxos,* however, is simply a Strauss opera with interpolations sufficiently burlesque to mark a sharp dividing line. In this respect the music fits all right, and the score is filled with those long tunes of which Strauss was such a master, and which, when written for singers, give them such glorious opportunities.

Strauss will live for certain constituent elements. One is his mastery of this long tune, which can be found everywhere, and it will suffice to mention the "Donna Anna" tune in *Don Juan* and the "Dulcinea" one in *Don Quixote,* the former serious in intention, the latter a parody. Another element is the shape of the themes, which have arc and breadth and, in the rapid moments, leap and bound energetically. Harmonically he said the final word in romanticism. While adhering firmly to tonality, he delighted in sudden changes of key, in many cases through a Neapolitan Sixth. However, best of all was his knowledge of the orchestra. Strauss' horn parts, like Elgar's trombones, are models for all time. The springy theme with which *Till Eulenspiegel* opens covers almost the entire range of the instrument; the magnificent horn theme in the last part of *Don Juan,* which shouts defiance to the Statue, and the opening of *Der Rosenkavalier* are striking instances of his melodic qualities on the instrument; in every work he makes the horns climb worm-like through the texture until they reach the climax upon the apex of their range. Strauss is owed a great debt by British composers of his period. He taught them how to write for the orchestra. He led their ideas away from the grey classical tints of Brahms and gave them a virtuosic directive. The danger of this lay in the fact that often the results were not commensurate with the labour entailed, but orchestral players found that for the first time they could regard themselves as orchestral soloists.

Strauss was a curious paradox. Apart from his personal dissimilarity to his music, he seems to have had little self-criticism and was happy in the thought that his orchestral virtuosity would draw attention away from certain commonplaces, and even raise the standard and quality of his banalities. *An Alpine Symphony* (1915), in which every type of weather, fauna and flora are experienced—never was there such an exciting day spent on any mountain—is typical of an elaborate score for a documentary film. There is hardly anything which can be singled out as first-rate except the graphic delineation of the subject, which is superbly done. The quality of a tune like that applied to transfiguration in *Tod und Verklärung,* written as early as 1889, shows that even at the time when his gifts were at their highest, he tried to make pure majesty of tone and grandiose presentation elevate a triviality to the height of magnificence. This is one of the signs which indicate his lack of a sense of proportion. It is possible that he suffered many things from the critics in his early days, for his ultra-Lisztian concept of programme music consorted oddly with the outlook of pure German music; but it is doubtful if the enormous battle in *Ein Heldenleben* really represents the matter in due proportion. If this shattering din, full of insistent rhythm and trumpet calls, represents merely critical vitriol, then a real battle to the actual death must be undelineatable. Similarly, the *Symphonia Domestica,* in accordance with its programme, is a distortion of the situations it attempts to delineate. Apart from its personal impulse, this is a work of real constructional mastery, and symphonic in the fullest sense of the term. Virtuosic it certainly is, but it is a real *symphony,* its programme not being as integral a part of the whole as Strauss imagined.

This family portrait album in the romantic style, where all modesty and domestic restraint are put on one side, which attempts to portray twenty-four hours in the daily life of the Strauss family, a period presumably typical of the routine of that household, culminating in the baby's bath after some Herculanean games, and ending with a conjugal love scene, proclaimed him as the complete egotist and confirmed the suspicions aroused by *Ein Heldenleben* in this respect. He said that he considered himself interesting enough to justify a musical autobiography: he may have said it in a spirit of mischief or bravado; but it was taken seriously. The answer lies in the fact that the work has received a great many performances and has been the argument-ground of critics and experts ever since it was first performed. However, the programme not being essential to a satisfactory musical comprehension and appreciation of the work, we can regard it as a well-planned and masterly symphony in which all the devices and processes of symphonic expansion are carried out in the classical manner, including that of double fugue.

The texture is flowery and Strauss pays little heed to traditional matters. This has always been one of his characteristics, but what was iconoclastic in the late nineteenth century is, of course, everyday technique in the twentieth. Strauss can provide examples of polytonality in various works, in *Elektra,* for example, while the screaming sevenths in *Salome* are every bit as "modern" as Milhaud—but Strauss did not use this type of progression consistently. He reserved it for specific occasions. With a lesser composer this might well have resulted in the upset of harmonic balance; but the process falls into line with the rest of the thought, owing to the exuberance of the orchestration. The combination of his own themes in *Ein Heldenleben,* which originally called forth the frenzied wrath of the critics and pedants, now sounds perfectly logical, and not in the least shocking. Richter's remark that one could combine a hundred themes provided that one did not mind what they sounded like is as true now as it has always been; but Strauss was too good a musician to adopt this easy way out. If, as has been suggested, he is the last of the tonal composers—it will be seen later that Mahler was the last of the diatonic ones—he is also the last of the ebulliently vulgar type. Vulgar music has, of course, been written by others since his last works, but no one has played so blatantly with vulgarity on the orchestra.

After the Hitlerian usurpation of power, when music became regimented to the Master State, Strauss developed into a mere Kapellmeister. His later works show a youthful polyphony in their return to the classical manner, and had memories of *Don Juan* (1888), *Till Eulenspiegel* (1894-1895) and *Don Quixote* (1897) not remained, he would have passed in the concert hall for a worthy composer of worthy German music, and one well within the tradition of the nineteenth century. The operas have disappeared—the recent production of *Salome*[1] indicated that they had more period than musical interest—but *Der Rosenkavalier* could stand as representative of any composer even if there were nothing else by which he could be judged. It is true to say that no other composer, not even Wagner, has so bestrode "the world like a Colossus".

There remains one more notable figure in the decline and death of German music, one who was content to work obscurely in the organ loft, like his more distinguished predecessor, Josef Rheinberger (1839-1901). Sigfrid Karg-Elert (1877-1933) was in the direct line from J. S. Bach. His books of *Chorale-Improvisations* contain chorale-preludes of great beauty and fine inspiration. They succeed where those of Max Reger fail, in that they are more evocative, more subtly wrought and more obviously inspired. The small genre of the *Chorale-Prelude,* one for scholars and church-goers, is capable of the highest flight of musical invention and resource. It represents an offering upon the altar to

[1] 1950.

Almighty God to His Glory. Within its limited range, it has the power
of placing men's minds upon a high spiritual plane through its spiritual
impulse. It elaborates and glorifies a simple tune yet fulfils its message
by reason of its simplicity of elaboration. The "Prelude on a Hymn
Tune", as composed by English organist-composers, is not quite the
same thing, although Parry and Charles Wood (1866-1926) utilised
many of the devices found in Bach. It has not the attraction to higher
things that is one of the *Chorale-Preludes'* strongest features, possibly
because the chorale has more dignity than the average hymn tune.

The genre appeals to the few, therefore, but in the doleful panorama
of German music, after the blare and bombast of the Grand Manner,
it indicated, through Karg-Elert, that Germany, if she would but turn
her eyes right back to the seventeenth century, was still capable of
producing small and beautiful gems. Perhaps the lessons of the 1914-
1918 War had not been in vain. These hopes, however, were frustrated
by the rise to power of Adolf Hitler.

Up to this moment Germany had been receptive to all the latest
ideas, and the most modern composers of Europe found no difficulty
in having their works produced there. Many operas from France were
performed with great success, and the German people, emancipated
from militarism (for the time being), were able to grasp that the old
nineteenth-century romanticism had gone for good. Hitler, however,
stopped all that.

Like the Kaiser, he posed as an artistic authority, but he became
obsessed with the idea that *le dernier cri* was communistic in origin. He
held everything outside the tradition of nineteenth-century German
romanticism to be degenerate—in other words, the new music made
people think, and this Hitler wanted to avoid as much as possible. His
Exhibitions of Degenerate Art in which the pictures of Paul Klee,
Picasso and other artists of the *avant-garde* were exhibited for derisory
purposes and gramophone records were available in cubicles for
playing the degenerate works of Stravinsky, Schoenberg, Milhaud
(but not Bartok, who protested vigorously at his exclusion[1]), had the
opposite effect to that which was intended. The Exhibitions were too
well attended and it gradually dawned upon the sluggish official Nazi
mind that possibly the interest was veering in the wrong direction.

Nazi music was deplorable because it was reactionary. Reaction is
all right if it works away from something really bad, but from radio

[1] Page 267.

performances of "Contemporary German Music" it seemed that everyone had gone back to a Schumann apparently incapable of giving vent
to any but the most commonplace ideas. This music was not for export;
that is to say, it remained a national product and was not exploited even
in those few countries sympathetic to the "ideals" of National Social-
ism. Perhaps the perpetrators were ashamed of it; perhaps they feared
scorn and derision, for the Nazi could not bear to be laughed at. In the
other direction Hitler was not prepared to let his followers be polluted
by foreign music, even if it were written by officially and physically
confirmed pure Gentiles. Once more the old idea of the superiority
of German art proclaimed itself and Hans Sachs' ringing line, "Despise
not then our German Masters"—as if anyone ever had—became a
political tag. German music in its own estimation was the acme of
excellence since it was concocted by the Master Race.

This probably had something to do with the fiat of the late Dr. Josef
Goebbels, who, in 1936, forbade all musical criticism save by duly
qualified people. Instead, the small critics were told to consider rather
than criticise. On the surface this does not seem a bad idea until it is
realised that the critics were thus coming within the circle of the official
directive and the officially approved article. It followed that not even
the qualified experts were allowed to praise any work by a Jewish
artist, but since such things were abolished altogether, the situation
could hardly have arisen. Looking at it from the constructive side, it
certainly forbade loose thinking and condemnation on any grounds
other than those arrived at after due consideration. The hacks, the little
people, the eternal condemnators-on-principle must have been made to
think rather more than was their wont, and it stopped the writing of
"Press notices" of new works on the bus between the concert halls and
the German equivalents of Fleet Street. However, as criticism has never
either harmed or strengthened a cause in the long run, the whole thing
was needless so far as the composers were concerned. It will not be
out of place to quote in entirety the extract from the *Neue Zeitschrift
für Musik* which appears in Dr. Percy Scholes' invaluable *Oxford
Companion to Music,*[1] since the National Socialist doctrine was never
publicly disclosed in full over here. The article appeared in March,
1933, and ran as follows:

"Since January 30th, when Adolf Hitler took over the leader-
ship of the German Government, there have come nearer to realis-

[1] Published by O.U.P.

ation all the hopes of German musicians in the Reich and those across the borders. . . . Soon again German opera houses will give bread to German opera singers, and become homes for the cultivation of German music. In our concert halls we shall witness the re-entry of German artists and German works. German universities and German music schools will give refuge once more to German scholars and German teachers who may be trusted to guide our youth to the great masters of German music. German schools will again become the cradle of German folk-song. German homes—freed from the alien pest—will resound again with works bequeathed to the German people by German masters. German publishers will feel renewed desire to encourage German composers and to issue German works. The German radio system will recognise its primary duty to cultivate German art. The German phonograph (*sic*) industry will finally be compelled to realise that only German music, performed by German artists, belongs to the German home. . . . A cycle and a new period of culture have begun. . . . Through Adolf Hitler's achievements a new epoch dawns in the German cultural life, and as a consequence, also in German musical life. [1]

The operative word will be found in the sentence dealing with the "phonograph business"—"compelled". The main idea was to prevent anyone showing the "Master Art" to its disadvantage, and as 90 per cent. of criticism is destructive anyhow, it prevented the totality rising to 100 per cent. The chief offences committed by the policy were the consequent banning of anything from abroad, and the restriction of composers to writing in a style at once comprehensible to the ordinary person. A similar situation arose in Soviet Russia, both political systems setting their faces resolutely against importation lest it might suggest that their "Art" was retrogressive in comparison with that of others.

Ever since the beginning of the foreign cultural invasion of this country by Germans, the general attitude has been to regard us as still being, figuratively speaking, stained with woad where creative art is concerned, and the position has been aggravated by the number of not in any way distinguished musicians who found refuge here and in America. It is true that among the dross much gold was to be found, but it has taken some considerable time to separate natural sympathy for humans in distress from recognition of genuine knowledge and

[1] My typewriter threatens to continue writing the word "German" of its own accord.

SIR WILLIAM WALTON (1902)

PAUL HINDEMITH

Jean Sibelius (1865)

Jean Sibelius
Hon. R.A.M.

merit. Comparatively few of these refugees have expressed any strong desire to return home and rebuild their native culture. In isolated instances the cultures of the receiving countries have gained by the presence of really prominent men and women in all branches of art and science, whether refugees of their own accord or from political impulse. Who shall say that America is not the better for the practice and teaching of Ernest Bloch, Igor Stravinsky, Arnold Schoenberg, Paul Hindemith, and Darius Milhaud? In reverse, it is certain that Milhaud returned to France with his own particular genius widened by sojourn in America, and his mixing with Americans and American ideas.

This country received only a few of outstanding note in their own lands. Certain musicologists have given us the benefit of their knowledge,[1] but this has in no way added to our culture. One notable exception, from Vienna, will be considered in his proper place.

To-day, Germany stands in an uncertain state. It will be some considerable time before Nazi stultification is overcome. Doubtless there are many composers with leanings towards a new Teutonism, based upon the realities of the technique of to-day rather than upon the heavy romanticism of the past: but these are as yet an unknown quality and quantity, and the future will depend upon whether the rising generation will consent to learn or not. The next fifty years will decide the matter. In the meantime, the leader of the present-day thought (for Germans seemingly must be led at all costs) should by right be Paul Hindemith; but his residence in America would appear to preclude any direct influence. He is the only German composer of the Hitler era with any distinctive qualities, and he alone is capable of taking up the threads from the point at which they were dropped.[2]

[1] This knowledge is, generally speaking, only second-hand and not the original thought which, after all, is what interests us in any writer. The prevalent custom of larding books with quotations from other writers, thus providing a résumé rather than an individual study, is to be deplored, even if it does satisfy the snobbish craving for "scholarship". Actually, it is only *one* aspect of scholarship, for this lies in the reasoning of the individual brain of the writer. Quotation from other people's ideas and discoveries is an easy way to fame.

[2] One is here up against a problem. None of these *émigrés* write like American or English composers, and the mere signing of a name on naturalisation papers does not turn an inherent culture into any other. Nationality has begun to count for nothing at all, and in the great upheaval which has resulted in the absorption of alien characteristics into every country's life and culture, it is the nationalism of the style and idiom which matters. Unfortunately, there is no necessity for the receiving countries to send their creative artists to war-destroyed areas. Consequently there is little chance of there being any direct exchange of ideas, or of deliberate reciprocation. In fact, as Sir W. S. Gilbert so aptly puts it, "In spite of all temptations to belong to other nations", the *émigré* remains whatever he happens to have been born.

CHAPTER SIXTEEN

GEBRAUCHSMUSIK

Kurt Weill (1900-1950)—*Paul Hindemith* (1895)

THE immediate aftermath of the 1914-1918 War saw an inevitable reorientation of musical values in Germany. It is usual to ascribe the "silly season" to the activities of the young French composers; but the high jinks which came from Paris were nothing in comparison with the stupidities with which the young Germans tried to indicate the "new music". However, there was some sense underlying the nonsense. The situation was perfectly reasonable. The Great War and the defeat of an arrogant nation meant that the general policy of life in Germany had to be altogether different. Unfortunately, things went too far, and instead of being evolutionary, they became revolutionary. Nevertheless, this revolution made Germany into an open market for music, and her liberality of thought towards what had become to be recognised as "contemporary music" (its real name should have been "temporary music") made it welcome and gave it every opportunity to flourish. For the first time, French music was accepted as within the canon, and taken for granted in Germany.

The period saw the rise of self-consciousness among artists. This brought forward cliques and coteries which, in themselves, did nothing but good because they kept up a vitalising stream of energy. They worked, however, on certain broad principles which had little foundation in fact. The musician began to humble himself. He proclaimed that he was the servant of the people, with the duty of providing the people with what (he said) they wanted. This kind of self-abasement maintained outright that the creative artist was not a superior kind of person or being apart from his fellow creatures. Exactly who had ever so regarded him was never explained, but the movement found quite a large number of followers. There came into being what was known as

Gebrauchsmusik, or utility music, music composed for certain *ad hoc* instruments and occasions. Some composers went so far as to state that no music should be written unless there was a demand for it; but the theory went further than this, and it became a standing principle that all art should be immediately comprehensible to everyone all at once. There were two aspects of *Gebrauchsmusik*, therefore, and it is noteworthy that while the principle of providing music for these specific purposes and occasions still holds as good as it did before the practice became a principle, that of writing immediately comprehensible music, as distinct from light music, did not have a very long existence.

In the first place, certain postulates were put forward which assumed a non-existent situation. The most vocal of its advocates was Kurt Weill (1900-1950), who came out with the most astonishing statements. We quote from the *Berliner Tageblatt*, in the translation by M. D. Calvocoressi, which appeared in the *Musical Times* for March, 1929.[1] The Editor of the *Berliner Tageblatt* had asked certain leading musicians to write down as in the form of a lecture to children what they considered their aspect towards their own musical activity to be. Kurt Weill wrote as follows:

> I have just played to you music by Wagner and by his followers. You have seen that this music consists of so many notes that I was unable to play them all. You would have liked now and then to join in singing the tune, but this proved impossible. You also notice that the music made you feel sleepy, and drunk, as alcohol or an intoxicating drug might have done. You do not wish to go to sleep. You wish to hear music that can be understood without explanation. You probably wonder why your parents attend concerts. It is, with them, a mere matter of habit; nowadays, there are matters of greater interest to all; and if music cannot serve the interests of all, its existence is no longer justified.

This impertinence would have been laughable if it had not been said in all seriousness. It was based upon a fortuitous assumption of insincerity formulated entirely upon wishful thinking and a false valuation of what has come to be known in high-brow circles as "Social Significance". The danger of it lay in the dictatorial prosody, which told the people exactly how they ought to feel and what they really wanted.

[1] It appears also in *The Oxford Companion to Music*, Scholes (O.U.P.).

Weill, who is regarded as a composer of some importance and significance by many intelligent authorities, tried to practise what he preached. His most well-known work was *Drei Groschen Oper* (1929), a perversion of *The Beggar's Opera,* which it only slightly resembles. Weill intended to write an opera in which the music played but an occasional part and, therefore, was easily assimilable by the audience. His other known work was *The Fall of the City of Mahagonny* (1929)— a city of great wickedness—a singularly cynical composition. Weill rated the common denominator of the people at a very low level, since the music is a debased form of jazz.

Hindemith, however, regarded *Gebrauchsmusik* from another angle. He saw the composer as a jobbing workman, prepared and able to carry out work of any kind for whatever resources might be available at any moment. The composer, therefore, became a craftsman, working to time for a set purpose, instead of an artist, taking his own time and offering something from his inner consciousness for which there was no specific demand and only possible acceptation. Hindemith was not greatly concerned with any aspect other than the practical one that the players and singers should be able to perform the music, if they so desired. The application of it to contemporary facets of life played a secondary rôle.

This composition of music for certain occasions and purposes is, however, nothing new. We may go back, for example, to the French Revolution and consider the numerous *ad hoc Hymns*—to *salpêtre* (*sic*), etc. (which the representative composers of the régime had either to write or be guillotined as enemies of the Republic)—to find a not so very early authority for this. We may also think of Berlioz' *Requiem* and *Symphonie funébre* (among others), although these are extreme instances. Serious composers have often written music outside their customary orbits: Sir Walford Davies (1869-1941) composed the *March Past of the R.A.F.,* Elgar's *Pomp and Circumstance Marches* were written for marching purposes, and were intended to apply a symphonic to a utilitarian principle, while no less a person than the intensely serious-minded symphonic Vincent d'Indy composed the *Marche du 76e Regiment d'Infanterie* (1903). To-day composers are invited to compete in innumerable competitions in honour of something or other (the number of rejected symphonies and overtures must be simply enormous).

Hindemith's attitude, however, was at once broader and more

practical. He set himself to write for almost every instrument in existence.

Even if only a piccolo and double bassoon were available, and they required something to play, Hindemith was always willing to provide the necessary article. Consequently one finds his *Gebrauchsmusik* divided into categories such as *Concert Music No.* —, and *Chamber Music No.* —. He has written music for every wind instrument, but his best achievement in utility music is undoubtedly the *Philharmonic Concerto*, which treats each "department" of the orchestra as a solo group, and each player as individual soloist. This has been copied by other composers, with indifferent success, and with no acknowledgement to the initiator of the principle.

It will be admitted by even the most ardent admirer of Hindemith that the level of these works is not consistently high, as well it may not be, in view of the speed and facility with which they were written. The principle, however, remains unassailable, provided that the composer writes sincerely and genuinely, without trying to put himself upon any higher or lower level. This music is cerebral and contrived entirely upon technique. No matter at what fever heat he may have written, nobody could possibly turn out as much as Hindemith has done from sheer emotional impulse. The practical side of this utilitarian principle can be illustrated by two cases, one general, the other local.

When the death of King George V was announced, Hindemith was rehearsing his *Viola Concerto* (1927) with the B.B.C. Symphony Orchestra. He immediately expressed a wish to write an "In memoriam", a tribute in harmony with the sorrow of the British people. A room was set aside for him at Broadcasting House, paper and pens were provided, and a copyist sat in waiting. The new work was performed the next day. This showed considerable nerve on the part of the B.B.C. because after all, King George V had had a Master of his Musick whose duty it was to celebrate such an event.[1] However, it illustrated the pliability of a technique so fecund as to be almost slick; but Hindemith has never been slick, for although a craftsman, he is a master of his art as well. Slick composers have simply a knack, which is not quite the same thing.

The other, the local instance, happened during the examination for

[1] It was reported that a number of British composers were contemplating an offer of similar services to the B.B.C., proposing to turn up singly, in rapid succession; but they were dissuaded from so doing. The situation, however, would have been provocative, to say the least.

the L.R.A.M. Diploma in Bandmastership. A trombonist told me that he would like to play Hindemith's *Sonata* for trombone and piano, if I did not mind. I certainly did not, and nor did my colleagues. After his really good performance, I asked him what he liked about the work, which is a very fine one. He said that it was a real *Sonata*, and real trombone music; it was interesting and stimulating to play and had obviously been written by someone who had practical knowledge of the instrument. Further, it was a valuable item in a limited repertoire. The soldier-pianist said the same thing. I think Hindemith would have liked that performance, and it certainly afforded convincing proof that his *Gebrauchsmusik* principle had a place in the scheme of things.

Hindemith's output is enormous and varied because he has provided so much music for so many media, each of which he has studied from the practical point of view, even though he may not be an expert performer on many of them. There has rarely been such an authoritative and practical composer. As a viola-player, he is supreme, and he is one of the few composer-performers able to play his own music without completely upsetting it. He appears almost casual at times—while rehearsing the *Viola Concerto* he wandered among the orchestra and sometimes left the platform, but never missed an entry or a beat. He said that in this way he could find out all he wanted to know about the balance of the orchestra. It need hardly be said that the music is brittle and inelastic, allowing for no rubatos or other means of "interpretation".

Those who buy his books, *A Concentrated Course in Traditional Harmony* (1944) and *The Craft of Musical Composition* (1945—a revised edition of an earlier work), thinking that therein they will find authority for every kind of licence, are sorely disappointed. They find that the basic technique and conformity with all the rules of the schools is a *sine qua non*, the general idea being that since traditional harmony is necessary, this is it, and it must be adhered to. He is often blamed for trying to teach composition from a book. This shows ignorance of the book itself. Hindemith does not pretend to turn out Beethovens; his idea is to give guidance to those who are trying to apply the basic technique, lodged in the subconscious, to their own means of self-expression. He does not pretend to provide "ideas" for composers; he only shows the means of both finding and expressing any ideas they may have. His approach is directly in opposition to that of Vincent d'Indy, who considered all craft to lie entirely in the basic training, and concentrated his *Cours de Composition Musicale* on the formalistic processes and their applications. Hindemith, therefore, tries to find a point of departure; d'Indy leaves that to the individual himself. Hindemith goes further in his *Ludus Tonalis* (1943), which consists of twelve fugues in all keys, with contrasting Interludes, and Prologue and Epilogue. This he explains as "Studies in Counterpoint, Tonal Organisations, and Piano Playing" thus providing a twentieth-century counterpart to the *Forty-eight*. Thus he practises exactly what he preaches, and if the result sometimes appears rather dry, it must be remembered that a similar point of view objected to the *Forty-eight* before their emotional qualities were realised. Hindemith, however, in his deliberately neo-classical manner suggests that there can be no such emotional qualities in this music; but the future will show, and few readers of this book will be alive when that moment is reached. It will be seen later that another composer-teacher has exactly the same strict views.[1]

Hindemith was very soon stigmatised as being an atonal composer. In those early days of "-alities" and "-isms" such terms were bandied about freely and at length, with little regard for their absolute accuracy. "Modern music" in general was described as "atonal", and shunned accordingly. At the time such idioms were fashionable it was nothing unusual for an unknown composer to be asked, before he even opened the case containing his score, if his music was atonal, because, if so, "we will have nothing to do with it". The composer was, consequently, nonplussed; he knew what the questioner was driving at, but could not say definitely to the contrary because it would have entailed a long explanation of the fact that, although it did not have any tonic and was not based on key relationships, it was, nevertheless, tonal. The word "atonical" had not yet been coined. It was some while, therefore, before Hindemith was welcomed with any degree of cordiality.

Neo-classicism has the danger of lacking all sense of contrast and variety. Hindemith's polyphonic outpourings did not superficially escape this danger. The music ran about in all directions when rapid, and, when slow, indulged in manifold quasi-baroque ornamentation. Ever present was a strong rhythmic impulse; this appeared out of the contrapuntal lines and was rarely impinged upon the music for its own sake. It seemed to talk much and say little—but right from the beginning, it was always abundantly clear and transparent. The polyphony

[1] Page 211.

was directed to one end only, the full expansion of interdependent melodic lines. The usual classical processes were used, but were not arbitrarily imposed; they all seemed perfectly natural and fell into the normal scope of the music.

That they seemed of an uniform dryness was to be expected, then; nowadays, this dryness has become slightly moistened because polyphonic listening has improved and increased beyond measure. Ears are now able to listen to simultaneous elements, and the orchestral or instrumental colouring there in Hindemith's music is so clear that the lines ere long become simultaneously distinguishable. It was sometimes laid against him in those days that he rarely moved his listeners to frenzies of emotion, but this was the reaction from the pre-1920 conception of heavy romanticism, which relegated neo-classicism to the classroom. It was some little while before it dawned upon the consciousness of concert-goers that there were two concepts of music, and that the romantic one was rapidly becoming stale and faded.

Hindemith's music, however, has never been simply "sound" and nothing else and therefore it has never actually repelled listeners. He has never subscribed to any type of systematic composition and there is no question of finding out where practice ends and creation begins. This polyphonic *Gebrauchsmusik* is always sane, reasonable, and non-problematical. In due time the idiom grew softer, and lately there has appeared a clearly marked subjectivity and objectivity. This can be seen to a marked degree in his so-called *Symphony* derived from the opera *Mathis der Maler* (1929) and the later *Symphonia Serena* (1946), a work full of exquisite music such as the early Hindemith appeared to despise. His association with the theatre undoubtedly played a large part in this partial reorientation.

This theatre music did not escape the early tendencies of the utilitarian purpose, and social significance played the entire part in the opera *Neues vom Tage* (1920) whose Overture—the only moment in the opera hitherto heard in this country—contains parts for typewriters, surely one of the most rhythmic machines ever invented. This innovation in the orchestra took place solely because the subject of the opera demanded it. It shocked and horrified the purists and was regarded as a joke by those who were otherwise prepared to take whatever Hindemith might write in all seriousness. The work is founded upon the advantages of electricity in the home—in one place the local Gas Company brought an action, because it appeared to show their amenity at a disadvantage. It will be seen at once that this was another period piece, expressive of a momentary attempt to bring concrete objects into the opera house and thus align music with everyday matters. Milhaud's seriously-intended *Machines agricoles* (1919) and *Catalogue de Fleurs* are other examples of similarly dated styles. The only work of the kind capable of maintaining interest to-day is Krenek's *Johnny spielt auf* (1927), but even this, alas! has faded, since jazz has taken a different course from that of the time.

Hindemith's fine opera *Cardillac* (1926) and the beautiful ballet *Nobilissima Visione* (1938) upon which Massine created such a fine work, have been placed in the background, mainly because each work has been succeeded by something equally fine which for the moment attracts attention to itself. However, the operatic repertoire of this country has never been remarkable for its enterprise and scope, and never will be until resources are available for risks allowing the production of a great many works and leaving the public to decide their merits.

Hindemith is an example of the fate attendant upon a composer who is over-prolific and whose output has grown to such proportions that one hardly knows what to play and what to omit. Consequently, even our less moribund concert-giving organisations omit nearly everything. Before Hitler's rise to power, Hindemith's works had established themselves in the repertoire of his own country. He was among those forced to leave Germany—Furtwängler was brave enough to protest at this—and after a short time spent in organising music in Turkey, he found himself in America, first at Berkshire Academy, Stockbridge, Massachusetts, and then at Yale University. America has accordingly benefited in no small degree. Whether he will become re-established in Germany is one of those questions which cannot be answered or even guessed at yet. Political impacts on art in general have a devastating effect. It is doubtful if reactionary Soviet Russia would welcome him in her zone any more than did Hitler, for Hindemith cannot be sung by everyone immediately after the first hearing. The Western Powers would in all probability set things musical upon their feet again (thus allowing the Germans to find their own level) had they not that constant and continuous interference from the East which holds up every gesture that offers any kind of independence. The solution may be for the Germans to re-start where they left off when Hitler took over control; in that case, Hindemith will surely find his niche again, but it is doubtful if he will become universal. He is as German as Vaughan Williams is English.

His emphasis upon the craft of composition places him amongst the theoreticians (who are not the same as the theorists). He is hardly creative, but is less constructivist than Holst.[1] His fecundity is purely technical, and one can find little purely musical justification for the greater number of his works. His style is personal but negative, his thinking perfectly logical, as logical as that of Kant, whose *Critique of Pure Reason* may be placed alongside Hindemith's *Ludus Tonalis.* The general atmosphere is a chilly one. Hindemith sees no reason to welcome his listeners and he seems disinterested in their aesthetic reactions.

The distinguishing marks by which he is recognised are general rather than particular. He is one of the few whose hand is detectable from the main layout and movement of the parts rather than from any cliché or little characteristic. Broadly speaking, there is more personality about the earlier *Gebrauchsmusik* than the later, but in neither can one pick out salient features. Quotation, therefore, becomes impossible in general, and only feasible when dealing with each individual work. One would be inclined to rate the *Philharmonic Concerto,* the oratorio *Das Unaufhörliche* and the *Symphonia Serena* as his most representative works, since they stand surety for three phases; but this is entirely personal and is neither more accurate nor more inaccurate than any other assessment. It suggests that the standard of his music is surprisingly level, but emphasises the negative qualities referred to.

In America Hindemith deals with a large number of young people. Not being a spectacular composer, and developing rapidly into what the French call a *Maître,* it is possible that he will take his place in history by the side of such people as d'Indy, Stanford, and Corder, and his compositions may be (wrongly) overshadowed by his pedagogy. His influence is now restricted to the confines of Yale and her students. As a world influence, Hindemith now plays a very small part, and his trend to romanticism has disappointed those who saw in him the seed of the renaissance of abstract classicism. His power falls below that of Arnold Schoenberg,[2] who, intentionally or otherwise, has altered the course of several young and extremely voluble composers, and has deviated music herself from certain well-established paths. Hindemith's

[1] See page 136.
[2] See page 211.

neo-classicism does not set up any difficulties. It pursues an even course, and neither Hindemith nor his followers feel constrained to issue apologia or detailed proclamations as to the exact situation of the canon at the latest moment.

His early European pupils have now arrived at maturity. Their work is always perfect in technique and construction, clear in texture and singularly lacking in feeling, and their acidity is easily assimilated into the normal course of the twentieth-century outlook. Hindemith is a figure to respect and admire; his lovable qualities escape the majority.

CHAPTER SEVENTEEN

THE AUSTRIAN DEBACLE
Mahler (1860-1911)—*Schreker* (1878-1934)—*Hauer* (1883)—*Wellesz* (1885)

THE difference between German and Austrian culture is not always appreciated, and people, from Hitler upwards, have often intermingled the two by reason of the common language. This confusion was fully illustrated by the *Anschluss*, one of Hitler's greatest errors of judgment, an error born of ignorance. The whole approach to life of the Austrian is completely different from that of the German. The Austrian is peace-loving and basically happy; the German is bellicose and lustful after power. There is a polish and a humanity about the Austrian which the German has never achieved. The quality of Austrian music is infinitely less violent and aggressive than is German; its romanticism is spiritual rather than subjective, its atmosphere equally erudite where erudition is necessary, but lighter. It may suffice to show the difference by saying that Mozart, Schubert and Bruckner[1] were Austrians, while Beethoven, Schumann and Brahms were Germans.

The leading Austrian composers towards the latter end of the nineteenth century were Anton Bruckner and Gustav Mahler (1860-1911). Mahler was by birth what is now called a Czech, having been born in Kališt, a village in Bohemia. He became an Austrian by residence and so easily absorbed Austrian culture that he is distinguishable for his land of birth only by certain little traits recognisable by the initiated, but otherwise passed unnoticed; these traits are aesthetic rather than technical or idiomatic. The *Symphonies* of Bruckner did not reach the turn of the centuries, but those of Mahler, from the *Fourth* onwards, belong definitely to the twentieth century. The last eleven years of his life were, therefore, the most prolific.

Mahler was in his way as big a figure as was Strauss in his, but he

[1] I do not suggest that Bruckner was a "light" composer; but he was never turgid.

preferred the harder path of Symphony to the spectacular one of Opera or Symphonic Poem. There is nothing hysterically sensational about Mahler. His was an intensely spiritual subjectivism. No matter what his private life may have been, there is no reflection of it in his music. He and Strauss, therefore, form the complete paradox. There is no concern with physical passion in his works and they are tinged with an overwhelming sadness and melancholy. Mahler was a man who suffered much, spiritually. His sympathies went with a burning idealism which he knew would be unattained. He shared his pity between humans and animals, and the future of mankind was a question of intense feeling with him. Jewish by birth, he was baptised into the Roman Catholic Church, but his Jewish love for humanity was never eradicated. His was a tortured spirituality and, unlike Bruckner (who was confident in the future and in the Hereafter), Mahler's philosophy seemed to be of little use to him, and he remained defeatist to the end. Any little persecution roused Mahler's sympathy. It has been said[1] that while Bruckner, seeing a hunt in full cry, ran with the hunters and hounds, Mahler immediately ran with the hunted. Bruckner did not look for death, but when it came, he followed its call with resignation. Mahler was obsessed with the fear of it. Consequently, Bruckner's music was one long glory to the Almighty, while Mahler's was a personal outpouring.

Although he wrote for large forces, Mahler never fell a victim to grandiloquence. For him the inflated orchestra was a necessity, not a luxury. In spite of several attempts, no one has succeeded in reducing his scores to any reasonable size commensurate with adequacy for the expression of the ideas. In this respect he showed his romanticism and his use and feeling for necessitous orchestral tints. The charge of vulgarity can be justified only if his circumstances are known and, therefore, appreciated. Mahler spent his youth among soldiers. He listened every day to bugles and trumpets from military barracks, and witnessed columns of men on the march, accompanied by the brilliant if somewhat coarse-toned military instruments. He imbibed the military musical tradition, and when he turned to subjective composition, this tradition became the basis of a philosophy. Mahler's so-called vulgarity represented the vulgar side of life. His stridency, allied to march-like and commonplace themes, all represent something over which he wished humanity to triumph. Consequently, there are few "noble" themes in

[1] *The Symphony: Its History and Development*, Demuth. (In preparation.)

his more powerful movements, and their actual substance is slight. Nevertheless, these works cannot be re-scored, for each instrument is used in accordance with its capabilities for delineation. The tenor horn in the magnificent *Seventh Symphony* (1904-1906) is as essential as the hundreds of voices in the *Eighth* (1906-1907). The choir in the latter cannot be reduced numerically any more than can the orchestra in the former, nor can the anvil be omitted from the *Second Symphony* (1894). His scores are too much of a piece to admit tampering.

It is in the massive slow movements that Mahler proves his greatness. In these heartfelt yearnings he showed himself the master of the "long tune", even a greater one than was Bruckner, and, conversely, showed that he was the last of a long line. It is true to say of Mahler that he closed an epoch and wound up a tradition. On no account and in no respect can he be considered "Teutonic". Teutonism played no part in his personal or musical make-up. Rhetorically he was short-winded and it was only when faced with a subjective emotional crisis, as displayed in these great adagios where rhetoric could find no place, that his genius allowed itself to languish. Mahler ruminated rather than conversed, and all the time appeared intensely sorry for himself. He was not at one with the world. There is nothing in any way sexual about his music. He himself was never repressed nor frustrated in this respect and therefore there was no need for him to find a sexual outlet in his music. It is all of the spirit and is sublimated to a high ideal and purpose.

His adagio themes have great poise and wide sweep. He knew how to hover over slowly moving harmony and to descend through a static chord to the lowest range of the instrument. Only careful handling can avoid a feeling of overclimax. This, in, fact, is a characteristic of much music of the early part of the twentieth century. Composers appeared over-anxious to show that their "climaxes were well attained" —a stock phrase with the ordinary musical journalist—with the result that climax follows upon climax with no interruption, the whole process being somewhat exhausting. This was the opposite principle to that of the Impressionists who at the same period were seeking after purely sensuous sound. The climactic ideal was an inheritance from *Tristan und Isolde,* and the early twentieth-century composers tried to produce innumerable little *Tristans,* forgetting that a Wagner comes only once in a while. Mahler did not altogether escape the vein in his use of the brass, which climbs martially and nobly through the texture. Nevertheless, he avoided the Grand Manner and even when hundreds of voices enter so broadly with "Veni, Veni Creator Spiritus" in the *Eighth Symphony*, there is no suggestion of bombast. Many composers, given these instrumental and choral resources could achieve magnificence by sheer weight of tone; but it is not simply within the compass of the first few bars that Mahler impresses. He does so throughout the movement, and in the second where he combines a slow movement, scherzo and finale through the medium of a text from Goethe's *Faust* and—here an interesting point arises—he succeeds in moving the listener by the sheer simplicity of banal material and commonplace arpeggii. There is no other composer of whom this can be said. The choir of boys' voices has its own atmosphere, and the pure treble[1] tone carries through the metallic harp in a wonderful manner. The harp arpeggio is a dangerous figure, and far too many composers have used it as a welcome means of getting over wastes of terrestrial technique, as well as finding it convenient for depicting celestial situations. It was another characteristic relic of the nineteenth century. Until the moment when Elgar showed the way in "Praise to the Holiest" in *The Dream of Gerontius*, quasi-celestial music easily takes the lowest place for quality and banality.

When Mahler reduces the faithful to tears, they are tears of sympathy, not of sentiment. In the unresigned despair of the *Ninth Symphony* (1912) and in the pessimistic *Das Lied von der Erde*, no less than in the wonderful and tragic *Kindertotenlieder* (1900-1902), his emotion is highly charged with sorrow. His despair is not hysterical as was Tchaikowsky's. He could not have written a *Symphonie pathétique*, for although he was (as I have said) sorry for himself, he aligned his sorrow with humanity in general. He was the last of the subjective romanticists.

He was, technically speaking, the last of the diatonic composers. Sensuousness and sensuality never entered his music as they did that of Franz Schreker (1878) whose operas and general approach to musical expression are pure sexuality and eroticism. This pathological psychology is turgid and superficially adolescent. It is no more physically stimulating than Scriabin's *Poem of Ecstasy*, which is an emotional and representational orgasm. Schreker's technique is, accordingly, highly romantic, sensuous and coloured. It is the complete antithesis

---

[1] Let us have done with the absurd description "boy sopranos" for good and all. Trebles they have always been, and trebles they will remain.

to Mahler. Mahler was "ill-conditioned", Schreker was frustration personified, and the present era regards this undressing of the emotions in public as either repellent or humorous. This is subjective romanticism brought to its ultimate and most absurd degree. There is nothing bestial about it, as in Strauss' *Elektra* or *Salome,* and it is simply the satisfying of repressed sexual appetite. By comparison, Salome is almost natural, since she is direct and uninhibited. Schreker tried to sublimate sex through music. This may have been all right at the time when inhibitions caused the whole thing to be regarded as "nasty" and "dirty", and, therefore, something to be concealed; but in these days of open-mindedness, when the so-called "sex mystery" has been proved to be no mystery whatsoever, Schreker can find no place. Indeed, the reading of some of his scores becomes intensely boring because they all harp on the same theme, without varying it. The heyday of sex-impelled art is over and has been destroyed by the stream of systematic composers led by Joseph Hauer (1883), and followed by Arnold Schoenberg.

The whole concept of music changed when Hauer devised his system which he called "atonality", but which was never more than "atonicality" or, as Schoenberg prefers to call it, "pantonality", meaning tonality all the time, but no actual tonic or home key. Hauer's use of the term was, therefore, misdirected. In his *Sinfonietta* (1927), for example, he opens in the true twelve-note manner and the note-row undergoes the usual permutations; but the feeling for tonality is never abolished and the music sometimes takes on an almost Gallic romanticism in its harmony.

Hauer, however, was convinced that European music had taken the wrong turning, and he tried to reorientate it along Chinese lines. He was convinced that the ordinary orchestra was wrong and that composers were misleading themselves in using it. Consequently, when he wrote for what he called *Kammerorchester,* he did not mean the ordinary traditional reduced symphony orchestra. Strings and wind he felt to be quite unsuited to his purpose, and his scores amount to a combination of as many pianos and harmoniums as the situations dictated.

He professed to eschew polyphony. What he called his "building materials" consisted of *Tropen,* containing all the possible combinations of the twelve semitones. Hauer commenced his researches with Goethe's *Farbenlehre* upon which he has constructed sets of tone-colour pictures. He is drawn to the large canvas, and the *Apocalyptic*

Anton von Webern (1883–1945)

Alban Berg (1885–1935)

Béla Bartók (1881–1945)    Igor Stravinsky (1882)

Fantasia for pianos and harmoniums may be taken as a fair sample; perhaps the musical research department of the B.B.C. and its Third Programme would take heed of it. That Hauer has not made any impression is another example of the fate of the pioneer, for this he is, and nothing more, and there have been many such. The principles of Schoenberg have been taken as being more reasonable, consistent and approachable.

Schoenberg shows an interesting descent from Wagner, and it is to be noted that not only was he one of Mahler's most devoted friends and admirers, but his first pupils also held Mahler in veneration. Among these must be mentioned Egon Wellesz (1885), whose advent to these shores in 1932 was one of the few happy results of Nazidom. Wellesz combines research into Byzantine music with scholarly composition of the finest kind. His is one of the greatest brains in this country at the moment, and he contributes to the universality of European music. Although a pupil of Schoenberg, he has shown that it is not necessary to write in the note-row manner. His studies with Schoenberg came just at the time when Schoenberg was about to change his technique. Wellesz, therefore, was fortunate in being with his master at the end of one period and during the inception of another.

His works are considerable and, consequently, are ignored for the most part. There is no native composer of his generation so completely symphonic in character. His *Symphonies*, particularly the *Symphony in C* (1945), are remarkable for their clarity. Wellesz is strictly classical. It is true that one finds evidence now and again of a literary programmatic basis, as in *Prosperos Beschwörungen*, based on Shakespeare's *The Tempest*, but in this particular case the orchestral work grew from the discarded idea of an opera upon that play. Generally speaking, he has acquired his lyrical state, which sometimes is considerable, from the close study of the Middle Ages, and the pliability of his thought suggests its foundation in the free rhythm of plainsong. His themes have magnificent breadth and range, just like so many of Mahler's, and in some cases they are akin to those of Roussel, which I feel sure to be absolutely accidental. His powers of continuity and sustained development are refreshing in a world which is just beginning to return to them.

It is possible that his reputation as a scholar has stood in the way of his music; otherwise it is impossible to see why it has not established itself in the repertoire of the B.B.C. He has been most successful in his settings of Fletcher, Dryden and Milton and has assimilated the spirit of the poems in a manner natural to the born Englishman. That Wellesz has not yet made any impact upon the music and musicians of to-day is regrettable; but the time must surely come when his presence will be felt. His style is not sufficiently "advanced" to recommend it to the notice of the "progressives", but at the same time it is too much so for the traditionalists, although the general layout and substance of Wellesz' symphonic music is distinctly traditional. It is easy to see certain traits of polytonality, but the music is mainly tonal, not in the Mahler manner, but in the fact that tonality is for the most part the basic element of the thought. As one sees the situation to-day, there are signs that twentieth-century tonality will before long declare itself, when sensationalism of every kind has had its day. In the meanwhile, perhaps that learning which Professor Weissmann draws attention to[1] is not being as sedulously acknowledged as it is being cultivated.

[1] Page 108.

CHAPTER EIGHTEEN

ARNOLD SCHOENBERG
(1874) [1]

SCHOENBERG'S output divides itself into three categories, with an intermediary period coming between the first and second. The first, the romantic, extended from 1897-1905; then followed the intermediary from 1906-1908. The second, the expressionist, ranged from 1909-1917; the third, the systematic, coming after a few years' silence, in 1920. Until 1949 his opus numbers amounted only to forty-nine, but these do not include certain unfinished works, transcriptions, and the *Harmonielehre*; thus he has not been in any way prolific in the 1951 meaning of the word. This is reasonable in one whose whole life has been spent in furthering and expanding his own technique and aesthetic and who has been sensible enough to realise when he has reached the apex of any particular manner. Schoenberg has always refrained from publishing anything new until he is satisfied that it represents the fulfilment of a newer technique; consequently, there are no experimental works, the beginning of a new period being achieved after considerable private travail. Thus all his music has been born out of deep conviction and burning integrity. Most composers show a difference between their first and second styles, but few have been so courageous as to forge themselves such a completely new technique that everything preceding the achievement sounds false—Delius may be placed side by side with Schoenberg in this respect. Schoenberg's intermediary period marks a gradual realisation of new aims, but the cleavage between the first and second is complete.

In the first period one finds such works as the string sextet *Verklärte Nacht* (1899) which breathes the whole atmosphere of delicate and decadent romanticism, and the enormous *Pelleas und Melisande* (1902-1903) for large orchestra, lasting one hour—surely the longest sym-

[1] Died 1951.

phonic poem in existence. In between these works came the even larger *Gurre-Lieder* (1900-1901), completed ten years later, the orchestration of the third part having been put aside.

In this period Schoenberg showed his descent from Wagner and his kinship with Strauss. These works appeared during the period of the Grand Manner, and Schoenberg, in common with other composers at the beginning of the century, indulged in the large orchestra which was tending to become the normal constitution at the time. *Pelleas und Melisande* is the direct antithesis to Debussy's opera of the same name. At this point it appeared to Schoenberg that he could go no further without either repeating himself or showing an increasingly turgid Strauss influence. Now and again, it is true, one finds a thematic use of the whole-tone scale in *Pelleas und Melisande,* and Schoenberg was the first Austrian composer to use it at all consistently. This was not going very far and was certainly not original; further, its limitations precluded individuality. He accordingly set his face against the heavy romanticism of the period and the intermediary years were occupied in not only changing his style from harmonic to polyphonic, but also in acquiring a strict sense of classicism founded upon polyphonic freedoms which, at the time, were almost iconoclastic. Nevertheless, until the actual dawn of the second period he maintained a strong feeling for tonality, although tonality relations slowly began to disappear until they were completely eradicated in the second period, known technically, and rather loosely, as atonal. The systematic manner did not appear until many years later, but the second style was declared in the *Three Piano Pieces,* Op. 11 (1909), where the music avoided tonality with as much fidelity as the traditional school maintained it.

Eventually he found himself at another *impasse.* Serving in the Austrian Army during the First Great War, he had little time for composition, but his brain was at work and he devised his own particular manner of using the twelve semitones. The first music to be written in this manner took three years (1921-1923) to come to fruition in the *Five Piano Pieces,* Op. 23. In the meantime he composed the *Serenade,* Op. 24 (1921-1923), and the *Dance Suite* for piano (1923). The composition of music, therefore, became a slower process with the fulfilment of the new manner.

Thus, briefly, can Schoenberg's creative activity be summed up. While the second period was a revolution, the third arrived as a natural evolution, through a negative to a widening positive, from a denial of tonality, concord, and discord, to a broadening of the tonal principle. All this was accomplished with only twenty-three works, some of which are remarkable for their brevity. That the revolution was complete may be evidenced by the fact that every work after *Pelleas und Melisande,* Op. 5, was greeted with a storm of violent and active abuse. *Pelleas und Melisande,* however, was always a success, and this is not to be wondered at, since it fell easily into line with the prevalent ideas. Music such as this, with its warm harmonic colouring, its purple orchestration, so graphically subjective, could not fail to make an impression on the minds of those now acclimatised to the tone poems of Strauss and familiar with the principles of the Mahler "adagio".

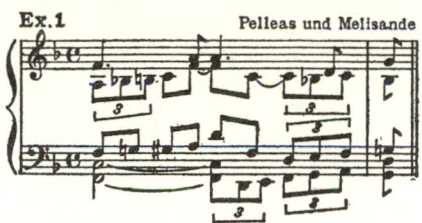

Ex.1   Pelleas und Melisande

It will not be out of place to give the list of the orchestral requirements of both this work and the *Gurre-Lieder* as they form a good sample of the contemporary orchestral approach :

Pelleas und Melisande	*Gurre-Lieder*
4 Flutes	4 Piccolos
3 Oboes	4 Flutes
Cor anglais	3 Oboes
E flat clarinet	2 Cor anglais
3 Clarinets in A and B flat	3 Clarinets
Bass clarinet	2 Bass clarinets in A or B flat
3 Bassoons	2 E flat clarinets
Double bassoon	3 Bassoons
8 Horns	2 Double bassoons
4 Trumpets	10 Horns
Alto trombone	6 Trumpets
4 Tenor trombones	Bass trumpet
Double-bass tuba	Alto trombone
2 pairs of kettledrums	4 Tenor trombones

Pelleas und Melisande	*Gurre-Lieder*
Percussion	Bass trombone
Glockenspiel	Double-bass trombone
2 Harps	Double-bass tuba
Augmented strings	6 Kettledrums
	Bass drum
	Cymbals
	Triangle
	Glockenspiel
	Side drum
	Tenor drum
	Xylophone
	Gong
	4 Harps
	Celesta
	Large iron chains
	Augmented strings
	5 Solo voices
	3 Four-part male choirs
	Mixed choir in eight parts

These works were written by a young man still with his name to make, and it cannot be said that Schoenberg made things easy for himself. Nevertheless, these enormous bodies are not extravagancies, or even luxuries. They are necessities. Naturally, his use of large iron chains came in for as much ridicule as Mahler's famous anvil—when the B.B.C. in a moment of expansiveness some years ago performed the *Gurre-Lieder*, it was almost depressing to read the allegedly humorous remarks made by the critics, one of them going so far as to say that as he could not hear them, or did not notice them, they were unnecessary. Taking the situation as a whole, however, it is worth noting that economics played a strong part in checking the trend towards orchestral inflation; but, in the opening years of the century, orchestral players were not paid as much as they are now, and, therefore, performance of these works was not the costly affair that it is to-day.

Schoenberg's early works are of but historical interest, in the light of the present, and this precludes frequent performance. That *Pelleas und Melisande* would be popular, cannot be doubted. Its value in a programme would be justified only if a work from each of the later periods were included as well; to suggest that it forms a good introduction to him (meaning that it is reasonably appreciable at a single hearing) is entirely erroneous.

The first work to cause an uproar was the *First String Quartet* in D minor, Op. 7 (1904-1905). It does not seem a very alarming affair, and one wonders what objections could have been raised to it, and it is difficult to understand why a man should have been constrained to blow on a latchkey during the performance of the first movement.

In this *Quartet* as well as in the *First Chamber Symphony*, Op. 9 (1906), we see the first breaking down of formal restraint.

This formal principle amounts to delaying the middle section until the actual second movement has been played. In the *First Chamber Symphony*, the scherzo follows the enunciation of the work. At its close, the material of the enunciation is fully developed in a process which includes a slow movement. This removes the inevitability of the established design while conforming with its formal requirements. A mere glance at a typical page of this work immediately demonstrates the remarkably full scoring, the independent polyphony of the part-writing, and the astonishingly Strauss-like contours of the material. Indeed, were it not for the acidity and keenness of the vertical entities, made so by the horizontal lines, the work in many places by its *look* might have been written by Strauss; but Strauss would not have been so consistently logical nor so persistently abstract.

The importance of the *First Chamber Symphony* cannot be over-estimated. It marks not only Schoenberg's first departure from both the Grand Manner and romanticism, but also his first use of a small orchestral force, in which the instruments are used individually. The orchestra required consists of flute (and piccolo), oboe, cor anglais, D clarinet, E flat clarinet, A and B flat clarinet, bass clarinet, bassoon, double-bassoon, two horns and string quintet—fifteen players in all. The musical thought, however, is so symphonic and closely wrought that Schoenberg permits performance with additional strings, thus obtaining a more satisfactory balance in large halls against the polyphonic wind writing.

Tonality remained, as I have said, but was approached from the angle of expansion. The work is described as being in E major. The conventional and conservative audiences of the time may be pardoned for doubting this when they heard the opening theme.[1]

(1) There was no doubt at the final cadence.

Ex.2

These rising fourths (they descend during the course of the work) made a sensation in 1907 and the audience showed its disapproval in the manner customary among audiences at that time. This theme offers opportunities such as the following, which sounded extremely stark then:

Ex.3

In contradistinction to this austerity, the second part of the first subject, with its whole-tone suggestion and Strauss-like curves and leaps, sounded almost romantic.

Ex.4

Schoenberg adopts an essentially polyphonic style of orchestration. Although there is complete individuality in the parts in *Pelleas und Melisande*, the harmonic aspect plays the important rôle. In the *First Chamber Symphony* it is of secondary importance, and in this respect an interesting situation arose. Concurrently with this *First Chamber Symphony*, Schoenberg worked at a *Second*. This he soon put aside, finding the preliminary sketches in 1911. He once again discarded the work, but in 1939 was persuaded to finish it. The reason for his ceasing to work at it becomes apparent from the opening bars:

The whole work is in this romantic vein and shows that Schoenberg had not as yet successfully re-orientated his mind towards the neo-classicism which the *First Chamber Symphony* was illustrating. When he came to complete it, he had completely mastered his principle of pantonality or, to use that clumsy word, "atonicality", which amounted to an extension of tonality, in that there was tonality somewhere all the time but no "home key". For the moment, however, the work found no place in the aesthetic gradually forming itself during the intermediary period.

It is worth while glancing backward for a moment to look at a melodic line in the first of the *Eight Songs*, Op. 6 (1905), "Traumleben", since it points in the intervals of the first two bars to the later distortion of line and displacement of interval which characterised the mature periods—let it be clearly understood that this second period was as mature in its way as the third since, as I have said, it reached a peak in its own style.

Two other works should be mentioned in the Intermediary period, the chorus *Friede auf Erden*, Op. 13 (1907), and the *Second String Quartet in F sharp minor*, Op. 10 (1907-1908). The former is a remark-able work in that it shows a combination of diatonicism and chromatic-ism. The voices move in thirds for a large part of the time, and in view of the *First Chamber Symphony*, this passage may be surprising:

The semitonalism becomes cloying and later faintly suggests that found in the *First String Quartet*.

The *Second String Quartet* indicates a still further departure from traditional formalism and also shows signs of thematic cohesion wrought through the germinal system. Here Schoenberg introduces a solo voice in the third and fourth movements. There is nothing really striking about this, except for the fact that it had not happened before in a classically-moulded string quartet. In the third movement, which is the so-called "slow" movement of the design, Schoenberg gives a striking example of what was to be the formal basis of his latest manner, that of variation. Thematic connection between the material of this work in general can be seen in the first three movements. The third movement, the "slow", condenses material from the previous sections in this manner:

Ex.8

The derivations are found to be from these germs.

Ex.9

Schoenberg did not take his ideas from the main material so much as from accompanimental fragments, and a study of the score will show that the themes themselves are mostly fragmentary in character; but it is not difficult to distinguish between the actual "theme", and the accompanimental "figure". Things become complex and considerably ornate in the fourth and fifth movements, which are settings of "Litanie" and "Entrückung", both poems by Stefan George.[1] The classical concept of quartet-writing vanishes and the music takes on an impressionistic tendency, especially in the fifth movement, parts of which in isolation could be mistaken for French Impressionism.

Here, of course, there is line and plenty of shape in the contour of the vocal music, but, generally speaking, this work shows a departure from the previous long tunes which Schoenberg inherited from Mahler and Strauss. Linear instrumental melody having disappeared, in its place one finds short and pointed fragments. Complete polyphony has been achieved.

[1] The parts of the last movement are so distinctive that they are here referred to as two movements.

At this point it should be remarked that Schoenberg's opus numbers do not coincide with the year of composition. It will make the position clearer if the works already mentioned are tabulated in the order of their opus numbers.

Op. 4. *Verkeärte Nacht,* 1899.
Op. ? *Gurre-Lieder,* 1900-1901.   Completed 1911.
Op. 5. *Pelleas und Melisande,* 1903.
Op. 6. *Eight Songs,* 1905.
Op. 7. *String Quartet in D minor,* 1904-1905.
Op. 9. *First Chamber Symphony,* 1906.
Op. 9A. *Second Chamber Symphony,* 1906.   Completed 1939.
Op. 10. *String Quartet in F sharp minor,* 1907-1908.
Op. 11. *Three Piano Pieces,* 1909.
Op. 13. *Friede auf Erden,* 1907.
Op. 15. *Das Buch der hängenden Gärten,* 1908.

From this it will be seen that in some cases Schoenberg made the opus numbers correspond with what he considered the true path of his progress. Thus the *Three Piano Pieces* show a more determinate situation than the Chorus *Friede auf Erden,* although it might well be considered that the latter is a reaction, temporary, perhaps, but possibly actuated by the circumstances of its medium. Officially, so to speak, the second period commences with the *Three Piano Pieces,* Op. 11.

Here is revolution with a vengeance. Certain interesting details of writing occur at once, the most notable being the fact that since there is neither tonic nor dominant, neither concord nor discord, the symbol for a natural becomes as essential as that for a flat or a sharp. The result is that the music becomes a complication of accidentals which tend to confuse the player not thoroughly familiar with the "look", or imbued with the technique. The second is the complete departure from harmony to polyphony. There are now no "chords" *per se,* these being formed incidentally at each point. Further, there is more classical approach to the material. Canon by inversion begins to play an integral part of the whole, and the thought is completely devoid of subjective emotion, although the listener has this conveyed to him through the shape of the melodic lines. These lines are extremely lyrical as a general rule. The abolition of tonality, concord, and discord, was, of course, nothing new in itself, for Debussy had abolished them years before; but he did so harmonically. Schoenberg abolished them contrapuntally.

It may be argued that the lines are not always completely atonal (hence his preference for the term "atonical"), but he succeeded in breaking down all tradition and convention.

The question of execution is indeed a difficult one. It requires close study on the part of the pianist to master a passage such as this:

No. 3 Three Piano Pieces Op. 11

Ex. 10

This is exasperating for the player who cannot or will not see the logic, and it is at this point that Schoenberg's music becomes extremely and undeniably logical, a natural progress from the *First Chamber Symphony*. One sees evidence of this at every point as in the elaboration of a simple progression, insignificant in itself in its original form, but which takes on thematic portent; one can be taken almost at random:

Ex. 11

No. 14 Das Buch der hängenden Gärten

The set of songs from which the above example is taken show a vocal point of view which demands intense musicianship and a keen ear for intonation on the part of the singer, who no longer sings to an accompaniment, but is one of the ensemble, as suggested in the *Second String Quartet*. The principle reached its peak in such works as *Erwärtung*, Op. 17 (1909), and *Die Glückliche Hand*, Op. 18 (1910-1913), and its final climax in the "sprechgesang" of *Pierrot Lunaire*, Op. 21 (1912). For the moment, we look at the intensely individual manner in which each orchestral instrument is used thematically, each player being regarded as a soloist.

This principle is maintained throughout the remainder of Schoenberg's works and each one is, paradoxically speaking, chamber music even when the full orchestra is used. The first of these, the *Five Pieces for Orchestra*, Op. 16 (1909), indicates the dagger aimed at the heart of the "interpreter" and tempo rubato conductor. Schoenberg states specifically that the conductor is not to "bring out" or otherwise emphasise any particular notes or instrument. The pieces are scored in such a manner that when anything has to be prominent, it will stand out on its own either by dynamic or by colour. This direction is emphasised by the symbols which he places to indicate which instrument is to be prominent, symbols necessary owing to the intensely polyphonic nature of the music. It becomes essential that the balance be maintained according to the composer's direction in the third of these *Five Pieces*, which consists not of themes, or even of fragments of themes, but the sustaining of harmony varied by constantly changing tone colours. This is a remarkable piece and defies classification. It is not classicism, because it uses no classical device. It is not abstract, because its sound is extremely moving and emotional. It is not Impressionism, because it is not in the least objective, and it is not romanticism, because it is neither pictorial or subjective. It is pure "sound" for orchestra. Its lowest dynamic is *PPP*, its highest *PP* and it is almost a mere whisper for full orchestra. The reader should study the score as it is impossible to give the slightest impression of it in a short extract.

From the constructional point of view, the *Five Pieces*, if not showing any definite use of the classical designs *in toto*, give many instances of the logicality of inversion and straightforward imitation. Little figures like this from the Fifth Piece, entitled "Das obligate Rezitativ", small in themselves, played

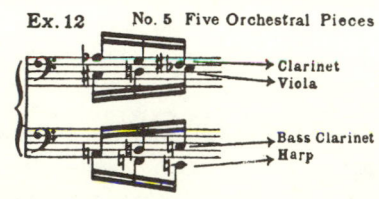

Ex. 12   No. 5 Five Orchestral Pieces

Clarinet
Viola

Bass Clarinet
Harp

an influential part with younger composers, notably Honegger. They indicate the manner in which so much of the later music, so much of *le dernier cri* evolved from and revolved round Schoenberg. The reader should study these pieces in detail from the score. They show a wonderfully cool and logically minded brain, which does not eschew a certain lyricism.

Schoenberg's dealings with the theatre are of the greatest interest. He contrived two stage works of an amazing complexity and power, *Erwärtung* and *Die Glückliche Hand*, of which the large apparatus required precludes frequent performance. There are not more than a handful of singers required in both works put together, although they require a large orchestra. They are intensely subjective, especially *Erwärtung*, which expresses in thirty minutes the emotional feelings of a woman awaiting her lover. Advocates of social significance decry this work as a shining example of "bourgeois subjective romanticism" of a personal nature of not the slightest public interest. They forget the wonderful texture and sombreness of the music. These are Schoenberg's so far only contributions to the "lyric" stage—they cannot be called operas. His mind was drawn much more towards neo-classicism and the connection of his manner with that of the classical past.

This can be seen in *Pierrot Lunaire*, a setting of twenty-one poems by Albert Giraud, translated by Otto Erich Hartleben. They are written for "Sprechgesang"—a midway point between song and speech—piano, flute (and piccolo), clarinet (and bass clarinet), violin (and viola) and 'cello. The seven poems which constitute each of the three parts are written in a scoring commensurate with its general spirit. For example, the piano is omitted in the fourth, "Eine blasse Wascherin", the seventh, "Der kranke Mond", the tenth, "Raub", and the twelfth, "Galgenlied". The third, "Der Dandy", is for piccolo, clarinet and piano; the seventh for flute alone; the ninth, "Gebet an Pierrot", for clarinet and piano; the thirteenth, "Enthauptung", for bass clarinet, viola, 'cello and piano—and so forth. The whole work is a fine lesson in economy of means and in the variety to be obtained from a handful of instruments. The texture is always clear even when the whole five instruments are playing. The classical designs are used—the eighth, "Die Nacht", for example, is a closely wrought passacaglia, while canon, canon cancrizan, and imitation play an important part in the general structure. One is not conscious of these devices and processes. It will suffice to look at four bars quoted on page 223 from the eighteenth, "Der Mondfleck", which demonstrate canon cancrizan between piccolo and clarinet, and viola and 'cello. The whole thing is carefully organised, even the frequent clef changes in the 'cello, which mostly seem unnecessary.

Schoenberg had no doubt in his mind that he was exhausting the possibilities of the atonal or atonical manner. During the 1914-1918 War he wrote no music except the sketches for an oratorio, *Die Jacobsleiter* (1915-1917), to his own text. For the remainder of the time he was occupied in finding a way out of the *impasse*. Eventually he came into the open with what he called his own manner of using the twelve semitones. From this moment begins the systematic period, which has had many copyists. This manner, peculiar to himself, consists of forming a series or note-row of twelve notes, these forming the melodic and harmonic basis of the whole work. Schoenberg has never taught this manner to any of his pupils and nothing infuriates him more than for a student to bring him a piece, exercise, or work, written in the so-called twelve-note-row system, for he maintains that as it took him twenty years' hard and progressive work to reach that system, it is not one upon which a basic technique can be formed.[1] He is a firm believer in the traditional basic technique, judging that this is the only foundation for logical musical thinking. (Many a student has had his early ardour damped through reading Schoenberg's *Harmonielehre*, thinking that therein he will start where Schoenberg himself has almost left off, but finding that the emphasis is placed upon traditional customs, although expressed in less of a text-book manner than is usual.) Schoenberg on these occasions always threatens to do all kinds of unimaginable things in the key of C.

The principle which Schoenberg has devised is that of pantonality, or the extension of tonality. No more is it to be self-consciously abolished. Pantonical implies that there is always a key suggestion in each harmonic entity when viewed upwards, but in no way does it include polytonality or a combination of different linear tonalities. He himself does not regard the process as anything but a means to making music, and does not claim any merit in the fact that a piece may be written in the system. He is the last to view his own technique as anything but a normal evolution. Not so the followers, who place altogether too much emphasis on the manner and too little on the matter. However, any new theory when advocated by a master is bound to be taken up with

[1] "Schoenberg in America", Dika Newlin (*Music Survey*, Vol. I, Nos. 5 and 6).

Der Mondfleck- Pierrot Lunaire

Ex.13

Piccolo

Clarinet
(actual sounds)

Viola

Cello

Q

enthusiasm and eventually be expanded beyond bounds. The disciples claim too much, much more than the master himself ever put forward. Regardless of any other aspect, they shout, " 'rah! 'rah!" whenever a work can be said to have been founded upon the note-row system. Thus a cerebral yardstick is applied to judgment, which ceases to be concerned with music. One might equally well cheer because a piece happens to be written in the key of E flat.

The note-row system consists of using a succession of twelve notes, which may or may not have any tonal suggestion, and may or may not consist of some technical and arbitrary principle. The note-row, thus, may be an independent succession in one line, or it may divide itself into groups of three or four notes, which have some intervalic relation to each other. This note-row is not a scale, although it may be said to represent one. The primitive survival known as the diatonic scale allows chromatic semitones, usable as passing notes; the note-row forbids anything which is not contained therein. Further, there are certain other rules which must be implicitly followed. The general principle is that no note may be repeated in any part until the whole series has appeared, in full, on each presentation.[1] The extremists go further and maintain that the notes must appear in their original order, being divided in the parts in strict succession.

Ex. 14   Valse— No. 5 Five Piano Pieces Op. 23

We may draw some deductions from this example, which is taken from the beginning of a phrase rather than from the opening bar.

It is not necessary that each phrase should end on the twelfth note, and overlapping of note-row is, therefore, permissible.

[1] Schoenberg does not tie himself down to this rule: see "Prelude" from *Suite for Piano*, Op. 25 (1924).

Enharmonic changes are allowed. The fifth and sixth in the series are altered at will or whim.

It is not necessary to read a chord serially from the bottom upwards.

This is one of the simplest and most straightforward cases. As time has gone on the whole thing has grown increasingly elaborate. The writer,[1] however, is free to indulge in any rhythmic variations he may choose; in fact, the basis of the system depends upon a lively rhythmic sense.

A more human theory allows immediate repetition in the same part at a different pitch, but the alteration of the order is frowned upon because this would make the series too similar to a scale. Even when this alteration is allowed, the series must be completed in all the parts before any of it is repeated, although overlapping is permitted.

It is claimed by the advocates that the writer is thus liberated from everything which has cramped creative activity for so many years, and the permutations run into hundreds—but so they do for the composer who uses his imagination and all the twelve semitones, regardless of tonal suggestions. The whole thing can very easily become mere "eye music", for the reason that on the keyboard and on wind instruments G sharp sounds precisely the same as A flat; the ears which can detect the difference on strings are in the minority.

To find the notes of a series upon which a piece is constructed is not at all times difficult, since all that has to be done is to reach that spot marking the twelfth note and arrange what has been heard in some kind of order.

This is not so easy when enharmonic changes occur. The writer has all the classical devices and processes at his command. The note-row can be inverted and retrogressed, and there can be retrogression of the inversion. The rhythmic changes include complete or partial augmentation and diminution in whatever order the row is heard. Canons of all kinds are not only allowed but encouraged, and the writer has perforce to abolish any hint of personal emotion while he is actually writing. No doubt with practice and experience he does reach that old-fashioned condition known as inspiration and can express it naturally by these means; but the very negations of the system preclude this, as far as one may judge, for inspiration gives place to impulse.

The actual use of the note-row goes back many hundreds of years, to the primitive plainchant and Oriental scales. The technique refers

[1] I use the word "writer" in a general, not a personal sense.

back to the days of the early Netherlandic canon writers whose efforts have but an antiquarian interest now. Under this system, as elaborated by the advocates, as long as one keeps within the confines of the note-row, one can never go wrong. Since these advocates claim the past as their authority, the whole thing has become reactionary and retrogressive and joins the list of the "back to" movements so fashionable in the 1920's. One can write canon after canon and utilise all the classical complexities, since the resultant sound plays no part whatsoever in the writer's scale of values.

It will be well at this point to examine some existent note-rows:[1]

The individual construction of Ex. 15A is of interest. At Nos. 4, 5, 6, and 7 the enharmonic change alters the augmented fourth into the diminished fifth; the actual keyboard sound is, of course, the same. The next example shows us the use of this bi-linear series:

[1] I have been unable to find out for certain if a note-row is copyright or not. Fairly expert opinion suggests that if it is definitely announced in equal notes as part of the piece, thus becoming a kind of motto-theme, then it is copyright; but if it appears simply from deduction, then apparently anyone can use it.

Ex. 16   Prelude– Suite for Piano Op. 25 (1924)

The series is completed in the right hand in its original order, the notes corresponding to the top line of the series. The left hand in the last two bars completes the series by going back upon itself when it falls into two lines. This is a straightforward instance. The next is a little different.

Ex. 17   Third String Quartet (1926)

I

Violins

II

Viola

Cello

While the first violin plays the series in retrogression, the second has it in its original movement (it is continued to the end after the quotation in question). The viola and 'cello present the series straightforwardly and divided between each other. Schoenberg does not hesitate at repetition, or at tying any notes he likes. The earlier restrictions, therefore, are thrown aside.

This is an ingenious arrangement of the series which, in itself, is divisible into four groups of three notes each. The finale 'cello note, the fifth in the series, appears without the fourth. The work is interesting, because it relies upon pitch and, consequently, timbre for its meaning. Its effect exasperates those who want some kind of line and

Ex.18   Krenek:— String Quartet Op.78

(1) Krenek composed the first note-row opera, *Karl V.*

after a short time its fragmentariness preys upon the nerves, since one is never quite sure from what pitch the next sound will emanate.

The next example, from Alban Berg, follows the original movement with a retrogression. Berg is much freer than either Schoenberg or Krenek, and does not adhere to any hard and fast rule. It will be noticed at once that there is an emotional feeling about the passage which has been absent from the other three.

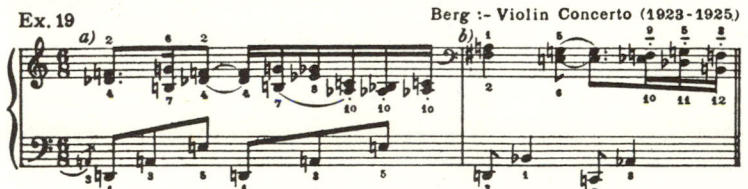

Ex. 19   Berg :— Violin Concerto (1923-1925)

The ultimate end of the note-row system appears to have been reached by Schoenberg in his magnificent *Variations for Orchestra,* Op. 31 (1927-1928), wherein all the resources of the system and all those of classical device are quite exhausted. It would take very much more than the space available here to analyse this work and the reader is referred to *Introduction à la musique de Douze Sons*, by René Leibowitz (1913)[1] who justifies the manner in three hundred and thirty-six pages. He is not always convincing, since some of the examples appear to have little connection with the note-row quoted as their foundation. It is, of course, the work of an enthusiast; but it is that of a specialist and one who has many note-row works to his credit. One hundred and eight pages are devoted to Schoenberg's *Variations*.

We have spent some while considering the optical aspect of this music. What of the aural?

The effect upon the listener varies. When the music moves slowly or is static, the ear is able to absorb the sounds; but when it moves rapidly and is consistently polyphonic, it sounds muddled and busy. Everything is too independent. Polyphonic listening has improved beyond measure in the last few years, but listening to this type of music will take a long time before it becomes instinctive. At the moment, it seems a jumble of sound. The aesthetic enjoyment is non-existent under these circumstances. In "Ars Viva", *News Bulletin*, No. 2, Andreas Briner writes as follows:

> The composers using Schoenberg's "tone-row" technique may be roughly divided into two groups, those who use the technique in order to express tensions by means of organised sound, and those who have given way to the temptation of regarding this seductive technique as an end in itself.

It is difficult to distinguish between the two, with all due regard. In both cases, there appear to be more constructive than creative principles. The completely detached manner in which the writer has to approach his work is forbidding. It is not without interest to notice the number of times the name BACH appears in this music, from Schoenberg's orchestral *Variations* down to the latest recruit to the system. This seems to beg for, and even claim, some authority.

Singers may be justified in regarding the intervals they are expected to sing with exact intonation as well-nigh impossible, and one never ceases to admire the apparent ease with which those sufficiently gifted attack the lines and succeed in getting exact intonation every time. The listener finds it quite immoderately difficult to attach any meaning,

[1] *L'Arche* (Paris). Ex. 11. 15B and C, 17, and 18 are taken from this book. Others appear in it, but were chosen before I came across it. I have adopted M. Leibowitz' manner of numbering the notes of the series and their corresponding examples.

in rapid music, to what is being sung. The passages hit the ear and pass on, the system allowing no respite. The tendency to write the vocal lines with notes joined together as instrumental music rather than to separate the notes save for single syllables indicates an ever-increasing anxiety to make the human voice into an instrument. The wide leaps and bounds which the systematic composers indulge in are nothing new; Rameau wrote them many years ago, although he did not use the same qualities.

Nevertheless, there are often very many beautiful and moving pages in Schoenberg's mature manner. One remembers the *Ode to Napoleon*, Op. 41 (1942), and certain moments in the *Piano Concerto*, Op. 42 (also 1942), and it would appear that the manner is open to softening. That it is neurasthenic cannot be denied. An evening of Schoenberg's third period chamber music to the uninitiated is sufficiently gloomy as to cause hysteria. The music must be received cerebrally and analytically until the whole mystery has been made clear. One can accustom oneself to anything in time, and doubtless familiarity will place this systematic music in the repertoire; but not just yet, and the more involved the devotees make the manner, the longer will it be. Problems are so often found where none exist. A twelve-noter would hate to be considered unproblematical.

There are dangers attendant upon the use of this system. What applies to traditional harmony applies in reverse to the twelve-note-row processes. In both traditions it is possible, by a logical pursuance of certain guiding rules, to concoct a work of any length without the necessity of hearing what is being written. This has always been an easy path for the mechanic. The rules to which the note-row advocates bind themselves in loving loyalty are more restrictive than ever were those of the traditional school. Departure from any of them, no matter in how small a degree, completely breaks down the system, for such a departure will entail an acknowledgement of tonic and dominant. Schoenberg does not eschew this principle when it happens to occur, but the advocates appear to flee in horror from it. Another danger is that anyone can do it. One need not be a musician. Given average intelligence, one can convey the impression of absolute sincerity. It is quite impossible to tell if the writer is hearing what he is writing, or not, but it is significant that the note-row can never be borne in mind like the old-fashioned scale, and this suggests that it forms a kind of architect's blue-print. It is not far from the habit of composing at the piano—which does not imply the playing of what has been written, but refers to the picking out of the notes with great labour and pain before writing them down. Bach called these people "harpsichord knights". I am not suggesting any personal criticism of any of the known adherents of the twelve-note-row system, but its use savours too much of the carpenter's shop and a lack of musical sensitivity. It is dangerous because it offers unlimited opportunities for insincerity.

This is another reason why Schoenberg refuses to teach it and will not look at anything brought him in the manner unless and until he is perfectly convinced that the writer has genuinely written the music from the basis of traditional craft and has heard it in his head. Schoenberg himself is a man of burning sincerity and a teacher with the fire of the zealot. He has suffered more than most other composers not so much from neglect as from bitter personal attacks. He might so easily have taken the easy path of *Pelleas und Melisande* and become speedily established as a great figure. That he turned his back to the smiters is something which even his enemies and those who do not see eye to eye with him always admire.

Did he come too soon? The answer is that he was both opportune and necessary. His influence has been made manifest over the whole of twentieth-century music, not only directly in those who follow him musically, but morally. He is the example of the musical martyr willing to sacrifice himself personally for the furtherance of his ideals. Had Schoenberg manifested himself in the 1920's for the first time, there is little doubt but that his impact would have been more general upon a world never so ready for change; whereas Les Six were concerned with lightening music, Schoenberg was directing it along very serious paths, and at that time the world certainly was not in a mood for such music.

To-day much that formerly astonished now only interests, even where it does not call for enthusiasm. In spite of claims made to the contrary by the advocates, the twelve-note-row system has not yet established itself. It may be true to say that a large number of writers use it, but it is truer to say that larger numbers of composers do not. Something more is required, a humanising element of some kind. This was nearly achieved by Alban Berg, but he was not a consistent adherent to the manner. He succeeded in combining the best of the not-very-old with the best of the very-new, thus accomplishing for central European music very much what Albert Roussel did for France. The present disciples out-mannerise the Master.

Schoenberg is a great man and a monumental figure in the history of music, no matter what one's own personal views may be. In his approach to his art, he resembles the passionate integrity of such men as Bruckner, Mahler, Franck and d'Indy and in these cynical days, when values have dropped and sincerity is at a discount, he can be regarded as almost a saint in this respect. Others have been equally far-seeing in their generations and have put into practice theories which later composers have expanded and taken to themselves. Whether Schoenberg will suffer the fate of a pioneer like Reicha, and find a Berlioz, remains to be seen.

No explanation for the inclusion of this discussion here rather than in the concluding chapter is offered, other than that the twelve-note-row manner and Schoenberg are indivisible, and all discussion must of necessity hinge on him. There are too many people who claim to be "pupils of Schoenberg" because they write in the note-row manner. Since he does not teach this manner to his pupils, these claims are exaggerated, and the most that can be said with any justification is that they are pupils of Schoenberg "by deduction". They forget that the world's greatest and best composer-teachers never allow their students to copy their style and idiom, nor do they help them over a difficult point by solving the difficulty in their own individual manner.

In this connection my friend Dr. Ian Parrott has shown me an "official" programme note explaining a certain work written by one of the Schoenberg copyists. This must be quoted since it confirms the opinions and theories expressed in this chapter. "All three movements are based on the same series of twelve notes. The first has the character of a sonata, the second of a passacaglia, the third of a rondo. The theme of the last movement is the original series of notes reversed, the sharp denominations being enharmonically transposed into flats". One may wonder how the writer can claim that this is a "composition". The act of composing seems to have played little, if any part, in the writing down of the work and it is certainly not in any way "creative". It claims more for the system than the originator of it himself ever put forward. To quote Vincent d'Indy in this context is strange, but it emphasises his dictum that "all processes are good provided that they are the means to an end (that is, the making of music) and not the end in themselves". For once d'Indy and Schoenberg find agreement. This explanation justifies the work only as the solution of a mathematical problem and it thus has no relation whatsoever to music.

CHAPTER NINETEEN

ANTON VON WEBERN

(1884-1945)

WEBERN was one of the most original composers of the last fifty years. His concept of music has found no copyist or disciple of distinction, and it remains unique to himself. Turning away from all established ideas on linear theme and symphonic expansion, he devised a technique of his own, founded upon the note-row, which stripped music bare of everything except pure sound. If one looks for line, one can find it, but to do so is to fly straight in the face of Webern's principles and intentions. He was concerned solely with placing each note in accordance with the particular "timbre" which he wanted at the moment. He was, consequently, one of the most expressive composers of the era. His scores are marvels of precision and detailed editing. It will be best to quote four bars from his *Sechs Bagatellen* for string quartet, Op. 9 (1913); these fully illustrate the whole concept of music as seen by Webern:

233

Points to notice here are, first of all, the meticulous care with which Webern indicates each dynamic, even, be it noted, putting crescendo and decrescendo marks under rests. This is not as absurd as it seems, for Webern is anxious that the player should have some expressive feeling all through the work. His state is to be one of tense and concentrated emotion, and unless he experiences this aesthetic in his own consciousness, the music may well result in a series of disconnected sounds. Webern is, therefore, an exceedingly subjective composer.

With this care of dynamic goes·care of manner, and it will be noticed that even groups of two notes are given a full directive in this respect. Nothing is left to the imagination, nor can it be, since "interpretation" of this pointillistic music is quite impossible without a directive, the player having mainly to content himself with single sounds, spasmodically realised. In no other music does the player have so to associate himself with his fellows. He hears the work being built up around him. He is neither complementary nor supplementary. It is impossible to refer to the compact body by the word "parts", for the music is cohesive.

The whole effect is one of sheer beauty of sound. It is true that it becomes a little disconcerting at times, more particularly in his orchestral works than in the chamber music; but his manner of splitting up a four-note chord by distributing the notes singly between four different instruments in four different registers does result in some most moving timbres. No other composer can so wring our withers by one single sound as can Webern; conversely, he remains unique in his ability to exasperate listeners with his static conglomerations of notes. His music gives the effect of having been written at the rate of not more than four notes as a maximum *per diem*, so considered does everything seem, and so final in its result. Sometimes he rasps at the instruments as if he hated them, and while other composers would give vent to feelings of hatred by lengthy melodic curves and strident progressions, Webern says all he feels in one entity—it can hardly be termed a chord.

Webern's variety and contrast, therefore, are obtained by timbre and placing, the former relying upon the choice of instruments from work to work. He never uses the normal constitutions and combinations, and his scores are of the greatest interest to students of tone-colour. The *Funf Stücke* for orchestra, Op. 10 (1913), require flute and piccolo, oboe, E flat clarinet, clarinet and bass clarinet, horn, trumpet, trombone, percussion, mandoline, guitar, celesta, harmonium, harp, and string quartet (one violin and double bass). The pieces last ten minutes in all. The *Funf geistliche Lieder*, Op. 15 (1922-1923), for high soprano require flute, clarinet and bass clarinet, trumpet, harp, violin and viola (this doubling of the string instruments makes things even harder)— these songs last ten minutes. The earlier *Vier Lieder*, Op. 13 (1916), have a different orchestration in each case—timings are five, three, two and five minutes respectively. A particularly charming score is that of the *Zwei Lieder*, Op. 19 (1926), for mixed chorus, celesta, guitar, violin, clarinet and bass clarinet, the timing for which I am unable to ascertain.

The condensation of thought which I have indicated precludes anything except straightforward statement, although in a formalised work like the *Passacaglia* for orchestra, Op. 1 (1908), there are twenty minutes of closely packed music—but this was his Op. 1, be it remembered. At the other end of the scale, No. 3 of the *Funf Stücke* for orchestra, plays for nineteen seconds.

Contrary to what is often thought, Webern did not use the note-row manner until 1924. His earlier works, therefore, are purely original thought contrived with no systematic technique and, consequently, impelled by sheer musical intuition. In the note-row manner, only the fully initiated "twelve-noter" can differentiate by listening, and it is left to the *reader* to distinguish between the works through the limitation of the note-range. This forms some justification for the description "eye-music" which has been given to this manner[1] and emphasises the undue stress placed by the note-row devotees upon the mere process.

Consider the note-row upon which the *Symphonie*, Op. 21 (1928), is founded:

Ex. 2

By use of enharmonic changes, the second strain will be found to be an inversion of the first. This adds another rod to the back of the writer already cluttered up with rules and regulations, because canon cancrizan simply results in an imitation of the first strain a diminished fifth higher; but since transposition is allowable, the restriction does not

[1] See page 225.

appear to be very dogmatic. We take this row as it appears in its free distribution among the instruments:

Ex. 3

Similar treatment of the row is meted out simultaneously in other instruments, at differing pitches.

Even the most whole-hearted admirers of Webern admit that the listener must hear this work several times before he can claim that he is familiar with it.

A similar difficulty awaits those who would try to grasp *Das Augenlicht* for mixed chorus and orchestra, Op. 26 (1935), the orchestra consisting of flute, oboe, clarinet, alto saxophone, horn, trumpet, trombone, percussion, harp, celesta, mandoline and strings; but the difficulties are increased several hundred per cent. for the voices, who have to pitch notes with no help from anywhere, and follow curves paying no attention whatsoever to vocal technique as formerly understood, with leaps far transcending all ideas of practicability from the point of view of human possibilities and which, were it not for the fact that it is the timbre which counts, would be easy of execution on wind instruments and possibly strings. Ex. 4 on page 237, is a fair quotation of what is expected from the singers. Their days are but labour and sorrow until the final revelation comes, and then they enter fully into the aesthetic. The listener is completely stirred by the moving sound of the combined effect. Yet effect for itself did not come within the scope of such a serious-minded musician as Webern. The result is emotionally overpowering, even if the text is not only unintelligible in language, but undetectable in performance. When performed at the 1938 Festival of the International Contemporary Music Society, it made a lasting impression on all, including those antagonistic to the aesthetic.

However, the question remains; to what end? This is rarefied music for the initiated. Those who wish to become so are faced with a hard and difficult, yet rewarding, task.

Webern actually is the only real atonal composer, since no tendencies

can be traced anywhere to invite even the slightest suggestion of a tonality. One may refer to him as a closed composer. He opened a particular outlook and on his death it closed up. Any disciple using Webern's manner must surely fail to produce anything individual to himself. Extension or variation of the principle can result only in the negation of the principle itself in some detail or other. It may not be out of place to refer to Schoenberg's Foreword to Webern's *Sechs Bagatellen*:

> Only they will be able to understand these pieces who hold the faith that tone can express something which nothing but tone can express. They can no more be subjected to criticism than this, or any other faith can be. Faith can move mountains, but disbelief is incapable of allowing that the mountains exist. Against this incapacity, faith is powerless. Do the players know how to play these pieces? Do listeners know what to make of them? Could faithful players and listeners fail to surrender to one another in perfect understanding? But what is to be done with the heathen? No need to resort to the sword or the stake; only the faithful can

be excommunicated. But may this stillness of Webern's convey its message to them all![1]

This applies to anything else in Webern's output. It has no future whatsoever outside its own particular domain, and only serves to intensify the impasse.

[1] Quoted from the programme of the Ninth I.S.C.M. Festival, 1931.

CHAPTER TWENTY

ALBAN BERG

(1885-1935)

THE débâcle which I have suggested as being accomplished by Schoenberg and Webern might well have been splintered and eventually completely broken by Alban Berg, had he been spared to finish his career—he died at the top of his creative span, and maturity had led him to an altogether human outlook upon systematic, atonical, atonal and even tonal music. In complete contrast to the severities of Schoenberg and the immobile expressiveness of Webern, Berg's music is full of the pathos of human nature. It never exults, it never laughs; but it does not wallow in eternal gloom. It is true that his two operas are studies in pathology, but they often reach pinnacles of great beauty and emotion. Berg himself suffered, as, indeed, did Schoenberg and Webern, but his path was more difficult than dangerous, more objectively hostile than personally so.

Berg was not consistently systematic, and when he did use the note-row manner, he bent it to conform with his intentions and never let his thought be subjugated to it. At times he found his deepest feeling in tonality, which is duly prepared-for and led-away from. Consequently, there is no feeling of topsy-turvydom, for the process both ways is gradual. Berg never really threw off the early romanticism which is exemplified in all its semitonalism and chromaticism in the *Piano Sonata*, Op. 1 (1908), emanating from *Tristan und Isolde* by way of Scriabin, of all people. It might have been written by almost any sentimental composer of the time, and no amount of revision has managed to alter its face. It is interesting to compare the tonal version of the song *Schliesse mir die Augen beide* (1907) with the duodecuple one of 1926. The latter has all the symptoms of self-consciousness about it. The *Piano Sonata* is hardly worth playing, were it not for the fact that its composer's name is Alban Berg and, since Webern wrote little music for the instrument, pianists are otherwise restricted to Schoenberg.

Berg's music refutes the statement that all duodecuple music is necessarily systematic. Such moments as indicate a tonic come in the natural order of things. They are neither deliberately cultivated nor avoided. Berg's music shows no negations of any kind. When aligned with a note-row, it is not bound by any rules forbidding anything, except the use of the series and none other. When convenient, he avoids the series altogether, and although there is a strong feeling for polyphony, vertical reading often suggests some tonality or other. The music was written under a strong musical impulse. The fact that the classical devices and processes appear is entirely incidental, and is of no more importance than with the older composers. Their use simply forms the technique upon which the work in question is written. That *Wozzeck* is built upon such designs as sonata, passacaglia and variation, means the binding of the thought into cohesive wholes rather than letting the ideas appear whenever the text suggests them. Each act, each scene, therefore, hangs together symphonically, and the whole work is formally satisfying.

The question of the note-row solves itself when one considers that upon which the *Violin Concerto* (1935) is built. For convenience' sake we repeat it here: [1]

It will be seen how this divides itself into triads. Its use, therefore, insists upon strong tonal suggestions which are more marked than would be the case were the series more conjunct. The interval of the third is, in itself, romantically suggestive, and takes away any austerity of feeling. Consequently, this *Concerto* abounds in warmth of emotion, semitonal if you like, but strongly redolent of the inevitable *Tristan und Isolde* through its trend to the appoggiatura. The series is also capable of some considerable width of leap. Omitting the intervening

[1] See page 226 for a transposition.

harmonies (in two parts) the permutations of the opening of this work are worth quoting at some length:

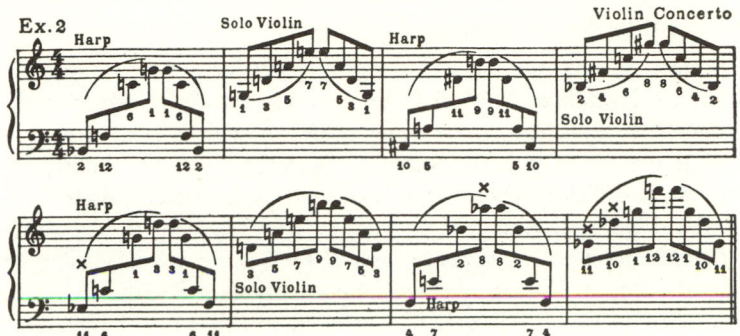

Notice that the enharmonic change appears at those points marked X. It may be remarked that bars 1, 3, 5, and 7 may be considered as transpositions of the original series, notwithstanding that the notes lie within the scope of the series.

It is upon this series that Berg composes this deeply-felt *Concerto*. It is an answer to those who maintain that emotion and the note-row are two distinct things, and the proof lies in the aesthetic of the whole work. It enabled Berg to find contrast between certain widespread themes notable for their lyricism and such a one as opens the *Allegretto* forming the second part of the first movement—up till that moment the music has formed an introduction stating the series as plainly as possible, both in its original state and in retrogression.

In the opera *Lulu* (1928-1935), which remains incomplete so far as the orchestration of the third act is concerned, Berg uses the following note-row:

which, again, has harmonic implications ascertainable by dividing the row into four groups or chord of three notes each. It may be significant of the note-row itself that the symphonic fragments available from this opera do not appear to have made the great appeal made by *Wozzeck*, either in whole or in part. However, this may be partly accounted for by the subject-matter, which, if anything, is more pathological and defeatist than that of *Wozzeck*.

Wozzeck stands sublime and alone in opera because of its intensity of pathos. Its difficulties seem to be unsurmountable on paper, but in practice they give the air of being achieved with perfect ease. It is possible that when each line seems to conflict with all the others, then there is no difficulty about individual clarity; it entails a matter of a different kind of listening, if, indeed, it is of any help to listen thus. Both ordinary vocal production and *Sprechstimme* are used, and the intervals, though frequently wide, are perfectly logical within the scope of vocal technique. It is largely the appearance of the music which repels at first sight.

The score is enormous, but every note is essential. This is no exaggeration or luxury; it is a necessity.

The technique of *Wozzeck* defies categorisation because it falls into every category. At moments it is frankly atonal; at others, it becomes atonical, and at others unmistakably tonal. Polytonal it rarely is; polymodal, never. Thus it might be considered by the unthinking to be a mixture of styles, but this it carefully avoids being, because the texture is uniformly thick although never obscure. It is interesting that at the time when Berg was writing the enormous semitonal crescendo and decrescendo, Milhaud was writing almost the same thing in his opera *Les Euménides*. This, of course, was pure coincidence; but whereas Milhaud was consistently polytonal in this work, Berg, as has been stated, varied the technique.

Berg's great tonal climaxes search out the very depths of our being. This is the result of contrast from the ever-pressing-onwards of the other type of thought. Listening to *Wozzeck* is a fleeting process. The ear absorbs very little at the moment, owing to the lack of poise. When the tonal moments come, the music rests upon a single harmony sufficiently long enough to allow complete absorption. This may be assisted by the fact that, for the moment, the ear finds repose in ordinary listening, as in a case like this:[1]

[1] I have omitted all accidentals irrelevant to the tonality although relevant to the atonal system.

where the key of F minor is driven home in a thoroughly traditional manner, by means of consonance. The music can be tonally dissonant, like this:

and diatonically dissonant, as in this passage:

which finds itself later at this situation:

Ex. 7   Wozzeck

The ear still has time to absorb the harmonic implications, and it is at such moments, particularly like Ex. 6, that Berg touches those heights of inspiration and depths of poignancy which I have mentioned. Whether he would have done so had the music been entirely in this somewhat turgid style, is doubtful, for the general texture would have become over-familiarised in the course of time. Berg, genius as he was, knew exactly what to do at the right moment to intensify a situation.

This tonal tendency has been regarded as showing up an atonal or atonical weakness, since in order to obtain his full effect, Berg had to go to the old-fashioned tonality to achieve it. I do not agree with this, because the process succeeds through contrast; and lack of contrast is a weakness of atonal music which few seem to be able to overcome. It may be said, therefore, that Berg has overcome it by avoiding the consistent use of the elements which go to make it. Berg's tonal instances appear all through his few works which, incidentally, amount to not more than seven opus numbers, and seven "other works". This is a small enough output in all conscience; but none of them is negligible in length or scope. Not one of "The Three" has ever written a hack work, or a piece deliberately written for gain—and it is rather doubtful if any of them could have done so, for their way of thinking was too enclosed. This is a striking testimony to their artistic integrity, for none has been gifted with a superfluity of this world's goods. From arousing hostility, they have moved through comparative indifference to recognition as a creative facet. The future is uncertain. Berg undoubtedly opened the *impasse* and provided a method and means of reconstruction. It is not as easy to write in his manner as may appear, and as so many people try to think. It requires concentration of thought and the ability to think along the system. This thinking must be impelled by musical instinct. Cerebrality is not enough; there must be feeling, but not the type envisaged and practised by Webern, for this is for the connoisseur alone and cannot result in anything but diluted Webern.

Austrian music requires someone who will continue the Berg tradition. There are many European copyists of the Schoenberg manner who thus deny their own culture in their endeavours to be universal. Unfortunately, universality in this case implies uniformity which in art, as in most other things, is an abomination. We await the moment when he that should come proves his descent while at the same time maintaining his native culture. It is in Vienna alone that these seeds can be replanted. At the moment, little new music comes to us from Germany or Austria, and what little does seep through bears only slight relation to the manner of "The Three". Their influence is to be found in France, although not necessarily among French-born composers. It is to be found to a certain extent in Italy, and to a small degree in England. It is possible that the New World under the influence of the great Schoenberg himself will send out disciples; but this cannot happen just yet, and it will be extremely difficult to differentiate between practice and maturity for some time. The omens seem to point to Berg rather than to Schoenberg or Webern as the apostle of the future, and it is as difficult to be distinct from Berg as it is from the others. The outlook is vague. It is some time since Berg died. Who is there in his own country to follow him?

THE AMERICAN NAISSANCE

[*Parker* (1863-1919)—*Macdowell* (1861-1908)—*Mason* (1873)]—*Ives* (1874)—(*Taylor* (1885)—*Hanson* (1896)) —*Cadman* (1881-1945)—*Still* (1895)—*Villa-Lobos* (1881)— *Chavez* (1899)—*Ruggles* (1876)—*Varèse* (1885)—*Cowell* (1897)—*Antheil* (1900)—*Thomson* (1896)—*Piston* (1896)—*Gershwin* (1898-1937)

THE American genius for publicity seems to have failed where her music is concerned. It is true that one may find scores here and there at agents, and that certain isolated works appear in our programmes from time to time; but no effort appears to have been made to publicise the music in a general way. This applies to both North and South America, particularly to the latter, whose musical output is enormous. The result is that American music is almost a closed book to the European music-lover and is confined to a few names, some of which play no part in the twentieth-century concept. At the end of the last century a certain impact was made by Horatio Parker (1863-1919), whose general musical outlook formed a clear parallel with the academic and university approach to music here, and Parker was one upon whose shoulders academic robes hung easily. The other name was that of Edward Macdowell (1861-1908), who made some considerable inroads into musical consciousness through his many piano pieces, all of considerable charm and romantic feeling. In this way he formed a counterpart to Edvard Grieg (1843-1907) in that pianists of limited ability were able to form a repertoire which made an instant appeal to themselves and their hearers, in the former case through the moderate standard of technique required for their performance, and in the latter through the simplicity of style and idiom.

Unfortunately, these drawing-room pieces of Macdowell took attention away from his more considerable works, among which the four

Piano Sonatas ("Tragica", "Eroica", "Norse" and "Keltic") and his two *Piano Concertos* are really notable works of their period. Macdowell had the right idea over the principle of creative isolationism, and it was unfortunate that his colony, where composers could live by themselves in picturesque surroundings, did not come up to expectations. He and other composers of his generation were mainly European trained and, therefore, their music does not carry any signs by which their Americanism can be recognised; indeed, these signs do not appear until well into the present century.

Towards the end of the nineteenth century, the German attraction seems to have faded somewhat and the orientation leant towards Paris and the Schola Cantorum. Vincent d'Indy was the best foil to the Teutonic tradition, because of his innate belief in classical form in combination with Gallic lightness. As a result, the composers coming under this influence were able to avoid Teutonic turgidity. Among the composers who found their musical feet under this aegis may be mentioned Daniel Gregory Mason (1873), a real *Maître* in the accepted sense, but one whose music has not penetrated European shores. However, more significant than the situation in North America is that in South, whose composers went to the same Schola Cantorum in great numbers and studied classicism and its association and possibilities with their natural folk-rhythms. The reason for this may be understood if Vincent d'Indy is placed alongside Nadia Boulanger (1887), the position of the two teachers in their respective generations being similar. Of the two, the latter may claim the distinction of having played a great part in the formulation of what may be termed the American style, because her teaching is less dogmatic from some points of view although the former was sufficiently objective to allow freedom of expression according to the natural inclinations of the individual pupil's culture. While it is true to say that a Boulanger pupil is recognisable anywhere, it is also true to say that that pupil's basic expression is never overpowered and her pupils do not write quasi-French music. With d'Indy and the principles of the Schola Cantorum, one realises the strong influence of style over that of process, and where the American students are concerned, this has resulted in a rather negative idiom. It should be acknowledged at once that the Schola principles have turned out a number of European composers of widely divergent points of view, and these include the American Edgar Varèse (1885) and the Czech Bohuslav Martinů (1890). However, American musical feeling at the end of the last century was not strong enough to maintain any individuality or even to formulate it, and the absence of tradition in these matters made things harder.

Nevertheless, one notes that Charles Ives (1874), a contemporary of Mason, but American-trained, eventually became an apostle of polytonality and split semitonality. Ives may certainly be said to be *of* as well as *in* the twentieth century, but owing to the weakness in propaganda, his music has played no part in the formation of contemporary thought. His influence, therefore, was purely local and even an avid desire for "culture" does not appear to have made a general impact upon musical styles and idioms. Ives, however, has always been far in advance of such composers as Deems Taylor (1885) and Howard Hanson (1896), whose music, although far from negligible, makes no appeal whatsoever to-day owing to its being too deeply rooted in European tradition. That America has some folk-lore tradition was evidenced by Charles Wakefield Cadman (1881-1945) who did for Indian folk-song what Bartok[1] did for Hungarian and Cecil Sharp for English. Not only did he make a large recorded collection of these tunes, but composed many works, including operas, based upon American-Indian folk-songs. Again, one has to chronicle the fact that these works do not bear any influence upon twentieth-century technique.

The situation, therefore, might be regarded as distinctly unpromising until one realises that in cultural matters America is still forming her traditions and that these very works which are confined to her shores will eventually be found to form the basis of what in time should be a great heritage. If one considers the eclecticism of the American race, one wonders why things should be as they are, for not only has she her North American Indian cult, but also the Negro element and the Hispanicism of South America to call upon.

The Negro element has indeed supplied a leaven of individual culture in the person of William Grant Still (1895), whose music is of a spiritual optimism which is in every way sincere. The so-called "spiritual" or sacred song, alternately nostalgic and optimistic, is as individual as a Somersetshire folk-song, but somehow or other Negro composers have not found it a basis for any permanent symphonic style. It may be that the wrong type of "spiritual" has reached Europe or that in the process of exportation it has become musically debased and otherwise distorted, but in actual fact the only striking influence

[1] See page 265.

of this Negro idiom has been realised in Delius' *Appalachia Variations*, for which he received the impulse from Florida, and in Dvořák (1841-1904).

In South America the situation appears quite hopeless, and the approach is hindered by the uncertainty expressed by those few writers who have discovered it. For our authority we turn to *Music in Latin-America*, by Nicolas Slominsky,[1] which fills the reader with doubts, not as to its authenticity, but as to the real value of what it propagates, for surely out of that vast and lengthy list of Latin-American works there should be a number which might be expected to reach Europe on their own merits. Of the Latin-American composers one can but take a handful, which includes only one who can be said to be at all familiar, Heitor Villa-Lobos (1881), a Brazilian composer, some of whose thirteen works called "Choros" have appeared in the B.B.C. Third Programme. Yet Villa-Lobos, like Carlos Chavez (1899) in Mexico, represents a culture which occupies an important place in music's panorama. Chavez, however, does not make things easy for himself, since he requires enormous orchestral forces for very little music. It may seem strange, but in Europe one has learned most about Brazilian music from a Frenchman, Darius Milhaud,[2] whose Soudades, or nostalgic pieces upon Brazilian rhythms, are full of sensitive delicacy.

This parochialism in a world only too anxious to learn is to be deplored, because it is actuated not by any political or parochial reason, but by pure laziness and lack of enterprise. It is all the more exasperating because what little one is able to pick up is infinitely more of the twentieth century than much of that emanating from North America.

However, the actual twentieth-century North American composers have indeed been in the maelstrom of contemporary thought, but they have not actually contrived anything permanent. Of these composers, one may point to Carl Ruggles (1876), whose *Angels* for six trumpets (this is the second movement of a work, *Men and Angels*) was apparently too much for the International Contemporary Music Festival of 1925, Edgar Varèse, whose pupilage at the hands of d'Indy, Roussel and Widor produced some amazing experiments in pure "sound" ("noise" might be more appropriate) which he called by such names as "Hyperprism", "Ionisation" (1931), "Equatorial" (1937) and "Density 21.5" (1936), Henry Cowell (1897), who devised a new

[1] Harrap.
[2] See page 81.

piano technique in terms of "clusters" played with the fist, elbow and forearm, and George Antheil (1900), who scored his *Ballet mécanique* for anvils, aeroplane propellers, two octaves of electric bells, motor horns, sixteen player-pianos controlled from a main electric switchboard, and some pieces of tin and steel. When Antheil had passed this adolescent foolishness his music developed into something perfectly normal and rather dull.

More permanent music, and in a legitimately musical manner, was that written by Virgil Thomson (1896), one of the earliest pupils of Nadia Boulanger, who combines a genuine creative facility with scholarly erudition. Living in Paris from 1925-1932, he spent a great deal of his time in the centre of *le dernier cri*, mixing freely and personally with Satie[1] and Les Six.[2] One result of this was the opera to text by Gertrude Stein, *Four Saints in Three Acts* (1938). Another trend he disclosed was also taken from the Parisian milieu, and on his return to America Thomson became one of her most valued and scholarly writers on music, a trait he picked up from the example of Paul Dukas[3] and others; in this way, Thomson, like Dukas and his fellows, writes with the benefit and advantage of a personal creative experience which has not been unsuccessful. He should not be confused with Randall Thompson (1899), a less astonishing composer, but in every way one equally important.

The parallel to Thomson the critic-composer is Walter Piston (1896) the composer-teacher who is the twentieth-century type of *Maître*. Piston's music bears all the marks of twentieth-century abstract classicism and his scholarship, which may be seen at its best in his chamber music and *Sinfonietta* (1940-1941), is of the highest. Piston, a pupil of Nadia Boulanger as well as of Harvard University, has written authoritative books on harmony and counterpoint which have the merit of looking and reading like books about rather than on music. The future of young America is assured at the hands of one who may be classed as the American Vincent d'Indy of to-day.

These names represent American music in its twentieth-century adolescence, and typify the state of confusion which reached her from Europe. It would not be wise to ignore a certain other facet of American music, which has been given an importance rather beyond its actual achievement. America may have been behindhand in her progress to the genuine twentieth-century thought in serious music, but she has

---

[1] See page 23.   [2] See page 70.   [3] See page 9.

always led the way in the century with new dance styles and in the realm of what is called the "musical". The influence of so-called jazz has penetrated the concert hall and its scintillating rhythms have found a place in the music of one or two composers who have had their minds upon higher things, but have not been found to have had the genuine musical ability at which they aimed. Of these, George Gershwin (1898-1937) is the most renowned through his *Rhapsody in Blue* (1923), which has circled the globe many times. Its popularity is due entirely to its orchestral colour and sensuous melodic fragments. It became available in many forms, for piano solo and for piano and orchestras of all sizes. It was followed by a *Piano Concerto in F* (1925), and Gershwin showed that he had ambitions; but he did not realise his limitations until he attempted to study with Ravel,[1] who could make nothing of him. The fact was that Gershwin had no symphonic abilities whatsoever, and his so-called symphonic works are mere scraps of music treated repetitively throughout. His most commendable orchestral work was *An American in Paris* (1928), which had elements of sharp wit about it, softened by nostalgia. This work had the honour of appearing in the International Contemporary Music Festival in London in 1931, when it was conducted by Alfredo Casella. After many concerts of weird and astonishing music, much of it neurotic and pessimistic, the unaffected simplicity of these naïve tunes cleared the air to such an extent that it even brought humour to the otherwise sedate proceedings. Gershwin was essentially a composer of the "musical", of the type of *Porgy and Bess* (1935), glorified by the name of "opera".

To say that the swinging tunes heard on so many sound-tracks are representative of American music is not altogether accurate; but composers of this kind who have had bands like that of Paul Whiteman "presenting" their concerts with a species of showmanship which in any other country would be utterly ridiculous can count themselves fortunate in having their music performed in such a perfect manner. Unfortunately, the cinema and the film-score have been the means of propagation and an altogether one-sided view of American music has been given to the world. That this particular one side is supreme in its own way cannot be denied, but the charge that jazz and this type of "musical" represent American music *in toto* is altogether inaccurate. One feels, however, that America has only herself to blame in this respect, since music is a commercial undertaking with her, like every-

[1] See page 50.

thing else. A series of serious symphony concerts, sponsored by some official body, is indicated, the concerts to be toured round the leading music centres of the world. The musical situation in America is almost limitless. There are foundations for this and that, research is encouraged in the most practical manner and prizes for compositions offered annually. American universities regard music as one of the primary studies; but of the results of all this activity, the world remains in partial ignorance and has infinitesimal knowledge.

It is time that the essence of American music declared itself more positively. Virility and rhythm alone are not sufficient. Claire Reis in the book, *Composers in America*,[1] defines an American composer as one "whether of European or Indian or African background—who has been woven into the American social fabric who thinks as his fellow-citizens do about accepted institutions and who conducts himself as they do"—which does not get us very far in determining American music.

Later, we shall take for consideration four names which seem to represent what the European mind may justly regard as being typically American composers, observing that they have certain parallels to themselves in their own styles and aims. It will be seen that American music offers much the same problem as that of British/English, yet in spite of the conglomeration of cultures which constitutes the American people, only one of the composers discussed seems to bear any entirely "national" traits. Their opposite numbers can be found in the music of our own country.

These four composers are not necessarily higher in value than any others. Indeed, the quality of American music in general is surprisingly level, and in some cases exceeds that representative of some European cultures. One may consider the future, when the work of the twentieth-century *émigrés*, Bloch (whose influence has not yet indicated any noticeable twentieth-century trend in spite of the unmistakable quality of his music), Schoenberg, and Hindemith shall have come to fruition, and America may reasonably be expected to be a world-leader in music; but this will not be for many years and will never happen unless the gospel is propagated in a practical manner to all and sundry.

[1] The Macmillan Company (New York).

CHAPTER TWENTY-TWO

COMPOSERS IN ISOLATION

1. *Jean Sibelius*
(1865)

THE position of Sibelius in this country is something quite remarkable. Although his opus numbers run into well over a hundred, not more than a dozen major works have ever been heard here. Few of these works which have served to place him among the greatest of the century, if not of all time (in the opinion of the experts), were composed later than 1935, and yet they seem to be perfectly new. It was not until the 1920's that realisation of him came to us; up till then he was known by the *First Symphony* (1899) and a few insignificant pieces, together with *Finlandia* (1900) and *En Saga* (1892). His *Fourth Symphony* made a surprising appearance at the Birmingham Festival in 1912, the year of its publication—and it is marked as Op. 35. The choice of this work, at once the least approachable of all the *Symphonies* which had already appeared, and were to appear, was actuated by much pioneer work on the part of (Sir) Granville Bantock, who had been the most fervent advocate of Sibelius up to that time, almost the only one, in fact. However, although this work made an impression by its solemnity and symphonic expansion, it cannot be said to have made an impact outside Birmingham, and London took Sibelius to her bosom in terms of the works named above, and of a certain *Valse Triste,* a movement in the incidental music to a play. This piece, excellent in its own setting, speedily came to a hackneyed death largely through its programme, the gloom of which was admirably portrayed in the sinuous and sinister music. Every café orchestra played it, and every listener hummed it at the same time. However, its popularity created no urge for enquiry or interest as to its composer's other works, except for the middle section of *Finlandia* (a magnificent tune, and hackneyed to death) and possibly for *En Saga* which, again, had a stirring theme. When, therefore, it was discovered that Sibelius had composed a number of *Symphonies*, a *Violin Concerto* and a *String Quartet* of enormous proportions, interest suddenly awoke, fanned by the enthusiasm of such people as Constant Lambert and Cecil Gray; Bantock's early advocacy was forgotten. One consequence was that each work in turn appeared as a brand new one, and the distinguished composer must have smiled to himself on many occasions when he found that from obscurity outside his own country, he had suddenly been proclaimed as a kind of musical saviour. This "discovery" of a composer who had already reached maturity and full individuality may be characteristic of the tendency to delayed exploration which is part of the English musical temperament, but it was of paramount importance. Its realisation came from the lack of a central figure which had the quality of stability not rooted in the outmoded styles prevalent in the early part of the twentieth century. At the same time, the music sounded as if it might have been written in the 1920's, although, in point of fact, none of it was really "new"; the harmonies were of the most elementary type being used and spaced in a manner not to be found in any other composer. Sibelius, therefore, might be considered as being only *in* the twentieth century, yet from other points of view he is distinctly *of* it. These include his isolation as a symphonic figure during a period fraught with uncertainty and superficiality.

Sibelius' position must be a constant source of embarrassment to him. He has completely swamped all the other Scandinavian composers. His position of primary significance he held with the Dane, Carl Nielsen (1865-1931), and since Nielsen's death he has reigned supreme and alone. It is as if Vaughan Williams were to exercise a similarly stifling effect upon the concept of English music. In Finland, the existence of others is naturally acknowledged, but the moment any music by another Finnish composer appears abroad, it is promptly laid next to Sibelius, and found wanting. Wanting it certainly is in all the elements which have made Sibelius significant; but there are other aspects of Finnish music which should be considered, and these are not deemed worth disclosing by our concert promoters. Like Vaughan Williams in this country, Sibelius is held in reverence by his juniors of all ages, and they continue to take their example and encouragement from the overpowering genius who presides at their head. Thus European recognition of one figure has halted recognition of all others of the same culture. However, because the situation is viewed from one side in this country, it must not be assumed that the same is the case in Finland herself, and the young generation there is probably quite contented with its lot, which need not, as ours need not, be necessarily universal and cosmopolitan. It is interesting that the prophet should come from such a small country, with history obscure and unknown to the West of Europe. Her topography is equally unknown, but, in accordance with the externals of Sibelius' music, is considered to be a land of mountains, forests, rain[1] and eternal snow. These externals, of course, are entirely fictitious, but the general impression received is one of grimness simply because Sibelius does not indulge in orchestral virtuosity and uses the instruments so often in their low registers. It is difficult to decide whether he is objective or abstract. The authorities hold that, generally speaking, he is the latter; but Sir Donald Tovey (1875-1940)[2] gives the following information apropos the *Third Symphony*—namely, that certain "passages . . . are said to represent the composer's impression of fog-banks drifting along the English coast". However, we need not take the suggestion[3] that the main or rondo theme of the *Violin Concerto* is "evidently a polonaise for polar bears" at all seriously. So much of his music seems to sing a saga of some kind and to paint magnificent pictures of rocky crags and booming seas; it must be remembered that he has written many symphonic works based upon the legends and poems from the *Kalevala* and *Kanteletar*. It is not unreasonable to suppose that he has had some of these in his mind when writing his *Symphonies*, particularly the *Fifth*. The technique is entirely his own and one can find no traces whatsoever of any influences from earlier composers. His music for the theatre has penetrated these shores in a very small quantity and much of it is not particularly remarkable or outstanding, although extremely suitable for its purpose. He must be regarded, therefore, as the composer of seven *Symphonies*, a *Violin Concerto*, and a *String Quartet*, together with a few *Symphonic Poems*, such as *The Oceanides* (1915), (a superb work), *Tapiola* (1925) and the two previously mentioned works. To these must be added the lovely little *Swan of Tuonela* (1895-1896) whose cor anglais solo sings the desolation of the lonely waters

[1] It is probably quite coincidental, but nearly every photo of Sibelius' house seems to have been taken after a heavy rainstorm.

[2] *Essays in Musical Analysis*, Vol. 2 (O.U.P.).

[3] *Idem*, Vol. 3.

of the lake leading to Tuonela, the Finnish equivalent of Hades, upon which the swan floats serenely, watching the souls which cross the waters after their journeyings over the nine seas. This work showed that the symphonic poem need not be bound up in terms of full orchestra.

It is in these pages that one realises the immobility of Sibelius' thought which, in the twentieth-century works, never hesitates to pause harmonically and dwell for long stretches on a single harmony. This little work, of course, has no connection with the twentieth century other than that it was "discovered" here during that period and since it bore no technical relation to any earlier processes, was thought to have been written after 1900. This is not a bad point, because it has allowed Sibelius to become recognised by both old and young; by the former, because they have been able to assimilate his style with no difficulty, and the latter, because there seems to be something in it which does not in any way suggest a date. The older generation admires the symphonic concepts of continuity and sustained development, while the younger rejoices to find means of expanding what to them tends to be an outworn design. Sibelius, therefore, has all the potentialities of one in the position of being able to please everybody; there are, of course, many who dislike his music, finding it to be neither ancient nor modern, neither traditional enough to come within the framework of the late nineteenth and early twentieth centuries nor "modern" enough to place it among the really noteworthy "experiments" of the 1920's. Sibelius seems to be a fixed taste. It does not seem possible to acquire it or to become fatigued by it. One either likes him or one does not. Another point which makes the music alien to the younger generation is its serious-mindedness, which came at the right moment over here, but seemed to be a definite reaction. Admiration as to its integrity and technical mastery over the processes of symphonic growth is general, and those who do not like the idiom at least find the style impeccable.

The usual stupid things have been said about the not absolutely mature works, particularly about the *First Symphony* and the *Violin Concerto*. It is often loosely said that the *Symphony* closed an epoch and that the *Concerto* is the best such work that Tchaikowsky ever wrote. Unfortunately, these dicta have remained fixed in the minds of the unthinking, and the two works are passed over with no thought to the fact that they contain the germs of the mature Sibelian outlook and technique. The *Symphony* closed no epoch; it bridged the gap from one to another and has nothing in common with what had become recognised as the standard type of romantic symphony. The *Concerto* could have been written by nobody except Sibelius. To ascribe it to Tchaikowsky is to admit ignorance of that composer, who was never so simultaneously subjective and objective and had no such highly-developed powers of symphonic expansion and continuity. The elements which gave Tchaikowsky his somewhat spurious feeling of continuity (repetition of fragment and passage work extraneous to the thematic content and written to fill up gaps) are absent from Sibelius, for when he repeats a fragment he does so in order to extend it slightly; the music is so continuous and cohesive that there are no short-winded phrases whose frequent cadences have to be filled up with rushing semi-quavers in order to keep the music moving. Further, there is not the slightest sign of hysteria in Sibelius' *Concerto* or, indeed, in any of his works. Finally, one finds none of the commonness which mars so many Tchaikowsky pages, particularly in the *Violin Concerto*. Sibelius' source of impulse is as "national" as that of Vaughan Williams, and his heroic sagas of Finland find their counterpart in the Celtic mysticism of Sir Arnold Bax.

If one attempted to explain Sibelius' harmonic thought, one would be hard pressed to find words which could convince the unknowing reader that there is anything noteworthy at all in this respect. When one has said ordinary common chords and discords treated in a non-semi-tonal manner, one has nearly covered the ground. Sibelius has never been either an inventor or an experimenter. He has followed no "-ism" or "-ality". He has merely twisted the ordinary basic technique to suit his own ideas and he obtains his individuality by these means in the matter of spacing. This management consists of using the lower registers of the instruments (as I have said) and of a fondness for thirds, which he gives often to the flutes, low down. This is a negative matter which cannot very well be illustrated in a short chapter, but it gives him his individuality as much as Berlioz' fondness for placing the first clarinet high up below the first flute, and for doubling the two instruments, immediately distinguishes his orchestration from anyone else's, at least, from the point of view of process.

While Sibelius is occupied in slightly expanding and extending fragments of themes, he often accompanies the process with an insistence upon some figure, repeated over and over again. This repetition drives orchestral players nearly frantic at times because it requires the highest control to prevent it being perfunctory and ill-balanced.

His melodic processes and attitude to Form are among the most remarkable of the century. His melodies are often expressive of moods, the effect being obtained both by means of shortness of initial phrase and its gradual widening, and by limitation of range. There is frequently a central note to which the theme returns again and again, and when this is not apparent, it is divided into spasms, as it were. The following may be taken as illustrating these facets of Sibelian melody:

These are quoted at length, to show the full implications of the process.

These themes maintain strict tonality, for Sibelius has not considered it necessary to throw this overboard or to propound new theories of extension. He is strictly evolutionary, not revolutionary.

Even with this centralisation of melody, Sibelius can rejoice over a moment of great spiritual exaltation. Without the surrounding texture, it is difficult to give a convincing proof of this, but the following will indicate the general attitude to what have been called "glorious outbursts":

Another melodic concept is his, and his alone. This is his attraction to a kind of Alberti treble which widens the scope of the theme but restricts its range:

This can be seen to a small degree in the penultimate bar of Ex. 2*b*. Consequent upon this, there is a tendency to repetition of a note, adding forcefulness of rhythm and turning the theme into a figure.

It suggests that Sibelius may have had a poem in his mind when he devised the process; this is stressed in a fragment like the next well-known tune:

Ex. 5   Finlandia

In parenthesis, so to speak, the middle tune in Holst's "Jupiter" from *The Planets* should be compared with Sibelius' quasi-folk-tune, which is in no way modal in technique although distinctly so in expression. Comparison will show two different cultural approaches to the tune suitable for "massed singing", and both have the effect of lifting the singers above themselves. Believe it or not, the writer heard of a church whose custom it was to sing "Abide with me" to Sibelius' tune. . . .

A particularly striking instance of the repeated note occurs in the Trio of the Scherzo in the *Second Symphony* where it is accentuated by the mark "Lento e suavo":

Ex. 6   Oboe   Symphony No. 2

The limitation of range gives certain themes a leaning effect, two good instances being found in the second movement of the *First Symphony* and the opening of *Tapiola*.

The concept of symphonic development is tied up with thematic expansion. Sibelius is not cyclical; his works do not revolve round a theme or evolve from permutations of it. They germinate from fragments, and the germinal process is often altogether unsuspected and unexpected. A very short incidental progression, or even an innocent interval, will be found to have been the germ of a final melody. Ex. 3b is the culmination of one of these. The first interval appears quite inconsequentially at first, and is absorbed into part of the main texture, although its quality attracts momentary attention to itself. The *Seventh Symphony* has its roots in the opening scalic passage. In this way the music never halts or falters and it is thoroughly symphonic, in the fullest sense of the term. This process does not appear in the *First Symphony*, which is completely conventional in form and construction and makes but a fleeting appearance in the first movement of the *Second*. The *Third* is the first example of its extensive use. The *Fourth, Fifth* and *Sixth Symphonies* are cohesive in this way, although the *Fourth* is entirely derived from thematic fragments. The *Seventh* is in one movement. This does not amount to a string of movements linked together by some little motto phrase forbidding any break, nor is it a one-movement symphony in first movement form, like Scriabin's *Poème de l'Ecstase* (1908), which is thus more in the nature of a subjective symphonic poem than of a symphony. Sibelius' *Seventh* moves steadily onwards, and the design is more a series of moods than movements. Its length is exactly right. It is concise and says not a word too many. Formally one distinguishes several "subjects", but these are not arbitrarily placed in any order of appearance, and the opening scalic passage does not "bring the work to a close" in a conventional manner.

This work gives the impression of having been composed with all the time in the world to spare. It is fruitless to listen in an impatient mood. The opening section progresses extremely placidly and smoothly and the concentration of thought and clarity of mind which went to its making are stamped on every bar. Like most of Sibelius' music, it appears to have been thought out and written down straight in terms of the orchestra, and straight into the full score, without any rough or preliminary notes in short score. One imagines that perhaps Sibelius is not altogether sure in what condition his material will finally disclose itself, or even of what his final material will consist, until he reaches the particular moments. Certain salient features appear to suggest themselves during the course of composition, striking him as possible germinals, to be brought into extension at the most suitable moments. Many of these fragments give the impression of being sudden ideas put into the texture on the spur of the moment. Formally, one can, with some imagination, divide each movement into the usual constituent elements, but justification for a "second subject" usually lies only in the fact that it comes after the opening, and, therefore, after the first. This whole symphonic principle fully illustrates the dictum of Vincent d'Indy that the material decides the form, not the form the material, a saying and practice evidently unknown to the vast majority of non-creative writers on music who live under the impression that composers "pour their ideas into moulds".

However, Sibelius gives no hint that he is extemporising on the orchestra and one can see the formal plan if unable to fit it into any preconceived and pre-established shape. The *First* and *Second Symphonies* offer no question in this respect, since Sibelius had not reached the stage when formal strictures hindered the freedom of his thought. Everything is well bound, and in this respect the *String Quartet,* "Voces intimae", may be studied not only from the point of view of its conjunct movement, but from its symphonic conception which goes as far along the traditional path as Sibelius wished to go, and applies the symphonic principle to the medium of the string quartet. No matter what the commentators may say to the contrary, this is not a work happier on the string orchestra, or one written in that medium and made available for performance by four players The writing is closely wrought and compact.

The reputation for gloom which has been grafted on to Sibelius' music is apparent and justified in one work only, the *Fourth Symphony,* which stands alone, not only in his output, but in that of the whole panorama of late nineteenth- and twentieth-century symphony.

I have suggested elsewhere[1] that many composers adopt a different scheme and approach to their fourth symphonies. I do not suppose that there is any psychological or physiological reason for this, but it happens to be so, and a moment's thought will call to mind some notable instances. Sibelius, in his *Fourth Symphony,* propounded a problem which has caused endless and indeterminable controversy and conjecture. He himself has never given any explanation of the impulse which drove him to such austerities as we hear in this work. Never a subjectively passionate composer, here Sibelius pours a jug of cold water upon his listeners, and the astonishing thing is that they seem to like it.

Throughout this work, which uses the leap of the augmented fourth extensively, one can see how the fragments of germinated material are woven together, but, as is always the case with fragmentation, a certain amount appears rather unconvincing and one is often not altogether sure of the thematic derivations. I admit that this places emphasis upon the analytical side of reading and listening, but in a composer whose technique shows so strong a trend towards the future of a truly symphonic concept of symphony, such cold thinking is necessary and inevitable; for Sibelius has already altered the whole face of symphony

[1] *The Symphony: Its History and Development.* (In preparation.)

and symphonic design. He has shown that the eradication of unessentials is not only possible, but feasible, if not essential for the true symphony of the present—and I say present and not future advisedly, because now seems to be the time when composers are finding the traditional designs no longer expandible within their present framework. In this respect Sibelius has accomplished exactly what Beethoven accomplished, and this outlook, anarchic though it was in some cases, now requires still further broadening.

However, Sibelius does more than indicate mere formal expansion. He presents a completely original approach to orchestration and melody. He has destroyed many conventions, and has shown in his treatment of the flutes, for example, that no instrument has a "normal position" any longer. He has found the happy medium between the fragmentary theme and the long tune, and this, not through any discovery of new secrets, but by laying bare the technique of germinal expansion and precision of construction. Harmonically, he has said nothing new at all. His harmonic bases are, quite frankly, completely traditional. Sonorities and researches into new aspects of chords have never troubled him. His originality may lie partly in this fact, but it has resulted in a clearly defined individuality, whose influence can be noticed in certain small ways. These do not in any degree imply plagiarism. To plagiarise Sibelius and, indeed, any of the leading composers who have so markedly indicated the trend of the present and future, would defeat its own ends. Fortunately, he is too well-established by now to suffer any eclipse, even after his death, as has been the case with Holst and Alfredo Casella (1883-1947). This has often been the fate of composers who have become fashionable; but it will be found that they usually suffer from excessive mannerisms which in time become monotonous. Sibelius is, to a certain extent, mannered, in that he does the same things so many times; but he does them in different ways, and what resemblance there is between one work and another is more often than not to be found in the orchestral technique peculiar to himself; for Sibelius is an orchestral writer *par excellence*. With no apparent effort or intention, he has shown how a composer, living away from the main stream of European experiments and fashions, can be original without being in any way iconoclastic or outré. He presents to the world a solid front against all prevailing tendencies and, as far as he is concerned, Schoenberg, Stravinsky, Les Six and every other kind of "school" might not have existed. It is said[1] that he admires the integrity of Schoenberg and feels that the fact that Stravinsky has gone through six periods may have been necessary to him, as were three to Beethoven.

The present-day younger composer who would seek to find his musical salvation from Sibelius will have to find some particular twists of his own in order to prove his individuality and to distinguish himself from his leader. What these can be, no one but the composer himself can say, but the lead given by Sibelius is clearly one of germinal growth and consequent thematic cohesion. He gives no lessons in form because he is indefinite in this respect and those who follow him must find their own paths.

---

[1] *Sibelius*, Cecil Gray (O.U.P.).

CHAPTER TWENTY-THREE

COMPOSERS IN ISOLATION
2. *Bela Bartok*
(1881-1945)

THE habit of pairing composers usually leads to curious anomalies, and although the result is not always far-fetched, there are instances when such pairing reveals a complete lack of the understanding of two aesthetics. Holst and Vaughan Williams is not quite so unknowing a pairing as it may superficially appear; Ravel and Debussy is an absolutely absurd one, but not so much so as Stravinsky and Bartok, whose particular aesthetics have never had anything in common. This coupling together was the result of an awareness which came into being at one and the same time as music's twentieth-century upheaval. The names of the two composers became inextricably locked up together as synonymous with everything which the conventional mind regarded as ugly and *outré*. "Modern music" came to be represented by these two names alone. In retrospect this is possibly understandable, for although Schoenberg had not at the time made any great impact over Europe, Stravinsky and Bartok were the most authoritative figures at the time, for the substance of their music was greater than that of any other composer of the time.

The history of music is formulated round figures which remain in the public eye and establish themselves in the concert programmes. These figures have usually found their level through conscious or subconscious propaganda on the part of the few. Schoenberg, Stravinsky and Bartok may justly be said to have disturbed the flow of tradition; the smaller figures, smaller only in the relative size of their works, have been passed over by the public as mere gnat stings, and public opinion has regarded them from a slightly superior angle because they did not emanate from a culture whose traditions had become established as the final authority for such matters. Schoenberg rose to prominence as a complete iconoclast and a composer of grim works, denying everything which had come to be represented by the term "music". Stravinsky had the popular backing of the Russian Ballet of Diaghileff, and no matter how startling the music may have been, it started with a certain advantage of being attached to another medium, for which it was admirably suited. Bartok came out of the blue, from a country whose culture was loosely tied up, in public realisation, in terms of Hungarian rhapsodies, Czardas, and Hungarian bands (so-called—many of the personnel were pure Englishmen). The only Hungarian composer to make any impact here was Ernst von Dohnanyi (1877) whose *Variations on a Nursery Tune* for piano and orchestra and *Suite in F sharp* for orchestra, proclaimed no little humour in the first instance and infinite grace and charm in the second, but whose technique and language were strongly rooted in the past. The arrival of Bela Bartok on the concert platform indicated a complete negation of everything which had become recognisable as Hungarian music, and even the well-written and masterly music of Zoltan Kodaly (1882) was viewed with suspicion at first, because it was altogether too genuinely Hungarian and not sufficiently "gipsy" to fall into line with the general point of view. In the days when Schoenberg sounded boring and heavy, and Stravinsky incompetent and crude,[1] Bartok struck the contemporary ear as being indescribably ugly.

Schoenberg's appeal was intellectual, Stravinsky's austere in its neo-classical approach, while Bartok combined the attributes of classical design and romantic feeling, of an uncompromising nature; it was generally felt that Bartok was the big bully of the three because he hammered his ideas home with a relentless love for the percussive elements of instruments. One could not dismiss his music as one could certain works of Stravinsky, or forget about him as one could forget about Schoenberg. Bartok had no ardent verbal or vocal propagandists and never came out with any public apologia or postulation of theory. He allowed his music to speak for itself. Schoenberg has been able to force his ideas upon the world through his pupils and disciples, while Stravinsky and his disciples have never hesitated to come into the open with proclamations and pronouncements of aesthetic ideals in order to justify each stage of his progress.

Bartok remained aloof from all musical polemics, and was rather a legendary figure. He was admired and respected by those who knew

[1] I refer to the post- *Le Sacre de Printemps* works.

him, but his following made no attempt at publicising his works and, indeed, Bartok's retiring nature would have withdrawn still further into itself at the mere thought of propaganda of this nature. Consequently, each work in his progress made a sudden impact which acted as a rude shock to the unprepared listener, for it came in the later part of Bartok's aesthetic progress; the early works have made but rare appearances here and the public heard his individual and mature "middle period" before anything else. This from one point of view was good, because there have not been any unfortunate "early works" to live down, but prejudice and the current approach of the moment made things difficult.

He was completely unpredictable from the very first moment that he became realisable as a composer of some force. It must be added here that although he did not make musical pronouncements or enter the lists of musical polemics, politically he was very different and his courage was supreme and proud. I have already told of his action with Dr. Goebbels;[1] when the persecution of the Jews started under Hitler, Bartok wrote and said that he wished to be considered as one of the persecuted race—actually, he had no Semitic blood at all. This courage, fortified and impelled by sincerity, made him an example to his contemporaries, and the artistic and racial defiance which he hurled at the hysterical Führer made life impossible for himself. His emigration to America was not voluntary, but was insisted upon by those who feared for him by reason of his outspokenness. Yet he complained of but one thing only—and his privations while in America were severe—and that was about the possible (proved later to be factual) destruction of his wonderful library of recorded Hungarian folk-music by the Nazis and their sympathisers. Deprived of everything, he lived a solitary and impoverished existence in America, and when he died his funeral was paid for by the Authors' Rights Society of America. His last days were lightened by the news that, after the fall of Nazidom, the new Hungarian régime had restored his former awards and decorations, and had made him a Member of the Senate; but his last illness prevented him from enjoying the situation.

Bartok has always been misunderstood and misrepresented. In an age when romanticism was scoffed at, he remained incurably romantic; when Impressionism had reached its dead-end, Bartok combined several Impressionistic trends with his own basically classical tech-

[1] See page 188.

nique. He himself admired Debussy and held the theory that, geographically, Hungary formed the meeting point of East and West. From the one side, he felt that French music with its warmth of feeling was the most closely aligned to that of Hungary, and, from the other, he detected a parallel with the colour of the nineteenth-century Russian composers, particularly Moussorgsky (the outsider can detect the influence of Borodin and Rimsky-Korsakov as well). This Russian influence was the splitting element of musical thought in Czechoslovakia, experienced, and proved beyond gainsaying, by the Czech composer Leoš Janáček (1854-1928).

Bartok was proud of being Hungarian and showed it in a practical manner. His vast collection of Hungarian folk-tunes was impelled partly through disgust. In 1911 the Committee of the Beaux-Arts in Budapest commissioned an opera from him. This resulted in *Bluebeard's Castle*, but when the work was handed in, the Committee refused to accept it, maintaining that it was unperformable. Bartok "took to the road" at once on his quest for folk-tunes and forgot all about this rebuff—young and old composers to-day may take comfort from the fact that he who eventually became recognised as one of Europe's glories failed in this respect. It was from the recording of many hundreds of these tunes that Bartok gradually acquired the type of short melody, which is the Hungarian characteristic. Hungary's folk-songs are not quite the simple-minded affairs that ours are, and while ours have a definite religious (if pagan) symbolism behind them, those of Hungary are full of barbaric brutality, as beseems a race which has lived sword in hand, surrounded by superstition. Bartok's uncompromising harmonic technique undoubtedly found its foundation in this uncompromising manner of life. While his themes are perfectly obvious and plain-sailing, his harmonies are the reverse, and the early antagonism to him may certainly be ascribed to the edge and acidity which characterised his harmonic thought. At the time when hostility was most rife, consequent upon his constant appearance in concert programmes, Bartok seemed to be unnecessarily keen and crude. One had not yet become thoroughly accustomed to the new underlining of themes in seconds and fourths which, after its heyday, became almost as dated as Brahms' thirds and sixths. Hence his piano writing, incisive and trim, repelled listeners by its absence of anything approaching the conventional type of lyricism. The piano became a percussive instrument, and accentuating this was his love of significant parts for percussion instruments. An interesting story is told of Sviatoslav Prokofieff, the elder of the composer's two sons, who described his father's method of composing as "first he writes music like everybody else, and then Prokofieffises it".[1] Bartok's music basically is no different from any-one else's. He used no harmonic cluster which has not been used by every other composer and which cannot be found in any text-book; but he used them in his own way. He succeeded in combining the best of two worlds and in so doing was always a step ahead of his contem-poraries. The "Bartokising" of traditional thought can be seen in nearly everything up to 1936, the year of the *Music for String Instruments, Percussion and Celesta* which heralded a thinning out of texture and a return to the atmosphere of Impressionism recognisable in the subtle-ties of the harmonies—there is little that can be described as "subtle" before that date. Note at this point the description of the work, which places a new point of view upon "strings". It is scored as follows:

> Double string orchestra
> Side drum without snares
>   ,,   ,,   with snares ⎫
> Cymbals   ⎬ One player.
> Tam-tam   ⎭
> Bass drum
> Timpani (chromatic)
> Xylophone
> Celesta
> Harp
> Pianoforte.

From this it appears that the harp and piano are included among the "string instruments". The care over details of percussion would have rejoiced the heart of Vincent d'Indy, himself a percussion "expert".

To return to the question of harmony; even as late as the 1930's, by which time one would have thought that ears had become accus-tomed to almost everything, hostility greeted Bartok in passages such as this

[1] *Bela Bartok*, Moreux, (Masse).

where the edge of the minor seconds proved too unrelenting for listeners, while the openness of the harmony of this

suggested that he was one of the hated "atonalists"—he, who never subscribed to any "-ism" or "-ality" but wrote simply "music".

Squareness of pianism appears all through his pages. It is obvious in the *Sonata for Two Pianos and Percussion* (1937), scored, in 1938, as a *Concerto for Two Pianos and Orchestra*, where the first movement moves solidly along in the manner of Ex. 3 for many pages.

It may be said that Bartok made himself first approachable with the *Music for String Instruments, Percussion and Celesta,* and from that moment his thought remained on a delicate plane which eschewed the former violence although staying faithful to classical processes and principles. From that moment he seems also to have been concerned with sonorities; previous to this, his orchestration was free from all feeling of orchestral effect, and even at this moment the exploration of

Ex. 3

{Sonata for Two Pianos and Percussion
{Concerto for Two Pianos and Orchestra

sonorities lies in the actual musical thought. The same attention to detail remained, but gained added importance the more he considered the orchestra from the "Concertante" point of view, and all the later works are imagined from this aspect.

The *Concerto for Orchestra* (1943) which Sir Adrian Boult took so much to himself (with such beautiful results) is a striking example of the combination of this research into sonorities and classical texture. It has acquired a reasonable amount of popularity and calls for applause with no dissension, this being the result of constant performance which has caused it to be absorbed into the listener's normal reckoning. This work, and the charming *Divertimento for Strings* (1939), place all violence on one side, and concern themselves with extreme clarity. The disappearance of the violent element caused the *Third Concerto for Piano and Orchestra* (1945) to become immediately acceptable and unassailable from the earlier points of view; there is no more instructive lesson to be learned in how a composer can, over a stretch of time, move from strength to strength and ultimately to refinement of thought and expression than through a study of the three *Piano Concertos* dated 1926, 1930-1931, and 1945 respectively. The opening bars of the last such work, completed by Bartok save for the final seventeen measures, will show almost a complete *volte face* from the ideals of the other two:

Ex. 4 — Third Piano Concerto

Of bi-modality there is plenty; of Bartok's fugal mastery there is every evidence (for Bartok from the point of view of classical design and texture was scholarly to a degree); the music is often lyrical in quality; there is hardly any of the earlier edgy harmony or block writing, although now and again we do find short passages; but these are not the main bases of the pianism. The same thing can be said of the *Concerto for Viola and Orchestra* (1945), composed under tragic circumstances and assembled by Tibor Serly, Bartok's pupil. Of this work, written for William Primrose, Bartok explained that "the orchestration will be rather transparent, more transparent than in the *Violin Concerto*" (1937–1938). The whole texture of the work is sparse to a degree, but nevertheless typically Bartok in technique.

One finds Bartok's progress to have been a normal advance from certain aspects of Richard Strauss, as in *The Wooden Prince* (1914), *Bluebeard's Castle* and, to a small degree, *The Amazing Mandarin* (1919), although the technique in this work shows a considerable advance upon the others. From this point it finds its way through an uncompromising vigour to a final clearing away of all signs of musical distemper, reaching its climax in 1936, and finishing in a world of infinite grace and delicacy, not unmixed with classic dignity.

In chamber music Bartok made no compromise with his performers, save in those many cases where he deliberately composed music for young players. Of these, mention should be made of the five pieces *Pour les enfants* (1908-1909) and the now well-known *Mikrokosmos* (1926-1937), consisting of a carefully graded "Course", from easy pieces for six-year-olds to concert ones for virtuoso pianists. Bartok succeeded in these works where Stravinsky in his *Les Cinq Doigts* (1921) failed because the latter tried deliberately to reduce his natural technique to a small scale and did not really understand the medium. Bartok wrote his pieces introvertly; Stravinsky did not convince because his efforts were too self-consciously manufactured for the purpose; further, they were not written from practical experience.

Bartok's *Sonatas* and *Rhapsodies* have been described as "fortresses of sound"[1] and this admirably describes them. Their severity does not invite immediate assimilation, but the musician regards them as monuments of artistic integrity and serious thought, the real enthusiasts placing them beside the greatest works of Beethoven; but it is as yet too early to make such an assessment. They are models of concentrated and closely wrought material planed down to the barest essentials. The earliest of these dates from 1921, from the time when his style had reached its second period, and was unique to Bartok alone.

This was no sudden change. The earliest signs of what the future might entail appeared in the fourteen *Bagatelles for Piano* (1908), although many of the authorities see this in the *Allegro barbaro* (1911), a piece requiring piano-hitting of some force and containing little of thematic interest outside the actual pianism. These *Bagatelles* may be regarded as experiments in certain processes which later were to become

[1] *Cyclopaedic Survey of Chamber Music*, W. W. Cobbett (O.U.P.).

normal aspects of his idiom. Thus we find examples of bi-tonality, and the use of single quantities of chords as the basis of different pieces. The *Bagatelles* hold much the same position in Bartok's canon as the *Six Piano Pieces* (1911) of Schoenberg, although Bartok was not to adopt his suggested points for some years. The pieces showed the early contrapuntal tendencies which were to appear all through his mature works. Their importance is probably higher than their musical value, which is confined mainly to points of interest.

As I have said, he is at his finest in the six *String Quartets* (1908, 1915-1917, 1927, 1928, 1934 and 1939). The dates will be seen to cover his whole creative career, and to represent each period. The most frequently performed is the *Fourth,* a work of remarkable tautness and precision. A comparison between the *Music for String Instruments, Percussion and Celesta* and the *Sixth String Quartet* will show a similar approach in their openings, and also the polyphonic orchestral style eventually thinned itself down to four instruments.

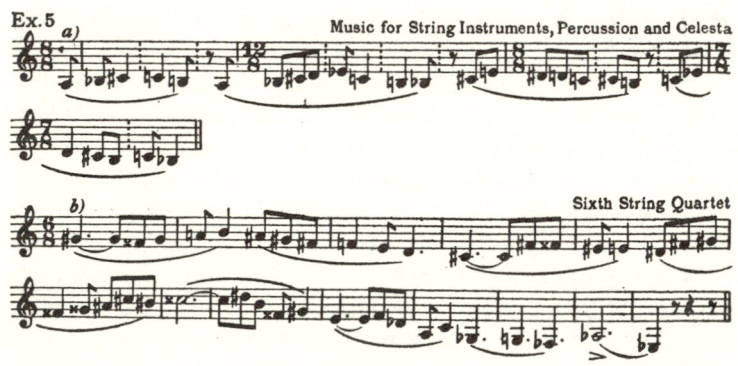

The *Quartet* is hardly a gracious work once the first movement has ended, and its spiky rhythms compel rather than attract by their thematic import. Formally, they extend the four-movement principle. The *Fourth Quartet* is laid out in five movements, the *Fifth* likewise, while the *Sixth* subdivides its second and third movements into two sections each, the first being slow passages rather than movements in themselves. The second section of the second movement is described as "Marcia" and that of the third "Burletta". Each complete movement ends quietly, and there is no gradual drawing to a triumphant close. "Fireworks" are conspicuous by their absence and when the music is not bitter, as in the "Marcia", it is gracefully sad. The medium allowed Bartok to exercise his extreme introversion and he sings very much for himself. These works are notable additions to the repertoire, but Bartok writes only for virtuosic chamber music players and thus slenders down his chances of performance. The music is for the connoisseur, consequently limited in appeal and anathema to the socially significant—but not all the countries behind the Iron Curtain appear to be so conscious, for the Czechoslovak radio broadcast a memorable performance on October 3rd, 1950.

Those who require their Bartok to be socially significant can find him so in his many transcriptions and arrangements of Hungarian folktunes, which include versions for voice and piano, alla capella chorus, chorus and piano, piano, violin and piano, orchestra and voice and orchestra. Here he has done very much what Cecil Sharp (1859-1924), Vaughan Williams, Holst and others have done for folk-tunes in this country.

Bartok's influence outside Hungary seems to be general rather than individual, for his style and idiom are not easy to particularise. All that can be done is to take certain little salient features and isolate them from the mass. Only a Hungarian wants to write in the terse Hungarian melodic style, and, if home-trained, he does this naturally. Bartok himself grew out of two composers, Debussy and Strauss, passing to his maturity through Schoenberg. His own individuality can be aligned with all three, although the second is not so easy to find in the mature works. From Debussy he got his latent Impressionism which became instinctive without being in any way arbitrarily used as a definite technique. From Schoenberg, he learned his uncompromising approach to harmony; but he never gave any suggestion of an iconoclastic trend. He has always strictly observed tonality, but his tonal moments are more than moments only, and it is simple to follow his key successions even in his most complex passages. It may be that one cannot easily hum or sing a Bartok theme, but this does not matter.

It appears, therefore, that he has no place in influencing trends in other countries. His music is universal because it is one facet of Europeanism. It travels well, since it combines its romantic and abstract elements so well. Bartok forms an interesting harmonic parallel with Roussel, in which connection one again draws attention to the musico-geographico theory. The parallel is only an harmonic one, for, melodically, Bartok was too patently Hungarian to show any similarity to the agile Gallic mind of Roussel. Roussel might have written like Bartok had he been Hungarian instead of French, and Bartok supplies the Impressionistic element absent in Roussel. Bartok's middle period is very much akin to Roussel's second.

It is peculiar that Bartok should be the theorists' hunting ground. Theories have been formulated far in advance of anything that Bartok either conceived or intended. Mahler, Scriabin, Stravinsky and Bartok have probably given rise to more theorising and blank-prose than any other composers. Is there a mystery about Bartok's technique, style or idiom? I think not. Bartok himself is perfectly plain to he who reads or listens. His problems were personal to himself and do not appear to have caused him much heart-burning, although there are plenty of signs of heart-searching (which is not quite the same thing). One can take Bartok in the normal stride of music without any theorising or philosophical thinking. Idiomatically, he is difficult to explain, but simple to understand. The qualities are distinctly positive, but inexplicable in words.

He is one of those who may well be found to form a major part of the basis of the music of the future, and his work shows every trend in that direction.

CHAPTER TWENTY-FOUR

COMPOSERS IN ISOLATION
3. *Igor Stravinsky*
(1882)

THERE has never been anything esoteric about Stravinsky's music, and if the influence of Bartok has been moral rather than directly musical, that of Stravinsky has been felt by almost every significant composer of the twentieth century, and, as in the case of Schoenberg, music has not been quite the same thing since he became established. Schoenberg's powers have directed a school, not a large one, it is true, but sufficiently so to make itself felt, the technique directing a trend which has not yet become general. Stravinsky's technique has influenced individuals rather than groups. Stravinsky has led a nomadic life and wherever he has pitched his musical tent, has succeeded in drawing a multitude to himself as the authority for a final break-away from traditional customs and restrictions without the necessity for the superimposition of substitutes. The former iconoclast, therefore, could regard him, or so he felt, as the final authority for complete freedom, and even for anarchy. That this was too wide a point of view was to be proved as time went on, for Stravinsky has always been able to justify everything which he has done, be it a new technical departure or a complete point of view. In a world unsettled and rocking with uncertainty, a man of Stravinsky's age and position was a godsend to youth who needed an example less austere than Schoenberg, but one equally full of integrity. That Stravinsky has sometimes come out with rather astonishing proclamations and declarations is beyond the point, although many have regarded them as showing a lack of stability. However, a little madness is a good thing now and again, and in an art situation which had become almost sterile for lack of freshness and impulse, these declarations of policy, so to speak, declared in both words and music, kept the waning flame alive. The immediate post-Great War years, therefore, had everything to commend themselves in respect of vitality, for everyone was necessarily living on his nerves and Stravinsky's ever-increasingly astonishing works played into the hands of the young generation.

Some influences are evil; others appear so on the surface, but when probed to their depths are found to be simply vitalisations. Stravinsky has never had an evil influence upon music or musicians. He has driven many to exasperation, but it is interesting to note that his works are performed constantly, with no regard to date, style, or idiom. It is not so much the case of one fine work following another in quick succession as being faced with a series of works which are so important and so varied, and which played such a controlling and directing influence upon the course of music, that none can be omitted, since their progress shows the progress of a complete reorientation of thought. The battles were not local battles, as in the case of Schoenberg; they were general, and took place everywhere because the music was more universal. Even to-day *Le Sacre de Printemps* is still exciting, but youth now takes it in its stride, finding it thoroughly in line with its own contemporary ideals. There are actually only two major works which reflect an immature Stravinsky. *L'Oiseau de Feu* still finds a welcome, and is still an object lesson in orchestral virtuosity; but it represents only momentary style. The other, *Le Rossignol,* is never played now (from what one can make out) and its circumstances forbid it. *Petrouchka* marks the first step to the representative Stravinsky, and here it should be noted that few composers have leapt to fame quite so easily or have found their own technique quite so quickly as Stravinsky. He was one of those caught up by Serge Diaghileff (1872-1929), to be used for his own ends. Diaghileff's perspicacity was remarkable, and although he made mistakes, these are in the minority. He chose his composers in some instances from the most meagre evidence, Stravinsky recommending himself through two early works which to-day sound not only tame, but make one wonder quite what they had to suggest his potentialities. Both the *Scherzo Fantastique* (1908) and *Fireworks* (1908) are in the Rimsky-Korsakoff tradition and might have been written by almost any Russian pupil of that composer. However, they have certain colouristic qualities which placed them in the forefront of a European music not notable elsewhere for its romantic approachability; this was to make itself apparent later, when the young French school impinged itself upon Europe in general.

Stravinsky, therefore, found himself bound up in the Russian Ballet, and soon proved it congenial to his sense of rhythm and the above-mentioned colouristic instinct which fell into line with the spectacularity of the whole Diaghileff concept of Russian ballet. For Diaghileff, Stravinsky wrote four actual ballets, although some of his other works were produced by that impresario. These ballets show a steady forward progress from the romantic spectacle of *L'Oiseau de Feu* (1909-1910) to the subjective humanities of *Petrouchka* (1910-1911), the religious expressionism of *Le Sacre de Printemps* (1911-1913) and to the realism of *Les Noces* (1914-1917). Stravinsky at this point set out to finish *Le Rossignol* which he had put aside in 1909, after writing the first act. The work was finished in 1914, by which time his style had changed so completely that a great seam appears at the join, and this otherwise charming "lyric tale" remains an ill-balanced work. After *Les Noces* came *Pulcinella* (1919), in which Stravinsky took pieces by Pergolesi (1710-1736), and strung them together in accordance with his own twentieth-century style. It is described as being "after Pergolesi"—it would be better to ignore the name of the original composer; albeit the whole work is charmingly done. To Diaghileff, Stravinsky owed the production of his opera *Mavra* (1922), a delightfully light and amusing work on a par with d'Indy's *Le Rêve de Cinyras* (1922-1923) and Roussel's *Le Testament de la Tante Caroline* (1932-1937), but is more successful since it was not necessary for him to turn his face against a natural style and idiom.

Stravinsky's flirtations with jazz, although not fruitful in the procreation of any really successful work, played a large part in giving him rhythmic polyphonic freedom, and assisted him in his pursuit of neo-classicism. This expressed itself in the *Symphonies d'instruments à vent* (1920), written in memory of Debussy. London may take the credit for the world première, which was greeted with indignation on the part of the public, the Press—and the composer himself. Stravinsky maintained that music should speak for itself, without any explanation or "interpretation". He insisted on obedience to marked dynamics, but objected to any expressive gradations of tone which were not indicated. Stravinsky took Koussevitsky to task because he said that that conductor put expression into the music. Koussevitsky held that the expression lay in the rise and fall of the notes and that it was impossible to eliminate it.[1] For this reason Stravinsky issued an embargo

[1] Other conductors seem to have been at work, because, on the MS. copy in front of me, from among the many pencil marks, can be deciphered the abbreviation *Espr* over an oboe part. . . .

upon any pianist save himself playing the *Piano Sonata* (1924), but this was impossible to carry out to the full. This neo-classicism was impelled largely by Stravinsky's horror of listening to music "with closed eyes". In his opinion the mechanism of performance should be part and parcel of listening to music.

Stravinsky's creative life has been spent in the process of paring things down to their essentials. In the course of this, his music has gradually lost much of its approachability, but every now and again one comes across some endearing moments which seem to turn back with wistful eyes to the long-forgotten romanticism. The *Sonata* for two pianos (1943-1944) and *Concerto* for string orchestra (1941) are examples of this. However, the main trend was towards a greater simplicity and a stripping down to the bare bones of the thought. Embellishment, however, has not been entirely eradicated and in the slow movements of the *Piano Concerto* (1923-1924) and the *Capriccio* for piano and orchestra (1929) there is quite a wealth of quasi-baroque filigree work. Stravinsky's course of thought is exceedingly easy to follow either by reading the scores or by playing them on the gramophone—"live" performance to-day is not of frequent occurrence. It only requires a few bars on the gramophone from *L'Oiseau de Feu,* followed by a few from *Petrouchka,* to indicate the great gulf fixed between the two successive works. The clearly defined tonalities of the former give place to the bi-tonalities of the latter. Follow this with a few bars from *Le Sacre,* and one sees the total disappearance of tonality and the use of the orchestra as a large percussive instrument. Only once does any romantic or pictorial feeling come into the work, and that is the interlude between the two parts delineating night, a movement full of sinister import and as cold as ice. Go further, and play a few bars from *Les Noces* (commenced in 1914 and finished in 1917; final orchestration completed in 1923) and the whole Stravinsky progress becomes apparent. In between times there are such works as the *Three Japanese Lyrics* (1912-1913), *Pribautki* (1914), *Reynard* (1914), *L'Histoire du Soldat* (1918), the *Concertino* for string quartet (1920), the *Symphonies d'instruments à vent, Mavra* (1922) and the *Octet* for wind instruments (1922-1923). This rather dull catalogue (which omits certain smaller works) indicates that Stravinsky was gradually paring down his conception of the classical orchestra and was finding groups of small combinations of instruments suited for the purpose of the particular work. His progress, therefore, is very easy to follow and in the light of retrospection, perfectly logical. During this time he was accused of inconsistency. He proclaimed several "back to" movements which, like everything he said and did, were held up to scorn, derision and misinterpretation. His "Back to Bach" cry did not call for music to be written in the language of Bach but in the style of his period. Stravinsky was seeking the complete abolition of extra-musical impulses, thus eradicating all use of "emotional" harmony *per se,* and executive interpretation. It was when he advocated a "Back to Gounod" movement that the situation became rather ridiculous since it veered in the opposite direction; but this only implied simplification of musical thought and reliance upon clarity and pure melody. In this case, as in the other, he was calling for the use of the technique rather than the language.

It was in 1912 that he heard Schoenberg's *Pierrot Lunaire,* and while deprecating the out-of-date romanticism of the poetry, was drawn strongly to the atonicality of the music and its neo-classical use of classical device and process. The choice of instruments in *Pierrot Lunaire* led him to the serious consideration of an *ad hoc* selection, and it is in *Renard* (1916-1917) that we find the first case of this approach to the selective principle in a work of any considerable size—certain chamber works like the song games *Pribautki* naturally require this selectivity. This was Stravinsky's only aesthetic contact with Schoenberg. It should be remarked that *Renard* was not performed until 1922. Darius Milhaud wrote the first of his *Petites Symphonies*—"Le Printemps"—in 1917, the second in 1918, the third and fourth in 1921—anterior to the production of *Renard,* therefore. Thus two divergent composers worked along similar lines, and Milhaud spent a great part of this period in Brazil.

The battles of *Le Sacre* and other works can be read of in many of the hundreds of books on ballet and were symptomatic of the prevalent state of excitement of the period. They were mainly due to misunderstanding. The *Symphonies d'instruments à vent* aroused a storm of indignation and sarcasm because the title was not read properly. It was assumed that the work was a "Symphony for Wind Instruments" in the established design, and the realisation that the title really meant "Wind Instrument Sounds" was not appreciated. Consequently, the frame of mind of the early audiences was wrongly directed and in this particular work, the instruments seemed to plod along rather inconsequentially, with little tone gradation and no clearly defined "melody".

Stravinsky's neo-classicism had become formulated, but it was not to remain at this point. He still sought for further eradication of expression and in the *Concerto* for piano and orchestra he abolished the strings, with the exception of the double basses, as being too expressive. A rather similar negation of expression took place in the following works for the concert hall, the *Piano Sonata* and *Serenade in A* (1925), also for piano. In 1926-1927 he returned to the approximately normal orchestra in *Oedipus Rex*, but in 1927-1928 he used the string orchestra alone in *Appollon Musagéte*, whose chaste and classic music is full of the deepest expression. However, just at this time Stravinsky had a curious harking after the Tchaikowsky concept of ballet, which resulted in *Le Baiser de la Fée* (1928), inspired by the Muse of Tchaikowsky himself. This ill-balanced work simply does not persuade the listener to which world it belongs and although the spirit may be that of Tchaikowsky, the letter swings first this way, and then, that. It is neither fish nor flesh, and its length militates against it. Even in the theatre the music is not interesting, nor is it sufficiently impersonal to avoid attracting attention to itself.

Stravinsky actually has never forsworn his early allegiance to the ballet and three later works indicate how far he has got from the tradition of his early stage music. *Jeu des Cartes* (1936) has an impulse which suggests some novelty of idea, but the music is flat and uninteresting save with regard to its position in the Stravinsky canon. The *Danses Concertantes* (1942), consisting of five individual movements or Divertissements—March, Pas d'Action, Theme varié, Pas de Deux, March— do not convince, even after repeated hearings, that Stravinsky is any longer suited to this type of music; what opulence there is does not sound natural. The *Ballet Scenes* (1944), written for the revue *The Seven Lively Arts*, are more successful, since their approach is not so empirical. The dancers are not handed some music out of the blue to dance, as in the *Danses Concertantes*, and the framework of the music is more essentially scripted. The *Circus Polka* (1942) written for the Elephant Ballet in the Barnum and Bailey Circus is a strange example of Stravinsky's approach to *Gebrauchsmusik*. This is amusing and suitable, but undignified. It served a momentary purpose, unlike *L'Histoire d'un Soldat* (1918) and the *Ebony Concerto* (1945), the latter composed for Woody Herman's Band.

None of these works, with the exception of *L'Histoire d'un Soldat*, is of the slightest importance. *L'Histoire d'un Soldat*, however, with its idea of the travelling theatre, its small orchestra, and its altogether quaint and unique set-up, propounded a practice which might well be followed up; but an ordinary audience in a village or market square might be forgiven for thinking that the whole thing were slightly mad, for, apart from the stage production with the Narrator drinking the health of the Conductor, the tautness of the harmony is not such as would make an immediate appeal to the heathen.

The landmarks of Stravinsky's maturity may be summarised in *Le Sacre, Les Noces, Symphonies d'instruments à vent, Oedipus Rex* (1926-1927), *Psalm Symphony* (1930), *Persephone* (1934), *Symphony in C* (1940) and the *Symphony in Three Movements* (1945). These works represent the several stages in Stravinsky's progress. Mr. Eric Walter White sees[1] in the *Symphony in Three Movements* an attempt to unite the "Dionysian and Apollonian elements in Stravinsky's nature". This is as may be, but the impression given to the general reader is that of repudiation and refutation of the former ideals. It is probable that others may consider the *Capriccio* for piano and orchestra, the *Violin Concerto* (1931) and the *Concerto* for two pianos among these landmarks, but this is a matter of personal assessment.

Later works show a trend to extreme graciousness and suave charm. The *Sonata* for two pianos and the *Concerto* for strings are almost Gallic in this respect, and this quality appears to have proceeded naturally from the earlier stark neo-classicism.

Le Sacre denotes the final break with all romantic and objective tendencies, and the fusion of tonal and non-tonal elements. *Les Noces* removes all polyphonic thought, and turns the *ad hoc* orchestra into a completely percussive body. In the latter respect it denotes the first important application of a specialised orchestration to the aesthetic requirements of a subject (and let it be noted that Stravinsky destroyed two previous schemes). Similarly, its use of four pianos confirmed that instrument finally and definitely as a purely orchestral entity and removed all necessitous consideration of it as a solo instrument for concertos. The *Symphonies d'instruments à vent* carry the selective principle still further and mark Stravinsky's entrance into the abstract concert hall. *Oedipus Rex* points an important combination of opera and oratorio which was to have a direct result in Honegger's *Jeanne d'Arc au bucher* and in *L'Apocalypse* (1946) of Jean Françaix (1912). It postulated a new form and style. The text of Cocteau's version of

[1] *Stravinsky: A Critical Survey* (John Lehmann).

the Greek play is in Latin, a universal language. A dramatic actor recites in French or in the language of the country producing the work an exact account of what is to happen; the action, incidentally, takes place off-stage. This dispenses with translation (so seldom really satisfactory) of the main text. The singers wear masks, not an altogether happy *décor*—one is reminded of Schoenberg's *Die Glückliche Hand,* in which the singers poke their heads and shoulders through the backcloth. The *Symphony of Psalms* is Stravinsky's great contribution to religious music. This made a sensation because, once more, preconceived ideas were disappointed. The text consists only of a few selected verses, which are treated in a vein of humility. The fact that Stravinsky was a member of neither the Anglican nor Roman Churches was ignored, and the particular qualities of Russian Church music were not appreciated. Instead of a Three Choir Festival outburst of joyful fugal "Alleluia's", there are awesome and reverent expressions of them. The work is redolent of solemn and stately ritual, in no way sacramental at that moment. The fatuous humour poked at the double dedication was purely malicious. Stravinsky composed the work to the glory of Almighty God and stated that it was dedicated to the Boston Symphony Orchestra. It pleased the little humorists and cynics to unite the two statements and regard the Boston Symphony Orchestra as being glorified.[1] There was no excuse whatsoever for this and it shows the self-conscious spite which can mar ordinary intelligence when occasion seems to require it to do so. *Persephone* postulates another unusual form, that of the melodrama, in France a work in which music forms the background for spoken dialogue—in this country it represents a double-dyed villain chasing some simple-minded family into the gutter and ultimately receiving his due reward, after a stream of hissing on the part of the audience. The two *Symphonies* show Stravinsky adapting his neo-classicism to full-length symphonic design, in a manner so complete that further trends would seem to be impossible—but Stravinsky has reached other seeming impasses and broken them down.

Stravinsky's scores are full of complicated time-signatures which appear every time he wishes to stress an accent. In many cases the bars all sort themselves out regularly in the end, and an ordinary emphasis mark would have the same result. It is when he indulges in sudden changes into 7/8 "allegro" that performers begin to despair.

---

[1] It seems that no journalist can read the words printed on the score accurately, and even in 1950 a *Radio Times* writer could still make this mistake.

The changes for the most part simply make life exceedingly uncomfortable for conductor and players, make little difference to the forward progress of the music, and in many cases resolve the question of the accents in the hardest possible manner. The same applies to *Le Sacre* and other works. A succession of time-changes like this 9/8-5/8-7/8-3/8-2/4-7/4-3/4-7/4-3/8-2/4-7/4-3/8-5/8 over-emphasises a rhythmic situation on paper; aurally, one is not aware of them and they settle themselves down perfectly logically. When the music is polyphonic the situation becomes difficult, because the accents naturally fall upon different beats of the bars in each part. In a work like *L'Histoire d'un Soldat* the effect becomes mechanical and jerky. The "March" which opens and closes *Renard* (1916) is in reality a straightforward 5/4, but it is written in alternating 2/4 and 3/4. Paradoxically enough, when the music goes in 7/8, Stravinsky does not alternate between 3/8-4/8-4/8-3/8, which would seem a logical process, but writes in the complete seven-pulse measure with bars subdivided by a dotted line. It is noticeable that the feeling of immobility is removed the moment the music remains in any time-signature for any lengthy stretch. Comparing these early works with the very latest, one sees that the rhythmic strength is still present, without any of these disturbing alterations and alternations.

In *Les Noces* the music is so essentially rhythmic that the changes do not make for so many difficulties. The texture is so taut, the melodic phrases (mostly Russian folk-melodies) so limited in range and set round a focal point, that the music rarely seems to have any real mobility at all and after a while it becomes almost a dope until, suddenly, the ear is rudely shaken by some astonishing explosion or by a moment of great beauty, like the Mother's farewell to the Bride. However, far too much has been said about Stravinsky's rhythm by commentators of all kinds to the neglect of other elements, and students in about sixty years' time may well be pardoned for considering that this twentieth-century composer was merely a machine. The quality of melody is in most cases short-winded, and although there is no literal repetition in the concert music (in the ballets this forms the main constituent) Stravinsky contrives much out of very little by means of his sense of balance. It is noticeable that when a Stravinsky admirer hums or whistles one of his idol's themes, it is never anything but a mere fragment, and one usually associated with some strong, emphasised rhythmic pattern which has remained fixed in the memory either for its extreme regularity of pulsation, or for its outstanding pattern. Stravinsky's lyricism is full of grace when he forgets to be self-consciously abstract. Moments in the *Concerto* for two pianos—the "Notturno"—the *Sonata* for two pianos—the opening—and the slow movement of the *Concerto* for strings, if not proclaiming him a melodist in the old style, show that beneath the intense vigour of the polyphony and the uncompromisingly tonal, yet acid, harmonies, there lurks a full realisation that it is sometimes necessary to be openly musical. Stravinsky likes to start a work with bold and widespread crotchets, as in the *Concerto* for two pianos and the *Symphony in Three Movements* (whose second movement is particularly lyrical and baroque in quality). He thus offers complete contrast in two ways of thinking. His lines are sometimes difficult to follow in their polyphonic textures because the parts cross and intertwine in a manner which if in no way obscure, is somewhat complex. The acute ear finds increasing satisfaction in disentangling the web. His abstract thought appears deliberately to preclude any emotional tendencies which may occur in the rise and fall of the notes, and on the surface he seems to lacerate himself with the efficiency of an Indian fakir. Yet, when the work in question is ended, one feels that an experience has been gone through, and the brain is cleared of all romantic cobwebs. While one is not aware of the Schoenbergian processes at the time, one is fully aware that there are never any in Stravinsky's concept of things; yet Stravinsky is often harder to listen to than is Schoenberg.

It is wrong to describe Stravinsky as "atonal" or "atonical". His music is both definitely tonal and "tonical". He uses harmony with no regard to tonal relations, and neither concord nor discord exist. There is no anarchy whatsoever except what may lie in a complete disregard of the interrelation of chords. That is why his music *looks* as if anything would do, and why it gave the early impetus to iconoclasm. Stravinsky's music frequently looks either as if it would not come off in performance, or that it would be exceedingly dull. Appearances are deceptive in many works by many composers, and the logic of the thought becomes apparent with closer reading and listening. It is not difficult to read a Stravinsky score, but invariably so to play it, owing to the constant multiplicity of polyphonic and rhythmic detail.

Stravinsky is always careful to show the progress of the separate parts, and one is faced with indications resulting in a puzzling series of lines which, if concerned with strings or wind instruments, would be

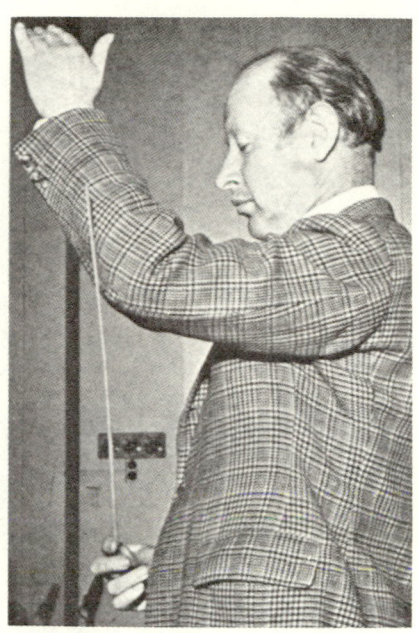

Willem Pijper (1884–1947)

Eugene Goossens (1893)

Cyril Scott (1879)

BERTUS VAN LIER (1906) LÉON ORTHEIL (1905)

EDMUND RUBBRA (1901) LENNOX BERKELEY (1903)

perfectly logical and simple in performance; but the pianist cannot differentiate in this respect, and no amount of polyphonic listening away from the printed music serves to clarify the situation.

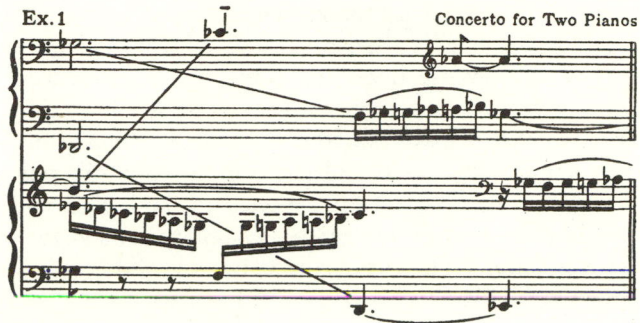

His pianism is a mixture of simplicity of thought and difficulty of technique. A passage like this is grateful to play, even in its limited range, because of its daintiness of aesthetic:

However, the neo-classic style requires a spiky technique, and so well managed is it that it is rare to find a spread-out awkwardness such as this:

Chordally, his jazz exercises offer no difficulties, and these lie well under the hands, putting forward rhythmic effects which come off perfectly naturally.

This is "Back to Bach" in the style of the twentieth century, and Stravinsky himself plays his works magnificently.

Stravinsky has always been unorthodox in his statements to the public. His opinions are frequently somewhat contradictory, and he takes up a cause with the greatest enthusiasm for the time being, regardless as to whether it may contradict a previous enthusiasm. This unorthodoxy, in an otherwise completely orthodox musical point of view, in a world in which everyone is expected to think alike and to hold common idols in extreme reverence, is stimulating, and the more so, because it is sincere. The lecturer or writer who is content to express opinions which he knows his hearers and readers already hold as their own merely confirms what is generally believed to be true. Such smugness, which, alas! is extremely common, has its opposing elements of snobbism; but of the two, the latter is the less dangerous since it forbids all tendencies to comfortable complacency. It does not follow because Stravinsky decries an idol or extols a fallen one, that his opinion is wrong; it merely suggests that there are two points of view of which one, smothered by the majority, is in the minority owing (very often) to the sheep-like manner in which musical commentators and musicians themselves follow their leaders. Stravinsky's music fully underlines his theories. He does not advocate anything which cannot be confirmed in his own works. When he suggests a "back to" movement, he shows how this can be accomplished in twentieth-century language. His precepts, therefore, are all borne out by his practices.

His output shows how tradition can be brought into line with contemporary technique. It shows a clear arrival from the point of departure. He has never been slick, but he has always been extremely neat and precise.

As I have suggested, it is impossible to say just where Stravinsky will go from here. His position at the moment is well established, whatever he may do in the future. His influence has been widespread, but his tonal freedoms and clearly defined tonality which back up the free use of diatonic dissonance, make it extremely difficult for anyone to follow in his neo-classic footsteps. This puts additional weight upon the arguments of those who maintain that tonal music has reached the end of its tether if it is to be abstract in expression. The disciples welcome every new work as a step forward. Curiously enough, these late works do not make listening to the early ones a disappointing or frustrating process, as in the case of some others. It is worth while to quote the closing lines of Mr. White's book, [1] which is the authoritative treatise in English up to date:

> There is much to admire and enjoy in works like the *Octet*, the *Capriccio*, the *Concerto* for two solo pianos and the *Symphony in Three Movements*; yet it seems probable that he reaches his fullest stature when his functioning as a composer has been set in motion by some extraneous factor such as a visual idea or a text, and that works like *The Rite of Spring*, *The Wedding*, the *Symphony of Psalms* and *Persephone* represent the high-water mark of his invention and form one of the most precious contributions to the musical treasury of the twentieth century.

This admits to a confession of failure. Certainly some works stand out from others, but it is too wide a sweep to relegate so many works, in an output as varied as that of Stravinsky, to the background. One feels that the late neo-classicism will come into its own when the writings of the systematic composers have become exhausted. Stravinsky's music may be for the few, but not for so few as the opposing school will eventually command unless some radical element is added. At present Stravinsky ranks among the highest of the twentieth-century hierarchy in that way, which, after all, is his and no one else's.

[1] *Op. cit.*

CHAPTER TWENTY-FIVE

COMPOSERS IN ISOLATION
4. *Eugene*[1] *Goossens*
(1893)

EUGENE GOOSSENS is one of those composers who make classification
in terms of culture extremely difficult. His position is altogether unique
in the music of this country, because he has never thrown over (and,
let it be said, we must be thankful that he has not done so) his basic
Gallic temperament towards music. The Goossens family is of Belgian
descent; the grandfather, Eugéne Goossens (1845-1906), and the
father (1867), who was also christened Eugéne, were both conductors
of the Carl Rosa Opera Company. Both studied at the Brussels Conservatoire, the latter completing his studies at the Royal Academy of
Music, London. The Goossens under consideration here commenced
his career as a student at the Bruges Conservatoire, later entering the
Liverpool College of Music and finally the Royal College of Music,
London, where he became a pupil of Stanford for composition and
Achille Rivarde (1865-1940) for the violin. Commencing his musical
life as a violinist in the Queen's Hall Orchestra under Sir Henry Wood,
he became one of Sir Thomas Beecham's conductors of what became
known as the British National Opera Company until 1920, finding his
spiritual home, so to speak, with Diaghileff, who appointed him his
permanent conductor for the London seasons of ballet. In the meanwhile he had formed his own Symphony Orchestra, but in 1930 he was
appointed conductor of the Cincinnati Symphony Orchestra and
remained in America until 1949, when he emigrated to Australia.

Belgium has never seemed to be able to keep a hold upon her most
promising composers, and from Grétry (1742-1813) and César Franck
(1822-1890) has managed to lose them in proportion to their notability.

[1] The composer himself has dropped the accent.

Things are rather different now, and she has kept several composers faithful to her flag whose reputation has but to cross the border with some frequency to establish itself in the hierarchy of twentieth-century music. In the case of Goossens, one wonders exactly what niche he found for himself in the tradition of the Royal College of Music, whose entire outlook at that time was strictly on the lines of Brahms, and whose musical policy was directed by Parry and Stanford. It says a very great deal for the latter that he was able to apply his point of view to a musical instinct which was at immediate variance to his own. Stanford was proverbially outspoken—"A lot of rot, my boy" was one of his favourite dicta—this spoke volumes to the students themselves who heard their latest and, to them, most original thoughts destroyed without any expression of sympathy. Thus is the respect and regard for a great teacher maintained, but one would give a good deal for recordings of some of the lessons given to the more iconoclastic students. Not all Stanford's pupils, of course, made a reputation of any note, and some fell by the wayside as time went on; but the enormous variety of expression emanating from that room in the Royal College of Music is something quite phenomenal.

Goossens probably did not fight with his teacher but was sensible enough to absorb the details of technique which Stanford passed on, into his own individual idiom, and of all that great man's students, Goossens stands out supreme in his individuality.

Of the two, one would say that Goossens was more English than British, for his music lacks the bluffness which characterises the latter while containing in its own manner some of the subtleties of the former which it in no way resembles in idiom. Goossens' Gallic expression served him well in his initial days as a composer; indeed, it can be said of him that he timed his entry into this world at exactly the right moment. His individualism was just the thing for the 1920's and, founded, as it was, upon a strictly classical formalism, it added an element of authority to an iconoclastic period. Such has always been his realisation of formal exigencies that some of his works, particularly the late *Symphonies,* suggest that he would have been an exemplary pupil of Vincent d'Indy at the Schola Cantorum which, in itself, suggests a point of contact between the Schola and the Royal College of Music. Coming to the fore just at that time when the native composer began to experience the possibilities of a hey-day, Goossens was helped and encouraged in a practical way by the far-seeing Otto Kling, whose publishing house had just the right Continental atmosphere and contacts for one of Gocssens' temperament. His music would not have been at home in a strictly English publishing environment.

Amid a whirlwind of folly, Goossens kept a clear head, and although he did not disdain a few trifling things for piano, he set himself the pleasurable task of living a practical life. His masterly conducting gave him perception for the unravelling of knots. At the time when *Le Sacre* was still postulating problems, the sight of the utterly cool Eugene Goossens leading the orchestra through all the intricacies with a perfectly clear beat and one devoid of all elaboration of gesture, gave both listeners and players perfect confidence. At the end of some stretch of complexities and complications, Goossens would turn round and bow, a smile on his face, as if to say, "What have you been worried about? It is all perfectly clear"; and this coolness of head which directed and controlled, outwardly at least, the inner emotions governed his musical composition. No matter how one may hesitate at the extreme chromaticism of the part-writing or at the ever-progressing richness of the seemingly unrelated harmonies, one soon realises the clarity of the whole thing, because there is always present a strong sense and feeling of tonality, atonical though it may be. In the decoration of his chamber music, which from his own experience he was able to think in terms of practicability and enjoyment of performance, the texture on paper appears crowded and complicated, but in actual sound it is perfectly logical and clear. The chromaticism presents no difficulties for the players, and Goossens can write phrases like this from the *Phantasy Quartet* (1915):

and another like this from the sketch *Jack o' Lantern* (1916):

with perfect ease and confidence, knowing that the semitonalism of the former can be easily solved in the general agglomeration of the music, and that the speed of the latter presents no difficulties of execution to capable players.

Goossens' versatility and mastery of medium is equalled only by those of the Italian composer Alfredo Casella (1883-1947) who ranked among the most efficient composers of the century; but Casella lacked the individuality which is one of Goossens' strongest features. Goossens is an example of an extremely sensitive musician who does not despise practicability and has both feet upon the ground, no matter how high his head may be in the air. If we may rank him as a native composer, it may be said that he is the sole instance of a convincing trend to Impressionism. This can be seen not only in a beautiful little piece like *By the Tarn* (1916) for string quartet (later made available for performance with clarinet doubling the viola part), but in the general vertical nature of the harmony, which takes entities as they come, with no reference to approach or departure. It is most marked in his attitude to the musical expression of silence[1] where the jangling of iridescent harmonies deliberately gives a musical effect to an element which is indefinable. Comparison with Holst[2] affords an interesting study. Goossens paints the tone colour of silence and underlines the indefinable quality of the text; Holst defines it by means of the text, clothing it with less elaborate but equally dissonant harmonies, albeit of another quality.

Goossens' melody often requires the background harmonies to give it justification, but in many cases the simplicity of the tune is disguised by the richness of the harmonies which constantly change, and are of an intensely chromatic nature. The melody is frequently of a lyrical quality, and flows along rhapsodically, as in the *Second Violin Sonata* (1931).

[1] See page 84.
[2] See page 139.

This depends entirely upon the harmonies to support it. On the other hand, we can find melodies which can stand on their own above a perfectly simple harmony.

The reader should turn to the rather sombre *Rhapsody* (1916) for 'cello and piano to find an ornamental lyricism of a different kind. This music shows a measure of how fashions change and idioms, at their time surprising enough, in due course become absorbed into technique which has not very far to go before becoming dated. The piano parts of the above examples illustrate the alteration of fashion in this respect. The reader need only consider the type of work performed now in the annual Festivals of the International Contemporary Music Society with that of 1931 which included this *Sonata*.

Goossens' music is universal and this prevents it from dating. Whatever harmonic outlook other composers may have adopted and however they may have tried to justify it in terms of "-ism" and "-ality", Goossens' style stands by itself because of his early classical training. This imbued him with a deep respect and acknowledgement of tradition, and gave him authority for breaking further away from traditional custom while, at the same time, maintaining a firm connection with that tradition. There is little which taken by itself cannot be traced to its traditional definition. His harmonies move along clangingly, the successive and simultaneous dissonances being well controlled and thought out.

As is the case with nearly every composer, Goossens' style became gradually simplified as he grew older, although it never lost its early individuality. His two operas, *Judith* (1929) and *Don Juan de Mañara* (1930), both to libretti by Arnold Bennett, made but sporadic appearances and suffered the fate common to most native operas of distinction. The barbaric splendour of the former, which challenged Strauss' *Salome* within its limits, made a deep impression on its first performance. There was no other native composer capable of writing in this colouristic manner. It separated him from the generality of his fellows in this country and yet did not fall beneath the sway of any European model. The latter, altogether a longer and more significant work, made a smaller attraction because it attempted to say a great deal more. Whether these works will ever appear on the English stage again is an open question, but one would suggest that instead of awarding prizes and giving commissions for new works which, in the nature of things, can have but a transitory life, the money should be devoted to the establishment in the new national repertoire of works which have languished because of the lack of financial backing but whose quality in any other country would entitle them to a permanent place in the repertoire.[1] Goossens in these works proved himself a man of the theatre, with a keen ear and eye for dramatic situations.

His more abstract works, if, indeed, the term can be applied to him, lie in the *Oboe Concerto* (1929), the *Concerto for Double String Orchestra* (1930) and the three *Symphonies,* of which the last-named works all bear testimony to a fully developed cyclical temperament which would do credit, as I have said, to the Schola Cantorum. They are well knit and in every way symphonically contrived, adding lustre to the many similar works of recent times.

Goossens, therefore, has a European appeal, but this is rather curbed by his unfortunate reputation of being a British composer, since foreigners are nonplussed at the lack of positive British or English qualities about the music which makes the complete comprehension of our music in their eyes something intangible and indefinite. His isolation is probably more marked than any of the others considered under this heading. It is a tragedy that his reputation should stand higher as a conductor than as a composer (in this country at least), for we should know better, and should place both upon an equally high pedestal. However, picturesque music is at a discount just now, and the inner romanticism of Goossens' individuality is regarded as faintly demoded and almost decadent. Nevertheless, there should be room for the chamber music if for nothing else, and players forget the inborn technical perfection displayed in these works. They complain, and not without some reason, at the fact that composers do not seem to take the execution or aesthetic enjoyment of the performer into any account nowadays; yet, when there is a host of works written from practical experience, they choose to ignore the catalogue.

The day for the revival and recognition of Goossens is not just yet, I am afraid; but it will come as soon as the present hankering after systematic neo-classicism has exhausted itself and its devotees. Goossens, more than any other composer, must bide his time for this consummation. He has been said to have completed the period of the ultra-romantic harmonic school, but this does not mean that it is not capable of revival or progression. Revival would not necessarily mean reaction.

[1] Speaking entirely offhand, one would mention the following in this respect. *The Wreckers* (Smyth), *Bronwen* (Holbrooke), *The Seal Woman* (Bantock), *Quentin Durward* (Maclean), *A Village Romeo and Juliet* (Delius), *The Travelling Companion* or *Much Ado about Nothing* (Stanford) as being an eclectic list capable of giving a representative facet of British opera. It is difficult to see how Covent Garden can regard itself as "national" and, in any case, two new native productions over a space of years hardly justifies a claim to enterprise.

In point of fact, there are a good many composers writing to-day who have distinct leanings to this style, but they are not brought into the limelight. Their sensationalism is not startling enough to suggest a new tendency; the neo-classical sensationalism, founded, as it would appear to be, simply on neurosis, must sooner or later find its achievement in the case of the followers of Schoenberg. In those of Stravinsky, it would seem to have already reached it. For the moment, Goossens remains important, and there the panorama of twentieth-century music must be content to let him stand. Belgium, England, America and now Australia gain honour by him. No one like him has yet come out of the last three, and perhaps it would be better to regard him as a high-light in Belgian music. Considered against that background, he continues the line from Joseph Jongen (1873) and shows a point of departure from the neo-classicism of Jean Absil. He is very much less ebullient and altogether of a different quality from Marcel Poot and less sombre than Norbert Rousseau or Raymond Chevreuille. Although Grétry and Franck are assimilable into the perspective of French music, Goossens does not show any real connection with it. The only French composer he can be placed alongside, so far as his latest works are concerned, is Vincent d'Indy, and one can see with a little imagination that d'Indy might have been the Goossens of the *Symphonies* had he been born later, or lived longer. However, he certainly would not have been the Goossens of the *Phantasy Quartet, Silence,* or the *Operas.* If it is going too far to say, as I have said, that nothing like him has ever or ever will emanate from this country, it is perfectly true to say that no one like him has as yet proceeded from the Royal College of Music. One might visualise him at the other side of the Park, since his romanticism is as strongly marked as that of Sir Arnold Bax in his own generation, and of Bantock in the earlier. One might be tempted to say that in his classification he follows the tradition of Bantock in his two operas, of Bax in his chamber and piano music, but his subjectivity and technique are Belgian through and through. I emphasise this point advisedly since he is not definitely and purely Gallic in the widest sense of the term. All of which proves his isolation, and shows how extremely difficult it is to put him in any cultural niche.

CHAPTER TWENTY-SIX

COMPOSERS IN ISOLATION
5. *Willem Pijper*
(1884-1947)

IF the question is asked as to why a composer almost unknown except by name outside his own country should appear in this study of the twentieth-century trends, the answer will be found in the position the particular composer holds in that country and the influence which he has exercised upon his native culture. In the same way that Vaughan Williams is essentially English and has exercised an influence solely upon English composers, so Pijper is essentially Netherlandic and has held sway over Netherlandic composers and no others; at the same time Pijper has the elements of universality which are lacking in Vaughan Williams. The fact that another prophet is found in a small country does not diminish either the stature of the prophet in question or imply a deficiency in the larger countries. Pijper for a few years, in the 1920's, unexpectedly found an English publisher,[1] but for some reason or other it did not tend to place him in any significant position here. Music publishing is done on a smaller scale in Holland than in most other countries, and is thus in a position similar to Finland and Belgium. It has become necessary for the Netherlandic composers to go elsewhere, and many of them have found a welcome in Vienna. To-day the position appears to be slightly worse than it was, but with the resourcefulness of a small nation, the composers have a system peculiar to themselves which eschews the printed page but places the same importance upon the photostat. Receiving a grant from the Government, the society known as "Stichting Donemus" makes every kind of music available, and to all extents and purposes plays the same rôle as a publisher. One advantage of this is that the composers are on an equal footing, and there is no question of some being publishers' pets

[1] Supported by the Dutch Government.

and the independent being left to fight their own battles. The dissemination of the works is not in any way different from the normal, but since the scores are free, gratis and for hire only, foreign agents make little profit out of them. Consequently, the music ceases to be an economic proposition for them and the scores languish on their shelves, seeing the light only on demand, which is seldom, owing to limitation of publicity. The position must be realised in order that Pijper's music, and, indeed, that of the greater part of the twentieth-century Netherlandic composers, may arouse interest about itself. The situation explains the whole question up to a point and carries us to the matter of the lack of interest and enterprise on the part of performers.

Pijper is the leader of a group of composers of whom many have been his pupils, whose approach to music is purely abstract and altogether free from romantic tendencies. The basis of the thought is a scholarly classicism which avoids systematisation, but owes everything to process. The descent of these composers from the early canonic composers is perfectly clear, but unlike the erudite primitive masters, those of the twentieth century are not entirely concerned with the production of musical puzzles. Pijper himself described the salient features of Dutch music to the composers' "love of counterpoint".[1] This is hardly a feature by which Dutch music can be recognised or set apart from that of other cultures. A cursory glance at the scores, however, reveals that the contrapuntal element is not the sole concern of the composers, and although they base their thought upon polyphony, they have a strong sense of harmony, of a thoroughly individual nature. In the 1920's Pijper was writing music fully in line with the then accepted facets of *le dernier cri* but lacking in the sensational and bizarre qualities which would have recommended it in those hectic days. Pijper wrote music which was entirely abstract in character and which did not deliberately flaunt established practices; it simply denied them, but the music carried a feeling of damning unobtrusiveness which kept it in the background. Self-effacement may have its ultimate reward, as in the case of a composer like César Franck, but this is of little use to the composer himself and a posthumous fame (over which no genuine creative artist ever bothers himself) is but poor reward for labours spent in the cultivation of art. The creative mind which so occupies itself may justly lay claim to the title of "artist"; this carries its own personal satisfaction, but, inwardly, surely tests a man's sincerity. Pijper died a disappointed and

[1] "Willem Pijper", Karel Mengelberg (*Music To-day*, Dobson).

disillusioned man, for even in Holland his music did not make the immediate appeal which its sincerity and proportions merited.

Pijper's music can be explained in two ways. It is possible to justify his processes in terms of devised scale and in the simpler ones of ordinary harmonic idiom. His style is a highly personal one and embraces several of the "-isms" and "-alities" without self-consciously proclaiming them. I, for one, doubt much of the theoreticians' claims to the use of this or that particular scale or system, and it seems to me that these are too often decided after the music has been written, and with little confirmation from the composers. It is, of course, perfectly easy to align anything with any process when it comes to being wise after the event, but I refuse to believe that a composer like Pijper cluttered himself up with blue-prints when in the actual course of composition. On the other hand, it is perfectly reasonable to believe in the polymodal and polytonal (although in Pijper's case, there are few signs of anything further than bi-tonal) moments. Pijper is perfectly easy to explain away, should one so wish, in terms of elaborate technique, but that technique is really too slender for this. Basically, it is triadic and its underlying technical thought perfectly obvious. Taking the music as we read it, we can make certain deductions (realising what has been said above, that it does not necessarily follow that Pijper himself thought in this way when he was composing the music).

Pijper's individuality is such that the same personal touches hold good in every work; but he contrives to avoid similarity of sound. Perhaps he could be described as a mannered composer, and certainly certain mannerisms do appear with frequency; but he can hardly be blamed for these, since in them lies the essence of his thought. Although we limit ourselves here to isolated quotations, parallel cases can be found in many other works.

The first point which strikes the reader is the transparency of the thought, and this emphasises its simplicity. A passage such as this

Ex. 1 Symphony No. 3

shows an extreme use of simple triadic means. The bass chases the treble and never actually catches it up upon a concord. Each impact shows some position of some chord of the seventh, the whole resolving upon an ordinary diatonic seventh on A flat. The treble is an alternation of major and minor triads, the bass being major throughout. At one moment there is a bi-modal clash. This may seem a lengthy commentary upon a mere matter of one bar, but therein can be found much of the salient Pijper thought.

The building up of harmony by means of sevenths broken into successions of fifths, offers the theoreticians every opportunity for finding devised scalic bases. This habit, for habit it has indeed become, appears frequently, and in effect usually sounds clumsy and sprawling; but Pijper is successful in avoiding this fault.

Observe in Ex. 2*b* that the right hand descends in major triads, the roots in succession eventually forming a dominant seventh.

A superimposition of perfect fifths, also forming a broken seventh, opens the *Third Sonatina* in this manner, the D major chord forming a triple pedal point, placing the whole in a bi-tonal background.

WALTER PISTON (1894)   ROY HARRIS (1898)

SAMUEL BARBER (1910)   AARON COPLAND (1900)

MARCEL MIHALOVICI (1898)

OLIVER MESSIAEN (1908)

JEAN LOUIS MARTINET (1912)

JERZY FITELBERG (1903–1951)

This also indicates what may seem to be a rather cussèd detail, but which is found to be a characteristic of his thought because of its frequency. It lies in the contradiction of flat and sharp chords. It can be found in a place such as this:

Here are both bi-modality and the contradiction mentioned. A more open use of this lies here,

but later he contrives, by means of the enharmonic change, to keep a broken contact between the two contradictory elements.

This, it may be argued, is but a divided use of an ordinary semitonal descent spread over a wide range, and I am inclined to the opinion that Pijper thought of it in this way.

Melodic and harmonic progression sometimes find themselves in contradiction.

Notice that in the second bar of Ex. 7*a* there is another example of the descending third principle, or progression through mediants. In Ex. 7*b*, having started the piano fair and square upon a concord, Pijper proceeds in contrary motion to a similar condition, thus emphasising Schumann's dictum: "Take care of the beginnings and endings; the middles will take care of themselves." The points of departure and arrival are safely dealt with in this case.

The logical progress of the harmony sometimes leads to surprising climaxes, and the conventional dominant seventh finds itself in bold relief in a passage such as this,

and Pijper makes no attempt to kill this result by contradicting it in the orchestra.

Melodically, he achieves a graceful lyricism on occasions, which will be found to include the mass of graceful sound as a whole, as well as to consist entirely of the melodic line. We quote at some length to show the former:

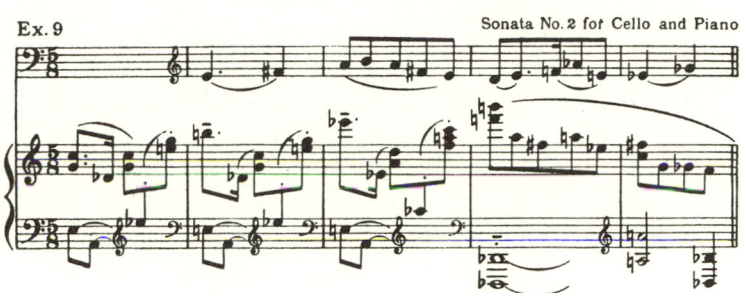

Ex. 9   Sonata No. 2 for Cello and Piano

Such melodies always move more conjointly than disjointly, but they often require their harmonic background to justify themselves. Indeed, sometimes one wonders whether Pijper did not derive or devise the melodies from the actual harmonies; but this is pure conjecture. There is, however, no sign that he ever drew his melodic lines from a systematic note-row, and no matter how brief or long his melodies may be, they are never scrappy in the former case or long-winded in the latter. One may, however, wonder if perhaps he did not flirt momentarily with a note-row in the opening bars of his *Trio No. 2* (1921) for violin, 'cello and piano.

Ex. 10   Trio No. 2 for Violin, Cello and Piano

This is entirely fanciful, but it does indicate a connection with the serial or with the principle used by Alban Berg in his *Violin Concerto*,[1]

[1] See page 240.

which should be referred to. It is seen at its clearest in a fragment such as this

and in the spread arpeggio of the opening bar of the same work.

Karel Mengelberg in his article on Pijper in *Music To-day*[1] gives a scale in four sections, which bears out the foundation in fact of Pijper's process of thought,

but I do not feel convinced that Pijper started from this point, and the general trend of his music suggests that it comes from the textures in the normal progress, being discoverable rather than foundational.

One other melodic feature may be mentioned, and that is the use of the inner thumb melody which plays an important rôle in Pijper's melodic pianistic concept. Tied up with this is his apparent obsession with tango rhythms which control much of the music's impulse. It must be confessed that during a detailed and consistent reading of

[1] *Op. cit.*

Pijper's scores the constant appearance of a pattern like this ♫♩
becomes somewhat wearisome; but so do other such clichés or personal
twists in other composers and to gainsay them is to gainsay the composers themselves. A commonplace may be such only by virtue of the
composer's frequent use of it; but as long as it is confined to the particular and not spread to the generality, there can be no objection to it
other than that it becomes an inevitable feature of the composer's ideas.

Although Pijper uses a large orchestra for his two existent *Symphonies*[1] (1921 and 1926) and a host of percussion in the *Piano Concerto* (1927), the scores being marvels of resource and detail, there is no
feeling of suffocation and all the details are perfectly clear. In the
Piano Concerto the piano, with its incisive triads, stands out in clear
relief from the flowing lyricism and rhythmic patterns of the orchestra,
while taking a place in the ensemble. There are two cadenzas which
make no concession to virtuosic display; indeed, this concerto is one
of the easiest of such works to play and the performer need but steep
himself in the idiom and then simply play the notes as Pijper directs.

Formally, Pijper is germinal and it is as difficult to align the form
with the traditional designs as it is with Sibelius. The two *Symphonies*
are models in this respect, and the influence of this free approach to
design is found in the massive symphonies of his pupil, Bertus van Lier.
Pijper's two great works do not make immediately attractive music,
and the reaction is more one of interest than of aesthetic uplift; but this
may be said of any symphony which is at all ambitious and which does
not set out to be comprehensible at first hearing. One of the principles
of symphonic music is that the music must be sought out, and its
repercussions can be experienced only after repeated hearings. Symphony is not one of those things to be taken in hand lightly and un-
advisedly, although there are many of the Schumann-Mendelssohn
variety, together with some composed to-day, which do set out with
this intention. Some composers attempt to clothe the paucity of their
ideas with grandiose and grandiloquent presentation, and overlay
their material with heroic orchestration. It is perfectly true to say that
the value of a theme lies not so much in its quality as such, as in what
the composer does with it during the course of the work. The truly
symphonic mind can do a great deal with next to nothing, and when
the particular symphonic principle is one of expansion or germination,

[1] The *First Symphony* (1917) was burned during the Occupation and the remaining
fragments are too inconclusive for reconstruction purposes.

the smallest fragment becomes of supreme magnitude. This has been seen in these pages during the study of Sibelius. In the case of Elgar the themes are always of significant scope in the first place. Further expansion becoming unnecessary and perhaps impossible, the process goes either in the direction of fragmentation or repetition, in most instances the latter. Pijper in his *Symphonies* announces a fragment and expands it not so much in the Sibelian manner (as he does not take any casual fragment) as in one peculiar to himself.

Pijper is never ponderous. His enormous orchestral forces move with the dignity of a stately habanera, but are in no way turgid or grandiloquent. The scholar can find great mental joy in reading these erudite scores, and the musician will not find himself empty of musical reaction at the end. Pijper may not consistently stir one's innermost feelings and one cannot listen to him in the frame of mind which expects intense subjectivity; but emotional music is not the sole type of music, and the sincerity of the thought conveys its message to the listener in no uncertain measure.

If one asks why this music has made so little impact outside Holland, the answer has already been given. In a culture which avoids sensationalism, this must be expected. In the panorama of music it will be found that Pijper holds the same position as Vaughan Williams here, Roussel in France, and Sibelius in Finland, but he lacks the universality of the two last-named. As a world influence, therefore, he is at present negligible; but so is Vaughan Williams. This does not matter in the least and in a world tending to a robot similarity of expression, Pijper will remain isolated; but in his own country which, after all, is the most important place for any composer, he stands as the leader of a great school of composers which unavailability alone restricts to their country's limits. Pijper, his pupils, and followers remain content in their position of insularity and their integrity is supreme.

Holding the balance between the older romanticism and the systematic note-row system, Pijper may well be found to provide an answer to the contemporary trend in his neo-classicism.

CHAPTER TWENTY-SEVEN

THE OUTLOOK

*Janácek (1854-1928)—van Lier (1906)—Badings (1907)—
Landre (1905)—Andriessen (1892)—Ortheil (1905)—Sessions
(1896) — Copland (1900) — Harris (1898) — Barber
(1910) — Schuman (1910) — Rubbra (1901) — Tippett
(1905) — Rawsthorne (1905) — Berkeley (1903) — Britten
(1913) — Leibowit\z (1913) — Krenek (1900) — Mihalovici
(1898)—Delvincourt (1888)—Fitelberg (1903)—L'Ecole de
Paris—Messiaen (1908)—Jolivet (1905)—Sauguet (1901)
—Martinet (1912)—Dallapiccola (1904)—Absil (1893)
—Poot (1901)—Chevreuille (1901)—
The Soviet Failure*

IN view of the many trends indicated since the beginning of the century, the present period may be regarded as one of consolidation. "-Isms" have come and gone; leaders of the *avant-garde* have retired into obscurity as honoured (and in a few cases, forgotten) names, and others have taken their places. There are probably no more composers to-day in relation to population than there ever have been. There are, and always will be, Hummels and Salieris to be found everywhere. These do not disturb the smooth flow of musical channels. The individualists of any period are in the minority and they always have a crowd of little Chorleys, Davisons, and Hanslicks on their tails. Indeed, it is a sure sign of individuality when this hunt gets up, and the panorama of musical criticism tells a remarkable story of misjudgment. Criticism does no harm and very little good, but at times taste takes the place of judgment, and all manner of unfair and unjustified comments are made. The worst of these is the charge of insincerity, the accusation that the artist is putting his tongue in his cheek. This should never be said of anyone unless strong conviction or certainty impels it.

It has become fashionable to categorise composers as "major" and "minor". This is to be deprecated for in so many cases the so-called minor prophet has become major. In what respects can this categorisation be made? A composer may be important in one particular line and, therefore, undoubtedly "major" in that line—which, in itself, may not be a very permanent one. Important composers of ballet or film music may be quite insignificant as symphonists, but they cannot be called "minor". Until the closing years of his life, it would have been justifiable to have described Delius as a "minor composer" for all the impact his music was making upon listeners and concert promoters. To-day, some "major composers" are judged solely by the quantity of their output, and some whose catalogue is small are rated as "minor" simply because their names appear less frequently than those of their more prolific brethren. A composer's position is often much higher in his own country than elsewhere. In this regard, one would point to Leoš Janáček (1854-1928) (whose position and influence in his native Bohemia was of the highest importance), as being a "minor composer" so far as the world in general is concerned, for it would be necessary to look far afield before finding anyone who could say with truth that he knew his music at all well. As far as Europe in general is concerned, even Vaughan Williams is "minor"—which is absurd. "Major" and "minor" are grades which simply do not justify their use and categorisation of this nature can come only in retrospect.

It may be conceded that both Impressionism and old-fashioned romanticism have now gone by the board, although certain elements constantly appear among even the most rabid neo-classicists. Poetry, however, will never disappear and poetic music will always find its niches in every era. To-day the emphasis is often moved from formal process and placed on derivation of theme. Earlier in the century it was considered righteous for a composer to have written his symphonic music in a manner which obeyed the customary usages of traditional design, and criticism was often levelled against any absence of it. To-day, some composers rejoice greatly at the discovery of some new note-series which, by simple processes of cerebral arrangement, can justly be stated to form the entire basis and material of a work. What was at one time spoken of as "visual counterpoint" is rearing its head again, but the process of consolidating the trends of the last fifty years will gradually settle these questions. We are witnessing a kind of résumé of the experiments and trends through which we have lived. One by one they are taken up again and re-discarded after due trial.

However, the truths of musical construction and symphonic design are still as firm as ever they were.

The present period in England may indeed be regarded as a reactionary one, for the greater part of the music written here to-day might very well have appeared fifteen years ago. The majority of the younger composers of all countries do not appear to be able to make up their minds whether to go straight ahead, to use the processes of the 1920's, or to try to mix the two. Only one composer of note has been able to take the best of the new and mix it with the best of the old,[1] and he succeeded in this because his maturity coincided with the 1920's. Young composers to-day fail signally in this attempt because they have not yet found their individuality. It is impossible to detect any trends whatsoever in the very young, although among those of the 1920's they were apparent almost from the first.[2] However, it is only with practice that individuality can be discovered, and as long as there are societies for the performance of new works (I refrain advisedly from using the term "new music") so will the young composers the sooner find their true style.

Meanwhile, what of the composers who may be said to represent their own cultures, men being neither young nor old and in some cases, hardly middle-aged?[3] In spite of the influence of the extreme neoclassicists and their insistence upon concentration of essentials, there are a large number of distinguished symphonists in all parts of the world who still see salvation in the established designs and processes and take pride in the workmanship displayed in symphonic expansions. It has been remarked that so often it is the small and unobtrusive countries who produce the Messiahs. Without in any way suggesting that the composers of Holland are the ultimate Messiahs of Music, one must give due credit to this learnèd set of scholars whose symphonies and other works carry the most marked signs of musical erudition, ingenuity, resource, and musicianship. The influence of Willem Pijper[4] is now fulfilling itself in the well-wrought and complete symphonic works of composers like Bertus van Lier (1906), Henk Badings (1907), Guillaume Landré (1905), Hendrik Andriessen (1892) and Léon Ortheil (1905). The first of these is a composer of prodigious sym-

[1] See page 59.
[2] Since going to press, an experience in Paris has caused me to modify my view of the situation.
[3] A scientist writing in one of the daily papers has envisaged middle age of the immediate future at—seventy.
[4] See page 299.

phonies which have all the stuff of symphonic construction. Van Lier's principles are those of germination and cyclicism. He is not content with letting the material grow from fragments alone, and his logical mind sees the value and possibilities of cyclical cohesion as well. Absolutely abstract and classical in approach, van Lier is masterly in his polyphony and symphonic continuity. His use of the passacaglia style refers him back to the days of the early Netherlandic writers. He does not write actual passacaglias, however, but in his *Second Symphony* he uses the style and method of the manner.

Van Lier, were he a native of a country with sufficient resources, would take his place in the generality of European music. Holland, however, is not as yet regarded as being a 100 per cent. musical centre. Her resources are limited, and her composers can find no publishers. (Later we shall discuss a composer whose reputation has been made very largely because of the availability of his scores.) Van Lier, had he been of German or Austrian birth, might well have held a position similar to that of Hindemith. His music is infinitely more resourceful and more distinguished by sheer musicality than that of Hindemith. As it is, his reputation is, for the moment, restricted to his native milieu.

There is nothing deliberately approachable about this music. On the contrary, at first glance it appears that the formal processes and the thematic derivations are too deliberately devised; but once one has got under the skin of the scores, there is a mastery of solid musical thought the like of which I can find nowhere else to-day. Like Willem Pijper, van Lier does not restrict himself in his orchestral requirements, and this may be a long-standing obstacle to performance outside Holland.

A similar integrity of purpose, but a far more serious and actually forbidding approach to music, is found in Henk Badings, who represents the very prototype of Emmanuel Kant, in music. It is quite easy to realise van Lier's ideals and to go the whole way with him; but Badings seems to invite one to avoid him unless one is possessed of an intellect of the calibre of Kant. Badings' philosophy seems frustrative, but I do not think that it is intentionally so. Reading the scores of his Symphonies, one is struck by their intellectual integrity and undoubted sincerity. He uses his material to its ultimate exhaustion; when the work is over, one rather wonders if there is any joy left in the world, and if any suggestion of it may not be altogether wrong and sinful. In a world which has been through a series of inconsequences and follies, Badings stands out for his consistency of thought, and there is little difference in the works written before 1939, those written during the Occupation, and those composed since the end of the War. A frivolous or flippant composition by Badings would be quite impossible.

He is not far removed from Schoenberg[1] in this respect, but his music is not systematically impelled. It has a strong tonal sense and moves with dignity. Schoenberg at times makes us feel that there is no future whatsoever for mankind. He may be right. Badings is a little more placid about the matter and does not weep over it. His is the music of the actual moment. Being unapproachable, it is unlikely to penetrate very far afield. His chamber works have appeared from time to time on the B.B.C. Third Programme and have made an impression for the reasons I have mentioned. One admires and respects them, but one feels that affection would be deplored by Badings himself.

The lighter side, as it were, of Dutch music is represented by Guillaume Landré whose Symphonies and other works are full of an almost Gallic lightness. Formally, he is as germinal and cyclical as van Lier, but his large-scale orchestral works are less powerful. His style, however, is very different from that of van Lier and Badings. His is a religious mind and his *Sinfonia sacra in memoriam patris* (1948) is in effect a Choral Symphony upon the text of the Requiem. His *Quatres mouvements symphoniques* (1949) form a complete symphony. The movements are played straight through without a break and are thematically connected in an unobtrusive manner. Landré's chamber music is characterised by a tranquil romantic charm. His music cannot by any stretch of the imagination be rated as "great", but it is infinitely approachable and does not attempt to explore any deep wells of philosophy.

Landré's religious tendencies are equalled by those of Hendrik Andriessen, who is essentially an organist and, incidentally, one of the most gifted extemporisers in Europe. Andriessen, who holds the appointment of Director at the Utrecht Conservatoire, has written some organ works which have not made a great impression over here owing to their rather Franckian approach. He is a convinced Franckist and d'Indyist and therefore it is not surprising that his symphonic outlook is cyclical. His Symphonies, while more harmonic than polyphonic, do not show any organ influence, a fact which is surprising. He is by no

[1] See page 209.

means Gallic in quality, although he manages to imbue his symphonic music with sufficient clarity and lightness to suggest a Latin background. He is less Gallic than Landré and infinitely less uncompromisingly abstract than van Lier or Badings. His *First Symphony* (1930) is in five well-connected movements, while the *Second* (1937) is constructed in the manner of an extended old-fashioned overture.

The fifth of the quintet of names which may be said to represent the present-day tendencies of Dutch music is Léon Ortheil, whose experiments in design are exceedingly interesting and convincing. In his *Second Symphony* (described as "Piccolo Sinfonia") (1939), Ortheil arranges each movement as if it were a section of first movement form. Thus the opening Poco Lento represents the Introduction, the ensuing Allegro stands for the principal subject and the connecting episode. The Meno Mosso (the actual slow movement) is the second subject, the Scherzando being the development section of the whole work or movement, whichever way one may consider the arrangement. The closing Meno Mosso and Allegro represent the recapitulation in reverse, the whole plan following the style of the "façade" in which the two subjects are placed opposite their first entries on the other side of the development section, this representing the keystone of an arch. The *Third Symphony* (1943) disregards all formal traditions until the fourth movement, which ties up the preceding cyclical movements in first movement form, concluding with a Funeral March whose material is solely and entirely permutations, and not very purposely concealed, of the themes of the whole work.

Ortheil, therefore, has spread the concept of symphonic design further than his fellow-countrymen. It is possible that this emphasis upon formal construction has given a wrong impression of Dutch music and that the general feeling may be that these scholarly composers are more concerned with cerebral variation than with musical impulse. The only way in which this can be proved wrong is by reading or hearing the music, and neither course seems likely to be possible in the immediate future. Dutch music, therefore, is behind a curtain through which information seeps only when enquiry is made, and this is not enough. One trouble about this music is that it has never been shocking or sensational, and the composers have all steadily avoided this easy way to popularity and recognition.

Similar evenness of purpose can be found in certain American composers of the younger generation, whose music survives because it has not subscribed to any fashionable trait. Some names have already been mentioned which took American music forward at the beginning of the silly season. These names played their part in that period, but in some instances failed to realise anything later. Their idioms have been too much of that decade and, having subscribed to fashion, they have been unable to continue their course. The names to be discussed here are, for the most part, familiar in Europe. One, Roger Sessions (1896), however, has not made the impact which his innate Americanism has merited. Sessions is 100 per cent. American; that is to say there are no European traces to be found in his music, which is generally hard and unsympathetic. This may be due partly to the basic hardness of the American character, yet a continent which lays such great store by symphonic music as does Europe should by rights have welcomed his *Piano Sonata* (1930) and his *Three Symphonies* (1927, 1937, 1938) with open arms. This may have been because his fellow-countryman Aaron Copland (1900) has also shown a more spectacularly full quota of Americanism.

Copland is regarded as even more than 100 per cent. American by his fellow-countrymen. His music proclaims it in many ways. His reputation has spread partly through the enormous amount of propaganda writing that he has done on behalf of American music which has, naturally, drawn attention to himself. A pupil of Nadia Boulanger (1887), Copland exemplifies once more the objective nature of this teaching which will be found in the English composer Lennox Berkeley—it has already been noted in the case of William Walton. Copland has not made counterpoint the basis of his music to the extent that others have. He has applied the prevalent tendencies in America to his serious music, and of all American composers he has succeeded best in his flirtations with jazz. Jazz rhythms abound in his earlier works, particularly in the *Piano Concerto. El Salon Mexico*, being a deliberately impressionistic portrait, naturally carries on the rhythmic impulse to its fullest degree. This remarkable work, ranking with the noisiest and most exuberant of the century, never fails to arouse a storm of excitement; this is probably all that it is intended to do. Copland is a serious artist in spite of certain whimsicalities. He does not regard himself as a Superior Being above the pettiness of commissioned work of a not very elevating character. His film music is exactly suited to the particular films and he does not fall into the temptation of writing a film score regardless of its suitability or otherwise. One cannot imagine any tenderness in his style, but its absence is mainly caused by the fact that it is never called-for from him. His *Symphonies* are not very notable and one cannot find a real symphonic impulse behind them. He is more suited for the shorter and more concise manner of the concert overture. One reads the unaffected *An Outdoor Overture* (1938) with considerable pleasure and sees in it certain healthy tendencies which are expressed by diatonic clarity. He does not slam his ideas about in this work. On the other hand, some do not consider it a characteristic composition for this very reason.

His early practice in complex rhythms has made him suitable for ballet, but ballet of an unromantic quality. The most uncompromising of these is *Rodeo* (1942) which, in the Preface to the score, states that it deals with "the problem that has confronted all American women, from earliest pioneer times, and which has never ceased to occupy them throughout the history of the building of our country: how to get a suitable man". This occupation, however, is not one which has been, or is, confined solely to America. In this work the women look for sheer athleticism and masculinity. As may be expected, the music is vulgar, but with an ebullient vulgarity characteristic of the subject. Copland here bounces about with great ado, but with perfect clarity, and although the rhythms appear complex, they all sort themselves out and fit into the general scheme. Different is the ballet *Appalachian Spring* (1945) which relates the wedding festivities of a pioneer settlement in the Pennsylvania Hills. Here the vulgarity is entirely proletarian and unstylised. It is less sophisticated, of course, but more complex. There is no tenderness about this work, either, but it is more realistic in that one can imagine its frequency more convincingly than that of the fun and games of the Sunday-afternoon Rodeo.

In all other respects Copland is abstract, and this can be seen in everything from the slight *Concerto for Clarinet and String Orchestra, with Harp and Piano* (1948) composed for Benny Goodman with all due knowledge of that player's versatility—Milhaud also wrote a *Concerto* for him—to the large-scale Symphonies. One imagines that Copland has human feelings and emotions, but he gives little indication of them in his music.

One may regard Copland as representative of the basic American life, but this is not the only kind of life in that vast continent, and her other composers have a definite European foundation, of the best kind, be it noted.

Of these, one singles out Roy Harris (1898), Samuel Barber (1910) and William Schuman (1910). In style these composers might well be Europeans. Harris is the most classically impelled of the trio, Barber the most romantic, while Schuman holds a balance between the two. Harris is a true symphonist. His remarkable *Third Symphony* (1938) in one continuous movement is a completely organic whole. Its considerable weight is engendered entirely by the rise and fall of the themes, and by their gradual growth. This is one of the most accumulative works that I have ever come across. Its balance is admirable and while the germinative fragments expand beneath one's eyes, so to speak, the music takes on an ever-increasing impetus in terms of diminution. That he has the gift of the long tune can be realised in the opening theme, which pursues an ever-increasing intensity not engendered entirely by the string tone-colour, which is always emotional under these conditions. This work is a real *symphony* and is one of the few really convincing one-movement works which do not sound like an isolated first movement. Harris' setting of Walt Whitman's "Sea Drift" (1936), described as a *Symphony for Voices*, cannot call for comparison with Delius' setting of the same words because the two approaches are completely different. Harris, yet another Nadia Boulanger pupil, is not concerned with the expression of the words so much as with vocal effect and, let it be said, with vocal gymnastics. His is an approach which strives after effect and this is fully achieved in a manner which should engage itself with choral societies for whom *Belshazzar's Feast* holds few terrors.

Harris' output is considerable. A man of great energy and one not content with letting his scores remain unplayed, he is the most musically athletic of the American group. In spite of his classicism, he does not despise human feelings; these appear in his music in the natural course of the material. He is a less complex William Walton, with whom he forms a parallel.

Barber is drawn to the romantic virtuosity of Strauss as viewed through late twentieth-century eyes. His music is not only emotionally charged, but picturesquely coloured. It might be said that he is a reactionary, until it is realised that he deliberately withholds himself from the trend to neo-classicism. His general outlook was undoubtedly impelled by his sojourn in Rome, and if a European parallel is sought for, it can be found in the later-Straussian style of Respighi. Barber has acquired distinction in Europe with his *Adagio* (1937) for strings and

Essay (1937) for orchestra, the former having become almost a standard work in this country. His *Symphony in One Movement* (1936)—composed the year after his award of the (American) Prix de Rome—is not as convincing in this respect as that of Harris, for its movements are separate and distinct and joined only by a link. Nevertheless, it is a noble work of its kind even if it is not very new; but Barber is not concerned with and does not show great interest in harmonic research. His chamber music is equally purple in colour, but one should not set it aside lightly for this reason. Barber is a connecting link between the old and the new. He has taken the elements of the former just before the period of its decay and has contrived to hook it to the fairly new; if he had hooked it to the *very* new it would have been a complete misfit. His music has power and stamina, like that of Harris, and the ideas do not have to be bolstered up for they stand by themselves, four-square. One is a little overpowered, perhaps, by the weight and richness of the colour; but although one is fearful lest sooner or later it may yearn, this never happens, and Barber's skilful avoidance of too highly charged emotion is masterly and natural.

It is refreshing to meet this unashamed romanticism to-day, and one hopes that Barber will have a little influence upon the young idea in this regard. If he can supply a leaven of softening to the hard American outlook and personality, he will achieve much.

His opposite number is William Schuman, whose European training took place in the Mozarteum Academy at Salzburg. Schuman supplies all the deficiencies of Harris and Barber. He is at once the "lighter" and least pretentious of these representative American composers. He, also is not in the least afraid of romanticism, and his symphonic music has a delicacy which is absent elsewhere. He has more delicate poetry about him than have the others. Schuman's romanticism is not unlike that of Mahler in places, but his means of expression are limited to the ordinary resources of the orchestra and they are not used turgidly or over-emotionally. The balance that he holds in American music softens the classicism of Harris and thins out the textures of Barber. He is, from what one can make out, isolated musically—but the enormous amount of American music which has not reached these shores and seems to be unobtainable, makes a dogmatic statement like this dangerous. Schuman's textures are slender and clear, and he is concerned with only one thing at a time. He might be placed as a parallel to Lennox Berkeley.

Schuman's music does not sound in the least American. Although this is not very positive, one can see traces of it in Harris and Barber. Schuman is definitely European, though he would probably be the first to say that it was quite unconscious. His tenderness is genuine, and of all the composers mentioned here, he is the most poetic, gentle and human.

It is not yet possible to see exactly what the American trend to-day really is. If one regards Sessions and Copland as being the typical article, then the others reflect nothing of American culture. However, no culture can be determined in a matter of a few hundred years. America is avid for learning. She has a notable number of great European composers in her midst. She welcomes lecturers with something to say, but will not tolerate dictatorial dogmatism or heavy preaching. It does not appear that she has as yet fully explored her vast and varied folk-lore, and the influx of foreigners may well impede this. However, if at the moment we welcome American music with more interest than affection, and see in it few signs as yet of any generally distinctive elements, eventually it will betray distinguishing qualities of the positive nature of the several European cultures. The trend is in that direction, although not yet plainly perceptible.

The trend in this country has been towards the formularisation of the English style. We now have our own clearly defined manner which is as distinctive in quality and quantity as that of any other culture; thus the work originated in our own time by Vaughan Williams in his *Pastoral Symphony* has reached its culminating point. Doubtless *British* music will continue to be written, but in due course it will merge into the more personal national idiom. Of the composers to-day who are definitely 100 per cent. in the English manner, the name of Edmund Rubbra (1901) is the most notable. Rubbra was a pupil of Holst, Vaughan Williams, and R. O. Morris. From Holst he obtained his sense of choralism, although there is nothing of that composer's constructivist style in Rubbra's technique. From Vaughan Williams he found his English manner, while R. O. Morris gave him his basic contrapuntal facility, founded upon the style of the sixteenth century. Rubbra, therefore, is the really typical English example.

Rubbra is a genuine symphonist. Strengthened by the sinews of counterpoint and backed up by a strong sense of resultant harmony, he is abstract in expression. His Symphonies place him in the direct line from Stanford, his technique being a later twentieth-century concept of that of the senior composer. Rubbra's style is not to everybody's taste. Many find it too redolent of South Kensington, for it could have emanated from nowhere else; but it is musical and one can see many points of individuality about it. Some maintain that it is not "modern", by which they mean that it does not startle or shock. It is true that it will never stir multitudes to frenzies of enthusiasm (I do not refer to the exuberance of Promenade Concert audiences), but it is all intensely well wrought and sensible. Formally, it is quite unassailable and the music hangs well together. Rubbra has a full sense of continuity and symphonic expansion simply because his thought is mainly polyphonic and not harmonic. It is impossible to discover any "new chords" or find any novelty in his methods of approach and departure; the technique is traditional, the "modernity", or whatever one likes to call it, lying in the incidental harmonic combinations which occur at various moments between the contrapuntal lines.

His choralism is in the line from that of Parry rather than that of Stanford, and he never aims for effect *per se*. His music is invariably singable and the voices are not exploited in any way. Indeed, one searches everywhere in vain for any experiments in sonorities and he does not write instrumental music for voices, or *vice versa*.

Rubbra is the scholar of his generation. His Englishness is not that of the "wodes so wylde", for he steadily avoids these glades and his music consequently has strength and stamina.

This sense of stamina is lacking in the music of Michael Tippett (1905) whose symphonic works are full of busyness but remain undistinguished by any recognisable feature. He walks along the edges of the "wodes so wylde", but his style makes it imperative that some time or other he must enter those "wodes", for it is there that he will find the missing element, and not until he has been well scratched and torn. Indeed, his Englishness is too sophisticated for its natural milieu and there are signs of too much deliberation. His *Concerto for Double String Orchestra* (1939) is admirable counterpoint, but it leaves little impression. Like the *Symphony* (1943), it does not sound as if it "damned-well had to be written"[1] and it just fails in its combination of intelligence, intellectualism and musicality to avoid the dangerous state of arty-craftiness. It is all rather precious and self-conscious. The Oratorio *Child of Our Time* (1942) made a deep impression chiefly through the circumstances of its impulse. Vocally, the writing is impec-

[1] I believe it was Vaughan Williams who first used this expression in a musical connection.

cable, as is the case with all such works composed in the English style and tradition. It is genuinely felt, but does not suggest any determination to be practically "up. and doing" in order to change a situation. It is altogether too resignedly pacific.

Tippett's musical mind is well ordered and his processes are all logical. His polyphony differs from that of Rubbra because it lacks that composer's strong harmonic sense. Another pupil of R. O. Morris, Tippett has been too loyal to sixteenth-century principles and he has not succeeded in combining these with the ideas of his other teacher, Charles Wood, who brought a rather scholastic nineteenth-century passion to bear upon twentieth-century thought. Nevertheless, Tippett has played a part in the establishing of the English manner and time alone will show if he is capable of making up the present deficiencies.

There are, of course, composers who consciously or otherwise model themselves upon the foreign article in some small respects, yet remain English and not British. Of these Alan Rawsthorne (1905) has shown a solidity of formal power which is even stronger than that of Rubbra. His *Symphonic Studies for Orchestra* (1939) and *'Cello Sonata* (1949) bear a distinct affinity with the formal and melodic contours of Albert Roussel. Nevertheless, there is nothing else which can be described as Gallic about his music, and in quality and expression it remains English. It suggests to us the time when Dover joined Calais, and, consequently, Rawsthorne has a Continental appeal denied the purely English traditional style. His *Symphony* (1950) proved a disappointment. It lacked drive, impulse, and continuity. This surprised many who thought that he might have proved himself a natural symphonist. It is said that he has composed many film scores. The fact that the *Symphony* was commissioned and, therefore, written to order should have proved no stumbling block to one experienced in turning out music "by the foot", but too much working to measure has proved the downfall of many other composers. In any case, the work cannot rank beside that of Walton or the *First* of Rubbra, both of which works are notable for the very elements that Rawsthorne's was deficient in. The salvation of English Symphony does not, alas! finds its roots in this work. Rawsthorne is probably the most gifted writer of variations in this country, a manner which calls for resource and invention and no symphonic continuity.

When Rawsthorne tries to be less serious, he becomes slightly trivial, as in *Cortèges* (1945) and *Street Corner* (1944) and these works show that the invasion of the territory of lighter (as distinct from light) music is not one which he can carry out successfully. Rawsthorne has as much stamina as Walton. While listening unknowingly, one realises that the music has been written by English composers in spite of certain technical twists. The chief difference between them is that Rawsthorne has none of the virtuosity of Walton. One can, and has, seen a certain connection between Walton and Berlioz; such a contact cannot be found in the case of Rawsthorne.

The gifts of polish and refinement can be found in the music of Lennox Berkeley (1903), who learnt the knack of clarity at the hands of Nadia Boulanger, and whose contrapuntal style and delicacy of harmony are Gallic in letter, but by no means so in spirit. Berkeley therefore is rather an isolated figure in English music to-day, and he may be said to form an opposing element to the subconscious Gallicism of Rawsthorne. The latter represents the strong formal uncompromising attitude of the French symphonists, while Berkeley superimposes the imaginative qualities of a Ravel upon his otherwise classical approach. There is, however, no lack of stamina, but it is more that of a slender and well-balanced long-stemmed silver vase than that of the oak tree which Rawsthorne suggests. It is his imagination which saves his music from being simply a series of pleasant sounds. This can be noticed in the *Nocturne* (1948) and the *Divertimento* (1946) for orchestra. His *Symphony* (1942) is tranquil, but not with the spiritual tranquillity of Vaughan Williams' *Fifth*. Berkeley's *Symphony* stands practically alone in its gentleness. It hangs together well and is symphonically derivative. Berkeley, however, is highly skilled in concealing his processes and they are worked from mere germinals; his gracefully poised melodies are fully complete in themselves, yet suggestive to the imaginative mind of many devices of expansion. His gift of clarity, which one suspects to have been latent in him rather than created by any process of teaching, never allows him to be ebullient or turgid. He rarely exults in a boisterous manner and his general style indicates a widely-cultured and placid mind. Nevertheless, in a work like the *Concerto for Two Pianos* (1949) he assumes a mantle of strength and vigour which lies more in the counterpoint than in the actual material. In this work Berkeley appears to have tried to be different, and it is a matter of personal opinion as to whether he has succeeded or not in being convincing; personally, I think that he has, but it is doubtful if another similar approach would be sufficiently varied.

His pianism is notable, and he is one of the few eclectic composers of to-day who manage the instrument with any sense of mastery. I except those who specialise in piano writing, of course, and Berkeley resembles John Ireland in his facility in this medium.

His choral works are all well written for the voices and do not ask for any ultra-musical effects. His one failure is his setting of the *Psalm* "*Domini est terra*" (1938) which is too subdued for the spirit of the text. Berkeley approached this more in a spirit of awe and wonder than in that of a song of triumph; but in any case, the music does not succeed. The early oratorio *Jonah* (1936) is better in this respect, while his *Stabat Mater* (1950) is a beautiful example of its kind.

Berkeley could write a good ballet because his sense of light rhythm is so highly developed and spontaneous. Reading a Berkeley score, one is immediately struck by the comparatively small number of notes per page, and this is something not often found in present-day twentieth-century music. His chamber music adds lustre to a genre gradually becoming more popular to-day.

One of the most remarkable trends of the period since the 1920's is the English composers' increased significance in this field. One may remark the chamber music of the senior composers, such as Armstrong Gibbs, Herbert Howells, Frank Bridge, John Ireland and E. J. Moeran, and see that the younger generation exemplified in Tippett, Rawsthorne, Walton and Berkeley, who have used this natural polyphonic technique, have established the string trio and quartet among the most universally important of the period. English string quartets make a Continental impression where the more elaborate symphonic work fails, because audiences, accustomed to polyphonic listening, regard the music in terms of lines rather than in those of general effect. The rise of practical interest among English composers is due entirely to the many splendid chamber music bodies which abound here, and which are more readily available for new works than orchestras. It seems that the future of English music on the Continent may rest with this rarified genre. Certain it is that the standard is uniformly high and several composers have proved their superiority here over their work in the orchestral medium. Although it is a natural ambition for a composer to aim at the Royal Albert Hall or Royal Opera House, Covent Garden, as the summit of his ambitions, he is but foolish and penny-wise who despises the smaller halls.

None of the composers discussed so far in this section has been in any way prolific, and the music suggests careful deliberation and thought in its making. At the same time none of it is forced. These composers have not been concerned with quantity at the expense of quality. This is not the case with Benjamin Britten (1913), who has accomplished much in his so far short life and bids fair to outvie that other shining example of facility, Camille Saint-Saëns. Britten has been exceedingly fortunate in that all his music has been published, publicised and performed. On the Continent, he is regarded as the representative composer of this country, a reputation gained entirely by the availability of his music. I refuse to believe that there are no other English composers who could not obtain similar repute had they the opportunities which Britten has enjoyed. In spite of all these advantages, Britten in the last ten years has written nothing better than *Les Illuminations* (1940), and a recent performance from an unknown radio station confirmed that they have the very stuff of music in them, with beauties and poignancies unfaded and unaffected.

Britten has been spoilt by the ease with which he has obtained success. With increasing facility his style has not crystallised itself, and there is nothing definite to which one can point as being essentially and specifically "Britten". He has been called the "twentieth-century Berlioz" and the "twentieth-century Mozart".[1] Both are completely wrong descriptions. He has neither the intrinsic power of Berlioz nor the profound thought of Mozart. The only ways in which the parallels can be justified lie in the fact that Britten can be just as noisy as Berlioz and nearly as prolific (in proportion to the labour entailed in the mere act of writing the music) as Mozart; but, as I have said, quantity is not enough.

Britten conveys an impression of stamina. This can be seen in the *Sinfonia da Requiem* (1940), but on examination it is found to lie simply in the weight of orchestral volume. The work bangs its way along with gong and cymbal, the orchestra tone and colouring supplying an impression of strength which the absence of musical content finally denies. It is undoubtedly effective—but anyone with a gift for scoring can achieve this quality. Britten is far more convincing in his chamber music—the *Serenade* (1944) and the *Sonnets of Michelangelo* (1943) are beautiful—and in works like the *Variations of a theme by Frank Bridge* (1937), and the *Violin Concerto* (1940); in other words, when he

[1] So many composers have at one time and another been given this Mozartean soubriquet that it is worth noting one solitary instance where it seems genuinely applicable. This is the French composer, Reynaldo Hahn (1875-1947), whose more important works have all the genuine Mozartean qualities of delicacy, deftness and grace.

is not pretentious. These works and their like are impeccable, but in no way worthy of being considered landmarks in the history of music. "Advance publicity" in the *Radio Times* anticipated that *A Spring Symphony* (1949) would be a work written on the Mahler concept. This claimed too much in advance and its extravagance gave rise to much disappointment. Earlier than this, in 1940, a writer in a magazine called *Tempo* implied of Britten's *Piano Concerto* (1937) that he had succeeded where such composers as Bartok, Bax, Schoenberg, Stravinsky, Hindemith, Ireland, etc., had failed. This particular *Concerto* appears to have long since passed into oblivion. It said very little which had not been said over and over again by other composers.

A Spring Symphony is a delightful if not a highly original work. Its choral writing and material are unquestionable; but its idiom is that of about five other composers. It is typically English in all its qualities, but falls into the group of typical recent twentieth-century works which have their place in the period without adding anything to the progress of music. It may be significant that so many critics commented upon the ineffable effect of "Sumer is icumen in" as sung by a choir of boys—but "Sumer is icumen in" was not composed by Britten, and the tune holds much the same position in English symphonic music as does the *Dies irae* in French. *A Spring Symphony* is a worthy contribution to English music, but it is not individual enough to justify it as a landmark, or as a work of world significance; it certainly has no Mahlerian proportions or propensities.

Britten is more likely to survive through the medium of such works as *Our Hunting Fathers* (1936) and *A Hymn to St. Cecilia* (1942) than through the pretentious and large-scale works. This survival will probably be a local one since he has provided our English choral societies with the very things which lie within their scope, and here we sing more than they do elsewhere.

One admires Britten's operatic accomplishments without being in any way convinced that he is the only composer to-day capable of writing such works. Again, opportunity has been the great thing and Britten has had most of that denied the vast majority of composers. This does not in any way detract from what value the works may have, which is considerable, but not unique. *Peter Grimes* showed that he had a strong sense of the theatre, but when all was played and sung, *Peter Grimes* said in its way no more than *The Wreckers* by Ethel Smyth said in its, and both works can claim merit for the same points.

It remains to be seen how soon *Peter Grimes* will go out of fashion.

The two chamber operas, *The Rape of Lucretia* (1946) and *Albert Herring* (1948) are interesting experiments which succeed and fail respectively. The former solves the problem of the double situation, and the idea is both cleverly carried out and convincingly conveyed, although it must be conceded that this is more the success of the librettist and producer than of the composer. The work, as a whole, is cleverly devised—and this is its weakest feature. Britten is so clever that he has forgotten to be musical. *Albert Herring* fails because its documentary message is misunderstood and because it is too good a play in itself. The music too often seems superfluous. Its seriousness underlines the stage situation with due cynicism, but these require no underlining. One actually should not laugh during this work, and were the music more deliberately poignant and less inherently clever, it would succeed in cancelling the farcical yet tragic stage business. Taking everything into consideration, *The Rape of Lucretia* is the most successful of the three works, provided that one likes this type of castrated, frustrated music, which has few positive qualities.

Let's make an Opera (1950) reminds one in title of Hindemith's *Let's build a City* (1930). The approaches of the two works are quite different. Britten brings the audience into the play itself; Hindemith provides a mimed show. The actuality of Britten's work has made an immediate appeal, since nothing like it in opera has ever been seen before, although the idea of appealing to the audience is as old as *Peter Pan*. However, it affords a jolly evening's entertainment and as far as can be seen, it has no moral or philosophical import. Many find it puerile, but there will always be a host of people older than their age.

The Beggar's Opera (1949) is quite pointless. Although it afforded Britten a fine opportunity for the exercising of technical processes and devices, the whole thing sounds a complete anachronism and it would have been better if a completely new work had been created. When Britten said at the first performance of his version at the Lyric Theatre that *The Beggar's Opera* had at last returned home, he was completely wide of the mark, for this sophisticated version has nothing to do with either the ideals or intention of the original.

It is significant that in many cases each new work of Britten supplants that immediately preceding it. This is not because from such a wealth of material it has become difficult, if not impossible, to be selective, and it cannot be ascribed to lack of opportunity, since Britten's name appears with frequency in concert and radio programmes. He is an isolated figure in himself, for he lives in an ivory tower, completely cut off from his fellow-composers. No great or lasting art has been cultivated by one so young under these conditions.

An objective assessment suggests that while Britten is a notable figure in English music, he is not as outstanding as might be thought in any respect save that of fecundity. Cleverness was a trait which marred the 1920's; it does not yet seem to have been altogether eradicated.

These names represent the present-day position of music in this country. There are many others who contribute to a smaller degree to our national culture and it must not be forgotten that in one particular style, so-called "light music", we have a number of first-rate composers, and that the English style of light music has a quality of its own. It may not be an important quality or style, but it is none the less "ours". At the other end of the scale there are those serious composers who go a-whoring after the strange gods of systematisation as practised in central Europe and elsewhere on the Continent. These are in a minority, and although they are filled with the commendable zeal of the missionary, have not yet given any really convincing proof of an inherent musical creativity or of very much genuine musical feeling.

This systematic trend has come to a halt. Its sudden rise to popularity among a limited number of composers has led towards its *impasse*, and with this in view the issues have become somewhat confused. Systematic composition in the twelve-note-row manner is not the same thing as twelve-tone composition. There are a great number of composers who write in the latter style without any regard to tonality or key relationships, and without deliberately denying both. With them discord and concord exist no more than they did when Debussy wrote *Pelléas et Mélisande*, but, unlike the twelve-noters, they do not run away from any incidental concord. These writers have not yet found any convincing expansion of the manner, and many of them write simply variations on preceding works.

Of the twelve-note-row advocates, René Leibowitz (1913) is the High Priest and represents the *maître par excellence* of the whole system. His compositions bear out his lucid writings, the latter being fully explanatory and dogmatic. He is the most sincere and most convincing member of the cult, but not even *he* is able to find the necessary manner of providing contrast and variety, although he is a master of variation —which is not quite the same thing as variety. The system is now going back upon itself. Strict conformity has cramped spontaneity and one is struck only too often at the prevailing influence of the chromaticism of *Tristan und Isolde*. When not being cerebrally abstract, the writers become ardently romantic; on these occasions it is only too patent that the system has been set aside for the nonce, and when an academic approach is denied, it proclaims its failure. The condensation of material to its briefest statements is nothing new; Darius Milhaud uncovered its secret in his *Petites Symphonies* and other works, and it may be noted that in maturity Milhaud has turned to the normal symphonic concept.

The twelve-note-row system has reached a position exactly similar to that reached by Impressionism, and has become merely an academic process similar in purpose to the traditional text-book. It is a means of breaking away from latent old-fashioned tendencies, but it is gradually resolving itself into public performance of classroom exercises. However, one must acknowledge the sincerity and consistency of the most austere of the systematic flagellants, Ernest Krenek (1900), who has passed through many musical tendencies before arriving at the forbiddingly restrictive and at the same time invitingly convenient field of his *Studies in Counterpoint* and the consistencies of his opera *Karl V* (1933-1935). These he reached by way of *Johnny spielt auf* (1925), a most engaging opera which says the last word in the combination of jazz and "straight" music. Krenek's *Symphonies* are masterpieces of technique and construction, but they contain few signs of any humanity or even of musical impulse. It will be interesting to see whither he will go from this point.

A very great number of composers acknowledge the mastery of Schoenberg without in any way desiring to write in his manner, or altogether approving it. In 1947 a festival was given in Schoenberg's honour in Paris, the programmes consisting of many works which bore not the slightest relationship to Schoenberg's own particular (and, one might almost say, patent) manner. Note-row and scale have now become slightly intermingled, the latter beginning to form an excuse for vagary from the former. The scale enables the composer to be perfectly free within its limits, and the extension of this basic principle lies in the free use of all twelve semitones, regardless of their incidental and ultimate constituents. The substitution of atonicality for atonality has now become fully re-established.

The practice of atonicality may be seen in the masterly works of a

Roumanian composer resident in Paris, Marcel Mihalovici (1898), a pupil of Vincent d'Indy who gave him his magnificent sense of variation and symphonic development. Otherwise, there is nothing in Mihalovici's music to suggest this pupilage, but in passing it may be noted that even the strict approach of d'Indy which, in its time, was regarded as unbending as the tenets of the Spanish Inquisition, has found its expansion along thoroughly "contemporary" lines and has thus given evidence of evolutionary elasticity. Mihalovici, therefore, shows continuity with tradition, while his technique is completely individual.

He is a composer of resource and invention, and he is at the same time profoundly musical. He has written nothing small, as far as can be ascertained, but although he wields a large brush, there is no extravagance. A broad view of his style can be obtained from three works, and these will serve to represent the approach in general to atonicality and the free use of the twelve semitones. The first of these is a *Toccata for Piano and Orchestra* (1938-1939) which has all the potentialities and essentials of a virtuoso concerto, with none of its vices. This healthy, vigorous music does not hesitate at an incidental consonance such as Ex. 1, which happens to be contradicted modally by the piano.

Ex. 1   Piano col 8ve   Toccata for Piano and Orchestra

The systematic composer would have to distort the consonance at all costs. The opening of the second movement demonstrates a manner of combining two worlds with no sense of incongruity—Mihalovici is exceptional in his ability to organise this.

Ex. 2

The prevailing athleticism and vigour of this work suggests the special attributes in these respects of Roussel, another d'Indy pupil; its resource is manifold. The pianism is sometimes percussive and often bravura, but in no sense conventional.

If there are few signs of a rhapsodic lyricism in this *Toccata,* this is not the case with the *Third String Quartet* (1946) or with the earlier *Ricercari* or "Variations libres pour Piano" (1941). The latter is a monumental work for the piano repertoire, worthy to rank with Dukas' *Rameau Variations* and d'Indy's *Sonata.* The music unrolls itself with great dignity and in places is almost unbelievably simple. The theme is suggestive of the type usually associated with the Passacaglia.

Ex. 3   Ricercari

The constructional influence of Vincent d'Indy is apparent on every page, but there is no harmonic resemblance whatsoever. It is distinctly a work which virtuoso pianists would enjoy playing provided that they have a strongly developed instinct and realisation of musical construction and feeling.

It may be said with some justification, perhaps, that the *Third String Quartet* is rather too full of busyness at times, and that the instruments behave in a fussy manner which says less than the appearance of the music suggests. Nevertheless, if the medium of the string quartet is indeed a testing-ground for the artistic restraint of an otherwise ebullient composer, Mihalovici may be credited with passing this test with ease, in spite of the above comment, for the texture is always perfectly open and clear. Some of the themes have a certain Rousselian quality about them.

Ex. 4
a)
b)
Third String Quartet

His opera *Phédre* (1948), commissioned by the French Radio, is a work of breadth and dramatic content which avoids all undue underlining of the tragic scenes, and convinces by its directness and clarity of expression. Mihalovici proves his mastery with the human voice, both in solo and in chorus. The singers top the orchestra without any sense of strain. He uses a smallish orchestra, with a plentiful amount of percussion, and enjoys rhythmic declamation with percussion background. In spite of the somewhat frightening (at first sight) texture, the main elements are all in easy relief, and questions of attack do not give the singers any anxiety.[1]

A prominent feature of these works is their inherent sense of scholarship which never becomes the uppermost element and never gets out of thematic control. Mihalovici could, and would, influence a large number of hesitant young composers if his works were to become familiarised to them. He can be placed in some respects next to the Czech, Bohuslav Martinů (1890), a pupil of Roussel and, therefore, imbued with the traditions of the Schola Cantorum. Both composers have an equal sense of vigour, but of the two, Mihalovici is the more' contrasted in style. Both have a sense of tenderness, although this makes but fleeting appearances. Martinů is the stiffer of the two and his lyricism is not quite so pronounced. He does, however, indulge in a kind of twentieth-century baroque rhapsodising on occasions, an element absent from Mihalovici.

Another composer to adopt a free approach to the twelve semitones,

[1] This opera is studied in detail in my *Paris and the Opera: the History of a Culture.* (In preparation.)

although drawn to a more distinct feeling for tonality, is Jerzy Fitelberg (1903)[1], son of a great conductor. Fitelberg, while being absolutely abstract, is not forbidding. His *Second Violin Concerto* (1937) and *Sonata for Two Pianos* (1939) are magnificent works. Fitelberg has his own ideas as to scoring. In the *Second Violin Concerto*, for example, he includes a thematic part for piano duet; this in itself is not an original idea—Saint-Saëns did it in his *Symphonie avec orgue*, but there the piano writing is perfunctory and supplies a "heavenly" arpeggio background, only. Fitelberg uses the players consistently throughout. He is essentially a polyphonic composer and this makes him admirable for the medium of the string quartet. His chamber music is very much musician's music and requires highly concentrated listening, but his *Sonatina for Two Violins* (1938) is a work of great charm and delicacy which neither makes the two players do the work of four nor sounds as if the pianist had not turned up. It is one of the few works in the medium which is entirely satisfactory and satisfying. In his slow movements Fitelberg shows an affinity with the baroque manner and they are highly decorated and rhapsodically melodious. His residence in America has removed a significant figure from European music, but America must be gaining by his presence.

It has become evident during the course of this study that it is increasingly difficult to regard a great many composers in terms of their innate cultures and not even naturalisation can change their natural expression. To describe Schoenberg, Hindemith, Krenek, Bloch or Fitelberg as "American composers" is as fatuous as describing Egon Wellesz as English or Martinů and Mihalovici as "French". The great migration started long before the rise of Hitler to power and a great number of composers lived or studied in any countries but their own; many, however, returned home after the completion of their studies. All through the nineteenth century until to-day Paris has been the Mecca of music, and musicians from all countries have either visited or settled there.   Here in the last century, we attracted German musicians, nay, invited them, and although French composers and performers appeared also, French music was never taken at all seriously.

London attracted by the power of the pound sterling—it still does, even if devalued. Fees paid in this country far exceed those obtainable anywhere else in Europe, but few artists take it seriously as a place of permanent residence or as an "art centre".[2] Paris is still the focal point

[1] Died 1951.   [2] Although there is actually as much "art" here now as anywhere else.

of artistic endeavour. The influx from other countries has resulted in what became known as "L'Ecole de Paris", consisting of those foreigners who reside there and play a part in Parisian musical activities without taking up French citizenship. Whether the French composers as a whole welcome this invasion is a moot point. The majority of the members of this so-called school maintain their basic culture and are content simply to take their places in the panorama. The whole artistic milieu of Paris, with her great traditions, make life and work infinitely more pleasurable and *sympathique* than London, which has seldom gone further than to tolerate the artist as an individual. Such a thing as "L'Ecole de Londres" would be a paradox. The foreigner is welcomed effusively and generously while he is a visitor. The moment he takes up residence or takes out naturalisation papers, he becomes part of the "barrack-room furniture", so to speak, and is henceforth taken for granted. The *avant-garde,* such as it is now, is still centred in Paris and all essentially cosmopolitan music finds its roots or its way there.

French composers, and, indeed, all those belonging to countries where musical activities are national affairs, have a certain *right* of performance; the "subvention" is granted chiefly for this purpose; in this country, composers have only the *favour* of one. This does not in any way impede the progress of those composers and students who feel that they have a vocation, and in due course they will make the necessary impact upon concert-giving organisations. The principle of allowing each Conservatoire teacher to teach in his own way, provided that the results are achieved, is working well for the future, distant though it may be. This is a principle which holds good everywhere. A still further benefit could be obtained by an exchange of professors, but financial difficulties make this almost insurmountable, I understand. Time was when certain text-books and musical works were taboo for their supposed unorthodoxy; the Paris Conservatoire was notoriously conservative at one time in this respect. Now everything is completely different. This may be placed to the credit of the present Director, Claud Delvincourt (1888), a composer of originality who is definitely *of* the century. Delvincourt's music covers a wide field and is all in the large forms. One singles out the *Bal Vénitien* (1934), *Pamir* (1948), *Radio-sérénade* (1937), a *Violin Sonata* (1941) and, best of all, *Lucifer* (1948), in which he returns to the ancient manner of the "Mystère" which is neither a ballet nor an opera, but a peculiarly Gallic combination of both. This is a monumental work which still awaits consideration by the B.B.C. and production at Covent Garden. It is "atonical", but by no means abnormally so, and has great power and dramatic force[1]Delvincourt is significant in French music as a progressive yet steadying element. That we do not hear his music in this country is another indication of the lack of enterprise marking our "programme planning" which is content with the narrowest view of French art.

Doubtless Ambroise Thomas (1811-1896) and Théodore Dubois (1837-1924) stirred uneasily with indignation in their graves when Olivier Messiaen (1908) was appointed Professor of Harmony at the Paris Conservatoire in 1941—he was given similar appointments in 1931 at the Schola Cantorum and at the Ecole Normale de Musique. The appointment to the Schola Cantorum was a venture on the part of Vincent d'Indy who was persuaded to it largely by Messiaen's orchestral work *Les Offrandes oubliées* (1930). Messiaen, a pupil of Paul Dukas and of Marcel Dupré (1886), has always been impelled by religious and liturgical subjects, and the devout mind of d'Indy, gently drawing to its close, may well have reached out to that of Messiaen, about to launch out on his career.

Messiaen resembles André Caplet (1878-1925) in his approach to the spiritual and mystical aspects of life. Caplet's few works, such as *Le Miroir de Jésus* (1923) show a deeply devout mind. He suffered in the 1914-1918 War and died from the effects of gas poisoning. Messiaen was interned in Stalag VIIIA, at Gorlitza in Silesia, from 1940 to 1941 and who knows what impression this may have made upon him. The physical sufferings of both men were relieved by their consummate faith, which strengthened them in adversity. During his captivity Messiaen composed a remarkable *Quartet* for violin, clarinet, 'cello and piano entitled *Quatuor pour le fin du temps,* in eight movements, the score being headed by the dedication: "En hommage à l'Ange de l'Apocalypse, qui lève la main vers le ciel en disant 'Il n'y aura plus de Temps'." One remarks this application to the pure style of chamber music, and remembers that d'Indy composed his first and second *String Quartets* upon Gregorian intonations.

This quartet of Messiaen continues his religious output, which includes *Hymne au Saint-Sacrément* (1923), *Neuf Meditations* "La Nativité de Seigneur" (1935), *Visions de l'Amen, Vingt Régards sur*

[1] This work is studied in detail in my *Paris and the Opera: the History of a Culture.* (In preparation.)

l'enfant Jésus and *Trois petites Liturgies de la Presence divine,* the last three being composed in the years following his release by the Nazis. On the other side of the picture there is a *Fantaisie burlesque* for piano (1932), *Theme and Variations* for violin and piano (1934) and *Eight Preludes* for piano (1930). Messiaen, like his teacher Dupré, finds his most natural medium in the organ, whose repertoire both composers have enriched with music which makes no compromise with the player. It is often said that the organ cannot "take" so-called modern harmony. This depends entirely upon the acoustical properties of the building. Where there is no resonance, the whole thing becomes tense and hard. However, such music to-day is composed with an actual building in view, a building in which the composers spend a great part of their musical life. Consequently, this music is suitable for this type of resonant building in which any stridencies dissolve in the height of the arches. It is, of course, a fact that if the initial stages of listening were based upon the present up-to-date concept of harmony, there would be no argument about this, and, indeed, the feeling might well be the reverse of what it is to-day; but what used to be termed "grinding discords" grind no longer, and the worst that can be said of a passage like this

Ex. 5

La Nativité du Seigneur

is that each entity makes too forceful an impact upon the ear.

The reader has come across some surprises in the course of this book. Prophets have sprung up in unexpected terrains. I have remarked that music no longer shocks or startles us to-day. From the Aix Festival of 1950 comes a small refutation of this. It is an isolated example, but augurs well for the future. According to the critic of *World Review,* Messiaen's *Turangalîla Symphony*—in ten movements—had a remarkable effect on the audience. The critic in question saw one listener go first white, then pale green, and then vanish altogether. After the performance, the crowd indulged in some light-hearted and also bitter obscenities about the work. The score of this intriguing *Symphony* is not available for study and, therefore, we cannot form our own judgment and opinion; but the critic stated that Honegger liked it and Poulenc did not. This may give an indication of what it is like. This is encouraging, but it in no way yet denies my statement that music does not drive anyone to fury to-day. That such a work should come from Messiaen is not remarkable if one studies his output, but one does not expect any such violent reaction as this latest work appears to have aroused.

Messiaen's principles of composition as laid down by him in his *Technique de mon langage musical* are perfectly logical and reasonable. His method is by no means arbitrary and is concerned more with scalic possibilities than with system. It is pliable and practical. This is the nearest approach to a system which can be found in Europe to-day, outside the twelve-note-row following (Krenek is in America).

The introduction included in the score of the *First String Quartet* (1934) by André Jolivet (1905) speaks of this composer's "system" and uses the term "atonal", again in the customary loose manner. It is difficult to understand why this work should have waited until 1950 before publication. Jolivet is a composer spoken of in this country, but so rarely played that one cannot remember any single performance, although there is a suspicion that the B.B.C. Third Programme must at some time have included one of his works.

It is not strictly atonal, although during its course it leaves the bounds of recognisable tonality at certain instants. It may be described as atonical in general, in spite of a definite concluding "home key". Jolivet, whose neglect leaves a gap in our knowledge of twentieth-century music, is a composer of some imagination and enterprise. It is possible to see certain processes in the writing—a fondness for diminished and augmented intervals, and a frequent superimposition of perfect fifths, for example—but these are not mannerisms. The *String Quartet* is a solid work, rather thick in texture, with the four instruments playing most of the time; but it is real quartet writing with a genuine impulse. The second movement, headed "Allant", is available as an *Andante for String Orchestra*, in which form it is even more convincing, since the composer has been able to spread his material wider and to add certain figurations which give an entirely different aspect to the aesthetic. In its original state this movement is rather strained and compressed in range, but when widened for double string orchestra, it immediately assumes a subjective tint which makes one think that perhaps it was reduced from this medium to that of the string quartet —there is no indication as to which came first. The string writing is impeccable in each version, and one may study the two scores with profit and pleasure. The width of the intervals naturally assumes greater significance in the orchestral version and although one must give the whole full marks for individuality, the larger version is not unsuggestive in timbre of some of the great "adagios" of Mahler, without their yearning.

Jolivet's music could take its place to-day in any programme and give no indication as to its date of composition. It is not over-profound, but it is infinitely less superficial than many works which have found a niche in the repertoire. Its composer is Musical Director at the Comédie Française, in Paris. His routine life, therefore, does not bring him into contact with anything very serious, and consequently we may guess that his serious music is the better part of him. This *String Quartet* is reflective and subjective; in scope and resource it combines classical processes with deep feeling, and Jolivet provides an opposing force to the classicism of a composer like Henri Sauguet (1901) whose *Second String Quartet* (1947-1948) takes the abstract principles of Milhaud to their present condition.

Sauguet, whose name will always be associated with his ballet *La Chatte* (1927), written for Diaghileff, and the long opera *La Chartreuse de Parme* (1932-1939), was one of the *enfants terribles* of the 1920's. Time has made us accustomed to the music of this period and has naturally sobered up many of the high spirits of its composers. In this *Quartet* Sauguet has attempted to penetrate the fastnesses of sombre gloom; in effect he has succeeded, but neither the style nor the music are attractive or really convincing. Sauguet lacks the spontaneity of Jolivet and he approaches the medium from a less polyphonic angle than one would expect; the music is square—the third movement is a "Tempo di Valse" of a cynical nature—and too often resolves into a tune with accompaniment.

This, of course, is but one point of view and there are many who do not regard polyphony as essential for the string quartet medium. Its individuality, however, is impersonal since it is impossible to indicate any positive qualities. Nevertheless, it is a useful work and indicates a step further in the Gallic concept of classicism.

Of the very much younger French composers one sees definite promise for the future in Jean Louis Martinet (1912) who with his symphonic poem in three parts, *Orphée* (1944–1945), has written a work which continues the tradition of Ravel's *Daphnis et Chloé,* is of the same size and scope and is worthy to rank beside it. Martinet (who makes no appearance as yet in any *Dictionary of Music and Musicians* that I can find—perhaps the new "Grove" will supply the deficiency) is evidently a composer of a seriousness of purpose which augurs well for the future of French music. Amidst the welter of neo-classicism it is refreshing to find one who does not hesitate at showing his Gallicism in terms of French romanticism. Ravel died in 1937, having ceased to shed any influence upon the young composers. Now, thirteen years later, he has suddenly been rediscovered, and Martinet may bid fair to replace Ravelian elements in French music.

Orphée is scored for an enormous orchestra which is used so comprehensively that charges of extravagance cannot reasonably be laid against it. Since this trend is towards the earlier Berliozian concept of the orchestra, it is worth quoting the requirements of the score in full, reminding the reader that the whole force is used poetically all through the work, with definite originality. Martinet is not concerned with Berliozian noise, but with Ravelian picturesqueness.

Piccolo	4 Kettledrums (one small)
2 Flutes	Whip
(one playing second piccolo)	Basque drum
Flute in G	Triangle
(or third flute in C)	Bass drum
3 Oboes	Side drum
Cor anglais	Cymbals
Clarinet in E flat	Gong
(or third clarinet in B flat)	Bells
2 Clarinets in B flat	Xylophone
Bass clarinet	Glockenspiel
3 Bassoons	Celesta
Double bassoon	Vibraphone
8 Horns	2 Harps
4 Trumpets	Piano
3 Trombones	Strings
2 Tubas	

The absence of a saxophone may be remarked, for this has for many years been a frequent occurrence in French scores, both large and small.

I know of no other work which opens with a xylophone rhythm, "solo", and no other composer who would think of doing this except, perhaps, Milhaud who has specialised in the percussion section of the orchestra. From this point of view Martinet finds his origin in the Greek operas by Milhaud which have been seen to be object lessons in resource of this nature.

Rhythmically, Martinet changes his time signatures freely and regularly, but unlike so many instances in Stravinsky's ballets, these changes are not so much eye-music. However, we are faced with real difficulties on occasions and it is for the conductor to control sudden "allegro" changes from 4/8 to 3/16 and 7/16. Listening to this work on a non-commercial record all these appeared to fall into place perfectly easily and the accents fully justified the means of obtaining them.

Melodically, Martinet is unashamedly romantic and some of the themes certainly find their origin and growth in *Daphnis et Chloé*, especially when they are placed in the 'cellos. Two short passages from Part Two, "La Descente aux Enfers" and Part One, "Orphée devant Eurydice", will illustrate this:

Martinet is more scholarly than Ravel, insomuch as he finds fugue and fugato a perfectly normal means of expression. The subject from the third movement is suave and on the viola extremely pathetic in effect.

The next example shows this subject and a counter-subject appearing at the final coda which is Bartokian in contour.

The coda of this work is interesting as it is an exposition in reverse, each part dropping out in turn at the end of the subject, leaving the violas "solo".

Let it not be thought that Martinet is but a pale reflection of Ravel, Roussel and Stravinsky, or that he has written music which in any way resembles that of those three composers. The style, the harmony and the formal construction are his, and his alone. This altogether remarkable work written by a young composer is yet another blow at those who maintain (still) that French music is something small and *délicieux*. This symphonic poem is a work of world importance, and its scope and invention, together with its supreme poetry, make it notable. Notability, however, may not come its way until economic resources are improved and concert promoters can afford the outlay of this large orchestra.

Fortunately, however, Martinet is accessible in small media, and one finds his *Variations for String Quartet* (1946) in every way suitable for confirming that slenderness of texture which is, indeed, a feature of *Orphée*.

This is a theme devised for variation. It has all the qualities which make for such treatment. The variations are fully amplified and the quality of the theme does not make its (perhaps inevitable) final return as irritating as is the case with many other sets. Martinet uses the resources of the instruments to the fullest degree, without considering effect or stunts. Everything is thematic, even two pages of quasi-arpeggio passages, and the thought is as clear as if the composer's name were Vincent d'Indy.

The future of French music is safe and sure if Martinet is a sample. There is no other culture which has shown such a marked trend from romantic picturesqueness to symphonic proportion as has the French. For the moment, we still hear mainly the older composers—Les Six, whose best music is always welcome and whose latest works have achieved all the early latent possibilities. We now expect to hear "Jeune France", and we do not mind if it is not particularly *jeune*. We should hear more Jolivet, as has been suggested, more Mihalovici and Fitelberg from "L'Ecole de Paris". From France herself Martinet claims our serious attention and one can say with perfect assurance that a country which can claim *Orphée* among its artistic achievements need have no fear of its future position. Martinet is far in advance of any other composer that we know of his own age, and he makes some of his immediate seniors and European contemporaries appear very small.

While Italian music continues to thrive in opera (although we have not heard any recent masterpieces) it is possible to point to one isolated figure who is outstanding in the symphonic concept of music. Luigi Dallapiccola (1904) uses the twelve-note series in the scalic manner without any restrictions. Since the death of Casella he is the most representative composer in Italy—the older Malipiero (1882) has not made very much impact elsewhere and composers of the calibre of Respighi (1879-1936) and Pizetti (1880) count for very little, since their music falls more into line with early twentieth-century romanticism. Dallapiccola's music takes its impulse from human experience, and has all the elements which the twelve-note-row composers lack. It is spontaneous, dramatic, and full of human emotion. His *Songs from Captivity* (1938) are among the most humanly poignant works of the era, and show him to be completely in touch with all the social tragedies of to-day. If he can find disciples, Italian music may stand a fair chance of taking a place among the best of the European symphonic countries; up till now its attempts in this direction have not been impressive or notable for originality. Dallapiccola is the only Italian composer showing any definite trend. Italy must find a second Ferruccio Busoni (1866-1924) and Alfredo Casella.

The Scandinavian countries and Spain play little part in any kind of *avant-garde*, and it is impossible to find any indications that this will take place in the near future. Belgium shows some promising signs, and of the older composers Jean Absil (1893) and Marcel Poot (1901) show individual traits towards neo-classicism in the former case and a cheerful and sane modernity in the latter. Of the younger composers, Norbert Rousseau and Raymond Chevreuille (1901) are serious-minded and intensely dramatic. Both these composers have collaborated with the Belgian dramatist Joseph Weterings (who wrote the libretto for Roussel's *Aeneas* (1935)) in works specially devised for radio. Chevreuille won the second prize in the 1950 "Italia" Competition with a symphonic fairy tale *D'Un Diable de Briquet* after Hans Andersen. This work was written from more than the normal point of view of actual radio musical presentation, for the composer consulted radio engineers and by means of a judicious wangle with turntable revolutions, produced a score which presented some interesting orchestral effects otherwise unprocurable. The first prize in this competition, an opera by Pizzetti, *Iphigenia,* might well have given place to this original score by Chevreuille, which is at once in every way more interesting, more original, and more "radiogenic". One wonders why Belgian music crosses her frontiers so seldom.

One more trend remains to be mentioned, a recrudescence from the eighteenth century. The Soviet Union has set an example in political music and we have from time to time been treated to a large number of works which do not appear to say anything very original. This hook-up between politics and art is nothing new; the French Revolution tried it all before, with the inevitable result that 90 per cent. of the *Gebrauchsmusik* written to order and to standard has completely disappeared, since its topicalities ceased to apply to everyday affairs. The general principle of Soviet art of all kinds is that it should be immediately comprehensible to all and sundry, and that it should have some basis of social significance. Subjectivity is vetoed with heavy penalties, and there must be no idiomatic or stylistic connection with Western Europe. Admirers of the Soviet system in other countries try to fall into line with the official rulings, but with indifferent success. Indeed, it appears that the whole thing in Soviet Russia herself has failed.

Reading the verbatim translation of the Central Committee's Decree on Music in August, 1948, certain points come into relief. It has always been a feature of the Soviet official that he has not minced his words in any way. He is outspoken in these matters at least, and one knows exactly where everybody stands. At the Committee's Congress, all the Soviet composers were roundly taken to task by Comrade Zakharov, a composer of popular songs. In spite of trying to follow the official directives, all so vague as to resemble any reactionary Western official document, and completely incomprehensible in terms of the art they set out to direct, it would appear that the leading Soviet composers amongst other crimes attempt to please Western audiences. To quote the comrade's own words:[1]

Shostakovich's Seventh, Eighth, and Ninth Symphonies are supposed to be considered as works of genius abroad. But who considers them as such? Who . . . apart from the reactionaries against whom we fight, apart from the bandits and imperialists? Do you think the people in foreign countries like these works? I can say quite categorically: "No; impossible." To-day the most popular composer in the world is our Tchaikowsky. His music is used in many foreign films.

Under the circumstances, we would not like to discuss in detail what is officially regarded as a failure, and since Tchaikowsky hardly comes within the scope of this book, and since Comrade Zakharov categorically states that we do not like the Soviet music, it would clearly be too destructive to write about it. Similarly, since in the event of our being appreciative and constructive we should be considered bandits and imperialists, it is best to draw a veil over this trend.

However, it is worth noting the Soviet opinion of some European composers. The following descriptions are given to certain composers —decadent, modernist, pathological, erotic, cacophonous, religious, and sexually-perverted monsters. I give the list of composers thus stigmatised without applying any of the labels to any individual one amongst them—Messiaen, Jolivet, Hindemith, Berg, Menotti, and Britten.

This kind of nonsense would be amusing if it were not pathetic and rather tragic, for it all comes from an *official ruling*. However, Western Europe and America will continue along their chosen paths untroubled by all this palaver, but since one side or other is bound to be offended, it is obvious that discussion of the Soviet composers and their trends may well complicate a world situation already sufficiently complex.

This present period being, as I have suggested, one of contemplation and consolidation, it is impossible to prophesy. It will be some while before Germany and Austria can take any place in the musical hierarchy of to-day. At the moment it is perfectly plain that in only two European

[1] *Musical Uproar in Moscow*, Alexander Werth (Turnstile Press).

countries are any prognostications possible, England and France. The former will certainly carry on its present English style and idiom and in due course it will penetrate to the Continent. The latter, as at so many times in the history of music, will again continue to lead European thought. In the meanwhile, France should hear some representative English works; but they must be of the right kind, the kind that a Gallic audience may reasonably be expected to react to favourably, and not just anything because it happens to be English. English music would make an impression in America, and here the choice of composers would be wider.

However, "art knows no boundaries" and, to quote Vincent d'Indy's statement at a Press interview, "Music will go whither the next composer of genius directs it". Will it follow Schoenberg, Sibelius, Vaughan Williams, Milhaud, Stravinsky (I quote only the living in this suggestion of a forward policy) or will it return to Debussy, Ravel, Roussel, Pijper, Delius? (I quote only those *of* the twentieth century and now departed). Can it effect a combination of the not-so-new and the quite new?—but "there is no new music; there are only new composers".[1]

[1] See page xviii.

INDEX OF MUSIC EXAMPLES

INDEX